The Zooarchaeology of the Late Neolithic Strymon River Valley

The case of the Greek sector of Promachon-Topolniča in Macedonia, Greece

George Kazantzis

BAR INTERNATIONAL SERIES 2908 | 2018

Published in 2018 by
BAR Publishing, Oxford

BAR International Series 2908

The Zooarchaeology of the Late Neolithic Strymon River Valley

ISBN 978 1 4073 1658 1

© George Kazantzis 2018

COVER IMAGE Cervus elaphus *(red deer) shed antler: Promachon sector, Phase I.*

Printed in England

PUBLISHING

BAR titles are available from:

BAR Publishing
122 Banbury Rd, Oxford, OX2 7BP, UK
EMAIL   info@barpublishing.com
PHONE   +44 (0)1865 310431
FAX   +44 (0)1865 316916
www.barpublishing.com

This book is dedicated to the memory of my father, Konstantinos Kazantzis (1944–2006)
I would like to thank him for believing in me until his very last day

Preface and Acknowledgements

Three years have already passed since I submitted my doctoral thesis at the University of Sheffield, UK. The circumstances under which, the decision was made to publish the thesis are not so important. What is important, is to acknowledge a number of people who supported me in many ways during the period of my studies and contributed to making me a more effective researcher and (I sincerely hope) a better human being.

This is why I decide to begin my acknowledgements section with a person characterized by a rare *ethos*: the supervisor of my doctoral research, Dr. Umberto Albarella. Proper acknowledgement of him, would require pages. I would like to express my sincere gratitude for providing much needed help, inspirational guidance, encouragement, and edifying instructions and criticisms throughout the whole period of my doctoral study. I would also like to thank him for teaching me that simple language rather than complicated jargon and superfluously ornate syntax is the key for being a good researcher.

Professor Paul Halstead has been a very understandable advisor. I would like to thank him immensely for his help, his valuable comments and suggestions, as well as for his permission to use some of the unpublished data from Makriyalos.

The Emeritus Director of Prehistoric and Classical Antiquities of Eastern Macedonia, Haïdo Koukouli-Chrysanthaki provided the faunal assemblage from Promachon sector for study without any hesitation. I would like to thank her for believing in me, and I also hope that some of her concerns have found their way in this book. Ioannis Aslanis (National Hellenic Research Foundation) provided useful comments on aspects of stratigraphy, structural features and phasing of Promachon. I would like to thank him for putting up with a lot of questions and emails during the writing of the second chapter of the book. Ivan (Ivo) Vajsov (National Institute of Archaeology, Bulgarian Academy of Sciences) has also provided useful information with regard to the phasing of the site and pottery typology. Thanks also go to Nikolai Spassov (Museum of Natural History of Sofia), who provided valuable information with regard to the faunal assemblage from the Bulgarian sector of Topolniča.

I would also like to give special thanks to the Department of Archaeology, University of Sheffield, for the pleasure of working in such a stimulating and fertile research environment. Dr. Sandro Sebastiani (University of Buffalo, USA) has been very helpful as he relieved the stress of the writing and the analysis with hourly smoking intervals. Special thanks go of course to the members of the Zooarchaeology Lab, who provided useful comments and contributed to various animal bone discussions. Mentioned in alphabetical order: Angelos Hadjikoumis, Hannah Russ, Lenny Salvagno, Angela Trentacoste, Silvia Valenzuela-Lamas, Sarah Viner and Lizzie Wright. Lastly, I would like to refer to the people who were closest to me personally and supported me in every way possible. First and foremost, I would like to thank my parents, Konstantinos and Soultana Kazantzi, who offered me education and limitless emotional and material support throughout the last 15 years of my studies. They are the people to whom I owe everything and I am grateful that they supported every choice that I have made in my life. I would also like to thank my uncle Nikolaos and aunt Theodora Kasapi, who, during a period of tremendous financial crisis in Greece, supported my three-year doctoral research: my moral debt to them is far more important than the financial, and I know that it cannot be reciprocated easily. I would also like to thank my partner, archaeologist Eirini Papadopoulou, who has shared with me the joys and the despairs, the good and the bad days. I would very much like to think that the former are more than the latter.

The structure of this book is fairly conventional. *Chapter 1* sets the scene in terms of the Neolithic in northern Greece and in Macedonia in particular and presents the history of the archaeological research undertaken in the area.

Chapter 2 introduces the site of Promachon-Topolniča, the history of the research on-site and the deposits from which the faunal material derives. This chapter brings together all available published sources with regard to the site and presents the latest absolute dating evidence.

Chapter 3 presents the history of the faunal research undertaken in the region of Macedonia and briefly introduces the faunal assemblage of Promachon before moving to the statement of the aims of the current project.

Chapter 4 outlines the methodology and the analytical techniques followed in the faunal study.

The study proper begins in *Chapter 5*; here, the results of the faunal material from Promachon sector are presented (*i.e.* taphonomic analysis, taxonomic, body part and contextual distribution, ageing and metrical analyses of the main domesticated species).

The main results from Promachon are then compared to the results obtained from a number of contemporary to Promachon northern Greek and Balkan sites in *Chapter 6*.

Chapter 7 discusses the case study, pointing to a number of key issues that arose from the previous chapters.

Finally, the conclusions of the faunal study are summarized in *Chapter 8*.

Contents

Please note that additional tables of data showing the full ranges of tooth and postcranial measurements for each species are available to download from www.barpublishing.com/additional-downloads.html.

List of Figures

Appendix: Animal Bone Material

List of Tables

Abstract

Excavations on the border between Greece (sector Promachon) and Bulgaria (sector Topolniča) in the basin of the river Strymonas, Central Macedonia, have revealed a 'flat-extended' settlement dating to the Late Neolithic. In addition to the rich array of material culture evidence, the excavation yielded a substantial quantity of animal bones, thus offering an unparalleled opportunity to study the human-animal relationships.

The current book focuses on the study of the faunal assemblage from the Greek sector of Promachon, and examines the role and the contribution of domestic and wild animals to the economy of the site. Within Promachon, the study of the animal remains indicates an economy particularly tuned to the production of meat; however, a small-scale exploitation of milk could also be inferred. This information is valuable, considering the scarcity of faunal data from contemporary settlements across the basin of Strymonas. Of particular interest is the presence of a large 'public' structure, rich in material culture evidence and animal bones, which creates an interesting contrast to the rest of the household deposits. In addition, the faunal evidence is consistent with the suggestion of the excavators of the site that significant changes occurred during the third phase of occupation at Promachon.

On the other hand, the substantially better representation of cattle in Promachon than any other settlement in Greek Macedonia, along with the evidence from pottery decoration and structural features, suggests that – to some extent – Promachon was linked to Balkan Late and Final Neolithic communities. Biometric analysis also provided interesting insights into the diverse husbandry practices among Late Neolithic sites in Macedonia and Thessaly. This information is particularly important, in view of the fact that the comparison of the size of domestic ruminants and pigs between Late Neolithic Macedonian and Thessalian sites has not been attempted prior to this study. In this respect, the collection of a larger body of metrical data from Late Neolithic Macedonian and Thessalian settlements should represent a priority for future research, in order to provide clarification to some of the issues discussed in this book.

The current research presents new information on subsistence strategies in an underrepresented area of northern Greece during a time-period (fifth and fourth millennium BC), that is considered one of the most dynamic eras of the prehistory of southeastern Europe. It also clarifies both temporal and regional trends in animal management, placing Promachon in the broader spectrum of contemporary agro-pastoral communities and creating an integrated picture of human-animal relationships that encompasses both the basin of Strymonas and northern Greece.

Prologue

1.1 The Neolithic

John Lubbock introduced the term 'Neolithic' [Greek Etymology: *Νέος* (New) + *Λιθικός* (Lithic) = New Lithic Age) in 1865 in order to distinguish that archaeological period in which polished stone axes and other stone tools were ground into shape, from the Old Lithic Age [Paleolithic; Greek Etymology: Παλαιός (Old) + Λιθικός (Lithic)], in which flints were shaped by flaking (Runnels and Murray 2001). Lubbock's differentiation was based solely on changes in the technology of lithic tools, but later prehistorians further differentiated the two time-periods on the basis of economic practices.

During the first half of the twentieth century, the science of archeology – and the study of the Neolithic in particular – were significantly influenced by the dialectical materialism and the Marxist theory, which were encountered in the work of the leading British archaeologist Gordon Childe. Childe's (1936) work, which was inevitably linked to his Marxist theoretical leanings, highlighted the regulatory role of the means of production and the material culture to the evolution of human society and had an immediate impact on archaeological science. Childe introduced to archaeology the well-established biological concept of 'monogenesis' (*i.e.* a novelty is only invented once, and then transferred from region to region). Plant and animal domestication, writing, irrigation, pottery and tillage are commonly considered as such contrivances today. The transfer of a number of novelties that took place during the Neolithic, is commonly referred today as 'diffusion' and it might have occurred in two ways:

1. directly, by moving populations
2. indirectly, by contact, exchange and trade

A frequently mentioned concept with regard to the Neolithic is the so-called 'Neolithic package'; the concept itself has been attributed to Chris Chippindale while an undergraduate at the Cambridge University in the 1970s (Sherratt 2005). By that time also, the concept of 'New Archaeology', which affected the study of the Neolithic in a profound way, was already taking the lead in archaeological science[1]. Its proponents argued that the study of archaeological data should by no means be influenced by the various historical and social conditions, but only by the accuracy of the method used to explain the archaeological record (Clarke 1973)[2].

The 'Neolithic package' was first used to refer to the material culture of the period of the Neolithic as a whole, since Neolithic assemblages from South-west Asia, Anatolia and Southeast Europe yielded similar types of finds, and these tended to occur together repeatedly in this vast geographical region (Çilingiroglu 2005; Özdogan 2001). Today, however, there is a general recognition that the term 'Neolithic package' implies something more than technological developments (*i.e.* the use of polished stone axes and querns, stone and adobe brick architecture, the use of pottery and woolen textiles and decorative arts in many materials). The 'Neolithic package' is closely related also to the appearance of domesticated plants (wheat, barley, beans and lentils) and animals (cattle, sheep, goat and pigs), sedentism, and the adoption of food production as the basis upon which, both social changes and technological innovations were founded (*cf.* Hodder 1990; Tringham 2000; Whittle 1996; Zvelebil 1998).

All in all, the term 'Neolithic package' is generally accepted to encompass the technological, economic, social and ideological aspects of the Neolithic period as a whole. Unquestionably, the beginning of the Neolithic is marked by fundamental changes in the economic mode of life and a dazzling burst of innovations in the sphere of material culture. In addition, the appearance of permanently inhabited farming villages was indeed an important step in human history and brought into existence a way of life that has remained the basis of the human society to the present day (Runnels and Murray 2001).

1.2 The Neolithic of Macedonia

One cannot refer to the research of the Neolithic of Macedonia, without first mentioning the research that was conducted in the Neolithic of Thessaly, which has a longer history. The pioneering work of Christos Tsountas in the first decade of the twentieth century at the Neolithic sites of Sesklo and Dimini shaped much subsequent research into the Neolithic of Greece (Halstead 2006; Theocharis 1993). Long before any systematic chronological framework was established in other parts of Greece, the archaeological research in Thessaly presented an elaborate chronological system suitable for describing the cultural history of the area (Andreou *et al.* 1996). To some extent, this privileged position of the Thessalian Neolithic is still held today and some of the central issues of the Greek Neolithic in general, such as the beginning of a farming economy and the emergence of social complexity, revolve around research in Thessaly – although questions of cultural

---

[1] Named shortly thereafter 'Processual Archaeology'.
[2] The main objective of the 'New Archaeology' (or Processual Archaeology) was to establish a number of scientific methods of analyzing the archaeological material in order to record patterns of human behavior.

history and chronology are still discussed (*cf.* Andreou *et al.* 1996; Kotsakis 2002; Perlès 2001).

1.2.1 A brief history of the research

Already at the beginning of the twentieth century, the prehistoric period of Macedonia became the subject of research by European archaeologists. The area of Macedonia was considered a key province for the understanding of European prehistory. The widespread view on the significance of Macedonia for the Neolithic in Europe followed the model of Gordon Childe (1936). According to this model, Macedonia was a natural channel for the expansion of the Neolithic into Europe, through the Axios, Morava and Danube rivers. However, a number of scholars recognized also a general tendency of the area of Macedonia to isolation (Andreou *et al.* 1996). The evidence, on which the latter view rested, was rooted in the underdevelopment of the research in the area of Macedonia, and thus, the general scarcity of archaeological information (Fotiadis 2001; Fotiadis *et al.* 2000). This led archaeologists to place and discuss Macedonia in the context of a Thessalian, rather than a local Macedonian Neolithic. It also led to the assumption that the Neolithic cultures of Macedonia were largely derivative from, and marginal to, those of Thessaly (Andreou *et al.* 1996; Perlès 2001). Inevitably, archaeologists studying the prehistory of Macedonia were considering it to be the 'province' of Thessaly during the Neolithic (Andreou *et al.* 1996).

This view of Macedonia changed with time, since the considerable number of Neolithic sites that were excavated as early as the early 1960s and 1970s gave important information with regard to the Neolithic of the area. The excavation of the site of Nea Nikomidia (in the prefecture of Veria in western Macedonia), which originally commenced in 1961 (Wardle 1996), yielded the earliest radiocarbon dating (6220 ± 150 BC) and the site represented at that time the oldest dated Neolithic community in Europe. Regardless of the fact that the excavation project of Nea Nikomidia was abruptly terminated[3], it marked the beginning of a significant archaeological research in the area of Macedonia and it was followed by the excavation project of another important site, which remains until today a point of reference for the Neolithic of the area: Sitagroi (Renfrew *et al.* 1986).

By the early 1990s onwards, the number of Neolithic sites in Macedonia had increased considerably (Figure 1.1). Sites such as Drosia (Kotsos 1992), Yiannitsa (Chrysostomou 1991), Dispilio (Hourmouziadis 1996), Makriyalos (Pappa and Bessios 1995; 1998; 1999; Pappa *et al.* 1998; 2003), Promachon-Topolniča (Koukouli-Chrysanthaki *et al.* 1997), Dikili Tash (Treuil 1992), Stavroupoli (Grammenos 2002; 2004), Metabgalo Nisi Galanis (Fotiadis *et al.* 2000), Toumba Serron (Fotiadis 1995), Limenaria (Malamidou 1996; 2006; Malamidou and Papadopoulos 1993), Aggitis

cave (Trantalidou *et al.* 2006), Arkadikos (Peristeri 2002; 2004), Vasilika and Dimitra (Grammenos 1991), Servia (Ridley *et al.* 2000), Kryoneri (Malamidou 1997; 2007; 2016), Mandalo (Papanthimou and Papasteriou 1993), Toumba Kremastis (Hondrogianni-Metoki 2001) and Avgi (Stratouli 2004) have provided important information with regard to the Neolithic of the area. A significant number of these excavations were staffed with scholars with different specialisms (*i.e.* anthropologists, zooarchaeologists, palynologists, geoarchaeologists), who had been trained in various European Universities and were introduced to archaeological research in Greece. This according to Andreou *et al.* (1996) had brought:

> "...a radically different set of questions and ethos of practice, a scientific humanism that had developed outside the area of the Aegean prehistory" (Andreou et al. 1996, 561-62).

The results of the archaeological research of the Neolithic (and Bronze Age) sites in the culturally and geographically distinct region of Macedonia were summarized about 20 years ago (Andreou *et al.* 1996). Their chronological framework, which was established for the Neolithic of Macedonia and northern Greece in general, is systematically used until today and it is presented in Table 1.1; this also includes the division of the Late Neolithic into two stages of development, following Gallis (1996) and Demoule and Perlès (1993).

1.2.2 The Late Neolithic of Macedonia: Promachon-Topolniča in context

In contrast to the preceding Early and Middle Neolithic periods, the Late Neolithic period of Macedonia is characterized by a considerable expansion of the number of settlements. These occupied either areas that were previously uninhabited or areas in which the environmental conditions did not permit risk-free agricultural production (*i.e.* swampy areas) (Hourmouziadis 1996). Examples of such Late Neolithic communities are represented by the site of Dispilio (Hourmouziadis 2002) near the lake of Kastoria and the site of Dikili Tash (Treuil 1992) in the plain of Kavala. On the other hand, a number of settlements, such as Vasilika (Grammenos 1991; Pappa 1993), Stavroupoli (Grammenos 2002; 2004) and Thermi (Grammenos *et al.* 1989; Pappa *et al.* 2000) covered large areas, which in some cases exceeded 20 hectares each (Pappa 1999; 2008). Despite the fact that the excavations in these settlements have uncovered a considerable number of structural features, it seems likely that the number of populations in each settlement did not exceed 100-200 people (Andreou *et al.* 2001; Pappa 2008).

As in the Early and the Middle Neolithic periods, there were two types of settlements during the Late Neolithic in Macedonia: tells (also known as toumbes in the area of Macedonia and magoules in the area of Thessaly) and open-air (also known as flat-extended) settlements (Perlès 2001; Souvatzi 2008). Prehistoric tells in Macedonia –

---

[3] For an overview of the significance of the Nea Nikomidia archaeological project, see also Fotiadis (2001).

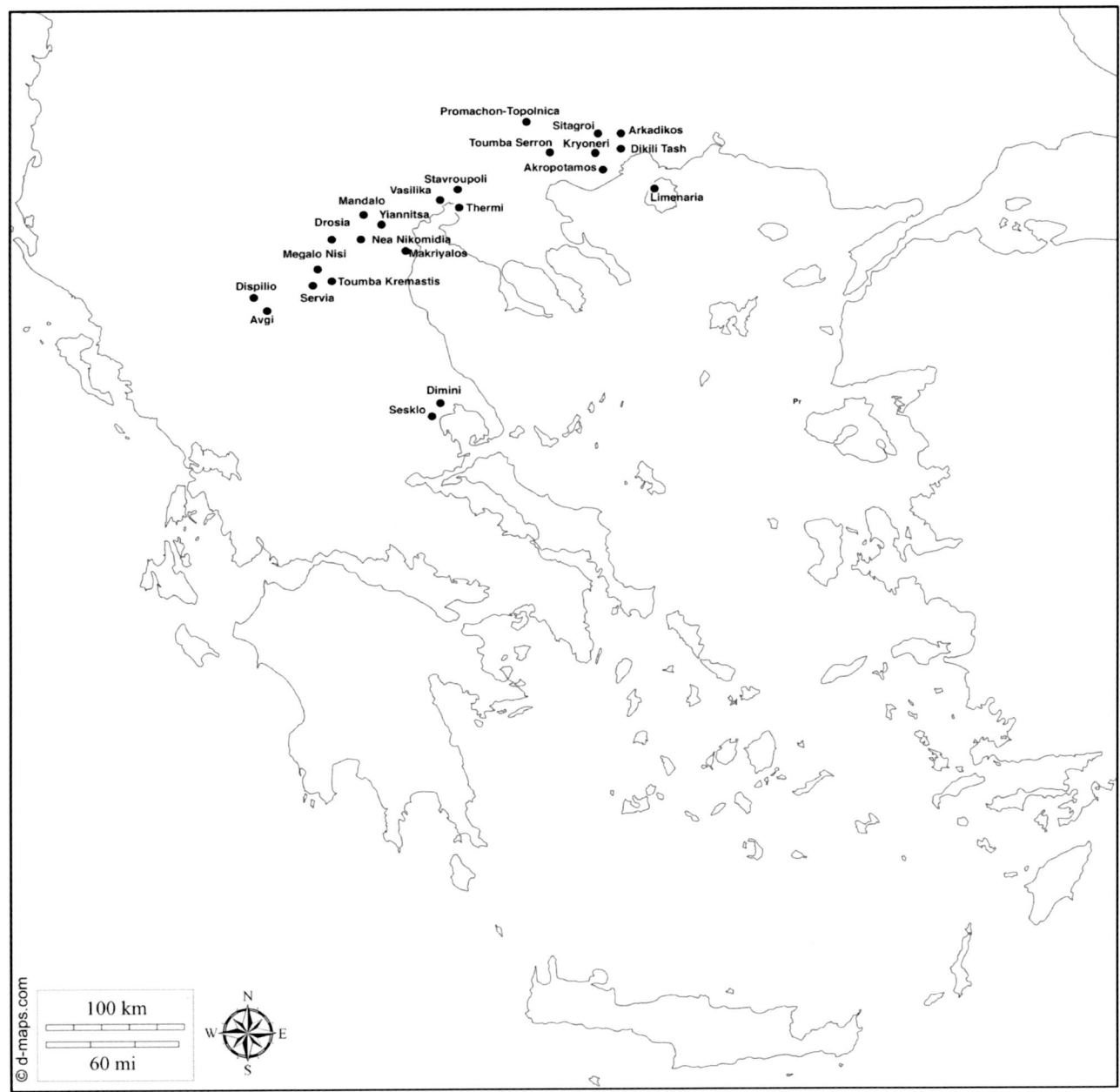

Figure 1.1 Map of Greek Neolithic sites mentioned in this chapter.

often confused with 'Macedonian tells', which are funerary monuments of the Hellenistic period – were formed by the accumulation of building materials, since the construction of any new building was based on the foundations of an older (Andreou *et al.* 1996; 2001). This practice ultimately resulted in the rapid elevation of the settlements and in some cases tells approached – or even exceeded – 20 meters in height. The persistence of the inhabitants to build their new structures on top of the foundations of the older ones, might have been associated either with the

Table 1.1 Archaeological phases and chronology for Neolithic northern Greece.

Cultural Periods	Cal. BC
Final Neolithic (Chalcolithic)	4700 – 4500 / 3300 – 3100
Late Neolithic II	4800 – 4700 / 4500
Late Neolithic I	5400 – 5300 / 4800
Middle Neolithic	5800 – 5600 / 5400 – 5300
Early Neolithic	6700 – 6500 / 5800 – 5600

declaration of the origins and the 'antiquity' of the group residing in the building, or with the close ties that this group shared with their ancestors who were perceived to support the longevity and the success of the household (*cf.* Andreou *et al.* 1996; 2001; Bailey 2000; Perlès 2001). In any case, practical considerations such as the availability of space or the easier construction of a new building might have also played a role (Bailey 2000).

In the case of the open-air (or flat-extended) settlements, the new structures were not constructed on the foundations of the previous ones. On the contrary, these were relocated within the framework of a wider area of the settlement, the limits of which, in most cases were defined by a circular trench (as in the case of Makriyalos) (Andreou *et al.* 1996; Kotsakis 1999; Pappa 2008). These buildings were not carefully constructed and they generally give the impression of more ephemeral structures, since they were often nothing more than pits dug into the natural soil (Souvatzi 2008). Like Thessaly, the density of the Late Neolithic buildings in Macedonian sites is extremely low, as there were extensive voids in-between structures – a practice, which is believed to reflect the establishment of the private space during the Late Neolithic (Pappa 2008). However, the large structural features, which are present in Thessalian sites of this time-period (*i.e* Dimini, Sesklo, Magoula Visviki) – possibly indicating a society with an enhanced hierarchical organization – are conspicuously absent from contemporary Macedonian sites (Pappa 2008). On the other hand, a considerable number of large circular or semi-circular structures, which were dug into the natural subsoil and are considered to represent communal structures with public functions, are present at a number of Macedonian sites (*i.e.* Stavroupoli, Makriyalos, Promachon-Topolniča).

In contrast to the faunal evidence from the preceding (Early and Middle Neolithic) and the subsequent (Early Bronze) periods, the faunal evidence from the Late Neolithic period of Macedonia suggests that wild species had a limited use. The economy during this time-period is mainly based on the breeding and keeping of domesticated animals (cattle, caprines and pigs). Mortality curves suggest a considerable potential for the production of meat, while a small-scale exploitation for secondary products, such as milk, wool and labour is also considered to have taken place (*cf.* Becker 1991; Halstead 1989a; 1996; Papathanasopoulos 1996; Theocharis 1993; Valamoti 2004). Widespread agricultural products are represented by wheat, barley, oats, lentils, vetch, beans and peas, while there is also evidence that Late Neolithic people were collecting wild figs, apples, pears, cranberries, grapes, almonds and acorns (Valamoti 2004). Charred seeds and skins that were found in the Late Neolithic deposits of Dikili Tash provide the first indication for the cultivation of the vine (Valamoti *et al.* 2007). Large storage pits and storage jars that were found either inside or outside the structures of almost all settlements from this time-period, have been considered to point to the existence of surpluses of products (Halstead 1989b). Evidence of technical expertise is also attested during the Late Neolithic in the area of Macedonia through a number of objects such as obsidian tools, high-quality pottery and marble vessels. The latter are present in a number of sites such as Limenaria in the island of Thassos (Papadopoulos and Malamidou 2012), Servia (Heurtley 1939), Dikili Tash (Treuil 1992) and Promachon-Topolniča (Koukouli-Chrysanthaki *et al.* 2007). Their manufacturing technology and their purpose of use are not yet fully understood, although the evidence from Limenaria suggests that these might have been used as colour containers (Papadopoulos and Malamidou 2012).

The considerable expansion of the number of Late Neolithic sites in Macedonia suggests a dense system of interacting communities that had proceeded from habitation sites to being villages in the functional sense. For instance, the impressive production of high-quality vessels with black paint on red background (also known as black-on-red or simply black-top) (Fotiadis 2001; Grammenos and Kotsos 2001; Koukouli-Chrysanthaki *et al.* 2007) – typical of Eastern Macedonia – have also been found in contemporary settlements from Thrace (Makri) and Thessaly (Pevkakia). In addition, the evidence indicates that a number of Late Neolithic Macedonian sites shared contacts with the wide area of the Balkan Peninsula. For instance, the Late Neolithic settlement of Mandalo in Yiannitsa (Chrysostomou 1991) yielded a considerable number of obsidian tools from the Carpathians (Grammenos and Kotsos 2001) and the well-known Aegean marine shell *Spondylus gaederopus* has been found in sites from Central and Northern Europe (Andreou *et al.* 2001).

Archaeological research has indicated that, in the beginning of the fourth millennium BC, settlements in Macedonia (*i.e.* Mandalo, Thermi, Stavroupoli, Promachon), which had been inhabited for several centuries, were ultimately abandoned (Andreou *et al.* 2001; Grammenos and Kotsos 2004). This constitutes a significant problem for the research of the prehistory of the area, as this means that the number of settlements which span the crucial transitional period between the Late/Final Neolithic and the Bronze Age are scarce.

Among recently excavated Late Neolithic sites in Greek Macedonia, the settlement of Promachon-Topolniča – with its rich array of material culture evidence – yielded a large assemblage of animal bones, which constitutes the focal point of this book.

The site of Promachon-Topolniča is introduced in the next chapter.

The Site

2.1 Location

The Promachon-Topolniča settlement is situated exactly on the border between Greece and Bulgaria. The site is located one kilometre to the west of the Strymon river (Struma in Bulgarian), two kilometres to the south of the Bulgarian village of Topolniča and almost three and a half kilometres northwest of the Greek border village of Promachon (Latitude: 41º 23.220`; Longitude 23º 19.725`; height: 80.5 meters) (Koukouli-Chrysanthaki *et al.* 2007) (Figure 2.1). This location was strategic and the site controlled the north-south traffic through the Promachon pass, which also provided an important link between the Neolithic cultures of northern Greece and southwestern Bulgaria. The locale itself benefited from the river's fertile alluvial grounds, which are still today used for agriculture and pastoral activities (Fotiadis 1995).

2.2 History of the research

The results of the thorough excavations carried out at the prehistoric settlement of Promachon-Topolniča are

of special importance for our understanding of southern European prehistory. Before 1981, when the investigations began on the Bulgarian part of the site (Topolniča sector), very little was known concerning prehistoric life in the middle Strymon river valley (Vajsov 2007). At the same time, published research from some of the relevant excavated sites in central Macedonia, northern Greece, was scanty. In 1980 the results of the excavations at Sitagroi (Evans 1986; Keighley 1986; Renfrew *et al.* 1986) had not yet been fully published. Excavation results from the nearby settlements of Dimitra and Vasilika were published early in the 1990s (Grammenos 1991), while the Dikili Tash (Seferiadis 1983) publication provided only some preliminary results of the excavations and an outline of the chronological sequence. Overall, research concerning the Late Neolithic in the middle and lower Strymon river valley was still in its infancy (Vajsov 2007).

Sector Topolniča was discovered in 1978 but it was not until 1981 that it was originally registered as a site of archaeological interest. Until the mid-1990s the site was referred to in the published literature as "Kremeniča" (Bailey 2000). The excavation on of Kremeniča (or Topolniča), which was directed by Henrieta Todorova from the Archaeological Institute of Sofia commenced in 1981 and lasted for 10 years. During the first few years, the excavation constituted mainly of test soundings extending up to the border with Greece. These were aimed at establishing the stratigraphy and chronology of the site (Figure 2.2).

Due to the existence of many different features, this proved to be a difficult task, leading to future excavations extending to the west and thus encompassing a large part of

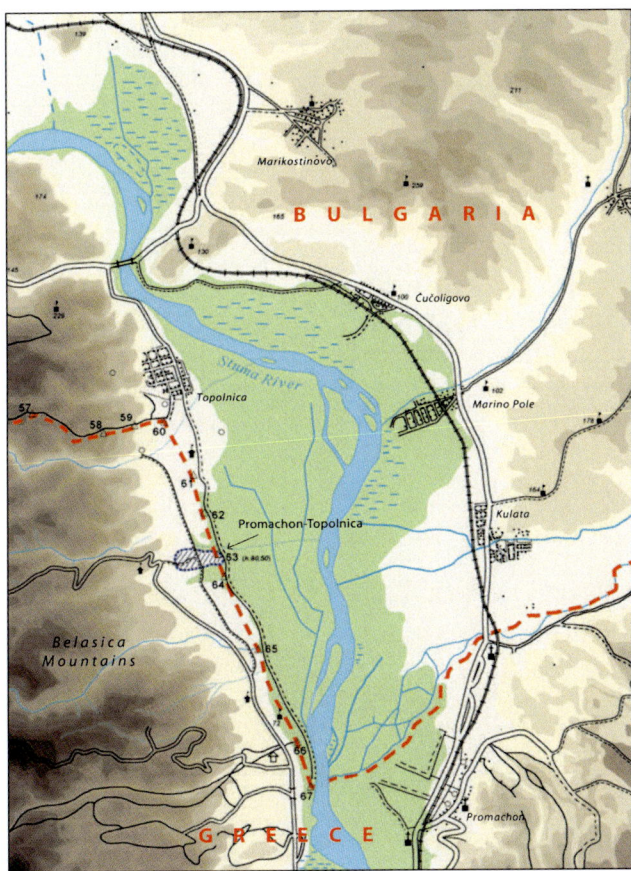

Figure 2.1 Lower course of the Strymon river and location of Promachon-Topolniča Late Neolithic settlement (after Koukouli-Chrysanthaki *et al.* 2007).

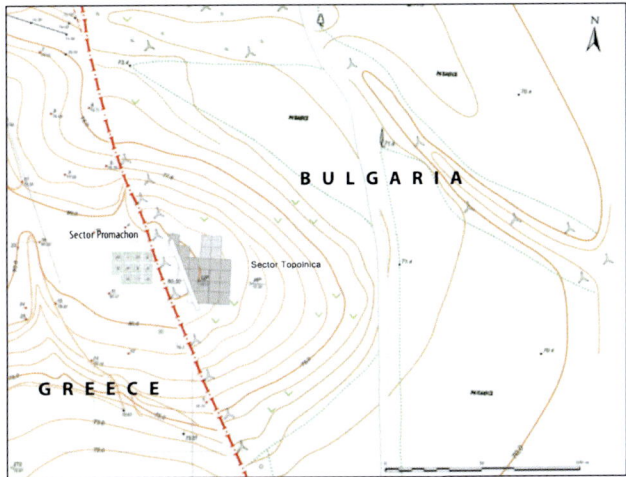

Figure 2.2 General topographic map of Promachon-Topolniča (after Koukouli-Chrysanthaki *et al.* 2007).

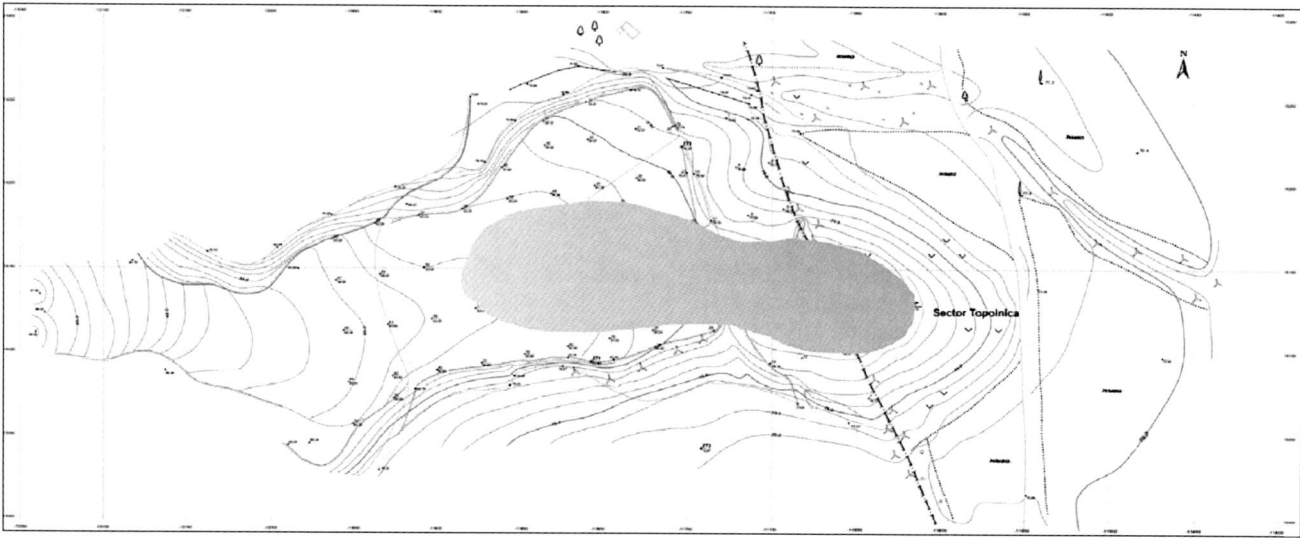

Figure 2.3 Topographic plan of Promachon-Topolniča depicting the estimated spread of the settlement (after Koukouli-Chrysanthaki *et al.* 2014). © Archaeological Museum of Thessaloniki.

the settlement on the Greek side (Koukouli-Chrysanthaki *et al.* 2007; Vajsov 2007). Finally, in 1993 a joint Greek and Bulgarian excavation research program began on the sector of the site located in Greek territory (sector Promachon). It was carried out under the auspices of the (now former) 18th Ephorate of Prehistoric and Classical Antiquities of Kavala (eastern Macedonia) and the direction of the archaeologist Haido Koukouli-Chrysanthaki in collaboration with Ioannis Aslanis of the National Hellenic Research Foundation. This further stage of excavation also lasted for 10 years (Koukouli-Chrysanthaki 2000; 2006; Koukouli-Chrysanthaki and Basiakos 2002; Koukouli-Chrysanthaki *et al.* 1992; 1993; 1995; 1996; 1997; 1998a; 1998b; 1999; 2000; 2001; 2003; 2007; 2014). The joint research program, which has combined excavations and surface investigation with archaeometric ground probe data (Koukouli-Chrysanthaki *et al.* 2007), has determined the existence of a Late Neolithic open settlement also known in the Greek literature as 'flat-extended' (Andreou *et al.* 1996; Chapman 1989), that covered an area of about five hectares (Figure 2.3), although dispersion of ceramic fragments indicates that the site covered an area as large as seven hectares (Koukouli-Chrysanthaki *et al.* 2014). The results after about 23 years of excavation on both sectors (Greek and Bulgarian) are discussed below and are of exceptional importance for the Late Neolithic of the Balkan Peninsula (Vajsov 2007).

2.3 The excavation on Promachon sector

Excavations on the Greek sector of Promachon originally commenced in 1993. The excavation methodology employed, broadly followed the system devised by Hänsel *et al.* (1989) for the Early Bronze Age site of Kastanas in western Macedonia (Koukouli-Chryssanthaki *et al.* 1993). It was flexible enough to be continuously modified as the understanding of the sedimentology and the dynamics of the deposited features gradually became clearer. The excavated area on Promachon sector consisted of 11

trenches with dimensions of 5 x 5 meters each (Figure 2.4).

The excavation involved the removal of soil in horizontal spits of no more than 10 centimeters in thickness each. These were later combined by taking into consideration the natural pattern of the layers, the occasional disturbances, the occurrence of pits and platforms as well as the storage areas and other features, which would lead to the recognition of the architectural and building phases (Koukouli-Chrysanthaki *et al.* 1993).

Material culture findings as well as organic remains deriving from various excavation contexts were given a Finding Units (F.U.) number and were placed inside plastic bags labeled with information regarding the trench from which they were excavated, the stratigraphic context to which they belonged, their coordinates of the excavated area, and the depth from which they were recovered (for instance, F.U. 1023 refers to the twenty third plastic bag

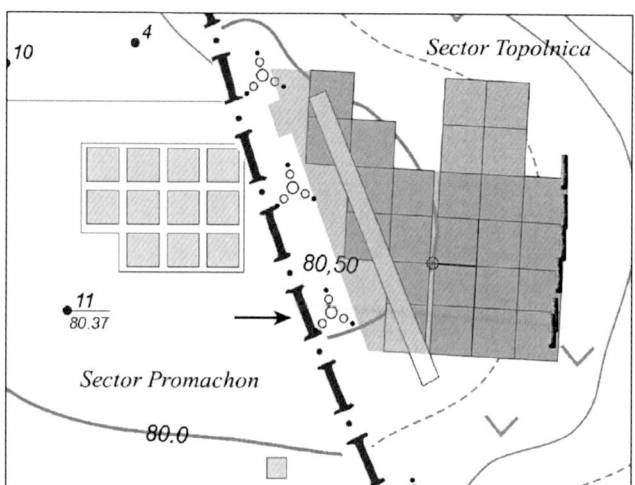

Figure 2.4 Topographic plan of the excavated trenches in both sectors (after Koukouli-Chrysanthaki *et al.* 2014). © Archaeological Museum of Thessaloniki.

of trench A). All trenches were fully excavated and the Neolithic deposits were dug down to the bedrock.

In the years 2003-2012 the analyses of the results from the Promachon sector have led to a good understanding of the stratigraphic sequence. Three phases of occupation have been identified on the basis of structural features and material culture. The latter evidence has also allowed subdividing the second phase into two stages of development (Vajsov 2007). The phasing, which is manifested most clearly in the horizontal plan but is also confirmed by the vertical stratigraphy, is based on the identification of eleven well-preserved layers. They all represent extremely rich deposits, which were either the result of levelling activities before a new house floor was built, or constituted habitation debris associated with human everyday activities.

2.3.1 Phase I (Layers 4 to 11)

Phase I (the oldest phase of habitation in the settlement), includes the deposits associated with layers 4-11. Layers 7-11 belong to a timber-framed structure (structure n. 4), which emerged in trenches IΣT and IZ. Structure n. 4 (Figure 2.5) was found under a timber-framed wattle and daub structure, which is unrelated and belongs to Phase II (Koukouli-Chrysanthaki *et al.* 2007). Structure n. 4 was roughly circular, with a radius of nearly 11 meters and a depth of nearly 7 meters. Excavation undertaken underneath a hearth that was found near the eastern wall of structure n. 4, revealed another layer (Layer 8) with pottery vessels *in situ*. Whitish traces on the floor probably came from a wooden structure, while a large posthole may have supported a wooden floor platform or simply the roof of the building (Koukouli-Chrysanthaki *et al.* 2001). Further excavations revealed the existence of a series of earlier layers (Layers 9, 10 and 11) plastered with yellowish clay, rich in finds. Among the findings, there were pebbles and grinding stones, intact and fragmented high-quality luxury vessels with incised, rippled and painted decorations, large quantities of animal bones, horncores and antlers (Figure 2.6), intact bucrania, as well as small objects including clay figurines, bone and stone tools, clay house models and jewellery, basket fragments and fragments of wooden barks with painted decorations (Koukouli-Chrysanthaki *et al.* 2003; 2007; 2014).

The next Layer (Layer 6) is represented by a thick deposit, occurring in trenches B, Γ, Δ, I, IA and IB. Here, the remains of three timber-framed structures (structures n. 1, n. 2 and n. 3) with internal pits along with mud bricks, hearths, plaster floors, pottery and animal bones were recovered. Structures n. 1, n. 2 and n. 3 along with structure n. 4, constitute the architectural remains of what is defined to be the first phase of habitation in the settlement (Figure 2.7)[1]. Timber-framed structures with

Figure 2.5 Promachon sector, Phase I. Structure n. 4 (after Koukouli-Chrysanthaki *et al.* 2007).

Figure 2.6 Promachon sector, Phase I. Bucranium and pottery vessels *in situ* (after Koukouli-Chrysanthaki *et al.* 2007).

Figure 2.7 Promachon sector, Phase I. Structure n. 4 and pit-houses (after Koukouli-Chrysanthaki *et al.* 2007).

internal pits (misleadingly defined in both Greek and Bulgarian publications as 'semi-subterranean structures' or 'subterranean structures' Koukouli-Chrysanthaki *et al.* 2007; Vajsov 2007) in some respects resemble – despite their geographical and chronological distance – the well-known Saxon 'sunken featured buildings' also known as 'sunken-houses' or 'Grubenhauser' (West 1985).

---

[1] At least six timber-framed structures with internal pits have been unearthed from the Bulgarian sector of Topolniča (Koukouli-Chrysanthaki *et al.* 2007).

The use of the timber-framed structures with internal pits, which are also referred in the bibliography as pit-houses, pit-dwellings and pit-huts (Bailey 2000; Halstead 2011; Pappa 2008), is a much contentious issue for the prehistoric archaeology of southeastern Balkans. In general, pit-houses – similar to those found at Promachon-Topolniča – have been identified as early as the Early Neolithic at Nea Makri in Attica (Pantelidou-Gofa 1991) and the Middle Neolithic in the northern Balkan peninsula (Bailey 2000). In addition, they have been unearthed from northern Greek sites contemporary to Promachon such as Makriyalos (Pappa and Bessios 1995; 1998; 1999), Thermi B (Grammenos *et al.* 1989; Pappa *et al.* 2000), Stavroupolis I-II (Grammenos and Kotsos 2002a; 2004), and Giannitsa B (Chrysostomou 1991). They all date to the early phase of the Late Neolithic (LN1) (Demoule *et al.* 1998).

There are currently two arguments with regard to the use of pit-houses. The first supports the idea that pit-houses were proper households, where a number of everyday activities, including grouping of families and food preparation and consumption were taking place (Bailey 2000; Pappa 2008). Proponents of the second argument emphasize the fact that the size of the pits of the pit-houses is rather small for a nucleated family to sleep, let alone perform other activities (Bogdanović 1988; Flannery 1972). At Promachon, each pit of the pit-houses comprises an area of nearly 10 square meters, while the floor levels were found 60-70 centimeters below the surface of the natural subsoil from which they were cut. According to the archaeologists of the site, the size of the pits of the pit-houses is rather small for a nucleated family to group. In this sense, they have suggested the presence of a raised upper structure, which would have been used as a living space, while the pits would have been used as storage facilities and workshop areas (Koukouli-Chrysanthaki *et al.* 2007) (Figure 2.8). It is worth noting, however, that the excavation on the lowest levels of the pit of the pit-house n. 1 from Promachon, revealed a hearth with distinctive traces of rebuilding and reuse (Koukouli-Chryssanthaki *et al.* 2007). It is therefore highly likely that pits of the pit-houses in Promachon might also have been used as actual living spaces. In addition, recent reconstructions of pit-houses based on two clay house models found in the Greek sector of Promachon (Figure 2.9), suggest the existence of pitched roofs.

Structure n. 4 significantly differs from the pit-houses n. 1, n. 2 and n. 3 in terms of size. In addition, the former structure can be differentiated from the other three in terms of functionality. The directors of the excavation of the site have proposed the use of structure n. 4 as a 'communal building' where activities of symbolic nature were taking place (Koukouli-Chrysanthaki *et al.* 2007), possibly involving the consumption of meat by a large number of participants as in the case of Makriyalos in Pieria, northern Greece (Mainland and Halstead 2005; Pappa *et al.* 2003). Additionally, the presence of the bucrania often covered in red paint or clay – which has parallels from Dikili Tash, eastern Macedonia (Darcque and Treuil 1997; Treuil and Darcque 1998) and the Vinča cultures of eastern Serbia (Chapman 1981) – could have added an element of symbolism to those activities.

Layer 6 is 'sealed' by a thick 20 centimeters deposit of white ash layer, marking a conflagration event that took place in the settlement. Evidence of the fire event is also documented on the Bulgarian sector of Topolniča in which, depending on the slope of the mound, the ash layer reaches almost 35-40 centimeters in thickness (Vajsov 2007). The next layer (Layer 5) was located above the successive layers of structure n. 4 and only in trench IΣT. Recent micromorphological evidence (Karkanas pers. comm.) suggests that this 15 cm layer might have been formed as a result of the collapsed wattle roof of structure n. 4 and its' ultimate subsidence after the conflagration event. Ultimately the debris covered that area.

Layer 4 represents a 25–30 centimeters thick destruction layer after the conflagration. It is found in trenches B, Γ, Δ,

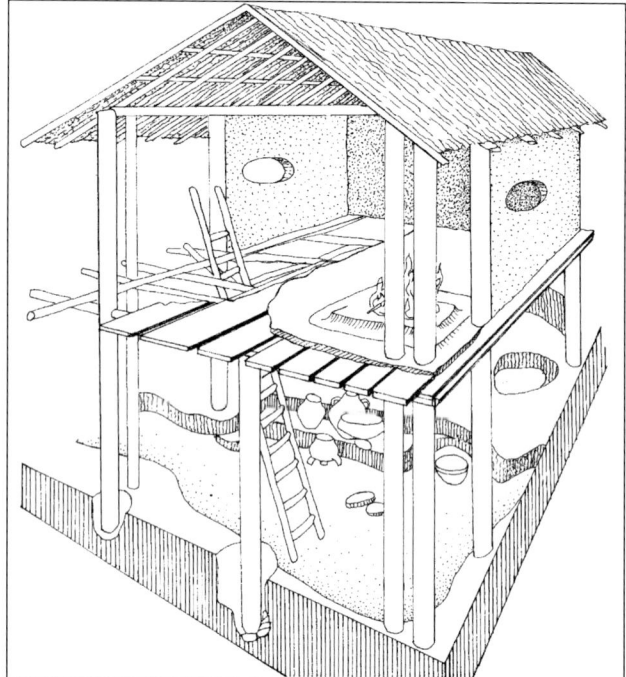

Figure 2.8 Promachon sector, Phase I. Reconstruction of a pit-house (after Koukouli-Chrysanthaki *et al.* 2007).

Figure 2.9 Promachon sector, Phase I. Clay house model with pitched roof and two depicted bucrania (after Koukouli-Chrysanthaki *et al.* 2014). © Archaeological Museum of Thessaloniki.

I, IA and IB. The deposits of this layer consist of a series of scattered debris of structures along with pebbles, a hearth, pottery sherds and animal bones, which may represent an incidence of leveling activity in order to form the floors of the structures in the next phase (Phase II). It is not yet clear whether there was a short phase of abandonment between Phase I and the subsequent Phase II (Koukouli-Chrysanthaki 2006), but evidence based on the continuity of the radiocarbon dates, suggest that the conflagration event did not substantially interrupt the settlement's occupation. To date, the causes of the fire incident are unknown.

2.3.2 Phase II (Layers 2 and 3)

The second phase of occupation includes the deposits belonging to layers 3 and 2. Layer 3 is found in all trenches of the excavation (trenches A, B, Γ, Δ, E, ΣΤ, I, IA, IB, IΣT and IZ). This level's thickness varies from 20 to 25 centimeters and consists of traces of floor surfaces, scattered mudbricks, pottery and animal bones from two aboveground timber-framed structures with internal hearths found *in situ* (Figure 2.10).

In general, aboveground timber-framed structures are found in almost all Balkan Late Neolithic sites (Bailey 2000). In the case of Late Neolithic Macedonia, aboveground timber-framed structures replace the previous structural features (pit-houses), as the interior pits are being filled and the floors are placed above ground (Gallis 1990; Koukouli-Chrysanthaki *et al.* 1997). Typical examples, contemporary to Promachon-Topolniča are represented by the aboveground timber-framed (wattle and daub) structures found at Limenaria on the island of Thassos (Malamidou 1996; 2006; Malamidou and Papadopoulos 1993; Papadopoulos and Malamidou 2012), at the Dikili Tash settlement in Kavala (Demoule 2004) and at the Arkadikos settlement in the plain of Drama (Peristeri 2002; 2004).

Excavation on both sectors of the settlement unearthed five such structures, three from the Bulgarian and two from the Greek sector. The largest of these structures was found in the Topolniča sector (structure n. 1). It was rectangular with dimensions of 8 x 5 meters and aligned roughly

along an east-west axis (Figure 2.11). A large posthole pit in the center may have been used to support the roof of the structure (Koukouli-Chrysanthaki *et al.* 1996; 2007; Vajsov 2007).

There is no certain interpretation on the function of structure n. 1 from the Bulgarian sector of Topolniča. Bulgarian archaeologists argue that the building was used as a 'sanctuary' (Vajsov 2007), since the conflagration event that took place during the previous phase may have forced the inhabitants of the settlement to move the 'communal' building (structure n. 4) from the western plateau (Promachon sector) to the eastern one (Topolniča sector) by constructing a new aboveground structure (structure n. 1). The Bulgarian publications base their interpretations regarding the 'communal essence' of the structure on the four bas-relieved schematic female figures (Vajsov 2007), which were found on the destruction levels of this building, and on the fact that the structure itself differs from the others in terms of size (Koukouli-Chrysanthaki *et al.* 1996).

Layer 2 was located only in trench IΣT. It consists of deposits made of a series of rocks, pebbles, pottery and animal bones, which accumulated in the negative features that formed as a consequence of the subsidence of structure n. 4 after the conflagration. Its thickness does not exceed 10 centimeters.

Radiocarbon analyses indicate that the site was abandoned by the end of the second phase of occupation (Koukouli-Chrysanthaki *et al.* 2014).

2.3.3 Phase III (Layer 1)

After the period of abandonment, the site was re-inhabited and it was used for a short period of time during the third

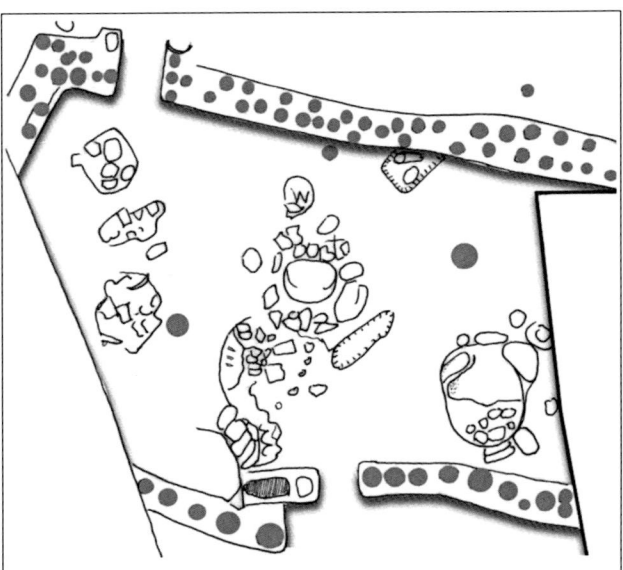

Figure 2.11 Topolniča sector, Phase II. Plan of the aboveground timber-framed structure n. 1 (after Koukouli-Chrysanthaki *et al.* 2014). © Archaeological Museum of Thessaloniki.

Figure 2.10 Promachon sector, Phase II. Aboveground timber-framed structures with hearths *in situ* (after Koukouli-Chrysanthaki *et al.* 2014). © Archaeological Museum of Thessaloniki.

(and last) phase of occupation. This phase is represented by the deposits of a single layer (Layer 1). Layer 1 is present in trenches B, Γ, Δ, I, IA, IB, IΣT and IZ. However, only a few pits and compacted debris of pottery sherds and pebbles appear in places where the structural remains of this last phase of habitation are present. These contexts probably came from the leveling of the ruins of the buildings from the preceding settlement levels, in order to form the floors of the houses of this last phase of habitation (Koukouli-Chrysanthaki *et al.* 1996; Koukouli-Chrysanthaki *et al.* 2007). Whatever the case, only tentative conclusions can be drawn, since pottery typology has indicated that this layer has been partly mixed with the preceding ones of Phase II, mainly due to intensive ploughing activity over the years (Koukouli-Chrysanthaki *et al.* 1996; Koukouli-Chrysanthaki *et al.* 2007; 2014).

Evidence of copper smelting is of particular interest in Promachon sector and it is documented in the deposits of Phase III (Koukouli-Chrysanthaki *et al.* 2000; 2007; Koukouli-Chrysanthaki and Basiakos 2002). According to the excavators of the site and the Archaeometry Lab Decmocritos in Athens, a clay crucible (Figure 2.12) that was found at the bottom of a small pit belonging to Phase III, contained traces of copper smelting with distinct also traces of heavy burning (Koukouli-Chrysanthaki *et al.* 2007; 2014). The excavation revealed also traces of copper on the floors of Phase III and a series of hollows with successive layers of burnt clay in their interiors, most likely associated with the extraction of copper (Koukouli-Chrysanthaki *et al.* 2007).

In general, the southeastern Balkan region is considered one of the independent centers of the adoption of metallurgy during the late stages of the Neolithic period (Jovanović 1980; Renfrew 1969). Similar to Promachon cases from northern Greece and the Balkan regions constitute the site of Sitagroi, with evidence of crucibles with copper slag during the third phase of occupation (Renfrew and Slater

Figure 2.12 Promachon sector, Phase III. Clay crucible (after Koukouli-Chrysanthaki *et al.* 2014). © Archaeological Museum of Thessaloniki.

2002), Dikili Tash, with evidence of hollows with burnt clay and traces of copper extraction dating to the first phase of occupation (Seferiadis 1983), as well as the sites of Rudna Glava (Jovanović 1980) and Ai bunar (Chernych 1978), with evidence of intensive copper extraction.

The settlement of Promachon-Topolniča was eventually abandoned by the end of the third phase of occupation.

2.4 Absolute dating

[14]C analysis from 11 bone and charcoal samples from both sectors (Maniatis and Fakorellis 2000; Maniatis *et al.* 2004) has shown a clear clustering of the absolute dates for Phases I and II (Table 2.1). Following calibration (Figure 2.13), the general chronological sequence that was

Table 2.1 ^{14}C dates from both sectors (after Koukouli-Chrysanthaki *et al.* 2007).

Lab number	Context	Material	[14]C	δ^{13}C	Cal. BC
HD-20459	Square ΣT (Phase II)	Bone	5999 ± 47	-19.3	4939 – 4805 / 5017 – 4733
HD-20462	Square IA (Phase III) / depth: 80.01 m	Bone	5530 ± 48	-19	4448 – 4337 / 4459 – 4254
DEM-1173	Square IΣT (Phase II) / depth: 79.30 m	Charcoal	5996 ± 25	-25	4910 – 4810 / 4940 – 4870
DEM-1185	Square IΣT (Phase II) / depth: 79.31 m	Charcoal	5895 ± 33	-25	4800 – 4720 / 4850 – 4690
Bln-3348	Square M14 (Phase II) / depth: 0.90 m	Charcoal	6000 ± 80		4970 – 4780
DEM-1250	Square IΣT (Phase II) / depth: 79.65 m	Charcoal	6068 ± 40	-25	5030 – 4860 / 5190 – 4810
DEM-1254	Square IΣT (Phase II) / depth: 78.99 m	Charcoal	6038 ± 40	-25	4990 – 4820 / 5040 – 4800
HD-20457	Square Γ (Phase I) / depth: 78.17 m	Charcoal	6188 ± 38	-25.77	5227 – 5061 / 5287 – 5002
Bln-3382	Square 2c (Phase I) / depth: 1.10 m	Charcoal	6100 ± 60		5200 – 5180 / 5080 – 4930
Bln-3349	Square O12 (Phase I) / depth: 1.20 m	Charcoal	6240 ± 90		5270 – 5060
Bln-3381	Square J11 (Phase I) / depth: 0.80 m	Charcoal	6270 ± 60		5270 – 5200 / 5170 – 5080

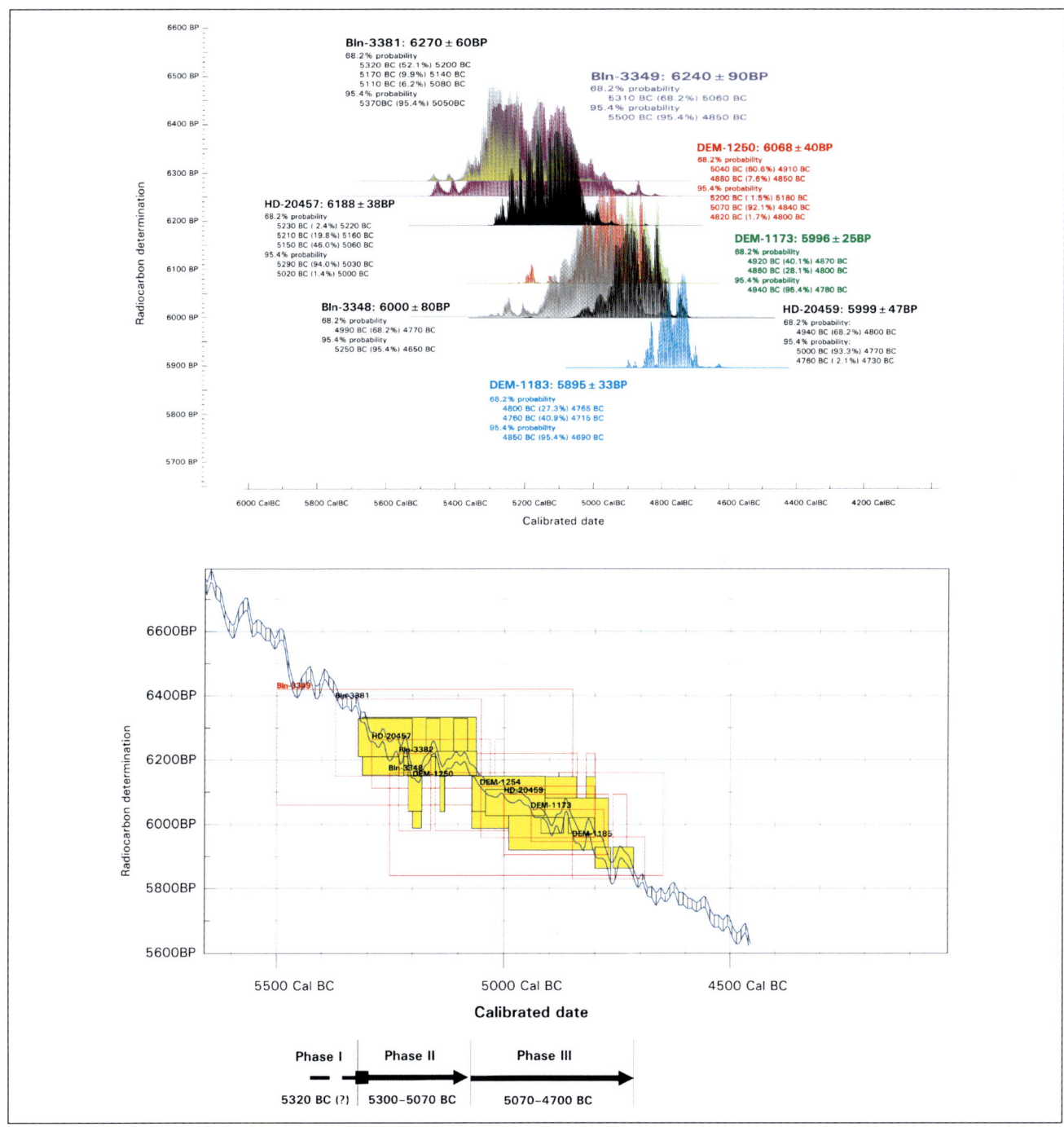

Figure 2.13 Calibrated ¹⁴C dates from Promachon-Topolniča (after Vajsov 2007).

established for the three phases in Promachon-Topolniča settlement is the following:

Phases	Cal. BC	Cultural sequence
Phase III	4460 – 4250	Late Neolithic II
Phase II	5070 – 4700	Late Neolithic I
Phase I	5320 – 5070	

We must, however, consider that the dating of Phase III is only based on one ¹⁴C date, which means that we must be cautious about its accurate chronological separation.

As mentioned above the deposit from this phase is mixed with the one from the earlier Phase II. It is, however, worth paying attention to the fact that the single ¹⁴C date from Phase III has produced the most recent date, which suggests that the finds from this phase are not entirely residual.

2.5 Material culture evidence

The analysis of the material culture from both sectors indicates that Phases I-II belong to the early stage of the Late Neolithic (LNI) (Demoule *et al.* 1998), which dates between the second half of the sixth and the beginning of the fifth millennium BC. Vessels painted in the 'Akropotamos type' of decoration (Mylonas 1941; Mylonas and Bakalakis

Figure 2.14 Promachon sector, Phase I. Single handed carinated bowl with black-on-top style of decoration (after Vajsov 2007).

Figure 2.16 Topolniča sector, Phase III. Sherds with incised Gradesniča type of decoration (after Vajsov 2007).

Figure 2.15 Promachon sector, Phase II. Bichrome painted Dimitra type pottery (after Koukouli-Chrysanthaki *et al.* 2007).

1938), as well as vessels with 'black on top' decorative styles (Figure 2.14) are typical of Phase I in Promachon-Topolniča (Vajsov 2007). Typical decoration styles from the following phase (Phase II) include pottery painted with wide bands of the 'Strumsko type' of decoration (Koukouli-Chrysanthaki *et al.* 1997) and 'Dimitra type' repertoire (Figure 2.15) (Grammenos 1991; Koukouli-Chrysanthaki *et al.* 1998a). This latter type can be subdivided into an earlier stage of development (typical of Phase IIa) and a later stage, which combines 'Strumsko and Akropotamos' types of decoration (Koukouli-Chrysanthaki *et al.* 2007; Vajsov 2007) (typical of Phase IIb).

Pottery typology and decorative motives link Phases I and II with Makriyalos I (Pappa and Bessios 1998; 1999; Pappa *et al.* 1998), Sitagroi I-II (Keighley 1986; Renfrew *et al.* 1986), Dimitra I-II (Grammenos 1991) Dikili Tash I (Seferiadis 1983; Tsirtsoni 1991; 2000; 2001) and Vassilika I-II (Grammenos 1991) from Greek Macedonia, Paradimi II-III (Bakalakis and Sakellariou 1981) and Makri II from Thrace (Efstratiou *et al.* 1998) Arapi Magoula from Thessaly (Hauptmann and Milojcic 1969) Damjanitsa (Pernicheva 1995) and Balgarčevo (Pernicheva 2002) from the Bulgarian part of the Strymon river valley, and 'Vinča B culture' settlements (Chapman 1981) from eastern Serbia.

The uppermost levels (Phase III) in the Promachon-Topolniča settlement can be dated to the late stage of the Late Neolithic (LNII) on the basis of pottery typology and decoration (Koukouli-Chrysanthaki *et al.* 1996; 1998a; 1998b; 2007). Typical examples of incised 'Gradesniča type' (Nikolov 1976) (Figure 2.16) and thin lined graphite painted pottery sherds, link this later stage to Dikili Tash II (Seferiadis 1983; Treuil 1992), Sitagroi III (Evans 1986), Dimitra III and Vassilika III-IV (Grammenos 1991), Makriyalos II (Pappa and Bessios 1998; 1999; Pappa *et al.* 1998), and Thermi B (Grammenos *et al.* 1989) from Macedonia, 'classic' Dimini and Larissa (Demoule 2004; Demoule and Perles 1993; Demoule *et al.* 1998) from Thessaly, Paradimi IV (Bakalakis and Sakellariou 1981) from Thrace, Slatino I-V (Chochadziev 1986) from the Bulgarian part of the Strymon river valley, Gradesniča (Nikolov 1976) from northwest Bulgaria, 'Marica-Karanovo' phase (Hiller 1989) from Bulgarian Thrace, and 'Vinča C culture' settlements (Chapman 1981) from eastern Serbia.

Table 2.2 presents the layers against excavation trenches at Promachon sector, while Table 2.3 summarizes the phasing of the site on the basis of structural features and material culture evidence.

Table 2.2 Layers against excavation trenches at Promachon sector.

Cultural sequence	Phases	Layers	Trenches										
			A	B	Γ	Δ	E	ΣT	I	IA	IB	IΣT	IZ
Late Neolithic II	III	1											
Late Neolithic I	II	2											
		3											
	I	4											
		5											
		6											
		7											
		8											
		9											
		10											
		11											

Table 2.3 Summary of the phasing on the basis of structural features and material culture evidence.

Layers	Structural features	Habitation phasing	Ceramic typology and repertoire	Material culture phasing	Cal. BC	Cultural sequence
1	Non-defined	III	Gradesniča type Graphite type	III	4460 – 4250	Late Neolithic II
2	Timber-framed aboveground structures	II	Strumsko type Akropotamos type	IIb	5070 – 4700	Late Neolithic I
3			Strumsko type Dimitra type	IIa		
4	Pit-houses	I	Akropotamos type Black on top Clay lamps	I	5320 – 4700	
5						
6						
7	Structure n. 4					
8						
9						
10						
11						

State of the Art and Aims

3.1 Zooarchaeology in Greece

The archaeology of classical Greece has been the main focus for research programs and excavations around the country for more than two centuries. The abundance of literary sources and the impressive archaeological discoveries from this period encouraged Greek archaeologists to focus strongly towards architectural and artistic features of the archaeological evidence, while social, economic and environmental aspects were largely neglected (Trantalidou 2001). Although there were a few cases of Greek archaeologists in the late 1920s and the early 1930s (Marinatos, Evans, Hatzidakis and Heurtley), who considered it necessary to have animal bones studied from their excavations, in most cases, excavation directors in Greece did not consider necessary to collect faunal material (Greenfield 1991; Reese 1994; Trantalidou 2001).

In the 1950s and in the 1960s, the proliferation of excavations at prehistoric sites especially from the Neolithic period in Thessaly, prompted the sporadic collection of faunal materials (Trantalidou 2001). In the two following decades, the study of animal bone assemblages from excavations in Greece began with the occasional work of zooarchaeologists of non-Greek origin, such as Boessneck and von den Driesch (Germany), Bökönyi (Hungary), Payne and Higgs (UK) and Gejvall and Larje (Sweden), who are today considered as the pioneers of zooarchaeology in Greece. Naturally, whatever progress was made in the study of faunal materials from Greek sites was affected by the methods and the theoretical orientation of these researchers' country of origin.

Although the study of faunal remains from Greek sites increased rapidly during the 1980s and 1990s, the number of zooarchaeologists of Greek origin studying faunal assemblages from Greek sites was rather scarce. At the same time, two comprehensive surveys of zooarchaeological work in Greece were published. The first was compiled in the mid-1980s by Payne (1985a). In his paper, Payne included 100 titles, with a summary description of the basic data provided in each study (site, region, time-period, and frequency of species). The second survey was compiled in the mid-1990s by Reese (1994). In his survey, he presented the zooarchaeological work conducted on Greek sites from 1985 to 1993, pointing out to the general scarcity of faunal reports dating to later than the Bronze Age, an issue which by and large still affects Greek zooarchaeology. In addition, Reese included a very useful table, in which he separated faunal materials deriving from settlements, sanctuaries and cemeteries from mainland Greece as well as the Greek islands. In the mid-1990s and the early 2000s, the potential of zooarchaeology was better understood by Greek archaeologists. By that time, scholars of Greek origins who, due to the absence of a Greek zooarchaeology curriculum had been trained in European Universities had already begun studying faunal assemblages from Greek sites (e.g. Grammenos 1997; Trantalidou 2001). Katerina Trantalidou provided a brief historiography of the science of zooarchaeology in Greece in a paper published in the early 2000s (Trantalidou 2001), before the publication of the monograph "Zooarchaeology in Greece: recent advances" (Kotjabopoulou et al. 2003), which contained a rich collection of zooarchaeological articles. The latter represents the first full survey entirely dedicated to Greek zooarchaeology and includes many contributions by Greek zooarchaeologists.

In recent years, papers on Greek faunal assemblages are regularly presented and published as parts of annual conference proceedings. However, a major drawback for zooarchaeology in Greece today is represented by the fact that there are no scientific journals dealing specifically with zooarchaeology – as there are for the more general field of archaeology (i.e. Archaiologiki Efimeris, Praktika tis Archaiologikis Etairias, Archaiologikon Deltion). However, and despite the availability of faunal remains from several recently excavated sites, there are still cases in which faunal assemblages are left unstudied, stored in the basements of various archaeological services and museums. The recent financial crisis in Greece has largely affected the entire discipline of archaeology and, with it, zooarchaeology.

There is however, another issue, which should also be considered. Even when faunal assemblages from Greek sites are studied and published, they tend to suffer from insufficient integration with other lines of archaeological evidence. There are cases however, in which the integration between archaeology and zooarchaeology has succeeded. This has given Greek archaeologists the opportunity to recognise the necessity of studying faunal assemblages as an important aid to the understanding of past human communities. It has also provided the opportunity to new researchers to move on from the classical tradition and explore new avenues of investigation, stimulating also the understanding of patterns of past human behaviour, which were previously explained solely on the basis of ceramic typology and architecture.

3.2 Faunal studies in Neolithic Macedonia

The bibliographic details that are provided in Table 3.1 (Figure 3.1) reveal an uneven spread of faunal research from Neolithic sites in Greek Macedonia as concerns space, time and the nationality of the zooarchaeologists involved.

Table 3.1 Neolithic Macedonian sites with published faunal assemblages. Only cases which include – at least – the proportions of the three main domesticated species are considered. Absolute dates for each cultural sequence follow Andreou *et al.* (1996). The cultural sequence at each site is not necessarily linked with the intensity of the faunal research conducted at it (*e.g.* the Early Neolithic levels of Dikili Tash have recently emerged, and consequently, no faunal research has been published until today). Each site is included in the broad geographical region in which it appeared to belong when first published. For instance, the village of Nea Nikomidia belongs to the administrative division of central Macedonia. However, in the publication of 1962 it is included in the region of western Macedonia. No efforts were made to state the nature of each site (open-air or tell), except for the site of Aggitis, which is a cave-site. This was decided since no general *consensus* has been reached in terms of defining the nature of some of the sites presented in this table.

Macedonian sites		Cultural Sequence				Sources
		Early Neolithic 6700–5800 Cal. BC	Middle Neolithic 5800–5400 Cal. BC	Late Neolithic 5400–4500 Cal. BC	Final Neolithic 4500–3300 Cal. BC	
Western	Dispilio				■	Cosmetatou-Phoca 2007; Samartzidou 2015
	Makriyalos			■	■	Tzevelekidi *et al.* 2014
	Megalo Nisi Galanis			■	■	Greenfield and Fowler 2003; 2005
	Nea Nikomidia	■	■			Higgs 1962
	Paliambela		■			Halstead and Isaakidou 2013
	Revenia	■				Halstead and Isaakidou 2013
	Servia	■	■	■		Watson 1979a
	Toumba Kremastis			■		Tzevelekidi 2012
Central	Stavroupoli			■		Yiannouli 2002a; 2004
	Thermi			■		Yiannouli 1989
	Vasilika		■	■		Yiannouli 1994
Eastern	Aggitis cave			■		Trantalidou et al. 2006
	Asprovalta			■		Samartzidou 2002
	Dikili Tash		■	■	■	Julien 1992; Helmer 1997
	Dimitra		■	■	■	Yiannouli 1994; 1997
	Kryoneri			■	■	Mylona 1997
	Limenaria (island)			■	■	Webb 2012
	Paradisos			■	■	Larje 1987
	Promachon-Topolniča			■		Iliev and Spassov 2007; Theodorogianni and Trantalidou 2013
	Sitagroi			■	■	Bökönyi 1986
	Kastri (island)				■	Halstead 1996

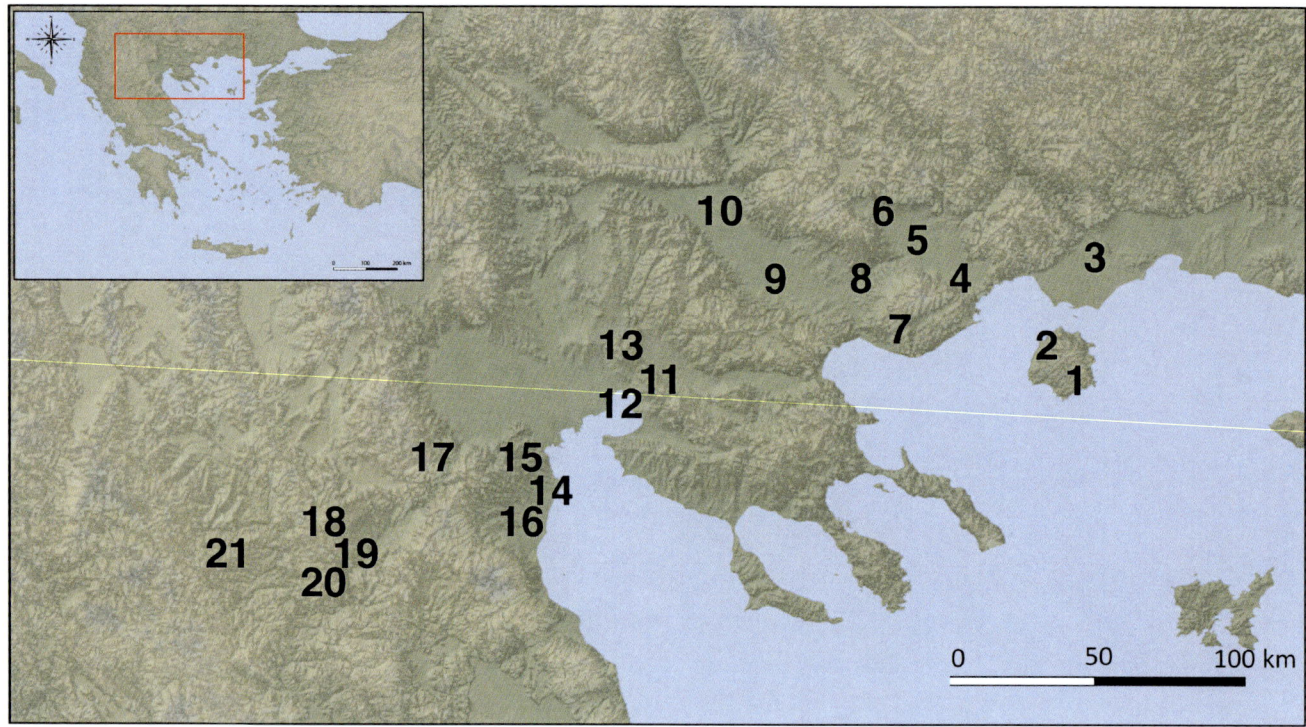

Figure 3.1 Map of Neolithic Macedonian sites mentioned in Table 3.1. Base map provided by the ASCSA©. 1. Limenaria (Thasos island); 2. Kastri (Thasos island); 3. Paradisos; 4. Dikili Tash; 5. Aggitis cave; 6. Sitagroi; 7. Asprovalta; 8. Kryoneri; 9. Dimitra; 10. Promachon-Topolniča; 11. Stavroupoli; 12. Thermi; 13. Vasilika; 14. Makriyalos; 15. Paliambela Kolindrou; 16. Revenia Korinou; 17. Nea Nikomidia; 18. Megalo Nisi Galanis; 19. Toumba Kremastis; 20. Servia; 21. Dispilio.

The first published faunal report regarding Neolithic Macedonia was undertaken by a non-Greek researcher and it dates back to as early as the early 1960s [*i.e.* Higgs' (1962) report for Nea Nikomidia]. In the following decades, zooarchaeologists of non-Greek origins continued to contribute to the study and publication of faunal remains from Neolithic Macedonia [*i.e.* Watson (1979a) for Servia, Bökönyi (1986) for Sitagroi and Larje (1987) for Paradisos]. These faunal reports were, however, published together with other archaeological materials, while the faunal report from Bronze Age Kastanas was – at that time – the only report which was published in a separate volume (Becker 1986). Only from the mid-1990s and the early 2000s Greek animal bone specialists started contributing regularly to zooarchaeological research (Grammenos 1997). However, the long tradition of non-Greeks doing faunal research in Macedonia continued to flourish, partly sponsored by the many archaeological schools and institutes established in Athens (Wiener Lab of the American School of Clasical Studies at Athens; Fitch Lab of the British School at Athens *etc.*). Yiannouli is considered one of the pioneers of Greek zooarchaeology in the area of Macedonia, since she started publishing faunal studies from Neolithic (Thermi, Dimitra and Stavroupoli) and Bronze Age (Skala Sotiros, Pentapoli and Mesimeriani) sites, as early as the late 1980s (Yiannouli 1989; 1997; 2002a; 2002b; 2004).

The coverage of faunal research in Neolithic Macedonia is inevitably linked with the intensity of archaeological research in the area. Most faunal analyses have been conducted on Late Neolithic remains from western and especially eastern Macedonia. On the contrary, sites dating to the Paleolithic and the Iron Age as well as sites from central Macedonia (and also Thrace), have received less archaeological attention (Reese 1994; Trantalidou 2001). With regard to the Neolithic, the scarcity of faunal assemblages from Early and Middle Neolithic sites in all three regions can plausibly be attributed to the absence of these early levels due to 'gaps' in the archaeological research. Excavation of the earliest Neolithic phases in western Macedonia were until recently confined to sites such as Nea Nikomidia and Servia (with already published faunal assemblages), whereas Early Neolithic horizons have recently emerged at Paliambela Kolindrou, Revenia Korinou (Maniatis *et al.* 2015) Fylotsairi Mavropigis (Karamitrou-Mentesidi *et al.* 2013), Pontokomi and Xirolimni (Karamitrou-Mentesidi 2014; Karamitrou-Mentesidi *et al.* 2014)[1]. With regard to eastern Macedonia, Early Neolithic horizons have recently emerged at Dikili Tash (Lespez *et al.* 2013), while the settlement of Mikri Volvi in the Langadas basin (Kotsos and Urem-Kotsou 2016) constitutes one of the few Early Neolithic sites in central Macedonia. It is therefore only a matter of time since analyses of faunal remains from these Early Neolithic Macedonian sites becomes largely available to the wider archaeological community.

The integration of such a diverse body of faunal literature – regardless of the time-period – presents a number of

---

[1] With regard to Fylotsairi and Xirolimni, the study of faunal remains has just been concluded by zooarchaeologist Stefania Michalopoulou as part of her PhD thesis.

challenges that should be articulated before making any comparisons. Taphonomy has important repercussions in the formation of the faunal assemblages, and naturally, it is a significant factor that we have to keep in mind. For instance, not all faunal reports contain information on patterns of both human and non-human modification (*i.e.* butchery, gnawing, burning *etc.*) on animal bones. The most important problem, however, is represented by the fact that the extent of recovery bias is not assessed in all cases. Differences in the recording methodology (identifications, recording protocols) and the analytical techniques (methods for the assessment of the age-at-death, biometry, sexing) used by the faunal researchers in a number of sites, are additional issues to be considered when conducting inter-site analyses (Albarella 1995). All of these issues will be further assessed for each site respectively, as we proceed with our comparison of Promachon to other contemporary sites in Macedonia. In addition, they will be taken into consideration when attempting to interpret the nature of human-animal relationships at a regional scale during the Late Neolithic.

3.3 Pilot study and doctoral research: two sides of the same coin

The animal bone material from the Greek sector of Promachon derived from contexts of sufficiently accurate dating and stratigraphic integrity to warrant detailed study. The excavation at the Greek sector of Promachon yielded a volume of animal bone equivalent to 296 boxes with dimensions of 45 x 28 x 18 centimeters each. Of these, 150 boxes derived from the five successive layers of structure n. 4 (Layers 7-11; Phase I), while 146 derived from the rest of the layers (Layers 1-6; Phases I-II-III). The faunal material from the excavation was divided and stored separately: material deriving from layers 7-11 was stored in the Amphipolis Museum, while the rest of the material (Layers 1-6) was stored at the Loutra Sanatorium in the village of Sidirokastro, Serres, Greece.

This book is based on the author's doctoral research at the University of Sheffield UK between 2011-14. The doctoral research was an extension of a previous study conducted as part of the dissertation associated with the MSc in Environmental Archaeology and Palaeoeconomy undertaken in the academic year 2008-09 at the same University (Kazantzis 2009). The Masters study only dealt with a sample of the assemblage and could therefore be regarded as a pilot study to the doctoral research: out of a total of 146 boxes of animal bone remains from the Greek sector of Promachon, the content of 16 boxes deriving from the floor levels of two structures belonging to the first and the second phase of the settlement's occupation [pit-house n. 2 (Phase I) and aboveground structure n. 1 (Phase II)] were washed and studied, and, in total, 1450 animal bone remains were recorded. Due therefore to the relatively small size of the sample once it had been divided into the two phases of occupation, the data (species, body parts and types of measurements) were merged and treated as a single sample (*cf.* Albarella 2002).

Consequently, no comparison was attempted between the two phases and the two structures of the settlement: the study mainly focused on a general assessment of the subsistence economy and animal use at both the site and regional levels.

Therefore, the results from the Masters study derived from a small sample, with the inevitable limitations of the case. In order to tackle questions for which the initial sample was inadequate, the doctoral research involved the study of a much larger assemblage. This consisted of faunal material from six layers (Layers 1, 2, 3, 4, 5 and 6; Phases I-II-III) belonging to trenches A, B, Γ, Δ, E, ΣΤ, I and IA[2]. On the other hand, the animal bones from structure n. 4 (trenches IΣΤ and IZ) and thus, Layers 7, 8, 9, 10 and 11 (Phase I), were not considered, since they were studied by zooarchaeologist Ourania Theodorogianni as part of her own PhD research.

Out of 130 boxes of animal bone remains used for the doctoral research, the content of 19 boxes derived from deposits placed between the topsoil and the first layer (Layer 1: Phase III). These were ultimately excluded from the analysis, since they could not be reliably dated. In overall therefore, the content of 111 boxes of animal bone remains were used for any analysis, and they constitute the basis of the zooarchaeological research presented in the current study. The bulk of the faunal material was unwashed, which made the cleaning of the bones a paramount necessity. Washing took place from March 2010 to September 2011 at the 'Bezesteni' Archaeological Museum of Serres, Greece. In September 2011, the washed faunal material was transferred from the 'Bezesteni' Archaeological Museum to the basements of the (now former) 28th Ephoria of Prehistoric and Classical Antiquities of Serres (KH ΕΠΚΑ Σερρών), where it was recorded. After the recording, the content of 111 boxes of animal bone remains was transferred back to the Loutra Sanatorium in the beginning of October 2012.

3.4 Aims

The main purpose of this study is to investigate human *versus* animal relationships in the Late Neolithic Strymon river valley, using the animal bone assemblage from Promachon as the main source of evidence. First, the general aims are presented. These are followed by a summary of the more specific aims be interpreted in the context of the broader questions highlighted before.

3.4.1 General aims

1. To understand the nature, scale and importance of pastoral activities at prehistoric Promachon

---

[2] Unfortunately, the faunal material from Trench IB was not included in the doctoral research (and therefore, it is not included here as well), since it was not possible to be detected at the Loutra Sanatorium, where the rest of the faunal material (not associated with structure n. 4) was originally stored.

This study will focus on husbandry strategies at the Greek sector of Promachon and will examine the role of the domestic livestock to the economy of the site. The integration of the faunal data with other lines of archaeological evidence will be instrumental in our understanding of the inhabitants' economic and social activities assessing also the significance and the relative contribution of livestock to subsistence. Ultimately the results from this local study will contribute to our understanding of prehistoric life as a whole and will also highlight the potential of zooarchaeology in the investigation of past human communities.

2. To contribute to the understanding of the nature of the site in its different phases of occupation, as well as the use of different areas and contexts

Comparison of different phases, contexts types and areas will be undertaken, as this will provide valuable information for the interpretation of the site. An element of particular comparative interest is represented by the interpretation of structure n. 4 as having been used for public functions (Koukouli-Chrysanthaki et al. 2007). As previously noted, the faunal material from structure n. 4 (Layers 7-11; Phase I) was studied by zooarchaeologist Ourania Theodorogianni as part of her own PhD research; the results from this study were published in a form of a preliminary report early in 2013 (Theodorogianni and Trantalidou 2013). It is therefore anticipated that the faunal evidence from this particular structure would make for an interesting comparison with the more likely household origin of some of the other deposits (Layers 4-6; Phase I). The animal bone material from the Bulgarian sector of Topolniča was published as part of a contribution dealing with the archaeological work in the area of the valley of the Strymon river (Iliev and Spassov 2007). Unfortunately, the publication is in Bulgarian, which limits the opportunity for the results to reach a broad readership. In this study, however, the results from the Bulgarian sector of Topolniča will be considered and, whenever possible, integrated with the author's work on the Greek sector of Promachon. This will provide valuable information for the interpretation of the site as a whole, since the two sectors belong to the same settlement, merely divided by modern political borders.

3. To document regional and chronological trends in the importance of domesticated and wild species at the site and beyond, incorporating the settlement in the broader complex of contemporary agro-pastoral communities in the Strymon basin and adjacent areas

This study will present new information on subsistence strategies in an underrepresented area of northern Greece during a time-period (fifth and fourth millennium BC), that is considered one of the most dynamic eras of the prehistory of southeastern Europe. The comparison between Promachon and other contemporary Macedonian, Thracian and Thessalian assemblages has the potential of shedding light on prehistoric life at both local (Strymon river valley) and regional (Macedonia) levels. In addition, the comparison between Promachon and other contemporary Balkan sites will clarify temporal and regional trends in animal management and will create an integrated picture of human-animal relationships that will encompass both northern Greece and the Balkan regions.

3.4.2 Specific research aims

1. To explore the effect of taphonomic modifications in the formation of the faunal assemblage
2. To explore the frequencies of the domesticated *versus* wild species, as well as the relative frequencies of three main domesticated species
3. To explore patterns of butchery on the bones of the three main domesticated species
4. To explore the body part distribution of domesticated and wild species
5. To reconstruct the age-at-death profiles of the three main domesticated species
6. To explore the size and shape of the three main domesticated species
7. To compare the relative frequencies of the domesticated and wild species, as well as of three main domesticated species, between structure n. 4 and the rest of the deposits of Phase I
8. To compare the age-at-death profiles of the three main domesticated species between structure n. 4 and the rest of the deposits of Phase I
9. To compare the frequencies of the domesticated *versus* wild species as well as the frequencies of three main domesticated species between Promachon sector and Topolniča sector
10. To compare the relative frequencies of the domesticated and wild species as well as the three main domesticated species between Promachon and other contemporary Macedonian, Thracian, Thessalian and Balkan sites
11. To compare the age-at-death profiles of the three main domesticated species between Promachon and other contemporary Macedonian sites
12. To compare the size and shape of the three main domesticated species between Promachon and other contemporary Macedonian and Thessalian sites

The methodology developed to address all of these aims is set out in the next chapter.

Methods and Analytical Techniques

4.1 Methodological considerations

Animal bone studies have developed in many ways during the past two decades, while methodological approaches and analytical techniques have been the subject of numerous debates (Lyman 1994). Variations in faunal samples and the realization that factors such as taphonomy and the level of preservation may influence the very nature of an animal bone assemblage, has led to a reappraisal of methodological techniques (Reitz and Wing 2008). It is the task of the zooarchaeologist to evaluate these factors, and, according to the research questions, to create a methodological protocol suitable to assess bias and enhance interpretation (Grayson 1984).

The methods used in this study were chosen due to their ability of commenting directly on animal exploitation in Promachon. Species frequency, body part distribution, sex ratios, age-at-death data and animal size and shape are focal points in assessing the economic importance and the cultural significance of both domestic and wild taxa on-site. In conjunction with these academic concerns, practical issues also influenced the selection of method. Particular attention was given to the timescale of the project and to the accuracy of the collected data.

4.2 Identification (challenges)

Promachon's faunal material is in an overall very good state of preservation, thus enhancing our chances of correct anatomical and taxonomical identification. A small modern reference collection created by the author and consisting of whole skeletons of sheep, goat, dog, cattle, pig and red deer, as well as a few roe deer elements, was used for identification. This was complemented by the use of a number of identification atlases (Gromova 1950; 1960; Hillson 1986; 1992; Pales and Lambert 1971; Schmid 1972). A small number of specimens that could not be identified *in situ* were eventually attributed to taxa with the help of the reference collection from the University of Sheffield's zooarchaeology lab. Identification challenges in temperate Europe Neolithic faunal material include distinction between similarly sized cervids and bovids, as well as wild and domestic forms of pigs, cattle and canids (Orton 2008). With regard to the latter, no wolves (*Canis lupus*) were positively identified at the time of the recording. However, metrical analysis has indicated the presence of the wild progenitor of dog in Promachon sector. On the other hand, discrimination between domestic dog (*Canis familiaris*) and red fox (*Vulpes vulpes*) presented a certain level of difficulty, since both species are present at the settlement with roughly the same size. In the Bulgarian site of Topolniča, domestic dog is represented by a small-

sized breed (Iliev and Spassov 2007), which confuses the pattern even further. Consequently, some canid elements could not be attributed with absolute certainty to either *Canis* or *Vulpes*. These were eventually identified as *Canis/Vulpes* (dog/red fox). Two wild ancestors of domesticated species were expected to be present in Promachon sector: *Bos primigenius* (aurochs) and *Sus scrofa* (wild pig). Theodorogianni and Trantalidou (2013) and Iliev and Spassov (2007) argue for the presence of the two species in structure n. 4 (Promachon sector) and in the Bulgarian sector of Topolniča respectively. In addition, the two species are reported in a number of contemporary sites in Greek Macedonia, such as Sitagroi (Bökönyi 1986) and Stavroupoli (Yiannouli 2002a; 2004). Even though metrical criteria can be useful in discriminating between wild and domesticated populations, sexual dimorphism as well as residual individual variation may confuse matters (Payne and Bull 1988). This approach was, therefore, used cautiously with very few specimens recorded as either wild or domestic at the time of recording – these were those whose size was obviously either very large or very small.

The sheep (*Ovis aries*) and goat (*Capra hircus*) distinction generally follows Boessneck (1969), Kratochvíl (1969) and Prummel and Frisch (1986) and it was attempted on the following postcranial elements: distal Humerus, proximal Radius, distal Metacarpal, distal Metatarsal, distal Tibia, Calcaneum and Astragalus. As for teeth, distinction between sheep and goat follows Payne (1985b) for deciduous teeth, and Halstead *et al.* (2002) for permanent teeth. However, the vast majority of *Caprinae* remains could not be identified to such a fine taxonomical level and were consequently identified as *Ovis/Capra* (sheep/goat).

Separation between cervids and bovids – in this case between *Cervus* and *Bos* and between *Capreolus* and *Ovis/Capra* – can be problematic on the basis of certain elements. The main references employed were Helmer and Rocheteau (1994) for the smaller species and Prummel (1988) for the larger. While this allowed the bulk of relevant specimens to be identified to taxon, a few were assigned to the categories *Ovis/Capra/Capreolus* (OCC) and *Cervus/Bos* (CB). The distinction of different cervids was mainly based on the criteria suggested by Lister (1996) and von Bosold (1968).

4.3 The recording protocol

The recording system adopted in this study falls broadly within the genealogy traced back to Watson's (1979b) 'diagnostic zones', but generally follows Davis (1992) with minor changes. The collected data were recorded using an Excel database for Macintosh. Only a number of bone zones of bones whose identity could be established with reasonable confidence was recorded (Albarella and Davis 1994; Davis 1992), using the recording criteria in Davis (1992) for mammals (Table 4.1). The aim was to produce a maximum amount of useful information, while avoiding recording low grade and redundant information.

The recording system is based on three main database structures: one for bones, a second for teeth and a last one for vertebrae and ribs. With regard to the 'Bones section', as well as species, element and side, fields were created for state of preservation, gnawing, burning, fusion status and pathology, with additional fields for measurements. The 'Teeth section' generally follows the same pattern as the 'Bones section'. However, additional fields were created to state whether a tooth was loose or within a jaw. The mandibular or maxillary status for each tooth was also recorded. No attempts were made, however, to separate first and second molars when isolated. These were recorded either as $M^{1/2}$ (maxillary) or as $M_{1/2}$ (mandibular). Presence was stated for vertebrae and ribs also, as these were recorded in a separate table into size groups (large, medium and small). Measurements were taken on teeth and on fused, fusing and unfused specimens

and generally follow von den Driesch (1976), with some additional measurements by Davis (1992), Albarella and Payne (2005), Albarella *et al.* (2005) and Payne and Bull (1988). Neonatal and juvenile specimens were measured following Prummel (1987) and flagged as such in an associated field. In this study, raw measurements are plotted on individual dimensions in order to find if size differences between domestic species occur. However, whenever the sample sizes are too small for any metrical comparisons to be conducted, we use two different methods: firstly, the metrical data from domestic species deriving from a number of sites contemporary to Promachon are superimposed in order to increase the sample size. Secondly, we use the log ratio technique. Log ratios are calculated to allow different measurements to be combined, maximizing the information potential of the data. The log ratio technique, first introduced in zooarchaeology by Simpson *et al.* (1960), is probably the most commonly used of the scaling techniques (Albarella 2002). The data from different measurements may be combined by transforming them into log-ratio scores relative to a standard animal. For each measurement on an archaeological specimen the natural logarithm is taken, and that of the equivalent measurement on the standard animal is subtracted to produce a measure of size difference

Table 4.1 The recording protocol used.

Anatomical elements	Articulation Criteria		Other Criteria	
	Proximal	Distal		
Antlers / Horncores			Complete transverse section	
Teeth			Occlusal surface	
Cranium			Zygomaticus	
Atlas			More than half present	
Axis			More than half present	
Scapula			Glenoid cavity	Articular end
Humerus	Yes	Yes		
Radius	Yes	Yes		
Ulna	Yes			
Carpal (2) + 3			More than half present	
Metacarpal		Yes		
Pelvis			Acetabulum	Ischial part
Femur	Yes	Yes		
Tibia	Yes	Yes		
Astragalus			Lateral half	
Calcaneum			Sustentaculum	
Scafocuboid			More than half present	
Metatarsal		Yes		
Phalanges	Yes			

between the archaeological specimen and the standard, allowing for comparability between elements. For instance, if the distance between the mean of each measurement and the 'standard' tends to be constant, we can assume that the animals of the archaeological population under analysis are similar in size to the standard (Albarella 2002; Payne and Bull 1988). The Cabeço da Arruda (Portugal) aurochs (Wright 2013) is used as a standard for *Bos* in Promachon, along with specimens of Shetland (UK) ewes (Davis 1996) for *Ovis aries*, and specimens of wild boar from Kizilcahaman (Turkey) (Payne and Bull 1988) for *Sus*. The two following tables show which measurements were taken on various postcranial (Table 4.2) and teeth (Table 4.3) elements.

4.4 Quantifying the faunal material

Methods of quantification have all been subjected to vigorous debates since the beginnings of the discipline. Regardless of the benefits and the drawbacks that each system presents, a consensus has been reached by a vast number of zooarchaeologists in using fragment count, or simply NISP (Number of Identified Specimens), as the basic measure of taxonomic abundance.

NISP suffers from a great deal of biases. It ignores some aspects that are related to animal anatomical representation (Ringrose 1993), while it is susceptible to differential bone fragmentation (Klein and Cruz-Uribe 1984). The system of 'Diagnostic Zones' proposed by Watson (1979b) and used here – with substantial modifications – partly circumvents *inter-taxon* anatomical differences by counting only certain key parts of the skeleton, and potentially reduces fragmentation bias since zones are counted only if more than half is present. Consequently, this prevents any single zone from being counted twice. NISP greatly suffers from recovery biases as well (Payne 1972a; 1972b; 1975). Much of the observed variation in anatomical representation between large animals, such as cattle, and small animals, such as sheep/goat and pig, can plausibly be attributed to retrieval biases. Indeed, NISP in Promachon might be biased against small animals, young age groups and small body parts since the bulk of the material was hand collected during excavation.

For this study, all recorded elements are used for quantitative analysis except for the proximal ends of the metapodials (metacarpals and metatarsals), the horn cores and the antlers, as well as the elements or parts of elements, which are not included in the list of the recording protocol, but were worth recording (*e.g.* anomalous size bones, bones with interesting butchery marks and bones with pathological conditions and/or abnormalities). All these 'non-countable' elements were recorded as 'others' (OTH). Similarly, the proximal ends of the four main long bones were recorded as OTHU (head of humerus), OTHRA (at least >½ proximal end), OTHFE (head of femur) and OTHTI (at least >½ proximal end). Since a considerable amount of studied faunal assemblages in northern Greece and the Balkan Peninsula have used NISP

as the basic measure of taxonomic abundance, we will also use it in this study as a mean of comparison. However, we have to keep in mind that since the vast majority of these reports do not assess the extent of recovery bias, we will have to be extremely careful with our interpretations.

Minimum Number of Individuals (MNI) is a method for estimating relative taxonomic abundance. It simply uses the most frequent anatomical element for each taxon as a predictor of this taxon's frequency (Lyman 1994). The relevance of the MNI in relation to the archaeological issues posed is generally questioned. One of the main problems of the method is that it assumes that each individual in an assemblage was fully consumed in relation to that assemblage. However, in the current study, MNI is used as a predictor of taxonomic frequency rather than a predictor of the number of animals that were kept in the settlement, which is by and large not a primary goal in zooarchaeology. In this study, the calculation of the MNI was conducted simply by dividing the total number of a single anatomical element of one species to the number of the same elements that the identified species has in its skeleton.

4.5 Ageing and sexing

Age estimation is based primarily on dental development and attrition as mandibles and teeth represent the most useful elements to extract age information (Grant 1982; Greenfield 2005; Hillson 1986; Payne 1973; Zeder 2006). It is important to bear in mind that the teeth of animals in different conditions / time periods may have different rates of tooth eruption. Tooth eruption was recorded following Ewbank *et al.* (1964) (Table 4.4).

Tooth wear stages were recorded following Grant's (1982) method for cattle and pigs, and Payne's (1973; 1987) method for sheep and goats. Tooth wear stages from a single mandible were then combined into age stages, using only mandibles with at least two teeth with recordable wear in the $dP_4 / P_4 - M_3$ row. For this study, O'Connor's (1988) age stages have been used for cattle and pigs (Table 4.5).

We also use Payne's (1973; 1987) age stages for sheep and goats (Table 4.6).

Despite epiphyseal fusion is susceptible to differential bone preservation, it is here used as a secondary source of ageing information in order to avoid the risk of relying only on a single indicator. Bone specimens were recorded as 'unfused', 'fusing', 'fusing / fused' and 'fused'. The approximate age of epiphyseal fusion for different skeletal elements of the common domesticates, follows the data of Silver (1969) for modern breeds.

Sex determination was attempted only on cervid antlers (all antler specimens can be assumed to be males) and pig canines. Dimorphism in adult pig canine teeth provides the most reliable basis for sex discrimination, as male canines

Table 4.2 Postcranial measurements taken and key to measurement abbreviations.

Postcranial elements	Measurements taken				
	Bovinae	**Caprinae**	**Suidae**	**Cervidae**	**Canidae**
Horn cores	W$_{min}$ W$_{max}$				
Atlas	H	H	BFcr	H	H
Scapula	SLC	SLC	SLC	SLC	SLC
Humerus	GLC BT HTC SD	GLC BT HTC SD	GLC Bd HTC SD	GLC BT HTC SD	GLC Bd HTC SD
Radius	GL SD	GL SD	GL SD	GL SD	GL SD
Metacarpal	GL SD BatF Bd a b 3 6	GL SD Bd a b 1 3 4 6	GL	GL SD Bd 3	GL
Pelvis	LAR	LAR	LAR	LAR	LAR
Femur	GL SD DC	GL SD DC	GL SD DC	GL SD DC	GL SD DC
Tibia	GL Bd Dd SD	GL Bd Dd SD	GL Bd Dd SD	GL Bd Dd SD	GL Bd Dd SD
Astragalus	GLl GLm Bd Dl	GLl GLm Bd Dl	GLl GLm	GLl GLm Bd Dl	GL
Calcaneum	GL GD	GL GD	GL GD	GL GD	GL GD
Metatarsal	GL SD BatF Bd a b 3 6	GL SD Bd 3 6	GL	GL SD Bd 3 6	GL

Measurements	Description	Sources
W$_{min}$	Minimum basal diameter of the horn core	Driesch, von den (1976)
W$_{max}$	Maximum basal diameter of the horn core	Driesch, von den (1976)
H	Height	Albarella and Payne (2005)
BFcr	Width of cranial articular surface	Driesch, von den (1976)
SLC	Width of collum	Driesch, von den (1976)
GLC	Greatest length from caput	Driesch, von den (1976)
BT	Width of trochlea	Payne and Bull (1988)
HTC	Minimum diameter of trochlea	Payne and Bull (1988)
SD	Smallest breadth of diaphysis	Driesch, von den (1976)
GL	Greatest length	Driesch, von den (1976)
BatF	Greatest width of distal end	Davis (1992)
Bd	Width of distal end	Driesch, von den (1976)
a	Width of left distal condyle	Davis (1992)
b	Width of right distal condyle	Davis (1992)
1	Depth of left distal condyle	Davis (1992)
3	Diameter of the internal trochlea of the medial condyle	Davis (1992)
4	Depth of right distal condyle	Davis (1992)
6	Diameter of the internal trochlea of the lateral condyle	Davis (1992)
LAR	Diameter of acetabulum	Payne and Bull (1988)
DC	Depth of the caput femoris	Payne and Bull (1988)
Dd	Depth of the distal end	Driesch, von den (1976)
GLl	Greatest length of the lateral half	Driesch, von den (1976)
GLm	Greatest length of the medial half	Driesch, von den (1976)
Dl	Depth of lateral side	Driesch, von den (1976)
GD	Greatest depth of the calcaneum excluding the sustentanculum	Albarella and Payne (2005)

Table 4.3 Tooth measurements taken and key to measurement abbreviations.

Teeth		Measurements taken			
		Bovinae	Caprinae	Suidae	Canidae
Maxillary	dP ^{4}	W		L WP	
	M ^{1}	W		L WA WP	
	M ^{2}	W		L WA WP	
	M $^{1/2}$	W		L WA WP	
	M ^{3}	W		L WA WC	
Mandibular	dP $_4$	W	W	L WP	
	P $_4$				L W
	M $_1$	W	W	L WA WP	L W
	M $_2$	W	W	L WA WP	
	M $_{1/2}$	W	W	L WA WP	
	M $_3$	L W	L W	L WA WC WP	
	P $_1$ – M $_3$				L
	P $_2$ – M $_3$				L
	P $_1$ – P $_4$				L
	P $_2$ – P $_4$				L
	M $_1$ – M $_3$				L

Measurements	Description	Sources
L	Crown length	Driesch, von den (1976); Payne and Bull (1988)
W	Crown width	Driesch, von den (1976)
WA	Width of anterior cusp	Payne and Bull (1988)
WC	Width of central cusp	Albarella *et al.* (2005)
WP	Width of posterior cusp	Payne and Bull (1988); Albarella *et al.* (2005)

Table 4.4 Tooth eruption stages (after Ewbank *et al.* 1964).

Abbreviations	Eruption stages
C	Crypt
V	Visible
E	Erupting
H	Half-erupted
U	Fully-erupted, yet unworn

Table 4.5 Age stages for cattle and pigs (after O' Connor 1988).

Stage	Tooth wear stages
Neonate	dP $_4$ not yet in wear
Juvenile	M $_1$ not yet in wear
Immature	M $_1$ in wear, M $_2$ not yet in wear
Sub adult	M $_2$ in wear, M $_3$ not yet in wear
Adult	M $_3$ in wear, not yet heavily worn
Elderly	M $_3$ heavily worn (stage j or beyond *sensu* Grant 1982)

Table 4.6 Age stages for sheep and goat (after Payne 1973).

Stage	Tooth wear stages
A	dP $_4$ not yet in wear
B	dP $_4$ in wear, M $_1$ not yet in wear
C	M $_1$ in wear, M $_2$ not yet in wear
D	M $_2$ in wear, M $_3$ not yet in wear
E	M $_3$ in wear, posterior cusp unworn (stages 1-8)
F	posterior cusp of M $_3$ in wear (stages 9-10)
G	M $_3$ stage 11, M $_2$ stage 9
H	M $_3$ stage 11, M $_2$ stage post-9
I	M $_3$ stage post-11

are considerably larger than their female counterparts and also morphologically different. Alveolar cavities were also attributed to sex. On the other hand, cattle horn cores were measured in order to define sex ratios. Measurements that were taken on cattle horn cores include minimum (W_{min}) and maximum (W_{max}) basal diameter, but no length measurements were taken due to absence of intact specimens.

For other taxa, any attempts to detect the sexual composition of the assemblage had to rely on metrical analysis.

4.6 Pathology, gnawing, burning and butchery

The identification of pathologies may provide important information on the treatment and management of animals but this is neither the only, nor the most reliable measure of the health of an animal population. Many diseases do not alter extensively the skeleton of the animals and we should also keep in mind that ailing animals might have been disposed of differently from the domestic debris. Animal pathological conditions were recorded – whenever visible – following details provided by Baker and Brothwell (1980) and notes were made in the 'comments' section of the database. The presence of linear enamel hypoplasia (LEH) on teeth was also recorded as one (P) or multiple (PP) lines, as this could provide useful information with regard to possible malnutrition and other forms of environmental stress (Kierdorf *et al.* 2006).

Gnawing provides information on peri-depositional damage, implying the exposure of an element to certain conditions before its ultimate burial into the archaeological record (Lyman 1994). Recognizing gnawing incidents in neonatal specimens can be extremely problematic due to these latter's relatively soft and porous surface. Therefore, in this study identification of gnawing incident is restricted to post-neonatal material. Human and pig gnawing is difficult to identify, let alone discriminate from other forms of gnawing (Greenfield 1988). Thus, it was not attempted. On the other hand, carnivore (Lyman 1994, 207-9) and rodent (Lyman 1994, 196) gnawing was relatively easy to identify and was therefore recorded when visible. Partial digestion of bones was also recorded (Lyman 1994, 211; Payne and Munson 1985).

Duration of exposure to a heat source, as well as its temperature and typology (*cf.* Nicholson 1993; Outram

2002; Shipman *et al.* 1984) can have different effects on the surface of the bones. In addition, the recognition of burned bones in the archaeological record may sometimes not be straightforward, since a black colour may be indicative of burning, but could also be due to staining by manganese and / or iron oxides (Shahack-Gross *et al.* 1997). Discriminating burnt and oxidized bones in the Promachon's faunal assemblage was difficult in some cases. Burning traces were therefore recorded only on specimens in which, the cause could unambiguously be identified. Consequently, it is possible that the rate of burning in the present study might be slightly underestimated. Three fields were created to record burning:

1. Singed, which referred to cases in which bones were only partially affected by heat.
2. Burned, which referred to cases were the incidence of burning covered the whole surface of the bones.
3. Calcined, which referred to cases in which bones presented white color on their surfaces.

The main reason for this separation is to try to identify the nature of the burning incidence on the bones from Promachon. For instance, burning traces (mostly bones which were recorded as singed) may well be the result of cooking activities. However, there are also cases of burned bones, in which burning traces are too severe to suggest only food preparation (*i.e.* calcined bones may be the result of the conflagration event at the end of the first phase of occupation).

Butchery is noticeable in Promachon sector, since the faunal material represents mostly consumption residues. Cutmarks and chopping marks were all recorded in the database and notes were made in the 'comments' section regarding their location on the surface of the bones. Cut marks referred to thin lines, which were inflicted by small tools and objects (mainly stone tools) for the dismemberment of the articulations and the joints. Chopping marks referred to traces inflicted by heavy tools and objects in order to divide the animal carcass into a great number of portions for processing. Attempts have also been made to attribute, where possible, butchery marks to dismembering, skinning and filleting, following Binford (1981). These notes were also stated in the 'comments' section.

Results

Note

This chapter is divided into 11 sections, each dealing with a single aspect of the analysis of the faunal material (*e.g.* taphonomy, body part distribution, biometry etc.). The various figures, diagrams and tables are located inside the main text; this was decided in order to facilitate the prompt comparison between the results and the raw data. It should also be noted that some of the results have already been published elsewhere (Kazantzis 2014a; 2014b; 2017).

However, they are presented here as well, as it was thought that it would have been unorthodox not to be presented at all.

5.1 Breakdown of the faunal material

The faunal material from Promachon sector consists of 11527 recorded specimens. Of these, 4470 (39 per cent) were recorded as bones, 3110 (27 per cent) were recorded as teeth, 3871 (34 per cent) were recorded as vertebrae and ribs and 76 (one per cent) were recorded as bone tools (Table 5.1).

Out of the total 11527 recorded specimens, 10159 (88 per cent) derive from undisturbed deposits (Table 5.2), while the rest of the material, which accounts for 1368 (12 per cent) recorded specimens, derives from mixed deposits (Table 5.3). Out of 10159 recorded specimens deriving from undisturbed deposits, a total of 6525 (64 per cent) represented 'countable' elements (Table 5.4). Of these, 4332 (66 per cent) were identified to species level, 2075 (32 per cent) were identified to subfamily level

Table 5.1 Faunal material breakdown. NISP counts.

Breakdown of the faunal material	NISP	%
Bones	4470	39%
Teeth	3110	27%
Vertebrae and ribs	3871	34%
Bone tools and objects	76	1%
TOTAL	11527	100%

Table 5.2 Faunal material from undisturbed deposits. Breakdown to phases. NISP counts.

| Breakdown of the faunal material | Undisturbed deposits | | | | | | TOTAL | |
| | Phase I (Layers 6, 5, 4) | | Phase II (Layers 3, 2) | | Phase III (Layer 1) | | | |
	NISP	%	NISP	%	NISP	%	NISP	%
Bones	1449	40%	1623	39%	900	37%	3972	39%
Teeth	902	25%	1063	26%	780	32%	2745	27%
Vertebrae and ribs	1231	34%	1401	34%	747	30%	3379	33%
Bone tools and objects	25	1%	17	1%	21	1%	63	1%
TOTAL	3607	100%	4104	100%	2448	100%	10159	100%

Table 5.3 Faunal material from mixed deposits. Breakdown to phases. NISP counts.

| Breakdown of the faunal material | Mixed deposits | | | | | | TOTAL | |
| | Phases I-II | | Phases II-III | | Phases I-II-III | | | |
	NISP	%	NISP	%	NISP	%	NISP	%
Bones	169	40%	317	34%	8	35%	494	36%
Teeth	94	22%	262	28%	9	40%	365	27%
Vertebrae and ribs	155	37%	335	36%	6	25%	496	36%
Bone tools and objects	3	1%	10	2%		0%	13	1%
TOTAL	421	100%	924	100%	23	100%	1368	100%

Table 5.4 'Countable' material from undisturbed deposits. Breakdown to phases. NISP counts.

Breakdown of the faunal material	Undisturbed deposits						TOTAL	
	Phase I (Layers 6, 5, 4)		Phase II (Layers 3, 2)		Phase III (Layer 1)			
	NISP	%	NISP	%	NISP	%	NISP	%
Bones	1386	60%	1538	59%	856	52%	3780	58%
Teeth	902	40%	1063	41%	780	48%	2745	42%
TOTAL	2288	100%	2601	100%	1636	100%	6525	100%

Table 5.5 'Countable' material from mixed deposits. Breakdown to phases. NISP counts.

Breakdown of the faunal material	Mixed deposits						TOTAL	
	Phases I-II		Phases II-III		Phases I-II-III			
	NISP	%	NISP	%	NISP	%	NISP	%
Bones	166	64%	297	53%	8	47%	471	56%
Teeth	94	36%	262	47%	9	53%	365	44%
TOTAL	260	100%	559	100%	17	100%	836	100%

(Caprinae) and 118 (two per cent) were identified as two or three most likely species: Red deer/Cattle (*Cervus/Bos*); Red deer/Fallow deer (*Cervus/Dama*); Sheep/Goat/Roe deer (*Ovis/Capra/Capreolus*); Dog/Fox (*Canis/Vulpes*).

The rest of the 'uncountable' material, which accounts for 3634 (36 per cent) recorded specimens consists of: 3379 (93 per cent) vertebrae and ribs, 63 (two per cent) bone tools and 192 (five per cent) specimens, which fell into the 'non-countable' categories as specified in the recording protocol (169 'others', 20 horn-cores and 3 antlers). Out of 1368 recorded specimens deriving form mixed deposits, a total of 836 (61 per cent) represented 'countable' elements (Table 5.5). Of these, 564 (67 per cent) were identified down to the level of species, 257 (31 per cent) to subfamily level (*Caprinae*), and 15 (2 per cent) were identified as two or three most likely species: Red deer/Cattle (*Cervus/Bos*); Red deer/Fallow deer (*Cervus/Dama*); Sheep/Goat/Roe deer (*Ovis/Capra/Capreolus*); Dog/Fox (*Canis/Vulpes*). The rest of the 'uncountable' material, which accounts for 532 (39 per cent) recorded specimens consists of: 496 (93 per cent) vertebrae and ribs, 13 (two per cent) bone tools and 23 (five per cent) specimens, which fell into the 'non-countable' categories as specified in the recording protocol (20 'others' and 3 horn-cores).

Table 5.6 provides the Latin names of the families, sub-families and species that are mentioned in this book in addition to their common English and Greek names. The last column on the right provides information on the species conservation status today (Legakis and Marangou 2009).

5.2 Agents affecting the faunal assemblage

Issues of preservation, fragmentation and general taphonomy of bones are varied and have been extensively discussed (Binford 1981; Lyman 1994). The main factors affecting the preservation of a faunal assemblage are butchery, disposal methods, scavenger activity, weathering, excavation methods, and sampling regimes. When any number of these processes are combined, their individual effects can be difficult to determine and the result not easy to interpret. However, as these processes can be very important in our interpretation and understanding of the site, at least some attempt has to be made to identify the major factors involved in the formation of the animal bone assemblage (Albarella *et al.* 1997).

5.2.1 Preservation

The faunal material from Promachon sector is in a very good state of preservation, thus enhancing our attempts of correct anatomical and taxonomical identification. A substantial number of bones were stained along their whole surface, presenting a dark red color due to the waterlogged deposits. Some bones present a light red to dark orange color, with dark stains due to the high concentration of charcoal in the soil. Cases of concretion along the surface of the bones are extremely low and they are present only in a part of the material from trenches I and IA near structure n. 4. Cases of weathering and root etching on bones have been recorded in the 'comments' section of the database. Their number, however, is extremely low (2 and 3 bones respectively).

It is generally difficult to assess if the faunal material derives from contexts representing primary or secondary deposition.

Table 5.6 Names of families, subfamilies and species that are mentioned in this book.

Latin name	Classification	Common name (English)	Common name (Greek)	Conservation status in Macedonia
Bos taurus	Species	Cattle	Αγελάδα	Domesticated
Caprinae	Subfamily	Caprines	Αιγοπρόβατα	-
Ovis aries	Species	Sheep	Πρόβατο	Domesticated
Capra hircus	Species	Goat	Αίγα	Domesticated
Sus domesticus	Species	Pig	Χοίρος	Domesticated
Canis familiaris	Species	Dog	Σκύλος	Domesticated
Cervidae	Family	Cervids	Ελαφίδες	-
Cervus elaphus	Species	Red deer	Κόκκινο ελάφι	Critical (30-50 individuals)
Dama dama	Species	Fallow deer	Πλατώνι	Critical
Capreolus capreolus	Species	Roe deer	Ζαρκάδι	Vulnerable/Endangered
Lepus europaeus	Species	Hare	Λαγός	Non-established status
Vulpes vulpes	Species	Red fox	Αλεπού	Non-established status
Rupicapra rupicapra	Species	Chamois	Αγριόγιδο	Vulnerable (remote populations)
Sus scrofa	Species	Wild Boar	Αγριόχοιρος	Least concern
Lynx lynx	Species	Eurasian lynx	Λύγκας	No data (unconfirmed presence)
Ursus arctos	Species	Bear	Άρκτος	Endangered (190-260 individuals)
Canis lupus	Species	Wolf	Λύκος	Endangered
Mustelidae	Family	Mustelids	Ικτίδες	-
Meles meles	Species	European badger	Ασβός	Non-established status
Mustela putorius	Species	Polecat	Βρωμοκούναβο	Non-established status
Mustela erminea	Species	Stoat	Ερμίνη	Non-established status
Martes foina	Species	Beech marten	Πετροκούναβο	Non-established status
Buteo lagopus	Species	Rough-legged buzzard	Αρκτικοβαρβακίνα	Non-established status
Anser anser	Species	Greylag goose	Σταχτόχηνα	Critical (declining nr. of individuals)
Grus grus	Species	Common crane	Γερανός	Non-established status
Corvus corax	Species	Raven	Κοράκι	Least concern
Aves	Class	Birds (indeterminate)	Πτηνά (αδιευκρίνιστα)	-
Testudinidae	Family	Tortoises	Χελωνίδες	-
Siluris glanis	Species	Sheatfish	Γατόψαρο	Least concern
Cyprinidae	Family	Minnows	Κυπρινίδες	-
Murex trunculus	Species	Banded dye-murex	Στρόμπος	-
Homo sapiens	Species	Modern human	Σύγχρονος άνθρωπος	-

For instance, a number of articulated bones in anatomical connection as well as a number of unfused diaphyses that were found together with their unfused epiphyses indicate the presence of at least some primary deposits (Table 5.7). However, the presence of gnawing marks indicates that some bones were re-deposited (*i.e.* bones were not found at the original place of discard) as a result of scavenger activity.

Gnawing was observed on the postcranial bones of cattle, caprines, pig, red deer and roe deer. Most of the gnawing

Table 5.7 Number of articulated bones and number of unfused epiphyses and unfused diaphyses found together for the three commonest taxa. All phases are considered. Caprinae subfamily includes *Ovis/Capra* (sheep/goat), *Ovis aries* (sheep) and *Capra hircus* (goat). NISP counts.

Prompt burial	Phases I-II-III	
	Articulated Bones	Unfused diaphyses & epiphyses
	NISP	NISP
Bos taurus (NISP: 1648)	5	4
Caprinae (NISP: 1208)	4	1
Sus (NISP: 590)	3	6
TOTAL (NISP: 3446)	**12**	**11**

Table 5.8 Incidence of gnawing among the postcranial bones of all species identified on the temporal level. Only 'countable' elements are considered. NISP counts.

Gnawing	Postcranial elements		
	NISP	Gnawed	%
Phase I	1386	79	6%
Phase II	1538	59	4%
Phase III	856	28	3%
TOTAL	**3780**	**166**	**4%**

traces observed were suggestive of gnawing by carnivores, dog being the species most likely to be responsible for most of the chewing. However, it is highly likely that pigs (Greenfield 1988) as well as humans (Brain 1981) might have contributed to the modification of bones. Traces of rodent gnawing are present in only two bone fragments (a proximal radius of a cattle and a caprine rib). No evidence of partial or complete digestion of bones was recorded whatsoever.

The gnawing incidence in Promachon is relatively low. Gnawing marks occur only on four per cent of all 'countable' postcranial fragments (Table 5.8), indicating that scavenger access to bone debris was often restricted. The frequency of gnawing at Promachon is close to that from other contemporary sites across Greek Macedonia. For example, in the Late Neolithic settlement of Kryoneri, gnawing is recorded on less than five per cent of the total postcranial bones (Mylona 1997), while in Dispilio (Cosmetatou-Phoca 2007) and Stavroupoli (Yiannouli 2002a; 2004) gnawing traces are found only on one per cent of the faunal material.

Only slight variations in the incidence of gnawing marks between the three main domesticates occur (Table 5.9), suggesting that carnivores did not have differential access to these species and that the latter were not disposed of in different ways. It should be noted, however, that the amount of gnawing on the bones of caprines and pigs could be underestimated due to the tendency for carnivores to completely destroy bones from small taxa.

Table 5.9 Incidence of gnawing among the postcranial bones of the three main domesticates on the temporal level. Caprinae subfamily includes *Ovis/Capra* (sheep/goat), *Ovis aries* (sheep) and *Capra hircus* (goat). Only 'countable' elements are considered. NISP counts.

Three main domesticates	Gnawing							
	Late Neolithic I				Late Neolithic II		**TOTAL**	
Bos taurus	Phase I NISP: 623		Phase II NISP: 671		Phase III NISP: 354		**Total NISP: 1648**	
	NISP	%	NISP	%	NISP	%	**NISP**	**%**
	23	4%	44	7%	12	3%	**79**	**5%**
Caprinae	Phase I NISP: 428		Phase II NISP: 487		Phase III NISP: 293		**Total NISP: 1208**	
	NISP	%	NISP	%	NISP	%	**NISP**	**%**
	13	3%	19	4%	3	1%	**35**	**3%**
Sus	Phase I NISP: 230		Phase II NISP: 226		Phase III NISP: 134		**Total NISP: 590**	
	NISP	%	NISP	%	NISP	%	**NISP**	**%**
	7	3%	13	6%	4	3%	**24**	**4%**
TOTAL	**Phase I NISP: 1281**		**Phase II NISP: 1384**		**Phase III NISP: 781**		**TOTAL NISP: 3446**	
	NISP	**%**	**NISP**	**%**	**NISP**	**%**	**NISP**	**%**
	43	**3%**	**76**	**5%**	**19**	**2%**	**138**	**4%**

Tables 5.10-5.13 present the anatomical distribution of gnawing for the three main domesticates as well as for cervids. The incidence of gnawing does not vary significantly between the different body parts of the different species, though the low numbers of gnawed specimens may not be suitable to highlight such differences. Nonetheless, there is no evidence that scavengers had differential access to specific body parts of cattle, caprines, pigs and cervids, although it is highly likely that the amount of damage inflicted may have differed between bones of high and low density.

5.2.2 Retrieval biases

As previously discussed, most of the faunal material from Promachon was hand-picked, flotation and sieving having been carried out only for the material deriving from the deposits associated with Layers 11-7 (structure n. 4). The skewedness of the composition of a non-sieved faunal material is well known: young age categories, small anatomical parts and small animals are underrepresented when systematic sieving procedures are not employed (Payne 1972a; 1975). Thus, before proceeding further

Table 5.10 *Bos taurus* (cattle) body part distribution of gnawing on the temporal level. Both 'countable' and 'uncountable' elements are considered. NISP counts.

Bos taurus		Gnawing			
		Late Neolithic I		Late Neolithic II	TOTAL (NISP: 1648)
		Phase I (NISP: 623)	Phase II (NISP: 671)	Phase III (NISP: 354)	
		NISP	NISP	NISP	NISP
Postcranial elements	Cranium (zygomaticus)			1	1
	Atlas		1		1
	Axis				0
	Scapula	1	1		2
	Humerus proximal	1			1
	Humerus distal	2	3	1	6
	Radius proximal	2		1	3
	Radius distal		1		1
	Ulna proximal	1			1
	Carpal 2+3				0
	Metacarpal distal				0
	Pelvis				0
	Femur proximal	1	5	3	9
	Femur distal	3	4		7
	Tibia proximal		1	1	2
	Tibia distal	1	1		2
	Scafocuboid		1	1	2
	Astragalus	1	4	1	6
	Calcaneum	5	9		14
	Metatarsal distal				0
	Phalanx 1	4	10	2	16
	Phalanx 2	1	3		4
	Phalanx 3			1	1
	TOTAL Countable	23	44	12	79
	TOTAL Uncountable	1	4	4	9
TOTAL		24	48	16	88

Table 5.11 Caprinae (sheep and goat) body part distribution of gnawing on the temporal level. Caprinae subfamily includes *Ovis/Capra* (sheep/goat), *Ovis aries* (sheep) and *Capra hircus* (goat). Both 'countable' and 'uncountable' elements are considered. NISP counts.

Caprinae		Gnawing			
		Late Neolithic I		Late Neolithic II	TOTAL (NISP: 1208)
		Phase I (NISP: 428)	Phase II (NISP: 487)	Phase III (NISP: 293)	
		NISP	NISP	NISP	NISP
Postcranial elements	Cranium (zygomaticus)	1			1
	Atlas				0
	Axis				0
	Scapula				0
	Humerus proximal				0
	Humerus distal	6	10	1	17
	Radius proximal	1	1	1	3
	Radius distal		2		2
	Ulna proximal	1			1
	Carpal 2+3				0
	Metacarpal distal	2		1	3
	Pelvis	1	1		2
	Femur proximal		2		2
	Femur distal				0
	Tibia proximal		1		1
	Tibia distal		1		1
	Scafocuboid				0
	Astragalus				0
	Calcaneum				0
	Metatarsal distal	1	1		2
	Phalanx 1				0
	Phalanx 2				0
	Phalanx 3				0
	TOTAL Countable	13	19	3	35
	TOTAL Uncountable	1	0	0	1
TOTAL		14	19	3	36

with our analyses, we should assess the significance of the quality of recovery.

A comparison between the frequencies of the distal tibiae and the astragali is considered to be a good indicator of the quality of recovery (Payne 1972a; 1975). Given their anatomical proximity and similar bone density and treatment in carcass butchery, these two elements should be found in almost equal frequencies in cases of comprehensive recovery. Figure 5.1 (Table 5.14) demonstrates that caprine

and pig astragali are underrepresented when compared to the larger tibiae, clearly indicating recovery bias. On the other hand, cattle astragali are very well represented, in fact even more so than cattle tibiae. This is not strange, since due to their density and size cattle astragali are not generally overlooked during excavation.

The ratio between the first and the second phalanges is considered to be an additional cogent test for assessing the quality of recovery in faunal assemblages (Table

Table 5.12 *Sus* (pig) body part distribution of gnawing on the temporal level. Both 'countable' and 'uncountable' elements are considered. NISP counts.

Sus		Gnawing			
		Late Neolithic I		Late Neolithic II	TOTAL (NISP: 590)
		Phase I (NISP: 230)	Phase II (NISP: 226)	Phase III (NISP: 134)	
		NISP	NISP	NISP	NISP
Postcranial elements	Cranium (zygomaticus)				0
	Atlas				0
	Axis				0
	Scapula	2	2	1	5
	Humerus proximal				0
	Humerus distal	1	1		2
	Radius proximal		4		4
	Radius distal	1		1	2
	Ulna proximal	1	2		3
	Carpal 3				0
	Metacarpal 3 distal				0
	Metacarpal 4 distal				0
	Pelvis		2	1	3
	Femur proximal				0
	Femur distal			1	1
	Tibia proximal	1			1
	Tibia distal				0
	Scafocuboid				0
	Astragalus		1		1
	Calcaneum		1		1
	Metatarsal 3 distal				0
	Metatarsal 4 distal	1			1
	Phalanx 1				0
	Phalanx 2				0
	Phalanx 3				0
	TOTAL Countable	7	13	4	24
	TOTAL Uncountable	0	1	1	2
TOTAL		7	14	5	26

5.15). Figure 5.2 demonstrates that small anatomical parts such as caprine and pig second phalanges are seriously underrepresented when compared to the larger first phalanges. On the contrary, cattle second phalanges are better represented in comparison to the larger first phalanges, indicating that recovery bias does not entirely apply to large animals such as cattle.

Thus, in the following analysis, we should strongly consider the fact that recovery bias is likely to have played a significant role in the formation of the faunal assemblage. It is not possible, however, to give precise estimates as to which aspects of the wider assemblage might be more affected, though species frequency, young age profiles and body part distribution are of obvious concern.

Table 5.13 Cervidae (cervids) body part distribution of gnawing on the temporal level. Cervidae family includes *Cervus elaphus* (red deer) and *Capreolus capreolus* (roe deer). Both 'countable' and 'uncountable' elements are considered. NISP counts.

Cervidae		Gnawing			
		Late Neolithic I		Late Neolithic II	TOTAL (NISP: 100)
		Phase I (NISP: 29)	Phase II (NISP: 51)	Phase III (NISP: 20)	
		NISP	NISP	NISP	NISP
Postcranial elements	Cranium (zygomaticus)				0
	Atlas				0
	Axis				0
	Scapula				0
	Humerus proximal				0
	Humerus distal				0
	Radius proximal				0
	Radius distal				0
	Ulna proximal		2		2
	Carpal 2+3				0
	Metacarpal distal				0
	Pelvis				0
	Femur proximal				0
	Femur distal				0
	Tibia proximal				0
	Tibia distal				0
	Scafocuboid				0
	Astragalus				0
	Calcaneum	1			1
	Metatarsal distal	1			1
	Phalanx 1				0
	Phalanx 2	1			1
	Phalanx 3				0
	TOTAL Countable	3	2	0	5
	TOTAL Uncountable	0	0	0	0
TOTAL		3	2	0	5

5.2.3 Fragmentation

In addition to the small number of articulated bones in anatomical connection, a number of complete bones untouched by fragmentation mechanisms were found. However, the majority of the material had been fragmented in antiquity. Old breaks may have occurred either before discard, most obviously in human extraction of marrow (Binford 1981), or after discard, for instance in gnawing by dogs or trampling by humans. In this study, the level of fragmentation on the bones of the three main domesticates is assessed using the ratio between the number of mandibles and the number of isolated mandibular teeth, as well as the ratio between fragmented and complete long bones.

The level of fragmentation varies between the three commonest taxa (Table 5.16; Figure 5.3). Cattle and caprine isolated teeth are represented with a higher frequency (87

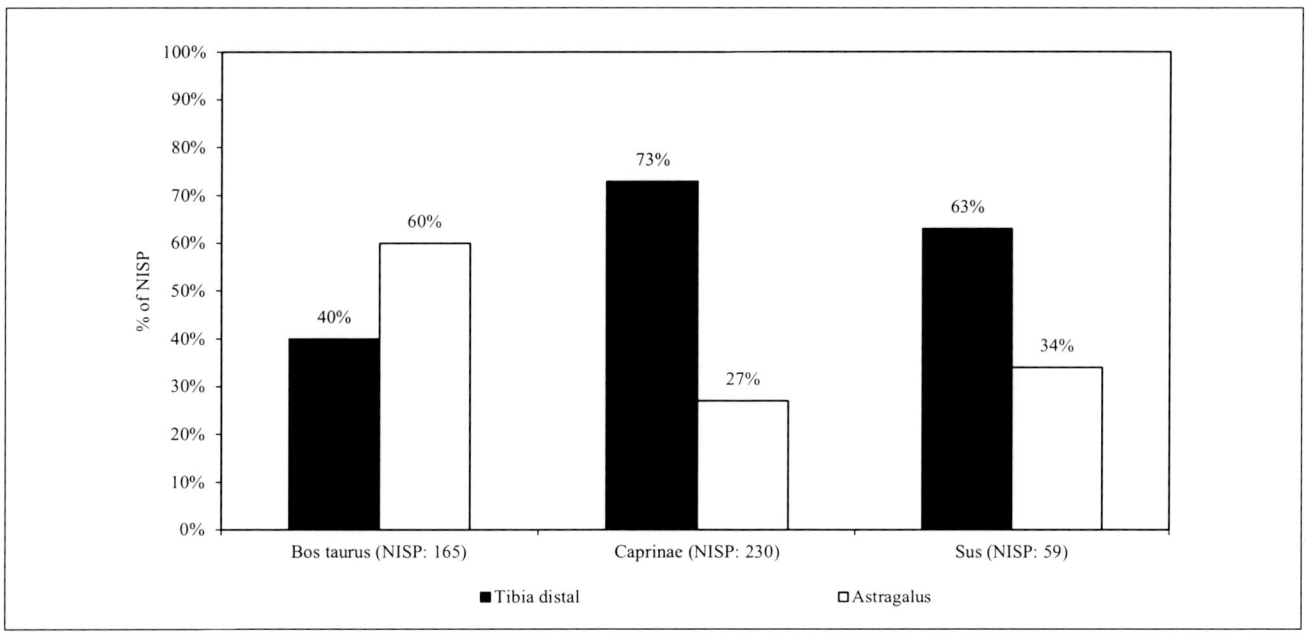

Figure 5.1 Ratio between the distal tibiae and the astragali for the three main domesticates. All phases are considered. Data in Table 5.14. NISP counts.

per cent for cattle and 71 per cent for caprines) compared to mandibles. However, the frequency of caprine mandibles is higher than that of cattle (13 per cent for cattle and 29 per cent for caprines). On the other hand, pig mandibles are represented with a higher frequency (54 per cent) than isolated teeth (46 per cent).

Table 5.14 Ratio between the distal tibiae and the astragali for the three main domesticates. All phases are considered. Caprinae subfamily includes *Ovis/Capra* (sheep/goat), *Ovis aries* (sheep) and *Capra hircus* (goat). Distal tibiae unfused epiphyses are not counted. Data for Figure 5.1. NISP counts.

Elements	Retrieval biases: astragalus *vs.* distal tibia					
	Bos taurus		Caprinae		*Sus*	
	NISP	%	NISP	%	NISP	%
Tibia distal	66	40%	167	73%	37	63%
Astragalus	99	60%	63	27%	22	34%
TOTAL	**165**	**100%**	**230**	**100%**	**59**	**100%**

Table 5.15 Ratio between the first and the second phalanges for the three main domesticates. All phases are considered. Caprinae subfamily includes *Ovis/Capra* (sheep/goat), *Ovis aries* (sheep) and *Capra hircus* (goat). Data for Figure 5.2. NISP counts.

Elements	Retrieval biases: first *vs.* second phalanges					
	Bos taurus		Caprinae		*Sus*	
	NISP	%	NISP	%	NISP	%
Phalanx 1	255	57%	43	83%	28	74%
Phalanx 2	184	43%	9	17%	10	26%
TOTAL	**439**	**100%**	**52**	**100%**	**38**	**100%**

Although the evidence seems to suggest that cattle remains were much more affected by fragmentation than any of the other main domesticates, the higher proportion of cattle isolated teeth can probably be explained on the basis of retrieval biases. Caprine and pig teeth are smaller than cattle teeth and they are frequently overlooked during excavation. On the other hand, the high proportion of pig mandibles is probably biased too, since the age-at-death data indicates a young age profile for pigs. It is suggested, therefore, that retrieval bias is probably the reason for the underrepresentation of small deciduous isolated pig teeth.

The ratio between fragmented and complete long bones (Table 5.17) provides a second method for the assessment of the level of fragmentation. In general, long bones have a better chance of survival than other anatomical elements (*i.e.* scapula, ulna, pelvis), which are particularly fragile and are rarely found complete. On the other hand, small

Table 5.16 Ratio between mandibles and isolated mandibular teeth for the three main domesticates. All phases are considered. Caprinae subfamily includes *Ovis/Capra* (sheep/goat), *Ovis aries* (sheep) and *Capra hircus* (goat). Isolated mandibular teeth include all deciduous and permanent incisors, canines and premolars, and all permanent molars. Data for Figure 5.3. NISP counts.

Three main domesticates	Rate of fragmentation: Mandibles *vs.* teeth			
	Mandibles		Isolated mandibular teeth	
	NISP	%	NISP	%
Bos taurus (NISP: 477)	60	13%	387	87%
Caprinae (NISP: 971)	285	29%	686	71%
Sus (NISP: 156)	84	54%	72	46%

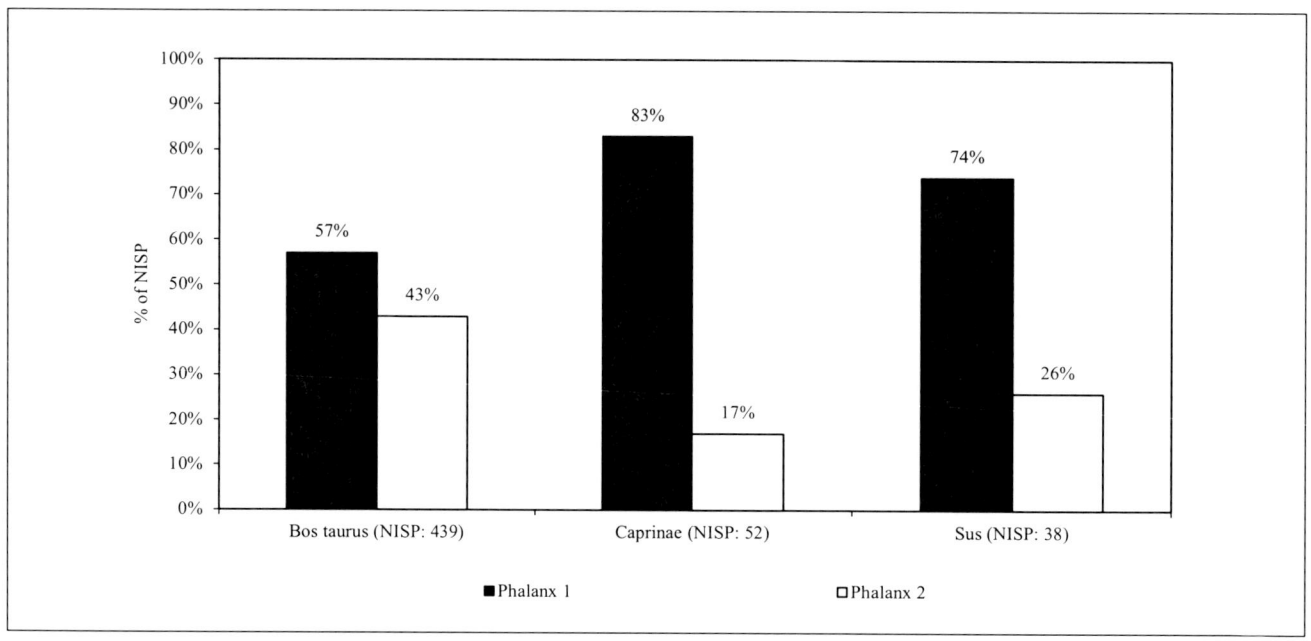

Figure 5.2 Ratio between the first and the second phalanges for the three main domesticates. All phases are considered. Data in Table 5.15. NISP counts.

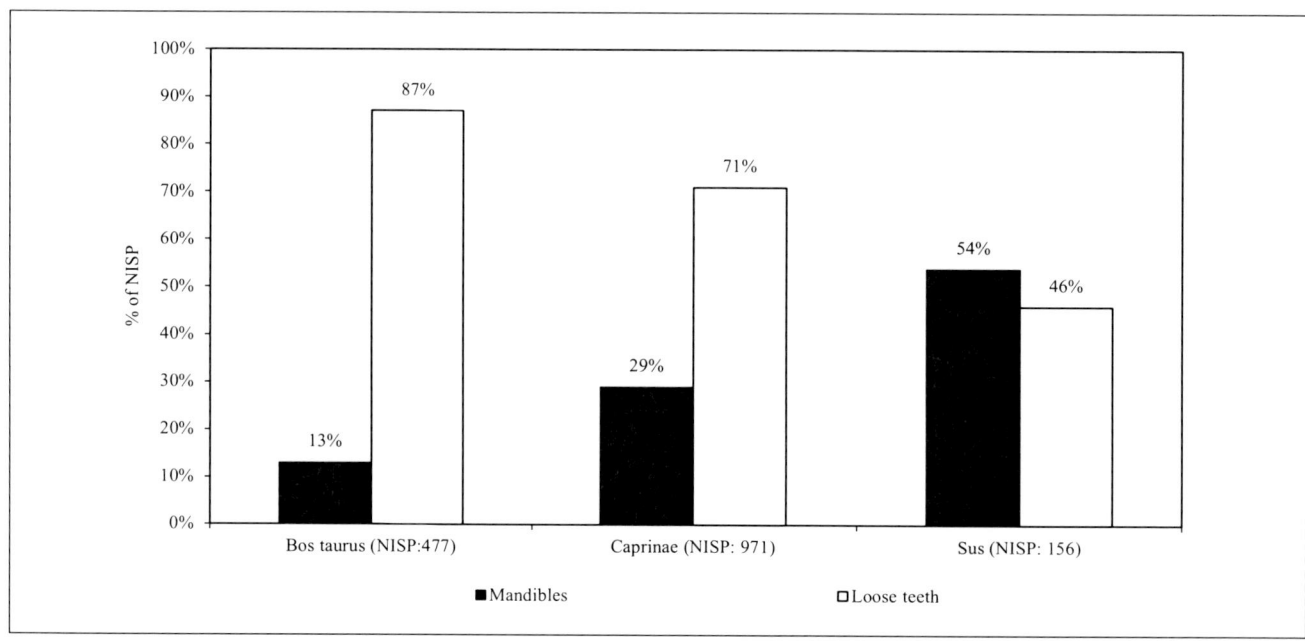

Figure 5.3 Ratio between mandibles and isolated mandibular teeth for the three main domesticates. All phases are considered. Data in Table 5.16. NISP counts.

compact bones such as the phalanges, the calcaneum and the astragalus, tend to be found complete. However, as we have already seen, small bones are subject to retrieval biases particularly in the case of small species such as caprines and pigs. Metacarpals and metatarsals are also excluded since their proximal ends, which in most taxa fuse before birth, were not recorded.In Promachon sector, out of 1053 recorded long bones deriving from the three main domesticates, only 31 (three per cent) complete long bones were found. This proportion is slightly higher than that found in the Late Neolithic assemblage of Dimitra,

where out of 323 recorded fragments of humerus, radius, femur and tibia, only six (less than two per cent) complete long bones were found (Yiannouli 1997). Figure 5.4 shows that cattle long bones were more affected by fragmentation than the long bones of the other domesticates. Out of 316 cattle long bones in total, only four (two per cent) were found complete. Fragmentation in caprine long bones is also high. Out of 545 long bones, only 10 (three per cent) complete long bones were found. Pig is the species less affected by fragmentation, since out of 192 pig long bones, 17 (10 per cent) complete long bones were recovered.

Table 5.17 Rate of fragmentation on the long bones of *Bos taurus* (cattle), Caprinae (sheep/goat) and *Sus* (pig). All phases are considered. Caprinae subfamily includes *Ovis/Capra* (sheep/goat), *Ovis aries* (sheep) and *Capra hircus* (goat). Proximal and distal ends include fusing/fused epiphyses and unfused diaphyses. Unfused epiphyses are not counted. 1. Both epiphyses fusing/fused, 2. One epiphysis fusing/fused, the other unfused, 3. Both ends of diaphysis unfused. Each proximal and distal end is considered half a complete bone. Data for Figure 5.4. NISP counts.

Bos taurus	Rate of fragmentation: long bones												
	Fragmented Bones						Complete Bones						
	Proximal end only		Distal end only		TOTAL		1.		2.		3.		TOTAL	
	NISP	%	NISP	%	NISP	%	NISP	%	NISP	%	NISP	%	NISP	%
Humerus	8	10%	75	90%	**83**	**100%**		0%		0%		0%	**0**	**0%**
Radius	55.5	64%	29.5	35%	**85**	**99%**	1	1%		0%		0%	**1**	**1%**
Femur	33	44%	39	53%	**72**	**98%**	1	> 1%		0%	1	> 1%	**2**	**2%**
Tibia	6.5	10%	65.5	89%	**72**	**99%**		0%		0%	1	1%	**1**	**1%**
TOTAL	**103**	**32%**	**209**	**66%**	**312**	**98%**	**2**	**1%**	**0**	**0%**	**2**	**1%**	**4**	**2%**

Caprinae	Rate of fragmentation: long bones												
	Fragmented Bones						Complete Bones						
	Proximal end only		Distal end only		TOTAL		1.		2.		3.		TOTAL	
	NISP	%	NISP	%	NISP	%	NISP	%	NISP	%	NISP	%	NISP	%
Humerus	9.5	7%	169.5	91%	**179**	**97%**	1	< 1%	1	<1%	1	< 1%	**3**	**3%**
Radius	115.5	75%	26.5	20%	**142**	**96%**	2	1%	2	1%	3	2%	**7**	**4%**
Femur	19	63%	11	37%	**30**	**100%**		0%		0%		0%		**0%**
Tibia	17	10%	167	90%	**184**	**100%**		0%		0%		0%		**0%**
TOTAL	**161**	**29%**	**374**	**68%**	**535**	**97%**	**3**	**1%**	**3**	**1%**	**4**	**1%**	**10**	**3%**

Sus	Rate of fragmentation: long bones												
	Fragmented Bones						Complete Bones						
	Proximal end only		Distal end only		TOTAL		1.		2.		3.		TOTAL	
	NISP	%	NISP	%	NISP	%	NISP	%	NISP	%	NISP	%	NISP	%
Humerus	5	12%	48	77%	**53**	**90%**		0%	4	7%	2	3%	**6**	**10%**
Radius	33	47%	28	41%	**61**	**89%**	2	3%	4	5%	2	3%	**8**	**11%**
Femur	2	12%	18	78%	**20**	**90%**		0%	1	5%	1	5%	**2**	**10%**
Tibia	4.5	11%	36.5	86%	**41**	**97%**		0%		0%	1	3%	**1**	**3%**
TOTAL	**44.5**	**25%**	**130.5**	**65%**	**175**	**90%**	**2**	**2%**	**9**	**5%**	**6**	**3%**	**17**	**10%**

Differences in bone fragmentation between the three main domesticates are most likely the result of the variation in the intensity of marrow extraction. It is suggested that humans preferentially fractured bones of large species such as cattle. The high fragmentation of cattle bones may be attributed to the species' large size: in order to obtain most of the marrow, cattle bones were subjected to intensive fracturing, thus resulting in a more fragmented material. In addition, the large cattle carcass needs to be separated out more: this leads to a greater amount of butchery-led fragmentation. Fragmentation in caprine bones is also high. Nevertheless, the proportion of intact caprine bones is higher than that of cattle. This is not strange, since caprine bones, being smaller than cattle bones, contain poor amount of marrow and offer relatively poor returns on processing labour (Binford 1978). On the

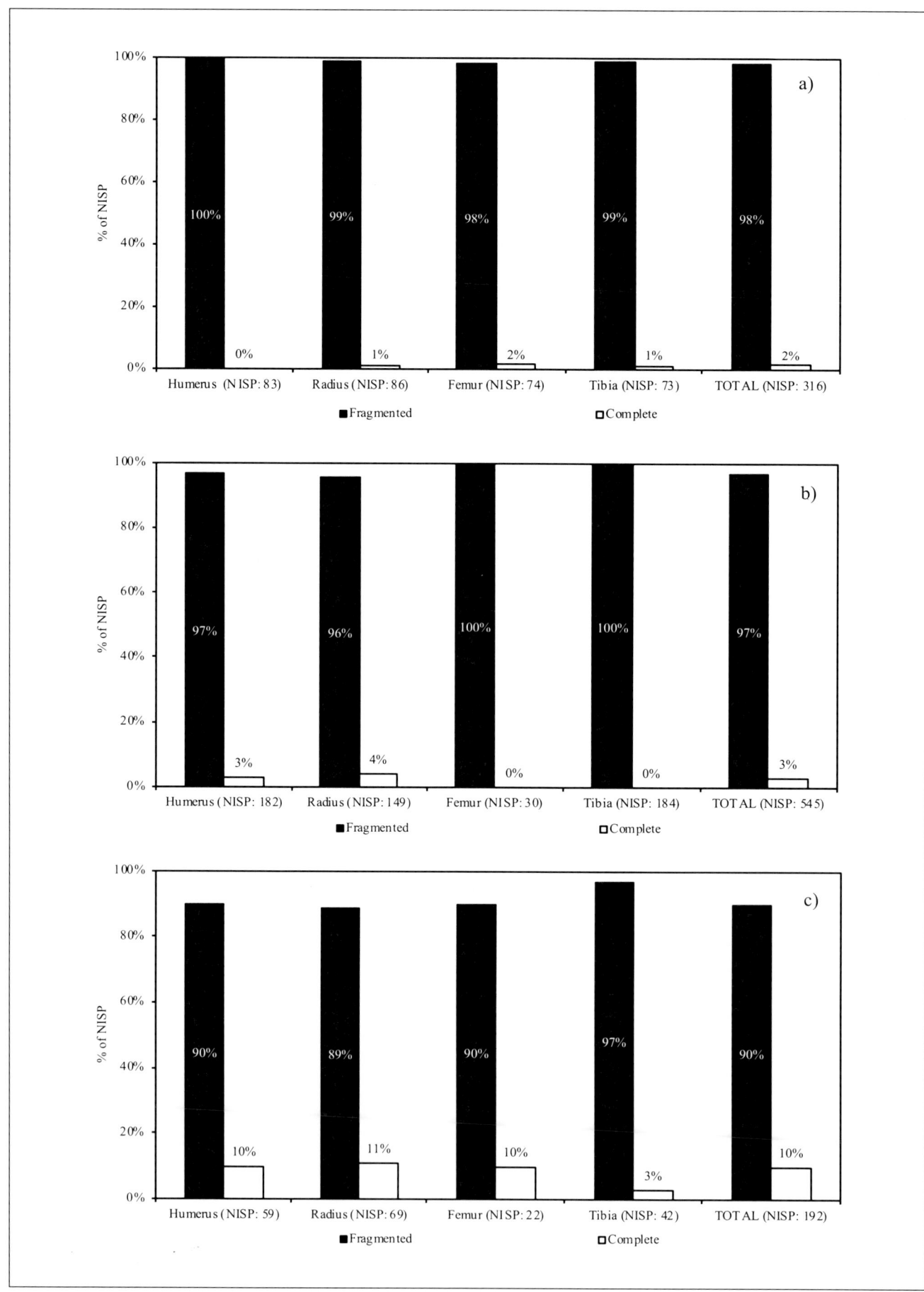

Figure 5.4 Rate of fragmentation on the long bones of: a) *Bos taurus*, b) Caprinae, c) *Sus*. All phases are considered. Data in Table 5.17. NISP counts.

other hand, the high proportion of unfused intact pig bones supports earlier arguments on the young age profile of the species. It is suggested, therefore, that unfused, immature pig bones were in some way 'protected' from intensive fragmentation since the content of marrow in young animals is considerably lower (Speth 1983).

5.3 Taxa representation

The fauna of Promachon is typical of the Late Neolithic of Greece. Domesticated animals constitute the overwhelming majority (Table 5.18). A glance at Figure 5.5 reveals that domesticates represent almost 97 per cent of the total NISP of all species identified considering all three phases. On a temporal level, no differences occur: domesticates are represented with 95 per cent during Phase I, increasing by one per cent during Phase II (96 per cent) and another two per cent during Phase III (98 per cent).

The domesticated fauna is dominated by the four species (cattle, sheep, goat, and pig) that are present during this time-period in almost all settlements from Greek Macedonia (Halstead 1994; Yiannouli 2002a; 2004; Table 5.19). No dramatic differences occur with time, but a gradual increase in caprines, paralleled by an equivalent decrease in cattle, is noticeable (Figure 5.6). In Phase I the two taxa are present with roughly the same frequencies (43 per cent for cattle and 42 per cent for caprines), but there is a slight change of the situation in the next two phases: during Phase II, caprines form the most abundant species (46 per cent), while cattle falls by almost three per cent of its former percentage (40 per cent). During Phase III caprine frequencies rise to 50 per cent while cattle frequencies drop to 36 per cent. It therefore seems that, with time, sheep and goat proportions increased while cattle proportions dropped. Chi[2] tests were also conducted to test whether the differences between phases in cattle and caprine

representation were statistically significant. The tests indicated that the two taxa representation is significantly different between Phases I-II (p= .015) and that it is highly different between Phases II-III (p= .003). Pigs are the least common of the three main domesticates. They are, however, consistently represented throughout the three main phases, with negligible differences between phases.

Attribution of specimens to either sheep or goat presented a certain level of difficulty. Regardless of the fact that the osteomorphological characteristics of a number of postcranial bones and teeth were used for the distinction of the two closely related species, the vast majority of caprine remains were not identified to the finest taxonomical level. These were eventually recorded to the level of subfamily (sheep/goat). Of those fragments that were identified as either sheep or goat, the majority belonged to sheep considering all three phases (79 per cent during Phase I, 82 per cent during Phase II and 83 per cent during Phase III; Table 5.20; Figure 5.7). Once again, Chi[2] tests were conducted in order to test whether the differences between phases in sheep and goat representation were statistically significant; these indicated that sheep and goat representation is not significantly different between Phases I-II (p= .47) as well as Phases II-III (p= .66). Further implications on the economic importance of these two closely related species will be assessed in other parts of the analysis (*e.g.* age-at-death).

Dog remains tend to appear in low frequencies in Greek Neolithic contexts (Trantalidou 2006). This is also the case for Promachon, where dogs are represented with the same number of fragments during Phases I and II (NISP: 48 respectively) and 28 fragments during Phase III. Their frequencies remain stable during all phases (two per cent among domesticates and two per cent among all species identified).

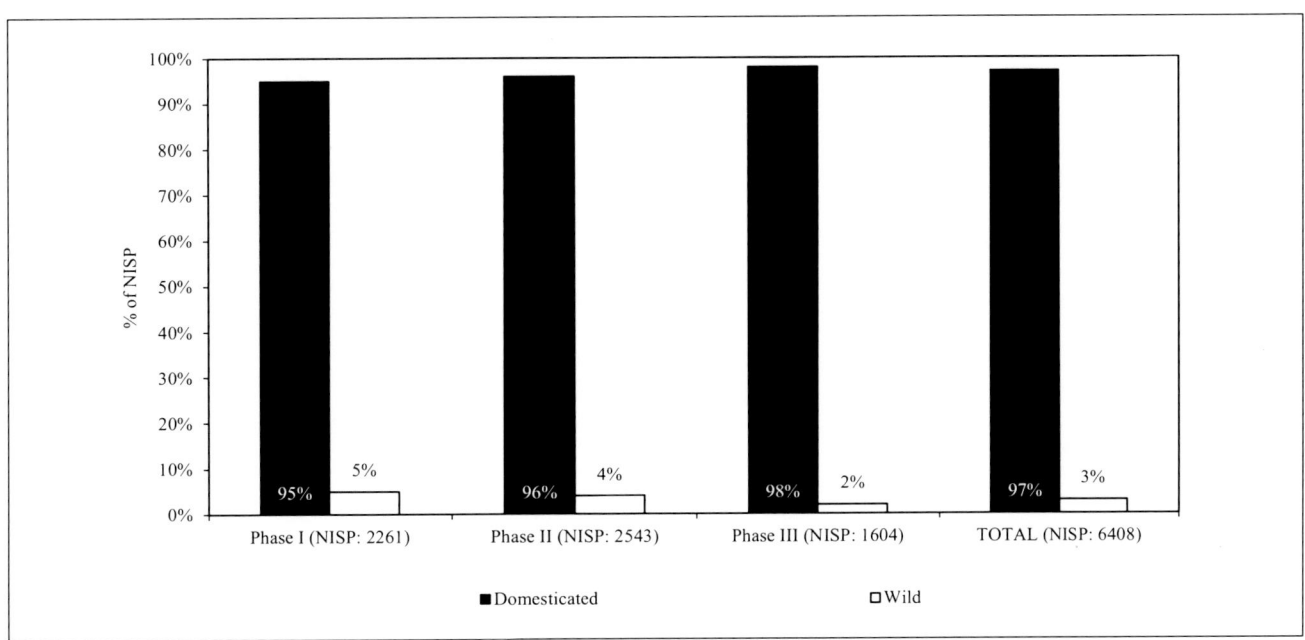

Figure 5.5 Domesticated *versus* wild taxa on the temporal level. Data in Table 5.18. NISP counts.

Table 5.18 Taxa present at Late Neolithic Promachon sector. Data for Figure 5.5. NISP counts.

Taxa present	Undisturbed deposits												Mixed deposits			
	Late Neolithic I				Phase II (Layers 3, 2)				Late Neolithic II							
	Phase I (Layers 6, 5, 4)								Phase III (Layer 1)							
	NISP		Total	%	NISP		Total	%	NISP		Total	%	NISP		Total	%
	Bones	Teeth			Bones	Teeth			Bones	Teeth			Bones	Teeth		
Bos taurus	623	295	918	40%	671	304	975	38%	354	197	551	34%	194	100	294	36%
Caprinae	428	460	888	39%	487	616	1103	43%	293	474	767	48%	150	189	339	41%
(Ovis aries)	(108)	(73)	(181)		(151)	(79)	(230)		(90)	(53)	(143)		(41)	(23)	(64)	
(Capra hircus)	(20)	(28)	(48)		(30)	(22)	(52)		(14)	(15)	(29)		(10)	(8)	(18)	
Sus	230	99	329	14%	226	107	333	13%	134	83	217	14%	82	57	139	17%
Canis familiaris	20	28	48	2%	34	14	48	2%	12	16	28	2%	6	7	13	1%
Total Domesticated	**1301**	**882**	**2183**	**95%**	**1418**	**1041**	**2459**	**96%**	**793**	**770**	**1563**	**98%**	**432**	**353**	**785**	**96%**
Cervus elaphus	19	11	30		33	10	43		11	4	15		17	8	25	
Dama dama	2		2		5	1	6		1		1		2		2	
Capreolus capreolus	8	2	10		13	2	15		8	1	9		5		5	
Lepus europaeus	8		8		6	1	7		6		6		2		2	
Vulpes vulpes	13	3	16		5	3	8		4	3	7			1	1	
Rupicapra rupicapra	1		1													
Sus scrofa		1	1													
Lynx lynx	1		1													
Ursus arctos	3		3													

Taxon	(1)	(1)	(1) Σ	%	(2)	(2)	(2) Σ	%	(3)	(3)	(3) Σ	%	Total	%	(4)	(4)	(4) Σ	%
Meles meles	1		1						1		1		2					
Mustela putorius		1	1										1					
Mustela erminea										1	1		1					
Martes foina									1		1		1			1	1	
Buteo lagopus					2		2						2					
Anser anser	3		3										3					
Grus grus	1		1										1					
Corvus corax					2		2						2					
Aves (indet.)					1		1						1					
Total Wild	60	18	78	5%	67	17	84	4%	32	9	41	2%	203	3%	26	10	36	4%
Domesticated & Wild	1361	900	2261	100%	1485	1058	2543	100%	825	779	1604	100%	6408	100%	458	363	821	100%
Cervus/Bos	12		12		27	2	29		9		9		50		6		6	
Cervus/Dama	1		1		6		6		2		2		9		1		1	
Ovis/Capra/Capreolus	8	1	9		14		14		18		18		41		6		6	
Canis/Vulpes	2	1	3		6	3	9		2		2		14			1	1	
Homo sapiens	2		2						1		1		3		1		1	
TOTAL	1386	902	2288		1538	1063	2601		856	780	1636		6525		471	365	836	

PRESENCE STATED

Taxon	(1)	(1)	(1) Σ		(2)	(2)	(2) Σ		(3)	(3)	(3) Σ		Total		(4)	(4)	(4) Σ	
Testudinidae					Present (non-countable)													
Siluris glanis					Present (non-countable)								Present (non-countable)					
Cyprinidae	Present (non-countable)				Present (non-countable)													
Murex trunculus	Present (non-countable)				Present (non-countable)													

Table 5.19 Three main domesticates on the temporal level. Caprinae subfamily includes *Ovis/Capra* **(sheep/goat),** *Ovis aries* **(sheep) and** *Capra hircus* **(goat). Data for Figure 5.6. NISP counts.**

Three main domesticates	Late Neolithic I				Late Neolithic II		TOTAL	
	Phase I		Phase II		Phase III			
	NISP	%	NISP	%	NISP	%	NISP	%
Bos taurus	918	43%	975	40%	551	36%	**2444**	**40%**
Caprinae	888	42%	1103	46%	767	50%	**2758**	**45%**
Sus	329	15%	333	14%	217	14%	**879**	**14%**
TOTAL	**2135**	**100%**	**2411**	**100%**	**1535**	**100%**	**6081**	**100%**

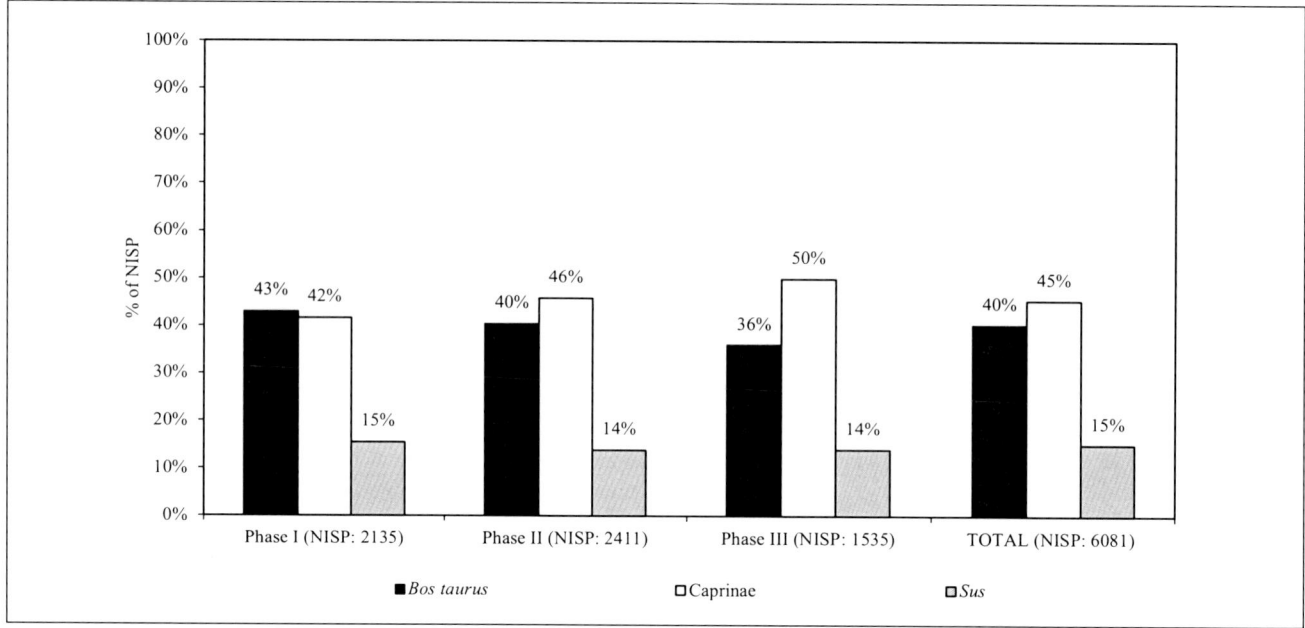

Figure 5.6 Three main domesticates on the temporal level. Data in Table 5.19. NISP counts.

Species frequencies for the three main domesticates calculated through MNI are not entirely consistent with those deriving from NISP (Table 5.21). The main difference is that caprines are substantially better represented when MNIs are considered (Figure 5.8). This difference between the two quantification systems represents a much-expected pattern due to the well-known effects of recovery bias. Anatomical elements deriving from smaller taxa such as sheep/goats (and pigs) are underrepresented in terms of NISP, which leads to their under-representation (in comparison to cattle)

in NISP counts. MNI counts are less affected by this bias as they only rely on the most common element.

It is therefore argued that it would be wrong to assume that NISP provides an accurate estimate on the frequency of species since it is seriously affected by differential recovery, a major factor in the formation of the Promachon assemblage. When MNI, which is less affected by recovery bias is taken into account, cattle frequencies are severely reduced while sheep/goat frequencies increase.

Table 5.20 *Ovis aries* **(sheep)** *versus* *Capra hircus* **(goat) on the temporal level. Data for Figure 5.7. NISP counts.**

Caprinae	Late Neolithic I				Late Neolithic II		TOTAL	
	Phase I		Phase II		Phase III			
	NISP	%	NISP	%	NISP	%	NISP	%
Ovis aries	181	79%	230	82%	143	83%	**554**	**81%**
Capra hircus	48	21%	52	18%	29	17%	**129**	**19%**
TOTAL	**229**	**100%**	**282**	**100%**	**172**	**100%**	**683**	**100%**

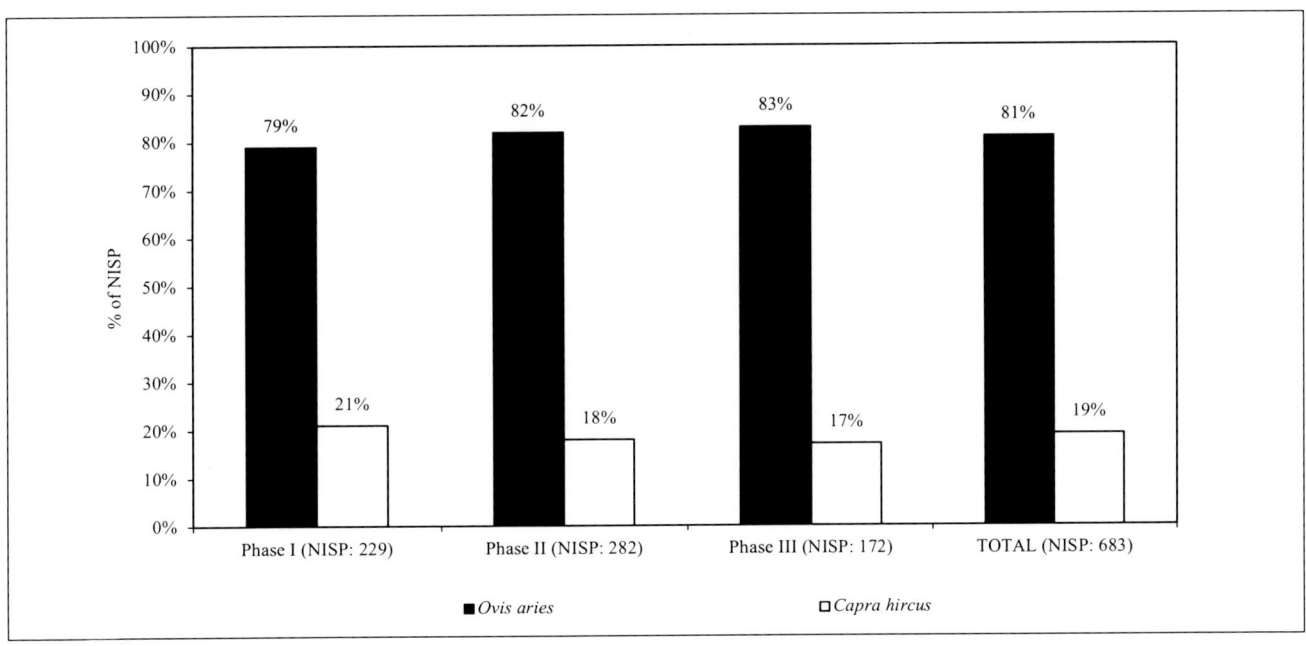

Figure 5.7 *Ovis aries versus Capra hircus* **on the temporal level. Data in Table 5.20. NISP counts.**

Table 5.21 Three main domesticates on the temporal level. Caprinae subfamily includes *Ovis*/*Capra* (sheep/goat), *Ovis aries* (sheep) and *Capra hircus* (goat). Data for Figure 5.8. MNI counts.

Three main domesticates	Late Neolithic I				Late Neolithic II		TOTAL	
	Phase I		Phase II		Phase III			
	MNI	%	MNI	%	MNI	%	MNI	%
Bos taurus	22	24%	25	24%	14	22%	**61**	**24%**
Caprinae	54	60%	62	60%	43	67%	**159**	**61%**
Sus	15	16%	17	16%	7	11%	**39**	**15%**
TOTAL	**91**	**100%**	**104**	**100%**	**64**	**100%**	259	100%

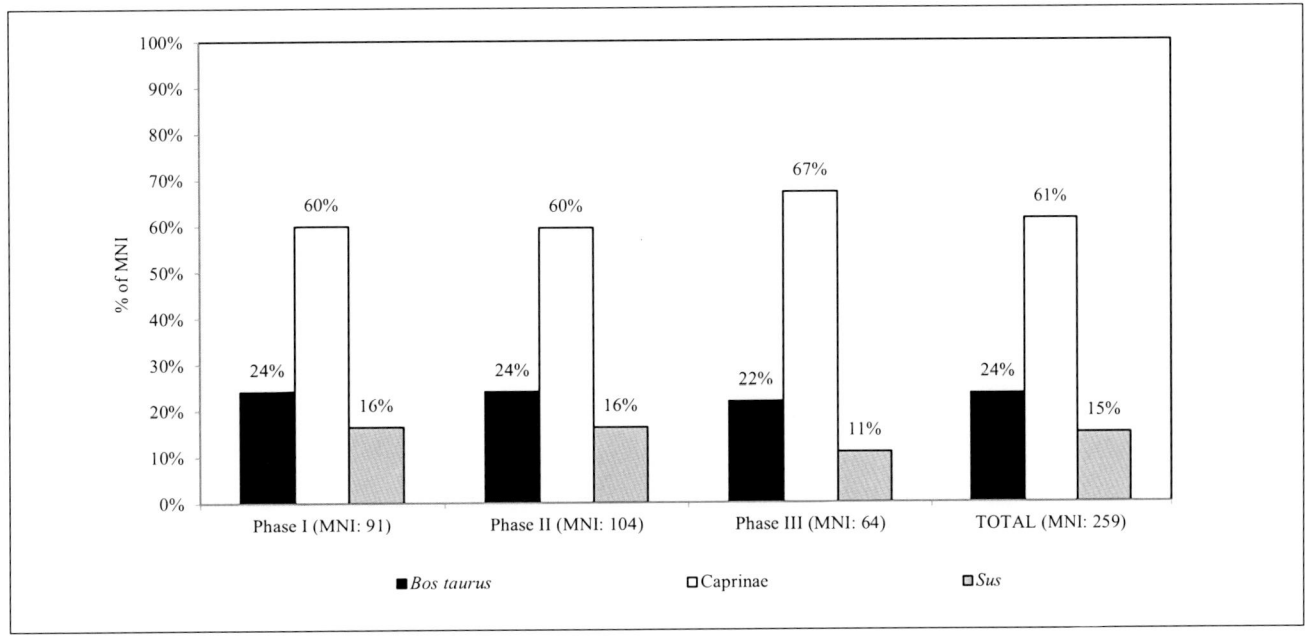

Figure 5.8 Three main domesticates on the temporal level. Data in Table 5.21. MNI counts.

41

Although by no means perfect, the MNI probably provides a more accurate estimate of the frequency of species (Albarella 1999; Johnstone and Albarella 2002), at least in assemblages that are substantially affected by recovery bias. MNI frequencies are generally closer to frequencies of NISP from sieved assemblages than hand-collected ones (Albarella *et al.* 1997), such as the Promachon assemblage. This would also indicate that the MNI count reduces the effects of recovery bias created by NISP.

Since a substantial number of studied and published faunal assemblages from contemporary sites have used NISP (rather than MNI) as the main predictor of taxonomic frequency, we will also use it for comparative purposes later on in the current study. In terms of diachronic trends, MNI counts are roughly consistent with the indications provided by NISP. The increase in caprine frequencies through time is confirmed, although, according to MNI, it does not emerge until Phase III, and this is not just at the expenses of cattle, but also pig. By combining the evidence of the two quantification systems therefore, the only safe conclusion to be drawn is the slight increase in the relative abundance of caprines through time.

Among wild taxa, cervids constitute the most common family and they are found in all habitation layers in Promachon sector. Red deer is represented with a total of 113 fragments (30 fragments during Phase I, 43 fragments during Phase II, 15 fragments during Phase III and 25 fragments deriving from mixed deposits). Roe deer, which is less frequent than red deer in almost all prehistoric sites in temperate Europe (Bökönyi 1986), is represented with a total of 39 fragments (10 fragments during Phase I, 15 fragments during Phase II, nine fragments during Phase III and five fragments deriving from mixed deposits). The presence of the fallow deer in Promachon's faunal assemblage confirms previous claims of the species reintroduction in the area of Greek Macedonia during the Late Neolithic, after its extinction due to hunting pressure by the end of the Lower Paleolithic (Bökönyi 1986; Curci and Tagliacozzo 2003; Yiannouli and Trantalidou 1999). Fallow deer remains are represented with a total of 11 fragments (two fragments during Phase I, six fragments during Phase II, one fragment during Phase III and two fragments deriving from mixed deposits).

Less common than cervids, but frequently represented in Promachon, are the brown hare and the red fox. Both species are frequently encountered in Greek prehistoric sites. While the brown hare appears as early as the Early Paleolithic in Greece, the earliest remains of the red fox derive from the Pre-ceramic Neolithic (Bökönyi 1986; Yiannouli 2003); In Promachon, brown hare is represented with 23 fragments in total (eight fragments during Phase I, seven fragments during Phase II, six fragments during Phase III and two fragments deriving from mixed deposits), whereas red fox is represented with a total of 32 fragments (16 fragments during Phase I, eight fragments during Phase II, seven fragments during Phase III and one fragment deriving from mixed deposits).

The deposits of Phase I have also yielded a right maxilla of a senile wild boar containing the tusk and the first, second, third and fourth premolars. The presence of the wild boar is reported from a number of contemporary to Promachon sites in Macedonia, such as Sitagroi (Bökönyi 1986) and Stavroupoli (Yiannouli 2002a; 2004). In Promachon however, apart from the maxilla, no pig postcranial elements presented the dimensional characteristics necessary for their attribution to the wild form. Nevertheless, the significance of the species will be further assessed later in this study through biometrical analyses. Chamois, whose presence is extremely rare in Greek Neolithic sites is represented in Phase I with a single specimen (first phalanx); the species' presence was also reported by Bökönyi (1986) in his study of the faunal material from the nearby site of Sitagroi.

Eurasian lynx remains are among the scarcest finds in Greek faunal assemblages (Yiannouli 2003). Lynx pesence was reported from two sites contemporary to Promachon: Dikili Tash (Julien 1992; Helmer 1997) and Dimitra (Yiannouli 1994; 1997) in Eastern Macedonia. At Promachon, the Eurasian Lynx is represented in Phase I by a single fragment of a distal humerus.

Brown bear remains are frequently reported from sites in northern Greece (Yiannouli 2003; 2013). Apart from Dikili Tash, brown bear remains have been reported from Sitagroi (Bökönyi 1986), Vasilika (Yiannouli 1994), Stavroupolis (Yiannouli 2002a), and Servia (Watson 1979a). Mountainous regions of the Balkans with dense forest surroundings, such as the area around Promachon provided an excellent habitat for the species. Brown bear is represented in Phase I by three fragments, a proximal radius, a third metacarpal and a proximal ulna.

The family of Mustelids (Mustelidae) is represented with four species: European badger, polecat, stoat and beech marten. The badger is the most frequently occurring mustelid in Greek prehistoric faunal assemblages (Yiannouli 2003). The current distribution of the species covers an area from mainland Greece to the island of Crete. At Promachon, the badger is represented in Phases I and III by two ulnae. Although the presence of the polecat during historic times is well documented, only recently it has been reported in Macedonian Neolithic faunal assemblages (Dikili Tas: Helmer 1997). At Promachon, the polecat is present in Phase I with a single mandible containing the fourth premolar and first molar. The deposits of Phase III have also yielded a stoat mandible containing the fourth premolar and the first and second molars as well as a distal tibia of a beech marten. The latter species is also represented in the mixed deposits with a mandible containing the first and second molars.

Bird bones are extremely scarce. Only nine fragments were identified down to the level of species: the rough-legged buzzard and the common raven are represented during the second phase of occupation with two proximal ulnae respectively. In addition, a distal tarsometatarsus, a proximal scapula and a proximal ulna were attributed to the greylag goose, while a proximal scapula was attributed to a common crane. All four fragments belong to the first phase of occupation. The deposits of Phase II have also yielded a single distal carpometacarpus of a bird, which, due to its poor preservation, could not be identified to any taxonomic level.

Reptiles, fishes and molluscs are also present in the assemblage with 'non-countable' elements. Reptiles are represented in Phase II by a carapace fragment of a tortoise. Molluscs are also represented in Phases I and II by one shell of a snail respectively. The deposits of Phase II have also yielded four vertebrae and a spine of a catfish, and three vertebrae of a species belonging to the family of minnows.

Modern human is represented in Phase I with two specimens (a proximal scapula and a proximal radius) and in Phase II with one specimen (a proximal ulna). The mixed deposits have also yielded a proximal scapula (glenoid cavity). The presence of human remains in the faunal assemblage is rather interesting. There are a number of possible reasons

that could potentially explain this presence, however, these will be further discussed later in this study.

Table 5.22 presents the relative frequency of all species – in terms of the Minimum Number of Individuals (MNI) – on a temporal level.

5.4 The human agent: butchery and burning

The preceding analysis, while recognizing that gnawing by carnivores (and pigs) played a significant role in the formation of the faunal assemblage, suggested that most of the bones represent material discarded by humans after some form of carcass processing for marrow extraction took place. In the following analysis, carcass processing is explored using more direct types of evidence, such as the incidence of butchery and burning.

5.4.1 Butchery marks

Because of the good preservation of the Promachon faunal material, butchery marks and burning could relatively easily be detected. Table 5.23 presents the incidence of butchery

Table 5.22 Taxa present at Late Neolithic Promachon sector. Caprinae subfamily includes *Ovis/Capra* (sheep/goat), *Ovis aries* (sheep) and *Capra hircus* (goat). MNI counts.

Taxa present	Late Neolithic I				Late Neolithic II		TOTAL	
	Phase I		Phase II		Phase III			
	MNI	%	MNI	%	MNI	%	MNI	%
Bos taurus	22	20%	25	21%	14	18%	**61**	**20%**
Caprinae	54	49%	62	52%	43	56%	**159**	**52%**
Sus	15	14%	17	14%	9	12%	**41**	**13%**
Canis familiaris	4	4%	4	3%	3	4%	**11**	**4%**
Total Domesticated	**95**	**87%**	**108**	**90%**	**69**	**90%**	**272**	**89%**
Cervus elaphus	1		2		1		4	
Capreolus capreolus	2		2		1		5	
Dama dama	1		1		1		3	
Lepus europaeus	2		1		1		4	
Vulpes vulpes	2		2		1		5	
Rupicapra rupicapra	1						1	
Sus scrofa	1						1	
Lynx lynx	1						1	
Ursus arctos	1						1	
Meles meles	1				1		2	
Mustela putorius	1						1	
Mustela erminea					1		1	
Martes foina					1		1	
Buteo lagopus			1				1	
Anser anser	1						1	
Grus grus	1						1	
Corvus corax			1				1	
Aves (indet.)			1				1	
Total Wild	**16**	**13%**	**11**	**10%**	**8**	**10%**	**35**	**11%**
Domesticated & Wild	**111**	**100%**	**119**	**100%**	**77**	**100%**	**307**	**100%**

Table 5.23 Butchery and burning on the cranial elements of *Bos taurus* (cattle), Caprinae (sheep/goat), *Sus* (pig), *Canis familiaris* (dog) and *Cervus elaphus* (red deer) on the temporal level. NISP counts.

Modification		Cranial elements										
		Maxilla				Mandible				Loose teeth		
		Cut	Chopped	Burned	TOTAL	Cut	Chopped	Burned	TOTAL	Chopped	Burned	TOTAL
Phase I	*Bos taurus*				**0**		4	3	**7**	1	2	**3**
	Caprinae				**0**		2	3	**5**		4	**4**
	Sus			2	**2**		1	3	**4**		3	**3**
	Canis familiaris				**0**	1		1	**2**			**0**
	Cervus elaphus				**0**				**0**		2	**2**
	TOTAL	**0**	**0**	**2**	**2**	**1**	**7**	**10**	**18**	**1**	**11**	**12**
Phase II	*Bos taurus*				**0**		6	2	**8**		2	**2**
	Caprinae				**0**		1	2	**3**		8	**8**
	Sus				**0**			2	**2**			**0**
	Canis familiaris				**0**	1			**1**		1	**1**
	Cervus elaphus				**0**				**0**			**0**
	TOTAL	**0**	**0**	**0**	**0**	**1**	**7**	**6**	**14**	**0**	**11**	**11**
Phase III	*Bos taurus*				**0**		2	6	**8**			**0**
	Caprinae				**0**			6	**6**			**0**
	Sus				**0**				**0**		2	**2**
	Canis familiaris				**0**	2			**2**		2	**2**
	Cervus elaphus				**0**				**0**			**0**
	TOTAL	**0**	**0**	**0**	**0**	**2**	**2**	**12**	**16**	**0**	**4**	**4**
TOTAL		**0**	**0**	**2**	**2**	**4**	**16**	**28**	**48**	**1**	**26**	**27**

marks and burning on the cranial elements (maxillae, mandibles and loose teeth) of the three main domesticates, dog and red deer. Chopping marks are present in a number of cattle, caprine and pig mandibles. More specifically, chopping marks were inflicted on the lower part of the mandible – beneath the tooth root line – suggesting marrow extraction. A number of chopped cattle, caprine and pig mandibles presented traces of burning, most likely to facilitate the extraction of marrow. Additionally, cutmarks inflicted on the articular process (*ramus mandibulae*) of four dog mandibles are most likely suggestive of skinning (Binford 1981). Almost five per cent of the total 'countable' postcranial fragments recorded, presented butchery marks (Table 5.24). The latter were observed on the postcranial bones of cattle, caprines, pig, dog, red deer

Table 5.24 Incidence of butchery among the postcranial bones of all species identified on the temporal level. Only 'countable' elements are considered. Both cutmarks and chopping marks are considered. NISP counts.

Incidence of butchery	Postcranial elements	
	NISP	%
Phase I (NISP: 1386)	61	4%
Phase II (NISP: 1538)	92	6%
Phase III (NISP: 856)	28	3%
TOTAL (NISP: 3780)	**181**	**5%**

and roe deer. Their absence from fallow deer is very likely to be the result of small sample size. This frequency is higher than that recorded in the Late Neolithic cave on the east bank of the river Aggitis, where less than one per cent of the total postcranial bones presented any traces of butchery (Trantalidou *et al.* 2006). In the Late Neolithic settlement of Dimitra, butchery marks are present on six per cent of the total postcranial bones (Yiannouli 1997).

Tables 5.25-5.28 present the incidence of cutmarks and chopping marks on the postcranial bones of cattle, caprines, pig and dog on a temporal level, while Figure 5.9 presents graphically the incidence of butchery on the postcranial bones of the three main domesticates at the temporal level. Cutmarks and chopping marks on the postcranial bones of red deer and roe deer were very few, and consequently, these two species are of necessity treated together (Table 5.29).

Table 5.25 Incidence of butchery on the postcranial bones of *Bos taurus* (cattle) on the temporal level. Only 'countable' elements are considered. Data for Figure 5.9. NISP counts.

Bos taurus	Modification: postcranial elements							
	Phase I (NISP: 623)		Phase II (NISP: 671)		Phase III (NISP: 354)		TOTAL (NISP: 1648)	
	NISP	%	NISP	%	NISP	%	NISP	%
Cutmarks	5	1%	13	2%	10	3%	28	2%
Chopping marks	26	4%	41	6%	6	2%	73	4%
TOTAL	31	5%	54	8%	16	5%	101	6%

Table 5.26 Incidence of butchery on the postcranial bones of Caprinae (sheep/goat) on the temporal level. Caprinae subfamily includes *Ovis/Capra* (sheep/goat), *Ovis aries* (sheep) and *Capra hircus* (goat). Only 'countable' elements are considered. Data for Figure 5.9. NISP counts.

Caprinae	Modification: postcranial elements							
	Phase I (NISP: 428)		Phase II (NISP: 487)		Phase III (NISP: 293)		TOTAL (NISP: 1208)	
	NISP	%	NISP	%	NISP	%	NISP	%
Cutmarks	2	1%	1	1%	5	2%	8	1%
Chopping marks	17	4%	14	3%	1	1%	32	3%
TOTAL	19	5%	15	4%	6	3%	40	4%

Table 5.27 Incidence of butchery on the postcranial bones of *Sus* (pig) on the temporal level. Only 'countable' elements are considered. Data for Figure 5.9. NISP counts.

Sus	Modification: postcranial elements							
	Phase I (NISP: 230)		Phase II (NISP: 226)		Phase III (NISP: 134)		TOTAL (NISP: 590)	
	NISP	%	NISP	%	NISP	%	NISP	%
Cutmarks	2	1%	1	1%	3	2%	6	1%
Chopping marks	7	3%	15	7%	2	1%	24	4%
TOTAL	9	4%	16	8%	5	3%	30	5%

Table 5.28 Incidence of butchery on the postcranial bones of *Canis familiaris* (dog) on the temporal level. Only 'countable' elements are considered. NISP counts.

Canis familiaris	Modification: postcranial elements							
	Phase I (NISP: 20)		Phase II (NISP: 34)		Phase III (NISP: 12)		TOTAL (NISP: 54)	
	NISP	%	NISP	%	NISP	%	NISP	%
Cutmarks		0%		0%		0%	0	0%
Chopping marks		0%	1	3%		0%	1	2%
TOTAL	0	0%	1	3%	0	0%	1	2%

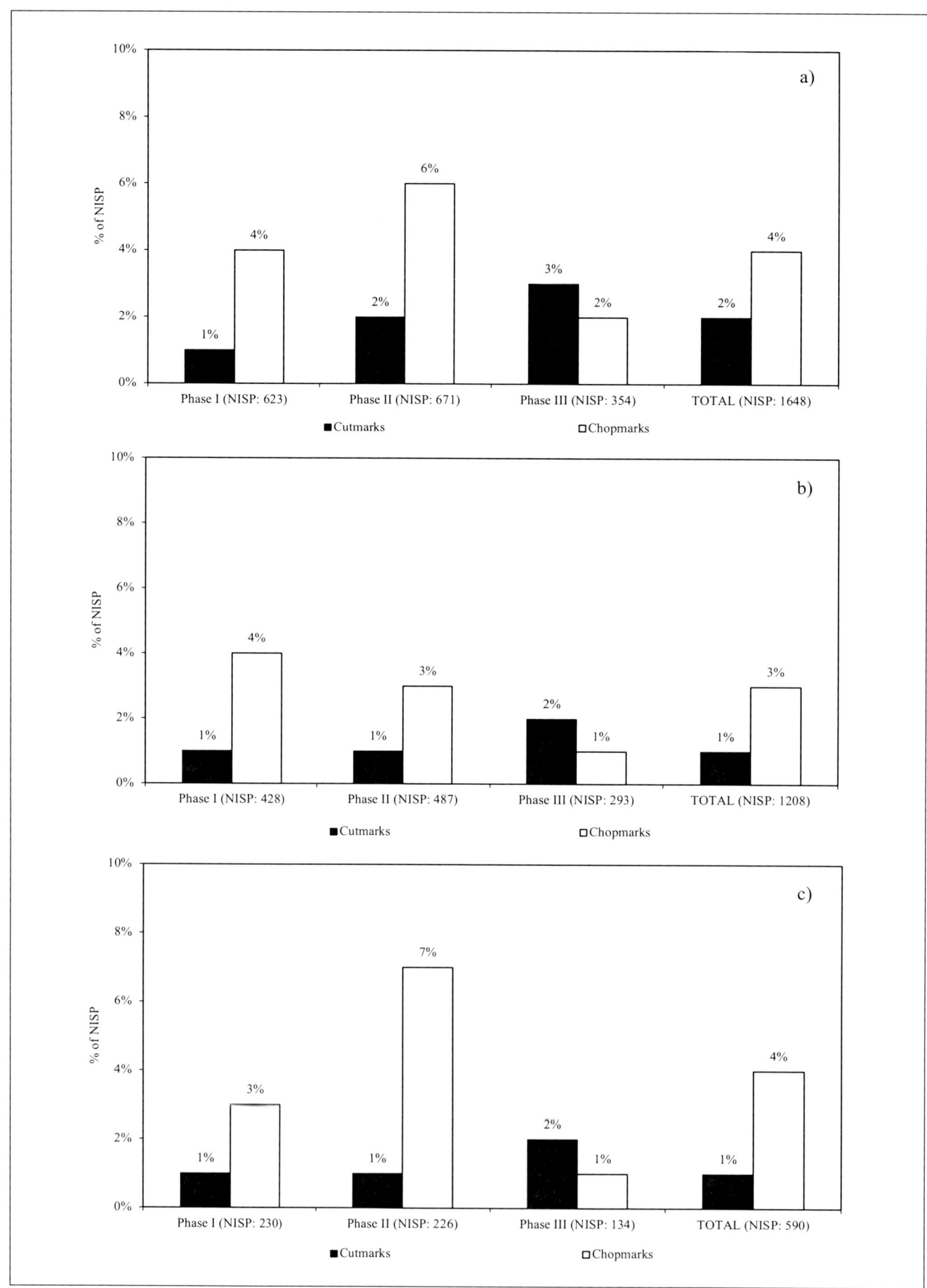

Figure 5.9 Butchery on the postcranial bones of: a) *Bos taurus*, **b) Caprinae, c)** *Sus* **on the temporal level. Data in Tables 5.25-5.27. NISP counts.**

Table 5.29 Incidence of butchery on the postcranial bones of Cervidae (cervids) on the temporal level. Cervidae family includes *Cervus elaphus* (red deer) and *Capreolus capreolus* (roe deer). Only 'countable' elements are considered. NISP counts.

Cervidae	Modification: Postcranial elements							
	Phase I (NISP: 29)		Phase II (NISP: 51)		Phase III (NISP: 20)		TOTAL (NISP: 100)	
	NISP	%	NISP	%	NISP	%	NISP	%
Cutmarks		0%	2	4%	1	5%	3	3%
Chopping marks	2	7%	4	8%		0%	6	6%
TOTAL	2	7%	6	12%	1	5%	9	9%

The overall frequency of butchery marks does not outstandingly differ between cattle, caprines and pigs. Butchery marks were recorded on about six per cent, four per cent and five per cent of cattle, caprine and pig postcranial elements respectively. Chopping marks are represented with a higher frequency than cutmarks in all three main domesticates during Phases I and II (and consequently for the whole cultural sequence of the Late Neolithic). This is rather unusual, as we would normally expect a greater difference in chopping between cattle and other species. The large size of the cattle body requires the use of heavy tools in order to divide it into a large number of portions for processing. On the other hand, we would normally expect cutmarks to be more frequent than chopping marks on caprine and pig bones: in most prehistoric faunal assemblages, carcasses of small animals such as caprines and pigs were usually dismembered using flints and stone tools to cut through the tendons and joints. However, this is not the case at Promachon, since cutmarks are much less common than chopping marks.

Carnivore gnawing could be a possible reason for the obliteration of cutmarks from the postcranial bones of caprines and pigs during Phases I and II. Cutmarks resulting from dismembering tend to be concentrated around bone articulations, which are particularly vulnerable to carnivore attrition. However, as we have already seen, the frequency of gnawing at Promachon is relatively low. Gnawing, therefore, cannot be considered as the main reason for the low frequency of cutmarks. It must also be considered that bone surface preservation is generally good at Promachon. It is therefore suggested that the small number of cutmarks on the postcranial bones of the Promachon animals is most likely to be the result of the processing of animal carcasses in large chunks (or even whole) as a consequence of communal consumption.

Another interesting pattern is that cutmarks are represented with a higher frequency than chopping marks on the postcranial elements from the deposits associated with Phase III. This is observed on the postcranial bones of all three main domesticates, which supports the view that the pattern is 'genuine', and that during Phase III heavy tools and objects were not used as regularly.

This is rather unusual and requires some explanation. As previously noted (chapter 2), evidence of copper smelting is of particular interest in Promachon sector and it is documented in the deposits of Phase III

(Koukouli-Chrysanthaki *et al.* 2000; 2007; 2014; Koukouli-Chrysanthaki and Basiakos 2002). In the light of this evidence, one would argue that during this time-period, metal tools and knives were most likely to have been implemented at Promachon. These new metal tools could have replaced heavy tools and objects that were used during the previous phases (Phases I and II) and could potentially explain the high frequency of cutmarks rather than chopping marks on the postcranial bones of the three main domesticates during the last phase of occupation.

The origins of metallurgy, and thus, the use of metal tools has long intrigued archaeologists. However, still very little is known about their rate of adoption (Greenfield 1999). In general, monitoring the importance of metal tools has been restricted to inferential suppositions based on their absence. This is also the case for Promachon, where no metal tools were eventually recovered. The argument therefore for the possible use of metal tools and objects in Promachon is based solely on the presence of a clay crucible with traces of copper extraction (and also traces of slag) (Koukouli-Chrysanthaki *et al.* 2007) during Phase III. There are a number of arguments that could potentially explain the absence of metal tools from the deposits of Phase III: these could have been either recycled by their users, or deteriorated in their post-depositional contexts, or deliberately deposited somewhere. However, we should not exclude also the possibility that metal tools might have been very few in Promachon, and therefore it is just chance that they have not been found. If this is the case, then it is highly likely that metal tools might have been regarded as prestigious items and therefore not used for 'humble', mundane, everyday tasks. In addition, there is also the possibility that the high frequency of cut marks during Phase III is the result of the use of small stone tools and flints, rather than metal tools, which as previously noted were not found on site. In any case, it should be noted, that no attempt has been made to identify metal *versus* stone cut marks on the surfaces of the animal bones from Promachon. In addition, tool manufacturing has yet to be investigated at Promachon: this should represent a priority for future research.

There is a further issue, which should also be considered. It is highly possible that the higher number of cutmarks during Phase III might be related with the more intensive butchery of animal carcasses, possibly for household consumption. This leads to the assumption that there was an increase in household-based eating during the third phase of occupation in Promachon. In other words, it is possible that during Phases I and II animal carcasses were processed in large chunks possibly for consumption by large social groups, whereas in Phase III, animal carcasses were butchered more intensively, possibly for household consumption. This issue will be further discussed later in this study (chapter seven).

Tables 5.30-5.33 present the anatomical distribution of butchery marks for the three main domesticates and cervids.

Table 5.30 Body part distribution of butchery for *Bos taurus* (cattle) on the temporal level. NISP counts.

Bos taurus		Late Neolithic I						Late Neolithic II			Body part distribution of butchery marks		
		Phase I (Layers 6, 5, 4)			Phase II (Layers 3, 2)			Phase III (Layer 1)					
		Cut	Chopped	TOTAL	Cut	Chopped	TOTAL	Cut	Chopped	TOTAL	TOTAL Cut & Chopped	Total NISP	%
Postcranial elements	Cranium (zygomaticus)			0			0			0	0		0%
	Atlas			0			0			0	0		0%
	Axis			0			0			0	0		0%
	Scapula			0	2	4	6	1		1	7	64	11%
	Humerus proximal			0			0		1	1	22	83	26%
	Humerus distal	1	7	8	3	7	10	2	1	3			
	Radius proximal		6	6	4		4			0	11	86	13%
	Radius distal			0	1		1			0			
	Ulna proximal		2	2			0			0	2	38	5%
	Carpal 2+3			0			0			0			
	Metacarpal distal	3		3	2		2			0	5	43	11%
	Pelvis	2		2	2		2	1	1	2	6	72	8%
	Femur proximal	1		1	1	1	2			0	5	74	7%
	Femur distal			0	2		2			0			
	Tibia proximal	1		1	1		1			0	11	73	15%
	Tibia distal	4		4	4		4	1		1			
	Scafocuboid			0	1		1			0	1	32	3%
	Astragalus			0	1		1			0	1	99	1%
	Calcaneum	1		1	2	2	4	1		1	6	73	8%
	Metatarsal distal			0	5		5		1	1	6	26	23%
	Phalanx 1	3		3	3	4	7	5	1	6	18	590	3%
	Phalanx 2			0	1		1			0			
	Phalanx 3			0	1		1			0			
	TOTAL Countable	5	26	31	13	41	54	10	6	16	101		
	TOTAL Uncountable	1	1	2	2	5	7	1	0	1	10		

The evidence suggests that scapula, humerus, radius, tibia and the metapodials were the postcranial bones with the higher percentage of butchery in cattle. Of interest is the fact that patterns of butchery seem to be different between cattle forelimbs and hind limbs. The high frequency of butchery marks on cattle humeri suggests an emphasis on the upper limbs of the forelimbs. On the other hand, the high frequency of butchery marks on cattle metatarsals

Table 5.31 Body part distribution of butchery for Caprinae (caprines) on the temporal level. Caprinae subfamily includes *Ovis/Capra* (sheep/goat), *Ovis aries* (sheep) and *Capra hircus* (goat). NISP counts.

Caprinae		Late Neolithic I						Late Neolithic II			Body part distribution of butchery marks		
		Phase I			Phase II			Phase III					
		Cut	Chopped	TOTAL	Cut	Chopped	TOTAL	Cut	Chopped	TOTAL	TOTAL Cut & Chopped	Total NISP	%
Postcranial elements	Cranium (zygomaticus)			0			0			0	0		0%
	Atlas			0			0			0	0		0%
	Axis		1	1			0			0	1	31	0%
	Scapula			0			0			0	0		0%
	Humerus proximal		1	1			0			0	9	182	5%
	Humerus distal	1	2	3		2	2	2	1	3			
	Radius proximal		2	2	1	1	2			0	7	149	4%
	Radius distal		2	2	1	1				0			
	Ulna proximal		2	2			0			0	2	61	3%
	Carpal 2+3			0			0			0	0		0%
	Metacarpal distal			0			0			0	0		0%
	Pelvis			0		1	1			0	1	147	< 1%
	Femur proximal			0		1	1			0	3	30	10%
	Femur distal	1	1	2			0			0			
	Tibia proximal			0		1	1			0	14	184	8%
	Tibia distal		6	6		6	6	1		1			
	Scafocuboid			0			0			0	0		0%
	Astragalus			0			0	1		1	1	63	2%
	Calcaneum			0			0	1		1	1	51	2%
	Metatarsal distal			0		1	1			0	1	20	5%
	Phalanx 1			0			0			0	0	0	0%
	Phalanx 2			0			0			0			
	Phalanx 3			0			0			0			
	TOTAL Countable	2	17	19	1	14	15	5	1	6	40	* Includes 1 *Ovis aries* horn core bearing cutmarks	
	TOTAL Uncountable	* 2	2	4	5	1	6	1	0	1	11		

suggests an emphasis on the lower limbs of the hind limbs. The pattern is rather complicated and butchery in cattle postcranial bones seems to be a combination of both dismemberment and fracturing for marrow extraction. More specifically, most of the cutmarks were inflicted on the articulations between scapula and humerus, most likely in order to severe the tendons.

Chopping marks on the other hand, were inflicted on almost all cattle postcranial bones. Transverse chopping marks, which may well have been inflicted in breaking the bone for marrow, were observed on the mid shafts of three humeri and two tibiae. Otherwise, characteristic examples of fracturing bones for marrow extraction were not observed, but such a diagnosis can only be attempted in extremely obvious cases. Analysis of the incidence of fragmentation, however, suggests that most cattle long bones were fractured during human extraction for marrow. Of particular interest is that no traces of cutmarks were detected on cattle metapodials. This is rather strange,

Table 5.32 Body part distribution of butchery for *Sus* (pig) on the temporal level. NISP counts.

Sus		Late Neolithic I						Late Neolithic II			Body part distribution of butchery marks		
		Phase I (Layers 6, 5, 4)			Phase II (Layers 3, 2)			Phase III (Layer 1)					
		Cut	Chopped	TOTAL	Cut	Chopped	TOTAL	Cut	Chopped	TOTAL	TOTAL Cut & Chopped	Total NISP	%
Postcranial elements	Cranium (zygomaticus)			0			0			0	0		0%
	Atlas			0		1	1			0	1	14	7%
	Axis			0			0			0	0		0%
	Scapula			0	1	3	4	1		1	5	76	7%
	Humerus proximal			0		1	1			0	9	59	15%
	Humerus distal	1	3	4		2	2	2		2			
	Radius proximal			0		2	2			0	3	69	4%
	Radius distal			0		1	1			0			
	Ulna proximal			0		1	1			0	1	64	2%
	Carpal 3			0			0			0	0		0%
	Metacarpal 3 distal			0			0			0	0		0%
	Metacarpal 4 distal			0			0			0			
	Pelvis			0			0			0	0		0%
	Femur proximal			0			0			0	1	22	4%
	Femur distal			0			0		1	1			
	Tibia proximal		1	1			0			0	6	42	14%
	Tibia distal		3	3		2	2			0			
	Scafocuboid			0			0			0	0		0%
	Astragalus	1		1			0		1	1	2	22	9%
	Calcaneum			0			0			0	0		0%
	Metatarsal 3 distal			0			0			0	2	29	7%
	Metatarsal 4 distal			0		2	2			0			
	Phalanx 1			0			0			0	0		0%
	Phalanx 2			0			0			0			
	Phalanx 3			0			0			0			
	TOTAL Countable	2	7	9	1	15	16	3	2	5	30		
	TOTAL Uncountable	0	1	1	1	0	1	0	0	0	2		

as evidence of skinning is implied by transverse knife marks on a single astragalus, four calcanei and eleven first phalanges.

Since the overall frequency of butchery on the postcranial bones of caprines is considerably low, only tentative considerations can be made. The anatomical distribution of butchery marks indicates an emphasis on hind limbs, which may be related to greater amount of meat carried by the hind limb. The anatomical elements of the caprine skeleton with the higher percentage of butchered bones were the femur and the tibia. On the other hand, forelimb bones with the higher frequency of butchery marks were the distal humerus and the proximal radius. The cutmarks inflicted on the latter anatomical elements possibly indicate the practice of the separation of the upper from the lower forelimb. Cutmarks were also present on a single astragalus and a single calcaneum: these could possibly be associated with the practice of skinning. Last but not least, chopping marks on a single axis suggest the removal of the head. Traces of butchery were not possible to be detected on other caprine postcranial bones, but this is most likely to be the result of both fragmentation and recovery bias.

The young age profile of pig may be the reason for the low frequency of postcranial bones presenting any butchery marks. Unlike caprines, there is no reason to suggest a particular emphasis in either forelimbs or hindlimbs. Pig postcranial bones displaying the highest percentages of butchery marks were the humerus and the tibia. Chopping marks on a single atlas also suggest that the head was severed, as in the case of the caprine example.

In general, cynophagy (*i.e.* eating dog meat) is considered to have been a common practice during the whole of prehistory. Comparative data from northern Greece indicate that dogs were used as a source of protein as early as the Early Neolithic [*i.e.* Achilleion (Bökönyi 1989)]. However, zooarchaeological analyses of the age distribution of dogs indicate their secondary role as meat animals, since very few bones from juvenile and sub adult individuals were eventually recovered (Trantalidou 2006).

Table 5.33 Body part distribution of butchery for Cervidae (cervids) on the temporal level. Cervidae family includes *Cervus elaphus* (red deer) and *Capreolus capreolus* (roe deer). NISP counts.

Cervidae		Late Neolithic I						Late Neolithic II		
		Phase I			Phase II			Phase III		
		Cut	Chopped	TOTAL	Cut	Chopped	TOTAL	Cut	Chopped	TOTAL
Postcranial elements	Cranium (zygomaticus)			0			0			0
	Atlas			0			0			0
	Axis			0			0			0
	Scapula			0			0			0
	Humerus proximal			0			0			0
	Humerus distal			0			0			0
	Radius proximal		1	1		1	1			0
	Radius distal			0			0			0
	Ulna proximal		1	1			0			0
	Carpal 2+3			0			0			0
	Metacarpal distal			0			0			0
	Pelvis			0			0			0
	Femur proximal			0			0			0
	Femur distal			0			0			0
	Tibia proximal			0			0			0
	Tibia distal			0		1	1			0
	Scafocuboid			0			0			0
	Astragalus			0			0			0
	Calcaneum			0	1		1			0
	Metatarsal distal			0		1	1			0
	Phalanx 1			0	1		1	1		1
	Phalanx 2			0		1	1			0
	Phalanx 3			0			0			0
	TOTAL Countable	0	2	2	2	4	6	1	0	1
	TOTAL Uncountable	0	1	1	0	0	0	0	0	0

Primarily, dogs seem to have been used in hunting, or as watchdogs (Bökönyi 1986; 1989).

At Promachon, cutmarks on dog mandibles (*ramus mandibulae*) are scarce and as previously stated, these occur only in four cases. However, as Gejvall (1969) notes, knife marks on dog mandibles, most likely suggestive of skinning, do not fully support the argument that dog meat was eaten, unless traces of butchery also occur on other anatomical parts such as the humerus and the pelvis. At Promachon, butchery marks on dog postcranial elements were scarce, since only a single dog calcaneum bears traces of chopping marks. This however, does not disprove the idea that dogs could have been eaten, especially if we consider that dog carcasses were not disposed of away from the site, but were dismembered, and their bones were fragmented in the same way as those of the other domestic animals. In other words, the distribution and the fragmentation of dog anatomical elements – despite the lack of intensive butchery marks – supports the argument that these represent food refuse.

It is quite possible that dog meat occasionally supplemented the meat diet of the community, a fact that largely conforms to the evidence obtained thus far from other contemporary settlements in Greek Macedonia, such as Dimitra (Yiannouli 1997), Sitagroi (Bökönyi 1986) and Thermi (Yiannouli 1989).

Evidence of butchery in cervids is rather scarce, due to the low frequency of bones of these animals in the faunal assemblage. Only two radii, an ulna and a metatarsal display evidence of chopping marks. On the other hand, a calcaneum and three phalanges display evidence of cutmarks, most likely suggestive of skinning.

5.4.2 Burning

Almost seven per cent of the total 'countable' postcranial bones bear traces of burning (Table 5.34). However, as previously noted the incidence of burning at Promachon could be underestimated since the discrimination between burned and oxidized material was difficult in some cases (due to staining on bones by manganese and/or iron oxides). Nevertheless, the frequency of burning at Promachon is higher than that from other contemporary

Table 5.34 Incidence of burning among the postcranial bones of all species identified on the temporal level. Only 'countable' elements are considered. NISP counts.

Incidence of burning	Postcranial elements	
	NISP	%
Phase I (NISP: 1386)	105	8%
Phase II (NISP: 1538)	90	6%
Phase III (NISP: 856)	72	8%
TOTAL (NISP: 3780)	267	7%

sites in Macedonia. For instance, burning has been recorded only on one per cent of the total postcranial elements from the Late Neolithic cave on the East bank of the river Aggitis (Trantalidou *et al.* 2006). In addition, burning at the Late Neolithic site of Stavroupoli (Yiannouli 2002a; 2004) was recorded on two per cent of the total postcranial bones. However, the incidence of burning in the Late Neolithic settlement of Kryoneri (Mylona 1997) is significantly higher than that from Promachon, since it has been recorded on almost 17 per cent of the total postcranial bones.

Burning traces were observed on the postcranial bones of cattle, caprines, pig, dog, red deer, roe deer and hare. The burnt bones were generally black and/or brown. Just eight per cent (105 postcranial fragments), six per cent (90 postcranial fragments) and eight per cent (72 postcranial fragments) of the total postcranial bones presented traces of burning in Phases I, II and III respectively. In addition, the overall frequency of burning does not substantially differ between cattle (six per cent), caprines (nine per cent) and pigs (eight per cent) (Tables 5.35-5.37).

The incidence of burned bones is a much contentious issue in almost all archaeological sites. There are a number of reasons that could be associated with the burning of the bones at Promachon. Undoubtedly, we should have expected a higher frequency of burned bones in Phase I than later phases, since the archaeological evidence suggests that a conflagration event took place at the end of Phase I. It seems however, that the fire incident during this phase did not substantially affect the discarded bone material and the bones were ultimately protected from fire. It is possible therefore that some bones were either buried relatively soon after disposal (the latter argument is also corroborated by the low incidence of scavenger gnawing), or that the fire during Phase I was not too long-lived to inflict substantial burning of the bones.

In any case, the presence of a number of calcined bones implying their exposure to very high temperatures, or to a source of heat for a prolonged period of time (Gilchrist and Mytum 1986) is not limited only to Phase I (eight per cent). Calcined bones are present also in Phases II (six per cent) and III (nine per cent). Therefore, even in Phase I, their presence should not necessarily be related to a fire that destroyed the settlement.

One could also argue that the burned bones were the result of cooking activities. Again, the presence of a number of calcined bones does not conform to this argument, simply because the meat would have become completely burned, and therefore inedible. However, we should by no means exclude the possibility that some of the burning traces – especially bones, which were recorded as singed – were inflicted during food preparation. In addition, as in the case of mandibles, a number of postcranial bones might have been intentionally heated on fire, before eventually being broken up to extract the marrow (Binford 1981). Such practice can, however, only be directly demonstrated

Table 5.35 Incidence of burning on the postcranial bones of *Bos taurus* (cattle) on the temporal level. Only 'countable' elements are considered. NISP counts.

Bos taurus	Burning: postcranial elements							
	Phase I (NISP: 623)		Phase II (NISP: 671)		Phase III (NISP: 354)		TOTAL (NISP: 1648)	
	NISP	%	NISP	%	NISP	%	NISP	%
Burning	36	6%	41	6%	23	6%	100	6%

Table 5.36 Incidence of burning on the postcranial bones of Caprinae (sheep/goat) on the temporal level. Caprinae subfamily includes *Ovis/Capra* (sheep/goat), *Ovis aries* (sheep) and *Capra hircus* (goat). Only 'countable' elements are considered. NISP counts.

Caprinae	Burning: postcranial elements							
	Phase I (NISP: 428)		Phase II (NISP: 487)		Phase III (NISP: 293)		TOTAL (NISP: 1208)	
	NISP	%	NISP	%	NISP	%	NISP	%
Burning	41	10%	29	6%	35	12%	105	9%

Table 5.37 Incidence of burning on the postcranial bones of *Sus* (pig) on the temporal level. Only 'countable' elements are considered. NISP counts.

Sus	Burning: postcranial elements							
	Phase I (NISP: 230)		Phase II (NISP: 226)		Phase III (NISP: 134)		TOTAL (NISP: 590)	
	NISP	%	NISP	%	NISP	%	NISP	%
Burning	26	11%	14	7%	9	7%	49	8%

in three cases (two cattle humeri and a caprine tibia). It is likely that the bulk of the burned bones represent material that ended up in the fire accidentally, or were randomly thrown in a fire, suggesting unsystematic waste disposal practices.

5.5 Body part distribution

Body part distribution (*i.e.* the relative abundance of different skeletal parts) has been calculated using the MNI values rather than NISP in order to eliminate the bias from elements that occur more frequently in the body (Johnstone and Albarella 2002). Even though parts of the skeleton, which are rich in meat content such as the vertebrae and the ribs are missing from the following body part analysis, this equally applies to all species.

In interpreting the skeletal distribution for all species in Promachon sector we will have to consider the following factors:

1. Differential preservation: variation in body part representation may be attributed to selective attrition of less durable parts
2. Retrieval biases: as already seen, this is likely to constitute a significant factor in the formation of Promachon's faunal assemblage
3. Human agency: skeletal parts may have been transported, deposited and processed differentially by the site inhabitants. Selectivity of elements brought on-site obviously applies primarily to hunted species, but also to domestic species killed off-site. The animal carcass may have also been subject to some subdivision within the site itself
4. Sample size: small sample size renders body part analysis on both temporal and contextual levels highly unreliable. This applies particularly to the deer species, but to some extent to pigs too

5.5.1 Bos taurus *body part distribution*

Table 5.38 and Figure 5.10 present the body part distribution for cattle. Cattle skeletal distribution in Phases I and III is similar; the highest MNI values are obtained from permanent first and second mandibular molars. The high representation of cattle teeth rather than cattle postcranial elements may be attributed to differential preservation between teeth and bones and it is expected.

On the other hand, there are no particular reasons to suggest that any cattle postcranial elements are missing because of pre-depositional factors. All postcranial bones are present, though less durable parts such as the cranium, the atlas and the femur are underrepresented. Scapula, humerus and pelvis are found in high frequencies, suggesting selection in body parts with high meat utility. Lower hind limbs (distal tibia and metapodials), as well as limb extremities (astragalus, calcaneum and phalanges) are quite common since they are better preserved due to their size and density.

Table 5.38 Parts of the *Bos taurus* (cattle) skeleton by number of fragments (NISP) and minimum number of individuals (MNI) on the temporal level. Data for Figure 5.10.

Bos taurus		Late Neolithic I						Late Neolithic II		
		Phase I			Phase II			Phase III		
		NISP	MNI	%	NISP	MNI	%	NISP	MNI	%
Teeth	Incisors	19	3	14%	13	2	8%	16	2	14%
	dP&P Maxillary	35	6	27%	45	8	32%	33	6	43%
	M1/2 Maxillary	72	18	82%	80	20	80%	32	8	57%
	M3 Maxillary	21	11	50%	15	8	32%	17	9	64%
	dP&P Mandibular	66	11	50%	59	10	40%	34	6	43%
	M1/2 Mandibular	88	22	100%	76	19	76%	53	14	100%
	M3 Mandibular	26	13	59%	28	14	56%	11	6	43%
Postcranial bones	Cranium	21	11	50%	21	11	44%	12	6	43%
	Atlas	4	4	18%	7	7	28%			0%
	Axis	12	12	55%	20	20	80%	8	8	57%
	Scapula	23	12	55%	25	13	52%	16	8	57%
	Humerus proximal	4	2	9%	1	1	4%	3	2	14%
	Humerus distal	34	17	77%	23	12	48%	18	9	64%
	Radius proximal	24	12	55%	24	12	48%	8	4	29%
	Radius distal	11	6	27%	18	9	36%	1	1	7%
	Ulna proximal	16	8	36%	13	7	28%	9	5	36%
	Carpal 2+3	18	9	41%	10	5	20%	10	5	36%
	Metacarpal 1 distal	16	11	50%	21	13	52%	6	4	29%
	Metacarpal 1/2 distal	4			2			2		
	Pelvis	28	14	64%	32	16	64%	12	6	43%
	Femur proximal	18	9	41%	10	5	20%	6	3	21%
	Femur distal	17	9	41%	16	8	32%	7	4	29%
	Tibia proximal	3	2	9%	3	2	8%	1	1	7%
	Tibia distal	28	14	64%	26	13	52%	12	6	43%
	Scafocuboid	11	6	27%	12	6	24%	9	5	36%
	Astragalus	33	17	77%	49	25	100%	17	9	64%
	Calcaneum	28	14	64%	30	15	60%	15	8	57%
	Metatarsal 1 distal	11	8	36%	13	10	40%	2	4	29%
	Metatarsal 1/2 distal	2			4			1		
	Metapodium 1 distal	2						1		
	Metapodium 1/2 distal	10			13			17		
	Phalanx 1	96	12	55%	95	12	48%	64	8	57%
	Phalanx 2	80	10	45%	97	13	52%	55	7	50%
	Phalanx 3	31	4	18%	49	7	28%	23	3	21%
TOTAL		912	MNI: 22		950	MNI: 25		531	MNI: 14	

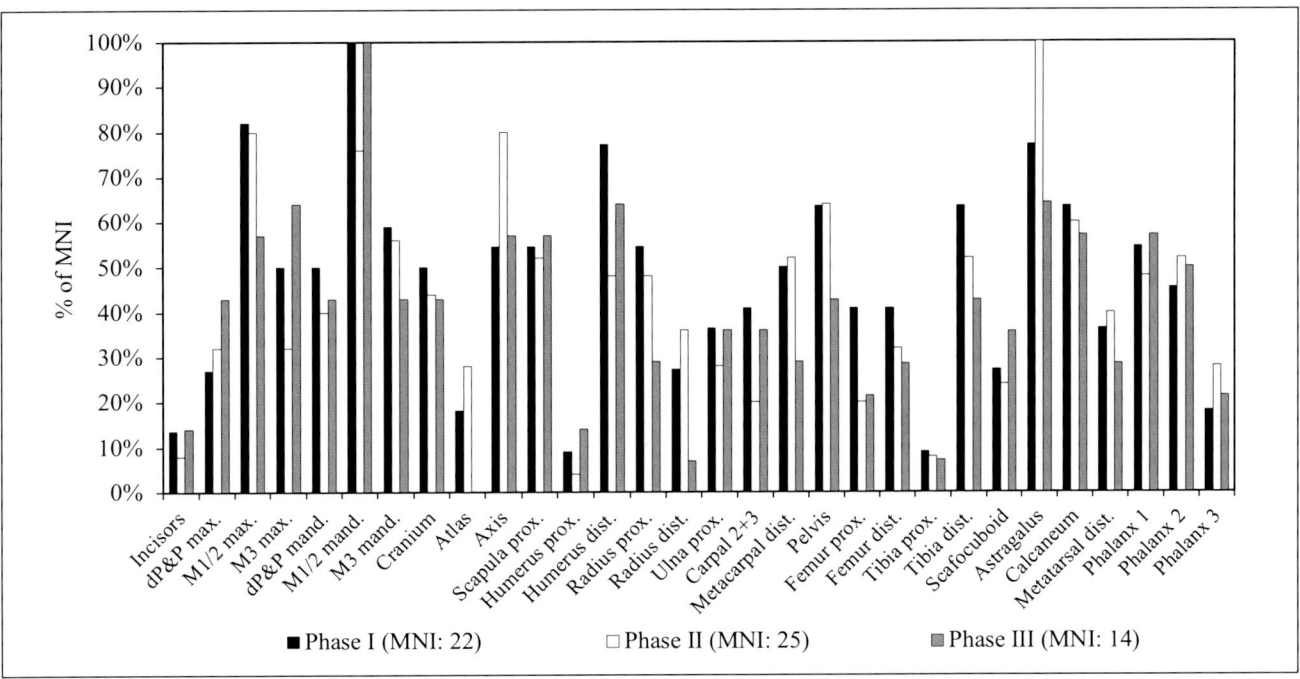

Figure 5.10: Parts of the *Bos taurus* skeleton on the temporal level. Data in Table 5.38. MNI counts.

The distribution of cattle body parts during the second phase of occupation provides a slightly different pattern. Unlike Phases I and III, the highest MNI value during Phase II derives from the astragali. The astragalus is a compact, durable bone, which would have survived well to taphonomic factors and in cattle is also large enough not to be easily overlooked. It is indeed the best represented postcranial bone in the other phases too. There are, however, no obvious taphonomic factors that could explain its better representation than teeth. We must therefore assume that this difference was in fact genuine at the time of the original formation of the cattle assemblage, and that, during Phase II, cattle heads were not as commonly introduced to the site with the rest of the carcass or may have been processed in areas of the site not affected by the excavation.

5.5.2 Caprinae body part distribution

Identification of caprine bones to the level of species was attempted on a limited range of elements (Table 5.39). However, as already discussed, the bulk of the caprine material was identified to the level of sheep/goat. Thus, in the following body part analysis these two species are of necessity treated together. Body part distribution for caprines exhibits a clear and unambiguous consistency throughout all phases under study (Table 5.40; Figure 5.11). Teeth are the most common elements, a factor most likely to be a result of differential preservation between bones and teeth, as in the case of cattle. In all phases, the highest MNI values derive from the first and second mandibular molars. The humerus and the pelvis are found in almost equal frequencies indicating preferences in body parts with high meat utility. It is therefore likely that whole caprine carcasses were introduced (or simply processed) on site. On the other hand, the overrepresentation of the radius and the tibia may be attributed to differential preservation. Elements that are poorly represented are those that do not easily survive in the archaeological record (*i.e.* cranium, atlas, axis, ulna, femur), or are less frequently recovered (*i.e.* carpals, tarsals and phalanges). Overall, the pattern for caprines appears to be mainly the result of preservation and recovery bias than of any specialized waste disposal practices. It is likely that all caprine body parts were equally represented on site before discard.

5.5.3 Sus body part distribution

Discussion of pig body part distribution (Table 5.41; Figure 5.12) is made rather difficult by the small sample

Notes for Table 5.38

Unfused proximal and distal epiphyses are not counted. Each tooth (loose or attached to maxilla/mandible) is considered. The MNI has been calculated as follows: Incisors and phalanges have been divided by 8, deciduous and permanent premolars (dP&P) have been divided by 6, first and second molars (M1/2) have been divided by 4 and all other elements -except for Metapodials- have been divided by 2. Metacarpals (Metacarpal 1 distal) and Metatarsals (Metatarsal 1 distal) have been calculated as follows:
Metacarpal = (Metacarpal 1 distal + Metacarpal 1/2 distal / 2 + Metapodium 1 distal / 2 + Metapodium 1/2 distal / 4) / 2.
Metatarsal = (Metatarsal 1 distal + Metatarsal 1/2 distal / 2 + Metapodium 1 distal / 2 + Metapodium 1/2 distal / 4) / 2.
Where Metapodium 1 distal: complete distal metapodial and Metapodium 1/2 distal: half distal metapodial.
%: Frequency of an element expressed in relation to the most common one (by MNI).

Table 5.39 Parts of the *Ovis aries* (sheep) and *Capra hircus* (goat) skeleton by number of fragments (NISP) on the temporal level. Only body parts that were regularly identified to species presented. Unfused proximal and distal epiphyses are not counted. NISP counts.

Regularly identified to species		Late Neolithic I				Late Neolithic II	
		Phase I		Phase II		Phase III	
		Ovis aries	*Capra hircus*	*Ovis aries*	*Capra hircus*	*Ovis aries*	*Capra hircus*
		NISP	NISP	NISP	NISP	NISP	NISP
Teeth and postcranial bones	dP&P Mandibular	117	38	116	32	65	19
	Humerus distal	26	12	23	8	16	7
	Radius proximal	3	1	10	1	1	
	Radius distal			4	2	1	
	Metacarpal 1 distal	2		3	3	7	
	Tibia distal	45	2	47	6	35	3
	Astragalus	8	1	24	2	13	
	Calcaneum	5	5	13	4	6	
	Metatarsal 1 distal	4		6		2	
TOTAL		210	59	246	58	146	29

size. Nevertheless, a number of trends can still be detected:

Teeth are underrepresented and the highest MNI values derive from postcranial bones (scapula and ulna during Phase I and scapula during Phase II). This possibly indicates, that some pig heads were disposed off-site

The high frequency of the upper forelimb bones (*i.e.* scapula, humerus) as well as the pelvis indicates preferences in body parts with high meat utility

One would argue that the scarcity of pig phalanges might be linked with the scarcity of the metapodials as well; this would lead to the hypothesis that limb extremities might have not been introduced to the site with the rest of the carcass and that the pig remains from the studied assemblage derive from dressed carcasses (*cf.* Albarella and Serjeantson 2010). There is, however, one issue, which must be considered in connection to this. The bulk of the pig population from Promachon was killed young,

making it more likely that pigs in Promachon would be moved around as complete carcasses. Therefore, it is highly likely that the underrepresentation of pig limb extremities is associated with recovery bias, rather than differential treatment of the pig carcass.

5.5.4 Cervidae body part distribution

Tables 5.42, 5.43 and 5.44 provide the body part distribution for red deer, roe deer and fallow deer respectively. However, their small sample sizes render any discussion on their skeletal representation highly problematic. In order to tackle this bias, the three species are of necessity treated together (Table 5.45). Though the bias is not entirely eliminated, we can still draw some basic conclusions.

The body part distribution of deer (Figure 5.13) resembles more that of pigs than of any of the other domesticates. The highest MNI values are gained from postcranial elements such as ulnae, astragali and first phalanges rather than teeth.

Notes for Table 5.40

Unfused proximal and distal epiphyses are not counted. Each tooth (loose or attached to maxilla/mandible) is considered. The MNI has been calculated as follows: Incisors and phalanges have been divided by 8, deciduous and permanent premolars (dP&P) have been divided by 6, first and second molars (M1/2) have been divided by 4 and all other elements -except for Metapodials- have been divided by 2. Metacarpals (Metacarpal 1 distal) and Metatarsals (Metatarsal 1 distal) have been calculated as follows:
Metacarpal = (Metacarpal 1 distal + Metacarpal 1/2 distal / 2 + Metapodium 1 distal / 2 + Metapodium 1/2 distal / 4) / 2.
Metatarsal = (Metatarsal 1 distal + Metatarsal 1/2 distal / 2 + Metapodium 1 distal / 2 + Metapodium 1/2 distal / 4) / 2.
Where Metapodium 1 distal: complete distal metapodial and Metapodium 1/2 distal: half distal metapodial.
%: Frequency of an element expressed in relation to the most common one (by MNI).

Table 5.40 Parts of the Caprinae (sheep and goat) skeleton by number of fragments (NISP) and minimum number of individuals (MNI) on the temporal level. Caprinae subfamily includes *Ovis/Capra* (sheep/goat), *Ovis aries* (sheep) and *Capra hircus* (goat). Data for Figure 5.11.

Caprinae		Late Neolithic I						Late Neolithic II		
		Phase I			Phase II			Phase III		
		NISP	MNI	%	NISP	MNI	%	NISP	MNI	%
Teeth	Incisors	11	2	4%	11	2	3%	14	2	5%
	dP&P Maxillary	48	8	15%	27	5	8%	28	5	12%
	M1/2 Maxillary	112	28	52%	156	39	63%	100	25	58%
	M3 Maxillary	51	26	48%	55	28	45%	58	29	67%
	dP&P Mandibular	203	34	63%	192	32	52%	94	16	37%
	M1/2 Mandibular	216	54	100%	248	62	100%	169	43	100%
	M3 Mandibular	82	41	76%	76	38	61%	70	35	81%
Postcranial bones	Cranium	18	9	17%	13	7	11%	3	2	5%
	Atlas	3	3	6%	10	10	16%			0%
	Axis	13	13	24%	13	13	21%	5	5	12%
	Scapula	21	11	20%	27	14	23%	6	3	7%
	Humerus proximal	6	3	6%	3	2	3%	2	1	2%
	Humerus distal	72	36	67%	52	26	42%	47	24	56%
	Radius proximal	43	22	41%	46	23	37%	30	15	35%
	Radius distal	9	5	9%	15	8	13%	6	3	7%
	Ulna proximal	23	12	22%	20	10	16%	18	9	21%
	Carpal 2+3	9	5	9%	5	3	5%	4	2	5%
	Metacarpal 1 distal	5	4	7%	10	7	11%	8	5	12%
	Metacarpal 1/2 distal	2			1					
	Pelvis	61	31	57%	70	35	56%	36	18	42%
	Femur proximal	8	4	7%	9	5	8%	2	1	2%
	Femur distal	5	3	6%	4	2	3%	2	1	2%
	Tibia proximal	6	3	6%	7	4	6%	4	2	5%
	Tibia distal	57	29	54%	65	33	53%	45	23	53%
	Scafocuboid	1	1	2%			0%	2	1	2%
	Astragalus	10	5	9%	31	16	26%	22	11	26%
	Calcaneum	15	8	15%	26	13	21%	10	5	12%
	Metatarsal 1 distal	7	6	11%	8	7	11%	5	4	9%
	Metatarsal 1/2 distal	4			4			3		
	Metapodium 1 distal				1					
	Metapodium 1/2 distal	6			10			3		
	Phalanx 1	10	2	4%	20	3	5%	13	2	5%
	Phalanx 2			0%	4	1	2%	5	1	2%
	Phalanx 3	2	1	2%			0%			0%
TOTAL		1139	**MNI: 54**		1239	**MNI: 62**		814	**MNI: 43**	

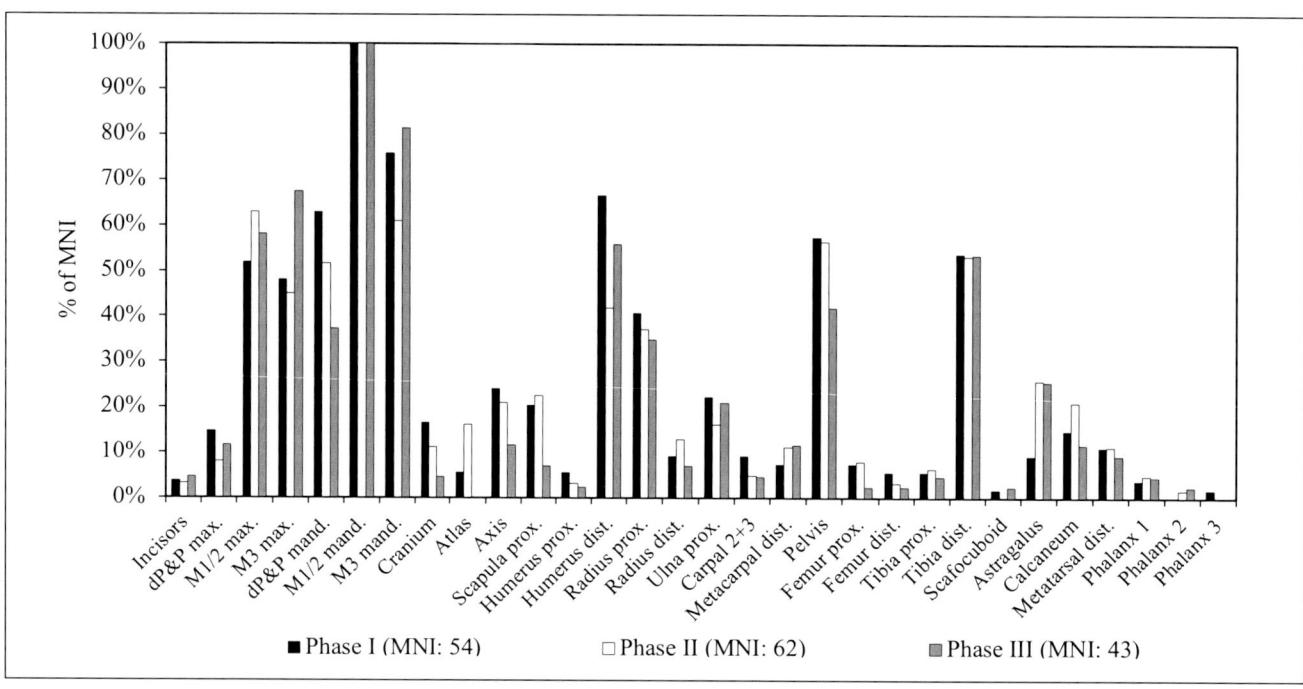

Figure 5.11 Parts of the Caprinae skeleton on the temporal level. Data in Table 5.40. MNI counts.

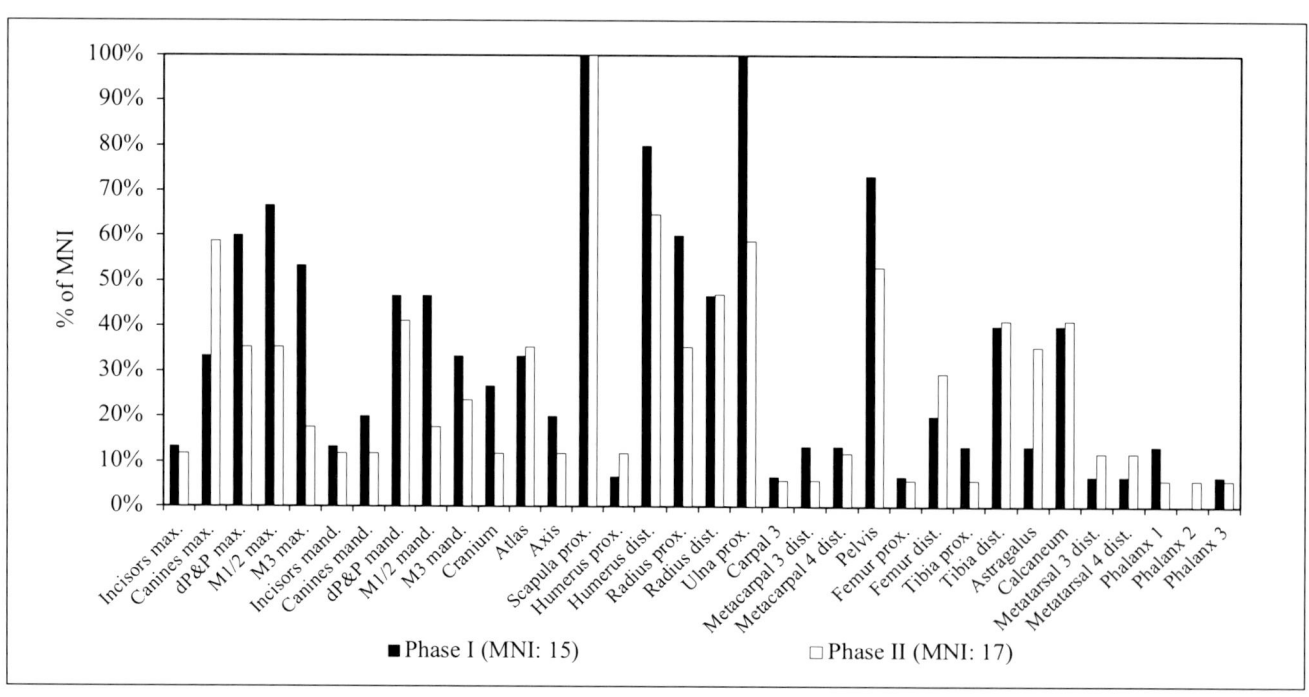

Figure 5.12 Parts of the *Sus* skeleton. Phase III (MNI: 8) is not considered due to small sample size. Data in Table 5.41. MNI counts.

Notes for Table 5.41

Unfused proximal and distal epiphyses are not counted. Each tooth (loose or attached to maxilla/mandible) is considered. The MNI has been calcualated as follows: Phalanges have been divided by 8, deciduous and permanent premolars (dP&P) and incisors have been divided by 6, first and second molars (M1/2) have been divided by 4 and all other elements -except for Metapodials- have been divided by 2. Metacarpals (Metacarpal 3 or 4 distal) and Metatarsals (Metatarsal 3 or 4 distal) have been calculated as follows: Metacarpal = Metacarpal 3 or 4 distal / 2. Metatarsal = Metatarsal 3 or 4 distal / 2.
%: Frequency of an element expressed in relation to the most common one (by MNI).

Table 5.41 Parts of the *Sus* (pig) skeleton by number of fragments (NISP) and minimum number of individuals (MNI) on the temporal level. Data for Figure 5.12.

Sus		Late Neolithic I						Late Neolithic II		
		Phase I			Phase II			Phase III		
		NISP	MNI	%	NISP	MNI	%	NISP	MNI	%
Teeth	Incisors Maxillary	7	2	13%	7	2	12%	3	1	14%
	Canines Maxillary	10	5	33%	19	10	59%	6	3	43%
	dP&P Maxillary	53	9	60%	35	6	35%	13	3	43%
	M1/2 Maxillary	39	10	67%	21	6	35%	11	3	43%
	M3 Maxillary	16	8	53%	5	3	18%	5	3	43%
	Incisors Mandibular	12	2	13%	11	2	12%	8	2	29%
	Canines Mandibular	5	3	20%	4	2	12%	3	2	29%
	dP&P Mandibular	37	7	47%	37	7	41%	24	4	57%
	M1/2 Mandibular	25	7	47%	16	3	18%	21	6	86%
	M3 Mandibular	9	5	33%	7	4	24%	5	3	43%
Postcranial bones	Cranium	8	4	27%	3	2	12%	5	3	43%
	Atlas	5	5	33%	6	6	35%	3	3	43%
	Axis	3	3	20%	2	2	12%	1	1	14%
	Scapula	30	15	100%	34	17	100%	12	6	86%
	Humerus proximal	2	1	7%	3	2	12%	3	2	29%
	Humerus distal	23	12	80%	21	11	65%	7	4	57%
	Radius proximal	17	9	60%	12	6	35%	8	4	57%
	Radius distal	14	7	47%	15	8	47%	3	2	29%
	Ulna proximal	30	15	100%	20	10	59%	14	7	100%
	Carpal 3	1	1	7%	1	1	6%			0%
	Metacarpal 3 distal	5	2	13%	4	1	6%	1	1	14%
	Metacarpal 4 distal	7	2	13%	5	2	13%			0%
	Pelvis	21	11	73%	18	9	53%	14	7	100%
	Femur proximal	1	1	7%	2	1	6%			0%
	Femur distal	5	3	20%	10	5	29%	4	2	29%
	Tibia proximal	3	2	13%	1	1	6%	1	1	14%
	Tibia distal	12	6	40%	14	7	41%	11	6	86%
	Astragalus	4	2	13%	12	6	35%	6	3	43%
	Calcaneum	11	6	40%	14	7	41%	8	4	57%
	Metatarsal 3 distal	3	2	13%	7	4	24%	2	1	14%
	Metatarsal 4 distal	4	2	13%	5	3	18%	3	2	29%
	Phalanx 1	11	2	13%	8	1	6%			0%
	Phalanx 2			0%	3	1	6%	7	1	14%
	Phalanx 3	3	1	7%	6	1	6%	3	1	14%
TOTAL		**436**	**MNI: 15**		**389**	**MNI: 17**		**215**	**MNI: 7**	

Table 5.42 Parts of the *Cervus elaphus* (red deer) skeleton by number of fragments (NISP) on the temporal level.

Cervus elaphus		Late Neolithic I		Late Neolithic II
		Phase I	Phase II	Phase III
		NISP	NISP	NISP
Teeth	Incisors	2		1
	dP&P Maxillary		1	
	M1/2 Maxillary	4	4	2
	M3 Maxillary	1	1	1
	dP&P Mandibular	3	4	
	M1/2 Mandibular	2		
	M3 Mandibular	1	1	
Postcranial bones	Cranium			
	Atlas			
	Axis			
	Scapula	1		
	Humerus proximal	1		
	Humerus distal	1	1	
	Radius proximal	1	1	1
	Radius distal	1		
	Ulna proximal	1	4	
	Carpal 2+3			
	Metacarpal 1 distal			
	Metacarpal 1/2 distal			
	Pelvis	1	1	1
	Femur proximal		1	
	Femur distal			1
	Tibia proximal	1		
	Tibia distal		2	
	Scafocuboid	1		
	Astragalus		1	1
	Calcaneum	1	1	
	Metatarsal 1 distal	1	1	
	Metatarsal 1/2 distal		1	
	Metapodium 1 distal			
	Metapodium 1/2 distal			
	Phalanx 1	3	9	3
	Phalanx 2	4	10	2
	Phalanx 3			1
TOTAL		**31**	**44**	**14**

Table 5.43 Parts of the *Capreolus capreolus* (roe deer) skeleton by number of fragments (NISP) on the temporal level.

Capreolus capreolus		Late Neolithic I		Late Neolithic II
		Phase I	Phase II	Phase III
		NISP	NISP	NISP
Teeth	Incisors			
	dP&P Maxillary		2	
	M1/2 Maxillary	1		
	M3 Maxillary	1		
	dP&P Mandibular	1		
	M1/2 Mandibular			
	M3 Mandibular			
Postcranial bones	Cranium			
	Atlas			
	Axis			
	Scapula			
	Humerus proximal			
	Humerus distal			1
	Radius proximal	1	1	
	Radius distal			
	Ulna proximal	3	3	
	Carpal 2+3			
	Metacarpal 1 distal	1		
	Metacarpal 1/2 distal			
	Pelvis		1	
	Femur proximal			
	Femur distal			
	Tibia proximal			
	Tibia distal			
	Scafocuboid			
	Astragalus	2	1	
	Calcaneum			
	Metatarsal 1 distal		1	
	Metatarsal 1/2 distal			
	Metapodium 1 distal			
	Metapodium 1/2 distal			
	Phalanx 1	1	5	7
	Phalanx 2		1	
	Phalanx 3			
TOTAL		**11**	**15**	**8**

Table 5.44 Parts of the *Dama dama* (fallow deer) skeleton by number of fragments (NISP) on the temporal level.

Dama dama		Late Neolithic I		Late Neolithic II
		Phase I	Phase II	Phase III
		NISP	NISP	NISP
Teeth	Incisors			
	dP&P Maxillary			
	M1/2 Maxillary			
	M3 Maxillary			
	dP&P Mandibular		1	
	M1/2 Mandibular			
	M3 Mandibular			
Postcranial bones	Cranium			
	Atlas			
	Axis			
	Scapula			
	Humerus proximal			
	Humerus distal			
	Radius proximal			1
	Radius distal			
	Ulna proximal			
	Carpal 2+3		1	
	Metacarpal 1 distal			
	Metacarpal 1/2 distal			
	Pelvis			
	Femur proximal			
	Femur distal			
	Tibia proximal		1	
	Tibia distal			
	Scafocuboid			
	Astragalus			
	Calcaneum			
	Metatarsal 1 distal			
	Metatarsal 1/2 distal			
	Metapodium 1 distal			
	Metapodium 1/2 distal			
	Phalanx 1	2	3	
	Phalanx 2			
	Phalanx 3			
TOTAL		2	6	1

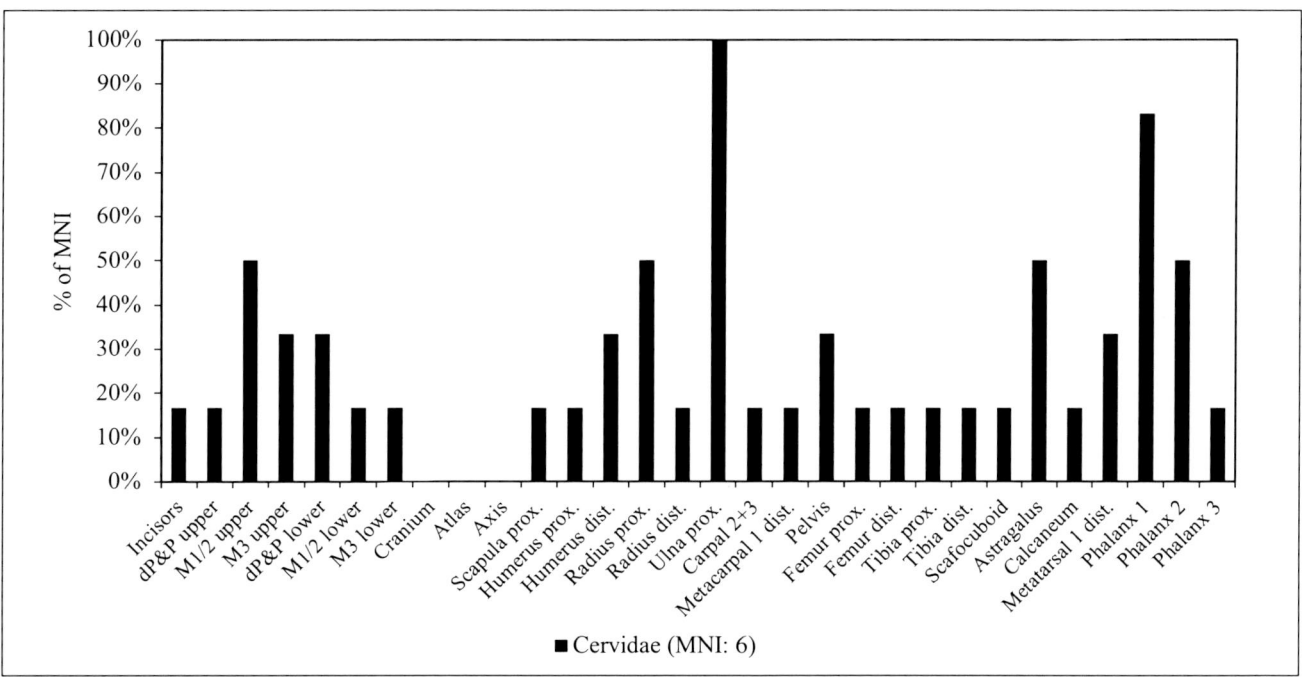

Figure 5.13 Parts of the Cervidae skeleton. All phases are considered. Data in Table 5.45. MNI counts.

The scarcity of deer teeth can be linked to the scarcity of antlers as well. Only four antler fragments with a complete transverse section were recorded, eventually representing 'non-countable' elements. Two were identified as red deer antlers and two as roe deer antlers. Although we cannot exclude the possibility that deer crania were disposed off-site due to their heavy weight and limited meat content, the pattern is most likely the result of the deer crania being kept elsewhere – at workshop areas – for the production of antler tools and objects. The latter hypothesis is further supported by two red deer tine antlers (lacking a complete transverse section and belonging to Phases I and III respectively), which also exhibit polished surfaces.

While the high frequency of deer astragali may be attributed to post-depositional differential preservation of less durable bones, the predominance of non-meat-bearing postcranial elements such as the ulna and the phalanges suggests that the species were exploited for a range of products besides meat. The high proportion of deer phalanges could be related to the presence or working of hides, although the small number of phalanges bearing butchery traits (only three) does not further support the latter hypothesis. Of more interest is the striking high frequency of deer ulnae, since it provides the highest MNI values. The abundance of bone tools with 'short active edges' made of deer ulnae (Christidou 2012) may provide an explanation as to the frequency of this specific body part. However, the study of bone tools falls into the task of the bone tools specialist currently working on the latter evidence.

5.5.5 Body part distribution of the remaining fauna

Dog, an animal rather more conspicuous by its destructive influence upon the bones (Albarella and Davis 1994), is not as common as the rest of domesticates both in terms of NISP and MNI (Table 5.46). As previously suggested, dogs were eaten in Promachon since four mandibles and a calcaneum bear butchery marks. Nevertheless, no clear distribution of dog body parts could be found, a pattern most likely to be the result of small sample size.

Body part distribution of red fox is presented in Table 5.47. Red fox elements are more likely to exhibit scavenger activity within the settlement, since there are no cases of reported use of red fox as a food resource. Table 5.48 presents the body part distribution for hare. Hare bones may well represent hunted food resources, although no human-agent modifications (*i.e.* cutmarks, burning) were eventually recorded. With regard to hare, the sample is too small to draw any firm conclusions, but various body elements are represented, including teeth. This is not surprising as the carcass of an animal of such relatively small size is unlikely to be subjected to successive stages of butchery process, which can be detected archaeologically.

5.6 Contextual distribution

Species and body part distribution per context type is presented on a layer-by-layer level rather than broad chronological periods. It is believed that each layer represents a distinct and separate entity with different formation processes and discrete activity areas. The following analysis aims to provide insights into the nature of different contexts as well as to reveal any patterns related to depositional practices. Excavators of the site have identified more than 35 different contexts, resulting in the assemblage from each context being very small to be properly analysed. For heuristic purposes, therefore, it

63

Table 5.45 Parts of the Cervidae (deer) skeleton by number of fragments (NISP) and minimum number of individuals (MNI). All phases are considered into a Late Neolithic aggregate. Cervidae family includes *Cervus elaphus* (red deer), *Capreolus capreolus* (roe deer) and *Dama dama* (fallow deer). Data for Figure 5.13.

Cervidae		Late Neolithic I		Late Neolithic II	TOTAL		
		Phase I	Phase II	Phase III			
		NISP	NISP	NISP	NISP	MNI	%
Teeth	Incisors	2		2	4	1	17%
	dP&P Maxillary		3		3	1	17%
	M1/2 Maxillary	5	4	2	11	3	50%
	M3 Maxillary	2	1	1	4	2	33%
	dP&P Mandibular	4	5		9	2	33%
	M1/2 Mandibular	2			2	1	17%
	M3 Mandibular	1	1		2	1	17%
Postcranial bones	Cranium				0	0	0%
	Atlas				0	0	0%
	Axis				0	0	0%
	Scapula	1			1	1	17%
	Humerus proximal	1			1	1	17%
	Humerus distal	1	1	1	3	2	33%
	Radius proximal	2	2	2	6	3	50%
	Radius distal	1			1	1	17%
	Ulna proximal	4	7		11	6	100%
	Carpal 2+3		1		1	1	17%
	Metacarpal 1 distal	1			1	1	17%
	Metacarpal 1/2 distal				0		
	Pelvis	1	2	1	4	2	33%
	Femur proximal		1		1	1	17%
	Femur distal			1	1	1	17%
	Tibia proximal	1	1		2	1	17%
	Tibia distal		2		2	1	17%
	Scafocuboid	1			1	1	17%
	Astragalus	2	2	1	5	3	50%
	Calcaneum	1	1		2	1	17%
	Metatarsal 1 distal	1	2		3	2	33%
	Metatarsal 1/2 distal		1		1		
	Metapodium 1 distal				0		
	Metapodium 1/2 distal				0		
	Phalanx 1	6	17	10	33	5	83%
	Phalanx 2	4	11	2	17	3	50%
	Phalanx 3			1	1	1	17%
TOTAL		44	65	24	133	MNI: 6	

Table 5.46 Parts of the *Canis familiaris* (dog) skeleton by number of fragments (NISP) and minimum number of individuals (MNI) on the temporal level.

Canis familiaris		Late Neolithic I				Late Neolithic II	
		Phase I		Phase II		Phase III	
		NISP	MNI	NISP	MNI	NISP	MNI
Teeth	Incisors Maxillary						
	Canines Maxillary	1	1			1	1
	dP&P Maxillary			1	1		
	M1/2 Maxillary	3	1				
	M3 Maxillary	1	1				
	Incisors Mandibular					2	1
	Canines Mandibular	6	3	2	1	4	2
	dP&P Mandibular	23	4	3	1	5	1
	M1/2 Mandibular	14	4	9	3	9	3
	M3 Mandibular	4	2	2	1	2	1
Postcranial bones	Cranium						
	Atlas	1	1	1	1	1	1
	Axis			3	3	1	1
	Scapula	1	1	5	3	1	1
	Humerus proximal	2	1	1	1	1	1
	Humerus distal	2	1	7	4		
	Radius proximal			1	1		
	Radius distal			1	1	1	1
	Ulna proximal	6	3	3	2	2	1
	Metacarpal 3 distal	1	1				
	Metacarpal 4 distal	1	1			1	1
	Pelvis			2	1		
	Femur proximal			1	1		
	Tibia proximal	2	1	1	1		
	Tibia distal	1	1	4	2	1	1
	Astragalus						
	Calcaneum			2	1		
	Metatarsal 3 distal	1	1			2	1
	Metatarsal 4 distal	2	1	2	1		
	Phalanx 1					1	1
	Phalanx 2						
	Phalanx 3						
TOTAL		72	**MNI: 4**	51	**MNI: 4**	35	**MNI: 3**

Notes for Table 5.45

Unfused proximal and distal epiphyses are not counted. Each tooth (loose or attached to maxilla/mandible) is considered. The MNI has been calculated as follows: Incisors and phalanges have been divided by 8, deciduous and permanent premolars (dP&P) have been divided by 6, first and second molars (M1/2) have been divided by 4 and all other elements -except for Metapodials- have been divided by 2. Metacarpals (Metacarpal 1 distal) and Metatarsals (Metatarsal 1 distal) have been calculated as follows:
Metacarpal = (Metacarpal 1 distal + Metacarpal 1/2 distal / 2 + Metapodium 1 distal / 2 + Metapodium 1/2 distal / 4) / 2.
Metatarsal = (Metatarsal 1 distal + Metatarsal 1/2 distal / 2 + Metapodium 1 distal / 2 + Metapodium 1/2 distal / 4) / 2.
Where Metapodium 1 distal: complete distal metapodial and Metapodium 1/2 distal: half distal metapodial.
%: Frequency of an element expressed in relation to the most common one (by MNI).

Table 5.47 Parts of the *Vulpes vulpes* (red fox) skeleton by number of fragments (NISP) on the temporal level.

Vulpes vulpes		Late Neolithic I		Late Neolithic II
		Phase I	Phase II	Phase III
		NISP	NISP	NISP
Teeth	M1/2 Maxillary			2
	M3 Maxillary			1
	dP&P Mandibular	3	7	
	M1/2 Mandibular	3	2	1
	M3 Mandibular			1
Postcranial bones	Atlas	1		1
	Axis	1		
	Humerus proximal	1	1	1
	Humerus distal	1	1	
	Ulna proximal	1	2	2
	Metacarpal 3 distal	1		
	Pelvis	2		
	Tibia distal	3	1	
	Calcaneum	1		
	Metatarsal 3 distal	1		
TOTAL		**19**	**14**	**9**

Table 5.48 Parts of the *Lepus europaeus* (hare) skeleton by number of fragments (NISP) on the temporal level.

Lepus europaeus		Late Neolithic I		Late Neolithic II
		Phase I	Phase II	Phase III
		NISP	NISP	NISP
Teeth and postcranial bones	dP&P Mandibular		3	
	Scapula		1	
	Humerus distal	3		1
	Radius proximal	1		1
	Radius distal	1		
	Pelvis	1	1	1
	Femur proximal		1	
	Metatarsal 3 distal			2
	Metatarsal 4 distal	1		
	Phalanx 1	1	2	1
	Phalanx 2		1	
TOTAL		**8**	**9**	**6**

5.6.1 Distribution of the faunal material per context type

Out of 6525 'countable' specimens, only 3628 (56 per cent) were attributed to contexts. The rest of the faunal material (2897 specimens: 44 per cent) derives from contexts of completely unknown origin (these should not be confused with the mixed contexts of Layer 1, which are described below). The part of the faunal assemblage, which derives from contexts of completely unknown origin, was left out was decided that a number of contexts with roughly the same characteristics should be grouped together into 10 major categories:

Contexts	Description
Pits	Containing refuse material. The excavators use the term "ditches" as well
Pits of pit-houses	Pits inside pit-houses n. 1, n. 2 and n. 3 (Layer 6/Phase I)
Floors	'Indoor' use surfaces, covered with clay. Scattered material culture objects and animal bones
Use surfaces	'Outdoor' use surfaces. Scattered material culture objects and animal bones
Hearths	Layer 3 (Phase II): four hearths, two *in situ*. Layers 4, 5 and 6 (Phase I): one hearth respectively, all *in situ*
Building foundations	Wattle walls daubed with clay
Postholes	Supporting timber-framed wattle and daub walls and roofs. Some found in pits/ditches
Ash layer	Ash covering a part of Layer 6 after the conflagration event
Patios	Paved area made with pebbles from the river Strymon. Present in Layers 3 (Phase II) and 4 (Phase I)
Cairns	Mound of rough stones present in Layers 3 (Phase II) and 4 (Phase I)
Mixed contexts	Include pebbles, rough stones, clay and pottery fragments. Present only in Layer 1 (Phase III)

Table 5.49 Distribution of the faunal material per context type on a layer-by-layer level. Data for Figure 5.14. NISP counts.

Context types	Late Neolithic I												Late Neolithic II		TOTAL	
	Phase I						Phase II				Phase III					
	Layer 6		Layer 5		Layer 4		Layer 3		Layer 2		Layer 1					
	NISP	%	NISP	%	NISP	%	NISP	%	NISP	%	NISP	%			NISP	%
Pits	128	34%	71	64%	147	24%	103	7%	22	100%	138	16%			609	17%
Floors		0%		0%	184	31%	236	14%		0%	8	1%			428	12%
Use surfaces	102	26%	9	8%	102	17%	627	38%		0%	110	12%			950	26%
Hearths	15	4%	21	19%	72	12%	453	28%		0%		0%			561	15%
Building foundations	1	1%		0%	18	3%	67	4%		0%	6	1%			92	3%
Postholes	5	2%	10	9%	43	7%	34	2%		0%	100	11%			192	5%
Ash Layer	122	33%		0%	7	1%		0%		0%		0%			129	4%
Patios		0%		0%	23	4%	39	2%		0%		0%			62	2%
Cairns		0%		0%	7	1%	75	5%		0%		0%			82	2%
Mixed contexts		0%		0%		0%		0%		0%	523	59%			523	14%
TOTAL	373	100%	111	100%	603	100%	1634	100%	22	100%	885	100%			3628	100%

of the current analysis. Table 5.49 presents the distribution of the faunal material per context type on a layer-by-layer level, and Figure 5.14 presents the results graphically, excluding however the material from Layer 2 (Phase II) and Layer 5 (Phase I) due to extremely small sample sizes. The analysis indicates that no particular context stands out for having being favoured regarding the disposal of butchered debris. On a gross scale, the examination reveals that use surfaces contain almost a quarter of the bone assemblage followed by pits, floors and hearths making up a further half of the assemblage. Other types of contexts such as postholes, ash layer and house pits produced more than 100 fragments each, while building foundations, cairns and patios produced less than 100 fragments.

Mixed contexts (these should not be confused with the contexts of completely unknown origin), which are present in Layer 1 (Phase III) provided a high number of remains (59 per cent of the faunal material from Layer 1), but unfortunately, their mingled nature (pebbles, stones, clay, pottery and animal bones) prevented any extensive analysis. Since the rest of the context types (pits, use surfaces, postholes) from Layer 1 produced very small quantities of animal bones, they will not be considered in the following analysis.

The contexts that produced the highest quantities of animal remains in Layer 6 (Phase I) were the pits of the pit-houses n. 1, n. 2 and n 3, the use surfaces and the ash layer. The high number of bones from the use surfaces was expected, since these were areas of everyday activities. On the other hand, the high number of bones recovered from the ash layer was also expected, as the sealing of parts of Layer 6 by a thick 20 centimetres deposit of white ash (see also chapter 2) guaranteed bone preservation. Of interest is also the fact that the pits of the pit-houses produced a large quantity of bones. In order to investigate the nature of the deposition of the faunal remains in these pits, we looked at the depths from which these bones derive. These indicate that a considerable number of bones were found at the lowest levels of the pits of the pit-houses. As previously argued (chapter 2), the archaeological evidence at Promachon indicates that each pit of a pit-house covered an area as large as 8-10 square metres (Aslanis pers. comm.), thus suggesting that it was large enough to accommodate a family. This evidence, combined with the presence of a hearth in the lower level of the pit of the pit-house n. 1 (square Δ) (Koukouli-Chrysanthaki et al. 2007) and the presence of animal bones, suggests that pit-houses were used as living spaces, where a number of activities – involving also food consumption – were taking place[1].

In addition to the faunal material that was recovered from the lowest levels of the pits of the pit-houses, a smaller number of bones were found at various depths above the lowest levels of the pits. These bones, probably mixed with soil matrix, could potentially represent backfilling material that was used by the Neolithic inhabitants of Promachon in order to fill the pits – after the conflagration event – of the

---

[1] We should not exclude the possibility that pit-houses were also used as storage facilities and/or workshop areas. Koukouli-Chrysanthaki *et al.* (2007) propose the presence of raised upper structures, which were separated from the lower levels (pits) with a raised (wooden?) platform.

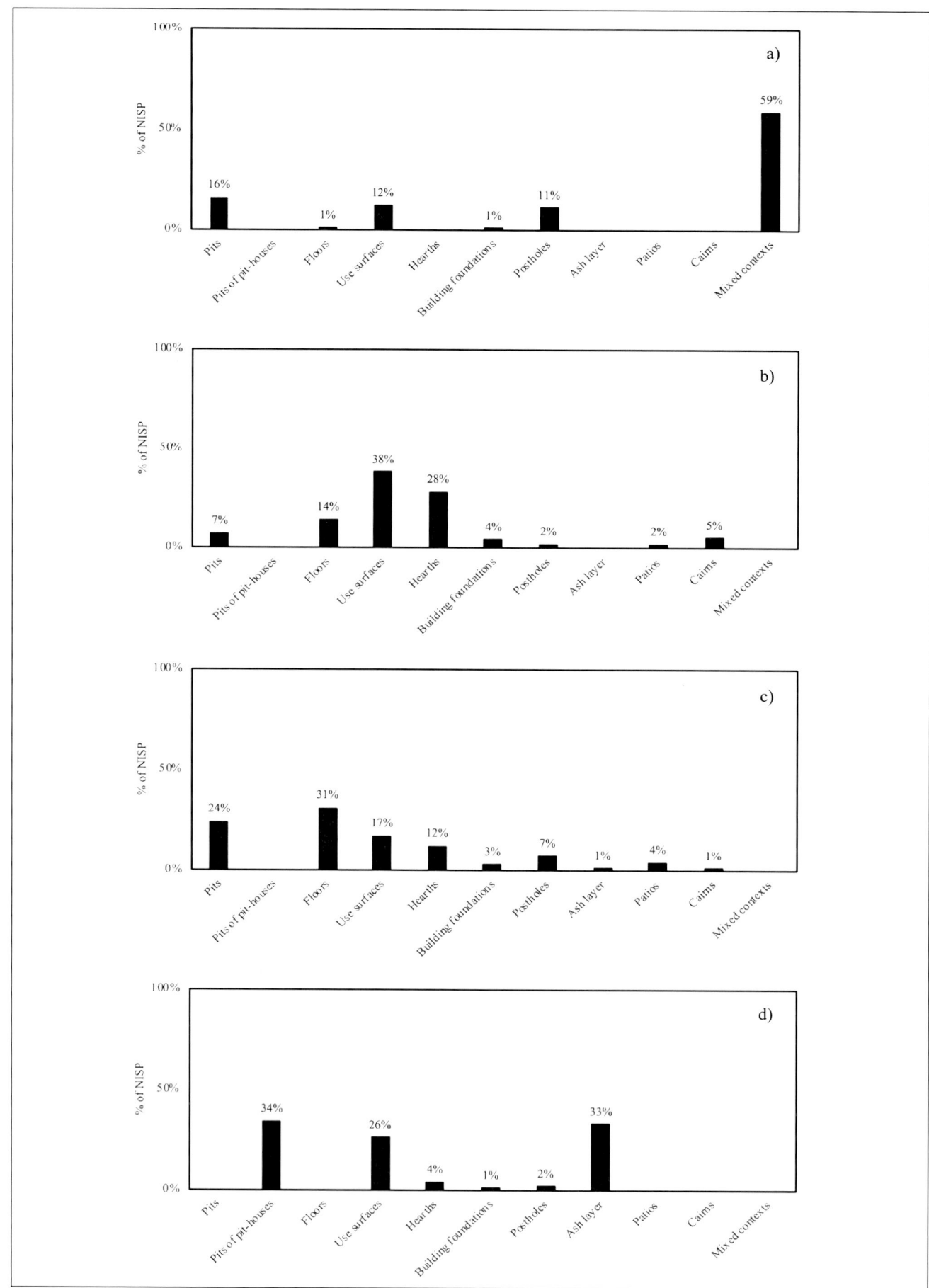

Figure 5.14 Distribution of the faunal material per context type: a) Layer 1 (Phase III), b) Layer 3 (Phase II), c) Layer 4 (Phase I), d) Layer 6 (Phase I). Data in Table 5.49. NISP counts.

pit-houses for the construction of the aboveground houses that appear in the next phase (Phase II).

With regard to Layer 4 (Phase I), the highest numbers of bones derive from floors (31 per cent), pits (24 per cent) and use surfaces (17 per cent). The high number of bones from the floors and use surfaces can – once more – be explained on the basis of the disposal of butchered debris on areas of everyday activities. In general, pits (*i.e.* external pits, also referred as 'ditches' and should not be confused with the pits of the pit-houses) have been considered to represent everyday deposition. This is also the case at Promachon. To be more specific, no particular preference on a single anatomical element or a specific age category was detected in any of the pits from Layer 4. In addition, there was no particular reliance to a single, either domestic, or wild, species. It can be suggested that pits from Layer 4 were not reserved for any particular events, and they were more likely to be the recipients of deposits containing material from everyday activities.

The contexts that produced by far the highest quantities of bones in Layer 3 (Phase II) were the use surfaces, the hearths and the floors. The frequency of bones from pits in Layer 3 is lower than the preceding layer (Layer 4), which is probably a result of the general scarcity of pits as a context type from this Layer. In addition, the two structures present in this layer are aboveground, and therefore, the discarded bone debris was most likely to end up in the use surfaces and the floors. This could potentially explain the highest frequency of bones from the latter contexts.

5.6.2 Distribution of the three main domesticates per context type

Only a number of contexts from each layer contained enough material to be properly examined. The threshold

Table 5.50 Taxa representation per context type. Pits of pit-houses, Layer 6 (Phase I). NISP counts.

Pits of pit-houses (Layer 6)	Bones	Teeth	TOTAL
	NISP	NISP	
Bos taurus	29	17	46
Ovis/Capra	17	15	32
Ovis aries	8	10	18
Capra hircus	1		1
Sus	12	7	19
Canis familiaris	2	2	4
Cervus elaphus	3		3
Lepus europaeus	2		2
Ovis/Capra/Capreolus	1		1
Homo sapiens	2		2
TOTAL	**77**	**51**	**128**

for this analytical purpose was set to 100 bone fragments per single context type. Most of the faunal material from individual contexts belongs to domesticated species (cattle, caprines, pigs). It seems therefore that there isn't any particular reliance to wild species in any of the contexts analysed. Additionally, no particular preference in a single wild species was detected in any of the contexts.

Due to restrictions of small sample size, frequencies between species are explored only for the three commonest taxa (cattle, sheep/goat and pigs). The results are presented in Figure 5.15 (Tables 5.50-5.75). Analysis of the distribution of the three main domesticates per context type shows that in most cases the observed pattern is similar to the distribution by phase. Almost all contexts stand out for having a higher proportion of caprines than cattle, while pig is consistently the third most frequently recovered species in all context types and layers.

Table 5.51 Three main domesticates, representation per context type. Pits of pit-houses, Layer 6 (Phase I). Caprinae subfamily includes *Ovis/Capra* (sheep/goat), *Ovis aries* (sheep) and *Capra hircus* (goat). Data for Figure 5.15. NISP counts.

Pits of pit-houses (Layer 6)	Bones	Teeth	TOTAL	%
	NISP	NISP		
Bos taurus	29	17	**46**	40%
Caprinae	26	25	**51**	44%
Sus	12	7	**19**	16%
TOTAL	**67**	**49**	**116**	**100%**

Table 5.52 Taxa representation per context type. Ash layer, Layer 6 (Phase I). NISP counts.

Ash layer (Layer 6)	Bones	Teeth	TOTAL
	NISP	NISP	
Bos taurus	27	13	40
Ovis/Capra	12	23	35
Ovis aries	5	2	7
Capra hircus	1	1	2
Sus	13	8	21
Canis familiaris		3	3
Cervus elaphus	2	4	6
Capreolus capreolus	1	1	2
Lynx lynx	1		1
Mustella putorius		1	1
Cervus/Bos	3		3
Ovis/Capra/Capreolus	1		1
TOTAL	**66**	**56**	**122**

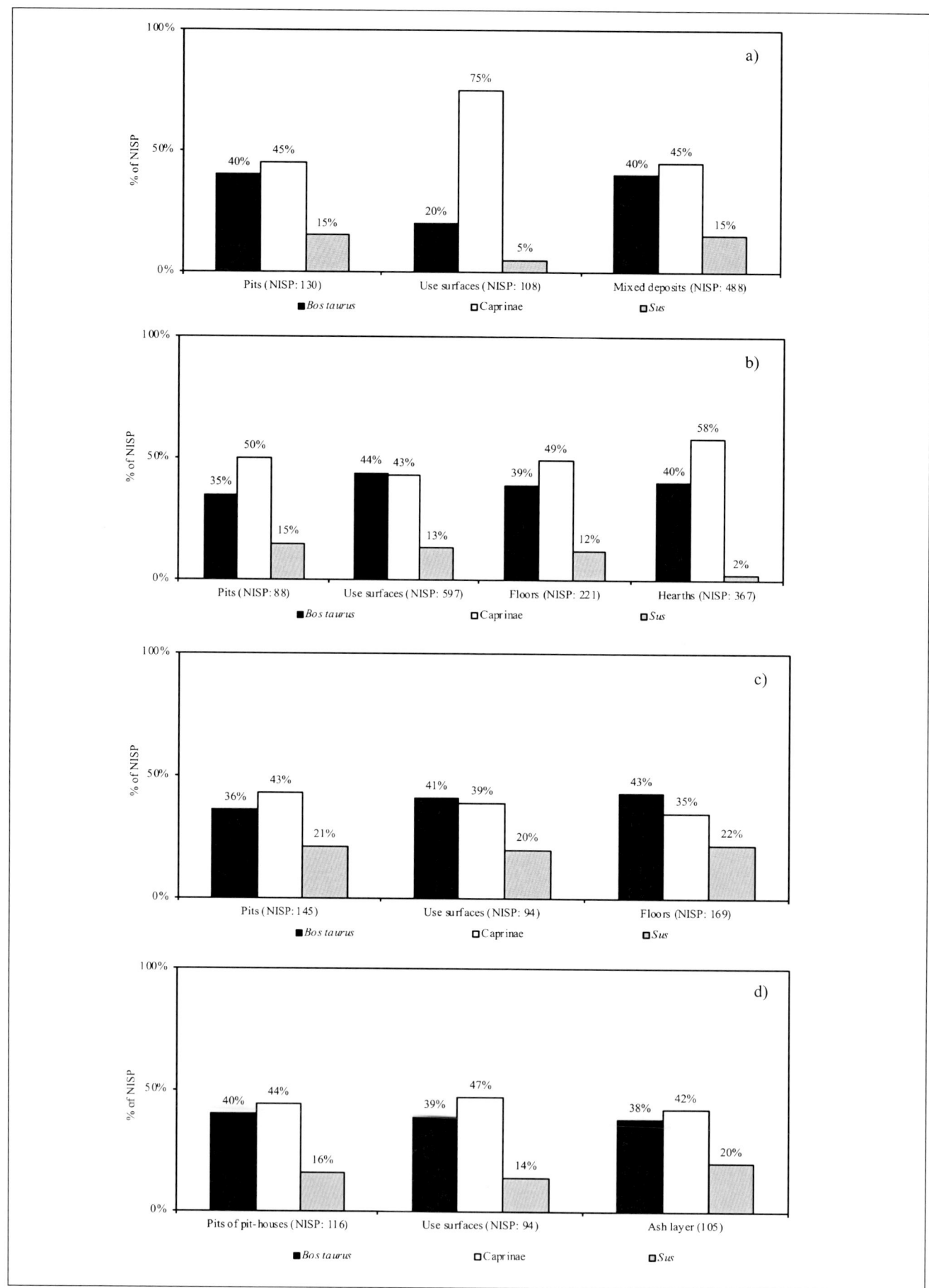

Figure 5.15 Distribution of the three main domesticates per context type: a) Layer 1 (Phase III), b) Layer 3 (Phase II), c) Layer 4 (Phase I), d) Layer 6 (Phase I). Data in Tables 5.50-5.75. NISP counts.

Table 5.53 Three main domesticates, representation per context type. Ash layer, Layer 6 (Phase I). Caprinae subfamily includes *Ovis/Capra* (sheep/goat), *Ovis aries* (sheep) and *Capra hircus* (goat). Data for Figure 5.15. NISP counts.

Ash Layer (Layer 6)	Bones NISP	Teeth NISP	TOTAL	%
Bos taurus	27	13	40	38%
Caprinae	18	26	44	42%
Sus	13	8	21	20%
TOTAL	58	47	105	100%

Table 5.54 Taxa representation per context type. Use surfaces, Layer 6 (Phase I). NISP counts.

Use surfaces (Layer 6)	Bones NISP	Teeth NISP	TOTAL
Bos taurus	30	7	37
Ovis/Capra	15	16	31
Ovis aries	8	5	13
Capra hircus		1	1
Sus	10	3	13
Canis familiaris	2		2
Cervus elaphus		2	2
Dama dama	1		1
Ovis/Capra/ Capreolus	1		1
TOTAL	67	34	101

Table 5.55 Three main domesticates, representation per context type. Use surfaces, Layer 6 (Phase I). Caprinae subfamily includes *Ovis/Capra* (sheep/goat), *Ovis aries* (sheep) and *Capra hircus* (goat). Data for Figure 5.15. NISP counts.

Use surfaces (Layer 6)	Bones NISP	Teeth NISP	TOTAL	%
Bos taurus	30	7	37	39%
Caprinae	23	21	45	47%
Sus	10	3	13	14%
TOTAL	63	31	94	100%

Table 5.56 Taxa representation per context type. Floors, Layer 4 (Phase I). NISP counts.

Floors (Layer 4)	Bones NISP	Teeth NISP	TOTAL
Bos taurus	46	26	72
Ovis/Capra	17	20	37
Ovis aries	9	8	17
Capra hircus	3	3	6
Sus	21	16	37
Canis familiaris	4	5	9
Dama dama	1		1
Vulpes vulpes	3	1	4
Ursus arctos	1		1
TOTAL	105	79	184

Table 5.57 Three main domesticates, representation per context type. Floors, Layer 4 (Phase I). Caprinae subfamily includes *Ovis/Capra* (sheep/goat), *Ovis aries* (sheep) and *Capra hircus* (goat). Data for Figure 5.15. NISP counts.

Floors (Layer 4)	Bones NISP	Teeth NISP	TOTAL	%
Bos taurus	46	27	72	43%
Caprinae	29	31	60	35%
Sus	21	16	37	22%
TOTAL	96	74	169	100%

Table 5.58 Taxa representation per context type. Pits, Layer 4 (Phase I). NISP counts.

Pits (Layer 4)	Bones NISP	Teeth NISP	TOTAL
Bos taurus	33	16	49
Ovis/Capra	18	25	43
Ovis aries	7	6	13
Capra hircus	2		2
Sus	21	7	28
Canis familiaris		3	3
Vulpes vulpes	1	1	2
Cervus elaphus	2		2
Cervus/Bos	1		1
Anser sp.	2		2
Grus sp.	1		1
Ovis/Capra/Capreolus	1		1
TOTAL	89	58	147

Table 5.59 Three main domesticates, representation per context type. Pits, Layer 4 (Phase I). Caprinae subfamily includes *Ovis/Capra* (sheep/goat), *Ovis aries* (sheep) and *Capra hircus* (goat). Data for Figure 5.15. NISP counts.

Pits (Layer 4)	Bones NISP	Teeth NISP	TOTAL	%
Bos taurus	33	16	49	36%
Caprinae	27	31	58	43%
Sus	21	7	28	21%
TOTAL	81	64	135	100%

Table 5.60 Taxa representation per context type. Use surfaces, Layer 4 (Phase I). NISP counts.

Use surfaces (Layer 4)	Bones NISP	Teeth NISP	TOTAL
Bos taurus	27	12	39
Ovis/Capra	12	15	27
Ovis aries	4	1	5
Capra hircus	3	2	5
Sus	16	2	18
Canis familiaris	1	1	2
Sus scrofa		1	1
Lepus europaeus	1		1
Cervus/Bos	3		3
Canis/Vulpes	1		1
TOTAL	68	34	102

Table 5.61 Three main domesticates, representation per context type. Use surfaces, Layer 4 (Phase I). Caprinae subfamily includes *Ovis/Capra* (sheep/goat), *Ovis aries* (sheep) and *Capra hircus* (goat). Data for Figure 5.15. NISP counts.

Use surfaces (Layer 4)	Bones NISP	Teeth NISP	TOTAL	%
Bos taurus	27	12	39	41%
Caprinae	19	18	37	39%
Sus	16	2	18	20%
TOTAL	62	32	94	100%

Table 5.62 Taxa representation per context type. Use surfaces, Layer 3 (Phase II). NISP counts.

Use surfaces (Layer 3)	Bones NISP	Teeth NISP	TOTAL
Bos taurus	185	76	261
Ovis/Capra	66	134	200
Ovis aries	27	20	47
Capra hircus	4	5	9
Sus	55	25	80
Canis familiaris	8	6	14
Cervus elaphus	1	1	2
Capreolus capreolus	2		2
Lepus europaeus		1	1
Vulpes vulpes	2	1	3
Corvus corax	1		1
Cervus/Bos	1		1
Cervus/Dama	1		1
Canis/Vulpes		2	2
Ovis/Capra/Capreolus	3		3
TOTAL	356	271	627

Table 5.63 Three main domesticates, representation per context type. Use surfaces, Layer 3 (Phase II). Caprinae subfamily includes *Ovis/Capra* (sheep/goat), *Ovis aries* (sheep) and *Capra hircus* (goat). Data for Figure 5.15. NISP counts.

Use surfaces (Layer 3)	Bones NISP	Teeth NISP	TOTAL	%
Bos taurus	185	76	261	44%
Caprinae	97	159	256	43%
Sus	55	25	80	13%
TOTAL	337	260	597	100%

Table 5.64 Taxa representation per context type. Hearths, Layer 3 (Phase II). NISP counts.

Hearths (Layer 3)	Bones NISP	Teeth NISP	TOTAL
Bos taurus	98	48	146
Ovis/Capra	57	94	151
Ovis aries	42	10	52
Capra hircus	5	4	9
Sus	41	20	61
Canis familiaris	5	3	8
Cervus elaphus	4	4	8
Dama dama	1		1
Capreolus capreolus	6	2	8
Lepus europaeus	2		2
Cervus/Bos	1		1
Cervus/Dama	4		4
Canis/Vulpes	1		1
Ovis/Capra/Capreolus	1		1
TOTAL	268	185	453

Table 5.65 Three main domesticates, representation per context type. Hearths, Layer 3 (Phase II). Caprinae subfamily includes *Ovis/Capra* (sheep/goat), *Ovis aries* (sheep) and *Capra hircus* (goat). Data for Figure 5.15. NISP counts.

Hearths (Layer 3)	Bones NISP	Teeth NISP	TOTAL	%
Bos taurus	98	48	**146**	40%
Caprinae	104	108	**212**	58%
Sus	5	4	**9**	2%
TOTAL	**207**	**160**	**367**	**100%**

Table 5.66 Taxa representation per context type. Floors, Layer 3 (Phase II). NISP counts.

Floors (Layer 3)	Bones NISP	Teeth NISP	TOTAL
Bos taurus	58	28	**86**
Ovis/Capra	30	54	**84**
Ovis aries	11	9	**20**
Capra hircus	4	1	**5**
Sus	12	14	**26**
Cervus elaphus	4	1	**5**
Dama dama	1		**1**
Capreolus capreolus	1		**1**
Lepus europaeus	2		**2**
Aves	1		**1**
Cervus/Bos	3	1	**4**
Ovis/Capra/Capreolus	1		**1**
TOTAL	**128**	**108**	**236**

Table 5.67 Three main domesticates, representation per context type. Floors, Layer 3 (Phase II). Caprinae subfamily includes *Ovis/Capra* (sheep/goat), *Ovis aries* (sheep) and *Capra hircus* (goat). Data for Figure 5.15. NISP counts.

Floors (Layer 3)	Bones NISP	Teeth NISP	TOTAL	%
Bos taurus	58	28	**86**	39%
Caprinae	45	64	**109**	49%
Sus	12	14	**26**	12%
TOTAL	**115**	**106**	**221**	**100%**

Table 5.68 Taxa representation per context type. Pits, Layer 3 (Phase II). NISP counts.

Pits (Layer 3)	Bones NISP	Teeth NISP	TOTAL
Bos taurus	23	9	**32**
Ovis/Capra	13	14	**27**
Ovis aries	7	2	**9**
Capra hircus	7		**7**
Sus	7	6	**13**
Canis familiaris	4	2	**6**
Cervus elaphus	2	1	**3**
Capreolus capreolus	1		**1**
Vulpes vulpes	1		**1**
Cervus/Bos	2		**2**
Ovis/Capra/Capreolus	2		**2**
TOTAL	**69**	**34**	**103**

Table 5.69 Three main domesticates, representation per context type. Pits, Layer 3 (Phase II). Caprinae subfamily includes *Ovis/Capra* (sheep/goat), *Ovis aries* (sheep) and *Capra hircus* (goat). Data for Figure 5.15. NISP counts.

Pits (Layer 3)	Bones NISP	Teeth NISP	TOTAL	%
Bos taurus	23	9	**32**	35%
Caprinae	27	16	**43**	50%
Sus	7	6	**13**	15%
TOTAL	**57**	**31**	**88**	**100%**

Table 5.70 Taxa representation per context type. Mixed contexts, Layer 1 (Phase III). NISP counts.

Mixed contexts (Layer 1)	Bones NISP	Teeth NISP	TOTAL
Bos taurus	140	58	**198**
Ovis/Capra	51	110	**161**
Ovis aries	28	15	**43**
Capra hircus	5	6	**11**
Sus	53	22	**75**
Canis familiaris	6	4	**10**
Cervus elaphus	7		**7**
Capreolus capreolus	4		**4**
Lepus europaeus	2		**2**
Vulpes vulpes	1	1	**2**
Homo sapiens		1	**1**
Cervus/Bos	3		**3**
Cervus/Dama	1		**1**
Ovis/Capra/Capreolus	5		**5**
TOTAL	**306**	**217**	**523**

Table 5.71 Three main domesticates, representation per context type. Mixed contexts, Layer 1 (Phase III). Caprinae subfamily includes *Ovis/Capra* (sheep/goat), *Ovis aries* (sheep) and *Capra hircus* (goat). Data for Figure 5.15. NISP counts.

Mixed contexts (Layer 1)	Bones	Teeth	TOTAL	%
	NISP	NISP		
Bos taurus	84	131	**215**	40%
Caprinae	140	58	**198**	45%
Sus	53	22	**75**	15%
TOTAL	**277**	**211**	**488**	**100%**

Table 5.72 Taxa representation per context type. Pits, Layer 1 (Phase III). NISP counts.

Pits (Layer 1)	Bones	Teeth	TOTAL
	NISP	NISP	
Bos taurus	34	18	**52**
Ovis/Capra	19	26	**45**
Ovis aries	11	2	**13**
Capra hircus		1	**1**
Sus	9	10	**19**
Canis familiaris	1	2	**3**
Cervus elaphus		1	**1**
Capreolus capreolus			**0**
Vulpes vulpes		1	**1**
Meles meles	1		**1**
Cervus/Bos	1		**1**
Ovis/Capra/Capreolus	1		**1**
TOTAL	**77**	**61**	**138**

Table 5.73 Three main domesticates, representation per context type. Pits, Layer 1 (Phase III). Caprinae subfamily includes *Ovis/Capra* (sheep/goat), *Ovis aries* (sheep) and *Capra hircus* (goat). Data for Figure 5.15. NISP counts.

Pits (Layer 1)	Bones	Teeth	TOTAL	%
	NISP	NISP		
Bos taurus	30	29	**59**	40%
Caprinae	34	18	**52**	45%
Sus	9	10	**19**	15%
TOTAL	**73**	**57**	**130**	**100%**

Table 5.74 Taxa representation per context type. Use surfaces, Layer 1 (Phase III). NISP counts.

Use surfaces (Layer 1)	Bones	Teeth	TOTAL
	NISP	NISP	
Bos taurus	11	9	**20**
Ovis/Capra	17	39	**56**
Ovis aries	13	8	**21**
Capra hircus	1	3	**4**
Sus	3	4	**7**
Canis familiaris	2		**2**
TOTAL	**47**	**63**	**110**

Table 5.75 Three main domesticates, representation per context type. Use surfaces, Layer 1 (Phase III). Caprinae subfamily includes *Ovis/Capra* (sheep/goat), *Ovis aries* (sheep) and *Capra hircus* (goat). Data for Figure 5.15. NISP counts.

Use surfaces (Layer 1)	Bones	Teeth	TOTAL	%
	NISP	NISP		
Bos taurus	11	9	**20**	20%
Caprinae	31	50	**85**	75%
Sus	3	4	**7**	5%
TOTAL	**45**	**63**	**108**	**100%**

However, there is an issue that should also be considered. To be more specific, it is worth noting that the slight decline in cattle frequencies that had been identified through the analysis of the combined assemblage is inconsistently represented in pits and use surfaces (the only context types that we can compare across layers). In pits it is not evident at all, while in use surfaces is not apparent until Layer 1 (where caprines are represented with 75 per cent and cattle with 20 per cent in terms of NISP). This may suggest that the decline of cattle with time is not only a product of changes in husbandry strategies but also of the differential use of context types across layers.

5.6.3 Body part distribution of the three main domesticates per context type

Due to restrictions of small sample size, body part distribution is explored only for the commonest taxa (cattle, caprines and pigs) from the use surfaces of Layer 3 (Phase II) and only for broad anatomical groups (cranium, axial skeleton, upper limbs and lower limbs). The results are presented in Figure 5.16 (Tables 5.76-5.78).

Analyses of the body part distribution of caprines and pigs from the use surfaces of Layer 3 (Phase II) show that the

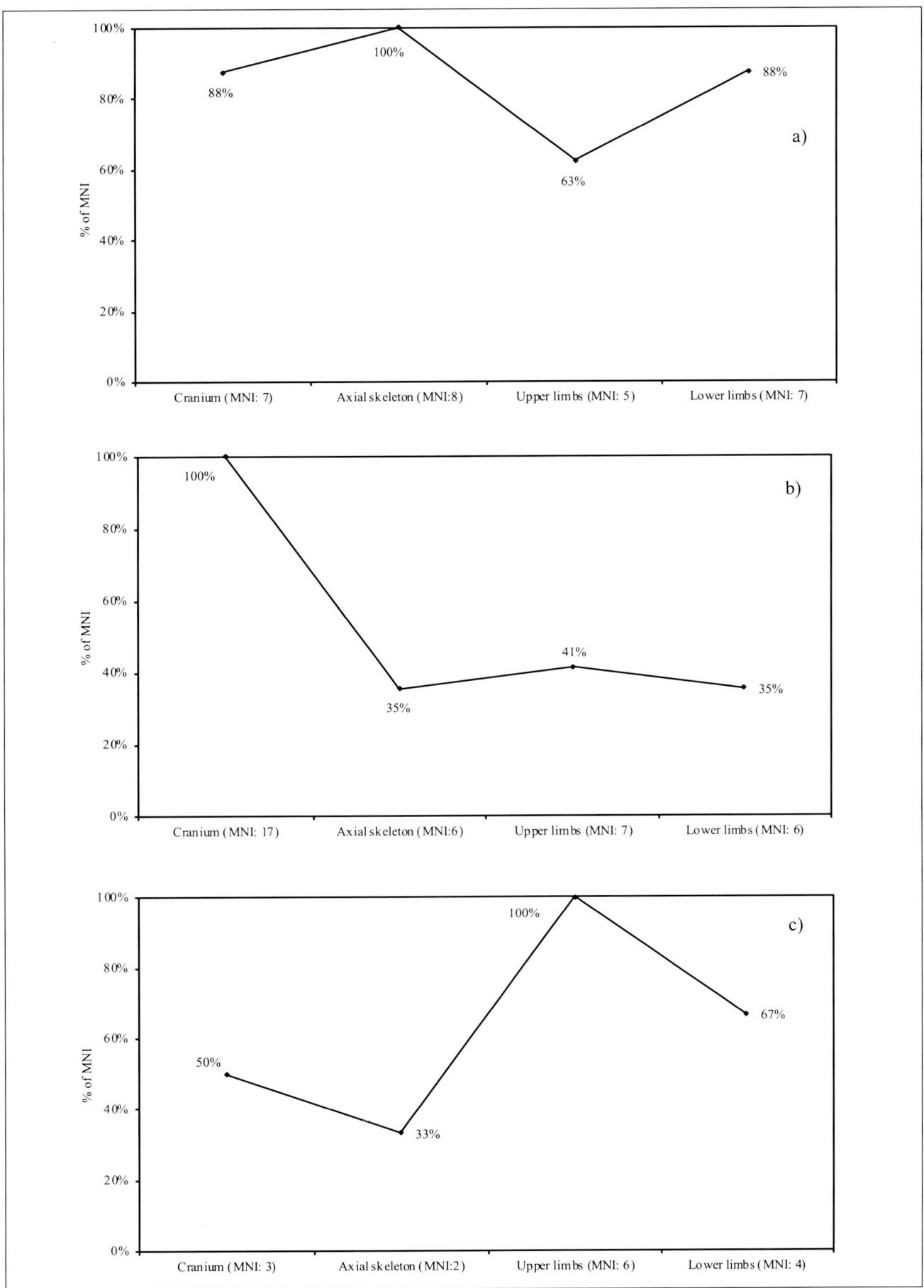

Figure 5.16 Parts of the: a) *Bos taurus*, **b) Caprinae, c)** *Sus* **skeleton from the use surfaces of Layer 3 (Phase II) using broad anatomical groups. Data in Tables 5.76-5.78. MNI counts.**

Table 5.76 Parts of the *Bos taurus* (cattle) skeleton by number of fragments (NISP) and minimum number of individuals (MNI) from the use surfaces of Layer 3 (Phase II) using broad anatomical groups. Data for Figure 5.16.

Bos taurus	NISP	MNI	HIGHEST MNI	%	BROAD ANATOMICAL GROUPS
Incisors	3	1	7	88%	CRANIUM
dP&P Maxillary	11	2			
M1/2 Maxillary	17	5			
M3 Maxillary	3	2			
dP&P Mandibular	19	4			
M1/2 Mandibular	27	7			
M3 Mandibular	5	3			
Cranium	5	3			
Atlas	1	1	8	100%	AXIAL SKELETON
Axis	8	8			
Scapula	9	5	5	63%	UPPER LIMBS
Humerus proximal	1	1			
Humerus distal	5	3			
Pelvis	4	2			
Femur proximal	4	2			
Femur distal	4	2			
Radius proximal	6	3	7	88%	LOWER LIMBS
Radius distal	2	1			
Ulna proximal	3	2			
Carpal 2+3	3	2			
Metacarpal distal	6	4			
Metacarpal ½ distal	1				
Tibia proximal	2	1			
Tibia distal	8	4			
Scafocuboid	3	2			
Astragalus	13	7			
Calcaneum	9	5			
Metatarsal distal	5	3			
Metatarsal ½ distal	1				
Metapodial distal					
Metapodial ½ distal	1				
Phalanx 1	28	4			
Phalanx 2	28	4			
Phalanx 3	17	3			
TOTAL	**262**	**HIGHEST MNI: 8**			

Unfused proximal and distal epiphyses are not counted. Each tooth (loose or attached to maxilla/mandible) is considered. The MNI has been calculated as follows: Incisors and phalanges have been divided by 8, deciduous and permanent premolars (dP&P) have been divided by 6, first and second molars (M1/2) have been divided by 4 and all other elements -except for Metapodials- have been divided by 2. Metacarpals (Metacarpal 1 distal) and Metatarsals (Metatarsal 1 distal) have been calculated as follows:
Metacarpal = (Metacarpal 1 distal + Metacarpal 1/2 distal / 2 + Metapodium 1 distal / 2 + Metapodium 1/2 distal / 4) / 2.
Metatarsal = (Metatarsal 1 distal + Metatarsal 1/2 distal / 2 + Metapodium 1 distal / 2 + Metapodium 1/2 distal / 4) / 2.
Where Metapodium 1 distal: complete distal metapodial and Metapodium 1/2 distal: half distal metapodial.
%: Frequency of an element expressed in relation to the most common one (by MNI).

Table 5.77 Parts of the Caprinae (caprines) skeleton by number of fragments (NISP) and minimum number of individuals (MNI) from the use surfaces of Layer 3 (Phase II) using broad anatomical groups. Caprinae subfamily includes *Ovis/Capra* (sheep/goat), *Ovis aries* (sheep) and *Capra hircus* (goat). Data for Figure 5.16.

Caprinae	NISP	MNI	HIGHEST MNI	%	BROAD ANATOMICAL GROUPS
Incisors	7	1	17	100%	CRANIUM
dP&P Maxillary	14	3			
M1/2 Maxillary	38	10			
M3 Maxillary	18	9			
dP&P Mandibular	45	8			
M1/2 Mandibular	65	17			
M3 Mandibular	18	9			
Cranium					
Atlas	2	2	6	35%	AXIAL SKELETON
Axis	6	6			
Scapula	6	3	7	41%	UPPER LIMBS
Humerus proximal		0			
Humerus distal	9	5			
Pelvis	14	7			
Femur proximal	1	1			
Femur distal	1	1			
Radius proximal	10	5	6	35%	LOWER LIMBS
Radius distal	9	1			
Ulna proximal	3	2			
Carpal 2+3	2	1			
Metacarpal distal	3	2			
Metacarpal ½ distal	1				
Tibia proximal	2	1			
Tibia distal	11	6			
Scafocuboid					
Astragalus	7	4			
Calcaneum	8	4			
Metatarsal distal	2	2			
Metatarsal ½ distal	2				
Metapodial distal					
Metapodial ½ distal					
Phalanx 1	3	1			
Phalanx 2	1	1			
Phalanx 3					
TOTAL	301	HIGHEST MNI: 17			

Unfused proximal and distal epiphyses are not counted. Each tooth (loose or attached to maxilla/mandible) is considered. The MNI has been calculated as follows: Incisors and phalanges have been divided by 8, deciduous and permanent premolars (dP&P) have been divided by 6, first and second molars (M1/2) have been divided by 4 and all other elements -except for Metapodials- have been divided by 2. Metacarpals (Metacarpal 1 distal) and Metatarsals (Metatarsal 1 distal) have been calculated as follows:
Metacarpal = (Metacarpal 1 distal + Metacarpal 1/2 distal / 2 + Metapodium 1 distal / 2 + Metapodium 1/2 distal / 4) / 2.
Metatarsal = (Metatarsal 1 distal + Metatarsal 1/2 distal / 2 + Metapodium 1 distal / 2 + Metapodium 1/2 distal / 4) / 2.
Where Metapodium 1 distal: complete distal metapodial and Metapodium 1/2 distal: half distal metapodial.
%: Frequency of an element expressed in relation to the most common one (by MNI).

Table 5.78 Parts of the *Sus* (pig) skeleton by number of fragments (NISP) and minimum number of individuals (MNI) from the use surfaces of Layer 3 (Phase II) using broad anatomical groups. Data for Figure 5.16.

Sus	NISP	MNI	HIGHEST MNI	%	BROAD ANATOMICAL GROUPS
Incisors Maxillary	3	1	3	50%	CRANIUM
Canines Maxillary	4	2			
dP&P Maxillary	10	2			
M1/2 Maxillary	11	3			
M3 Maxillary	3	2			
Incisors Mandibular	4	1			
Canines Mandibular	1	1			
dP&P Mandibular	8	2			
M1/2 Mandibular	3	1			
M3 Mandibular	3	2			
Cranium					
Atlas			2	33%	AXIAL SKELETON
Axis	2	2			
Scapula	11	6	6	100%	UPPER LIMBS
Humerus proximal	2	1			
Humerus distal	4	2			
Pelvis	1	1			
Femur proximal	1	1			
Femur distal	1	1			
Radius proximal	2	1	4	67%	LOWER LIMBS
Radius distal	5	3			
Ulna proximal	8	4			
Carpal 3					
Metacarpal 3 distal	1	1			
Metacarpal 4 distal	1	1			
Tibia proximal	1	1			
Tibia distal	5	3			
Scafocuboid					
Astragalus	1	1			
Calcaneum	2	1			
Metatarsal 3 distal					
Metatarsal 4 distal	2	1			
Phalanx 1	2	1			
Phalanx 2	1	1			
Phalanx 3	2	1			
TOTAL	**105**	**HIGHEST MNI: 6**			

Unfused proximal and distal epiphyses are not counted. Each tooth (loose or attached to maxilla/mandible) is considered. The MNI has been calculated as follows: Phalanges have been divided by 8, deciduous and permanent premolars (dP&P) and incisors have been divided by 6, first and second molars (M1/2) have been divided by 4 and all other elements -except for Metapodials- have been divided by 2. Metacarpals (Metacarpal 3 or 4 distal) and Metatarsals (Metatarsal 3 or 4 distal) have been calculated as follows:
Metacarpal = Metacarpal 3 or 4 distal / 2. Metatarsal = Metatarsal 3 or 4 distal / 2.
%: Frequency of an element expressed in relation to the most common one (by MNI).

highest MNI values are gained from the cranium (caprines) and the upper limbs (pigs). This is consistent with the information that we have from the body part distribution of caprines and pigs from the combined assemblage for Phase II, where teeth (in the case of caprines) and the scapula (in the case of pigs) were represented with the highest MNI values.

On one hand, there are no particular reasons to suggest that any caprine postcranial elements are intentionally missing from the use surfaces of Layer 3. It is therefore safer to attribute the observed variations in the proportions of caprine postcranial elements to differential preservation and recovery bias rather than any specialized waste disposal practice. On the other hand, the low representation of pig crania from the use surfaces of Layer 3 is supporting earlier suggestions that these might have been disposed off-site during Phase II.

Before moving to the body part distribution of cattle from the use surfaces of Layer 3 (Phase II), it is worth discussing what has been suggested for the body part distribution of this species from the combined assemblage for Phase II. This indicated that the highest MNI values were gained from cattle astragali rather than teeth. The pattern was considered peculiar, since there are not obvious taphonomic reasons, which could support the better representation of cattle astragalus in comparison to teeth. To be more specific, the astragalus is a very durable bone, however, teeth are dense and can easily survive in the archaeological record. It was therefore suggested that during Phase II, cattle heads were not as commonly introduced to the site with the rest of the carcass or may have been processed in areas of the site not particularly affected by the excavation.

On the other hand, the body part distribution of cattle from the use surfaces of Layer 3 indicates that the cranium and the lower limbs are evenly distributed. However, the highest MNI values are gained from the axial skeleton. The bone contributing to the high representation of the axial skeleton is the axis, while the atlas, adjacent to it, is poorly represented. The atlas is placed between the head and the axis, both well represented, and since there do not seem to be obvious taphonomic factors that could explain its under-representation, and it seems unlikely that they would purposefully be removed by humans, this rather odd pattern can only be explained with the vagaries of small sample size.

5.6.4 Distribution of taphonomic modifications per context type

Patterns of taphonomic modification and attrition may indicate differences in assemblage formation at a contextual level. Figure 5.17 (Table 5.79) presents the incidence of gnawing, butchery and burning from a number of contexts where human modifications were most frequent: pits, use surfaces, floors and hearths. The context types are analysed by combining layers (and phases) in order to increase sample size, though at the expenses of a loss in chronological resolution.

To a considerable extent, the incidence of gnawing across different context types is consistent with the information from the combined assemblage. To be more specific, there are no differences in the frequency of gnawing between individual contexts. Scavenger gnawing is rather low in pits, use surfaces, floors (three per cent respectively) and hearths (four per cent), indicating that scavengers did not have differential access to areas of the site. This is

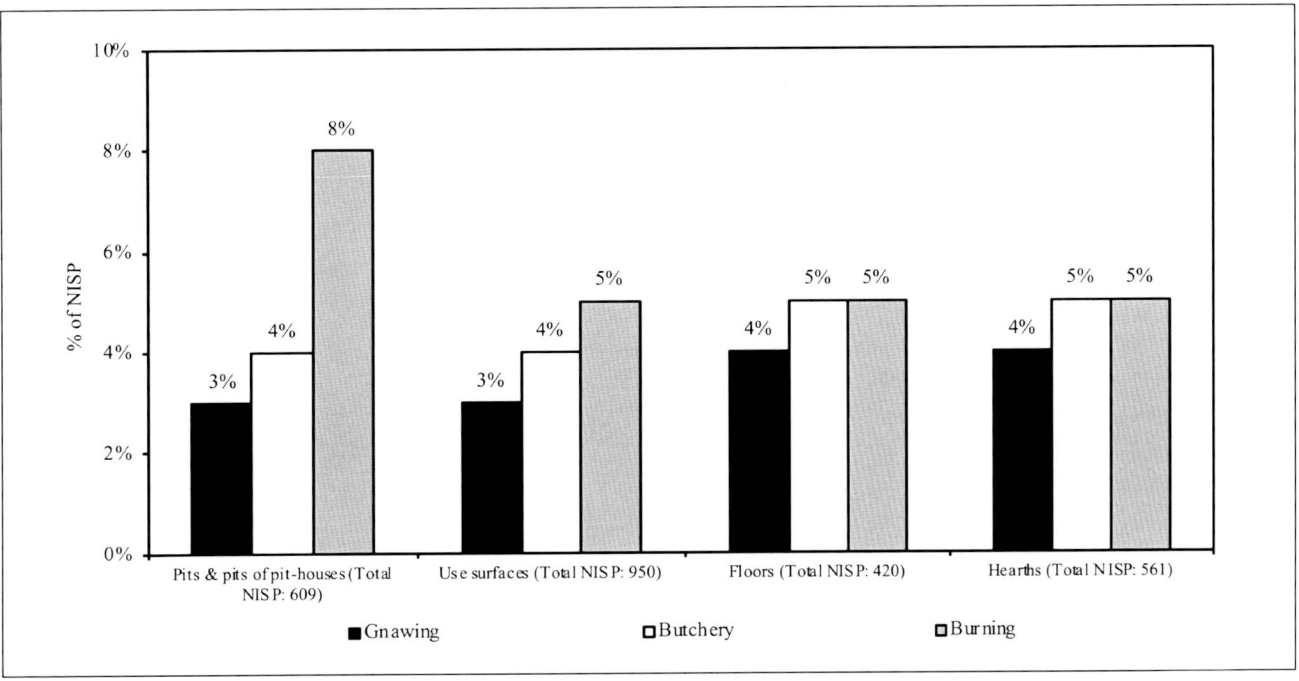

Figure 5.17 Distribution of gnawing, butchery and burning per context type. All layers are considered. Data in Table 5.79. NISP counts.

Table 5.79 Distribution of gnawing, butchery and burning per context type. All layers are considered. Both 'countable' and 'uncountable' material is considered. 'Gnawing' includes gnawing marks attributed with safety to carnivores. 'Butchery' includes both cutmarks and chopping marks. 'Burning' includes burnt, singed and calcined material. Data for Figure 5.17. NISP counts.

Modification	Pits & pits of pit-houses (NISP: 609)		Use surfaces (NISP: 950)		Floors (NISP: 428)		Hearths (NISP: 561)	
	NISP	%	NISP	%	NISP	%	NISP	%
Gnawing	16	3%	25	3%	15	4%	20	4%
Butchery	22	4%	36	4%	21	5%	26	5%
Burning	49	8%	50	5%	21	5%	29	5%

consistent with the information from the combined assemblage, which suggested that scavenger access to bone debris was by and large restricted. In addition, the frequency of butchery does not vary substantially across different contexts. Butchery marks are represented with four per cent on bones from pits and use surfaces and with five per cent on bones from floors and hearths. There is no indication therefore from butchery marks that butchered debris from various stages of carcass processing was preferentially discarded in pits, use surfaces, floors or hearths.

As previously noted, the overall incidence of burning at Promachon is rather small (only seven per cent of the total 'countable' postcranial bones). There seems however, that burning is slightly higher in pits (eight per cent) than any other analysed context (use surfaces, floors, hearths: five per cent respectively). The difference in the burning incidence between pits and other contexts is rather small for any definite conclusions to be drawn, but we cannot exclude the possibility that burned material was preferentially discarded in pits rather than in use surfaces, floors and hearths.

5.7 Age-at-death of the three main domesticates

Bone fusion and dental eruption and wear were recorded to assess kill-off patterns of cattle, caprine and pig populations from Promachon. In this section, these two main lines of evidence are presented independently. However, wherever possible, bone fusion and dental eruption and wear are integrated and evaluated.

5.7.1 Bos taurus *age-at-death*

Examining the data concerning the epiphyseal fusion evidence first (Table 5.80), it seems that there is an inconsistency regarding the fusion of middle and late fusing bones. Figure 5.18 shows that 67 per cent of the middle fusing bones (24-42 months) were fused. This indicates that 33 per cent of the middle fusing bones were unfused and thus, a considerable part of the cattle population did not survive beyond the second and the first half of the third year. On the other hand, 89 per cent of the bones in the late fusing stage (42-48 months) were fused, indicating that the overwhelming majority of the cattle

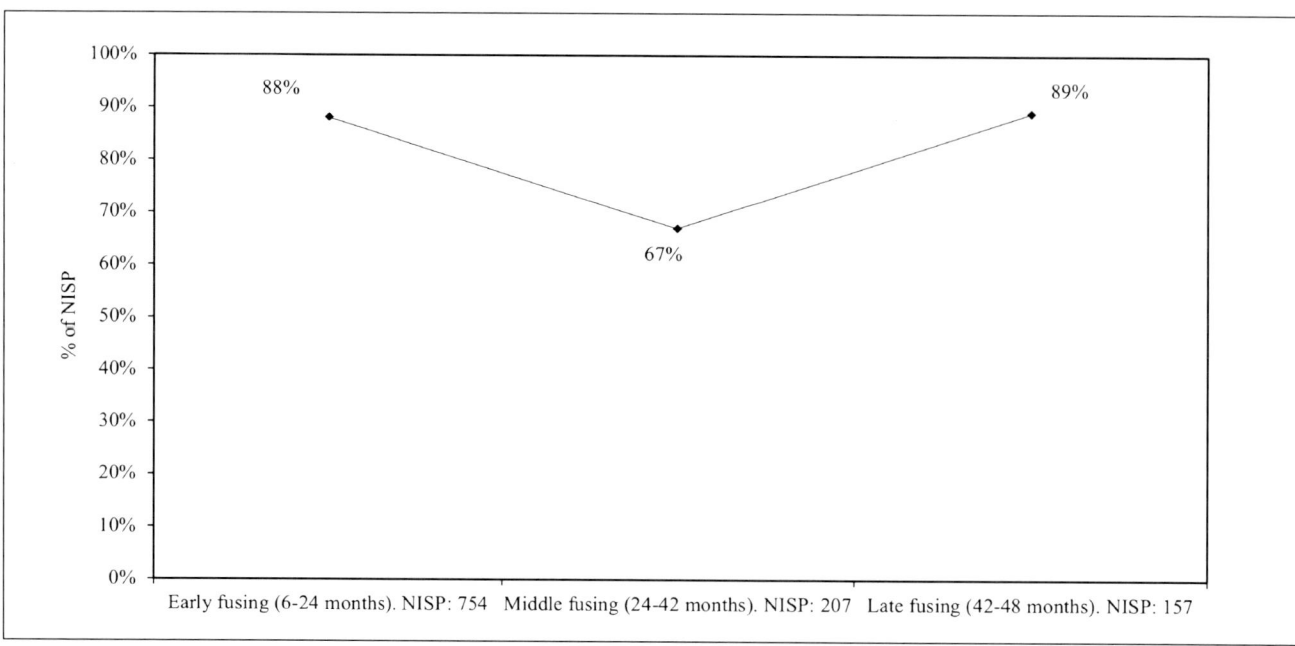

Early fusing (6-24 months). NISP: 754   Middle fusing (24-42 months). NISP: 207   Late fusing (42-48 months). NISP: 157

Figure 5.18 Epiphyseal fusion data for *Bos taurus*. All phases are considered. Data in Table 5.80. NISP counts.

Table 5.80 Epiphyseal fusion data for *Bos taurus* (cattle). Fused (F) column includes fused, fusing and fusing/fused specimens. Unfused (UD) column includes unfused diaphyses. Unfused epiphyses are not counted. Data for Figure 5.18. NISP counts.

Bos taurus		Late Neolithic I										Late Neolithic II										TOTAL				
		Phase I					Phase II					Phase III														
		NISP	F	%	UD	%	NISP	F	%	UD	%	NISP	F	%	UD	%	NISP	F	%	UD	%
Early Fusing	Scapula	23	20	87%	3	13%	25	19	76%	6	24%	16	15	94%	1	6%	64	54	84%	10	16%
	Humerus distal	34	21	62%	13	38%	23	14	61%	9	39%	18	13	72%	5	28%	75	48	64%	27	36%
	Radius proximal	24	24	100%		0%	24	24	100%		0%	8	8	100%		0%	56	56	100%		0%
	Pelvis acetabulum	28	16	57%	12	43%	32	24	75%	8	25%	12	10	83%	2	17%	72	50	69%	22	31%
	Phalanx 1	96	89	93%	7	7%	95	88	93%	7	7%	64	60	94%	4	6%	255	237	93%	18	7%
	Phalanx 2	80	75	94%	5	6%	97	91	94%	6	6%	55	54	98%	1	2%	232	220	95%	12	5%
	TOTAL	285	245	86%	40	14%	296	260	88%	36	12%	173	160	92%	13	8%	754	665	88%	89	12%
Middle Fusing	Metacarpal distal	16	13	81%	3	11%	21	15	71%	6	29%	8	7	88%	1	12%	45	35	78%	10	22%
	Tibia distal	28	20	71%	8	29%	26	16	62%	10	38%	12	9	75%	3	25%	66	45	68%	21	32%
	Calcaneum	28	13	46%	15	54%	30	18	60%	12	40%	11	5	45%	6	55%	69	36	52%	33	48%
	Metatarsal distal	11	8	73%	3	27%	13	12	92%	1	8%	3	2	67%	1	33%	27	22	81%	5	19%
	TOTAL	83	54	65%	29	35%	90	61	68%	29	32%	34	23	68%	11	32%	207	138	67%	69	33%
Late Fusing	Humerus proximal	4	4	100%		0%	1	1	100%		0%	3	2	67%	1	33%	8	7	88%	1	12%
	Radius distal	11	10	91%	1	9%	18	18	100%		0%	1	1	100%		0%	30	29	97%	1	3%
	Ulna proximal	16	9	56%	7	44%	13	10	77%	3	23%	9	8	89%	1	11%	38	27	71%	11	29%
	Femur proximal	18	17	94%	1	6%	10	10	100%		0%	6	6	100%		0%	34	33	97%	1	3%
	Femur distal	17	16	94%	1	6%	16	14	88%	2	12%	7	7	100%		0%	40	37	93%	3	7%
	Tibia proximal	3	3	100%		0%	3	3	100%		0%	1	1	100%		0%	7	7	100%		0%
	TOTAL	69	59	86%	10	14%	61	56	92%	5	8%	27	25	93%	2	7%	157	140	89%	17	11%
TOTAL		437	358	82%	79	18%	447	377	84%	70	16%	234	208	89%	26	11%	1118	943	84%	175	16%

population in Promachon had reached skeletal maturity before death.

The pattern is rather confusing, as we would have expected a lower frequency of fused late fusing bones than fused middle fusing bones. This unusual pattern has also been observed at the Early Neolithic site of Runnymede bridge, UK (Viner 2010) and in the Late Jomon (equivalent to the Early Bronze Age) site of Tohoku region in Japan (Hongo *et al.* 2007). Due to the small sample size of cattle (in the first case) and pig (in the second case) postcranial elements, those two cases may be due to chance and do not necessarily require to be explained on the basis of a pattern of human behaviour.

The observed inconsistency at Promachon cannot be explained on the basis of taphonomy. If taphonomy was the reason, we would have expected the vulnerable late fusing bones (proximal and distal femur, proximal humerus, proximal ulna, proximal tibia and distal radius) to be more affected by attrition than the robust and dense middle fusing bones (metapodials, calcaneum and distal tibia). However, this is not the case at Promachon, since the fused late fusing bones are very well represented (89 per cent), in fact slightly more so than the fused early fusing bones (88 per cent).

The high frequency of fused late fusing bones may in fact have different origins: it is possible that some skeletally mature (older) individuals were killed off-site and that the inhabitants of Promachon transferred to the site only some parts of their carcasses. These partial skeletons of skeletally mature individuals might have been mixed with complete skeletons of skeletally immature (younger) individuals, thus significantly complicating the pattern. This might also explain the complete absence of mandibles belonging to 'elderly' individuals, further discussed later in the current section. One would argue that it is highly unlikely that only the fused proximal humeri, distal radii, proximal ulnae, proximal and distal femora and distal tibiae were transferred into the site thus significantly inflating the frequency of fused late fusing bones, but this does not need to be the case. What the fusion evidence probably highlights is that, although all body parts are present, this does not necessarily indicate that all animals were introduced whole to the site. Perhaps specific meat cuts were also imported, deriving from animals of different ages, therefore confusing the fusion pattern.

In view of the fact that the fusion data is not entirely clear, mandible wear data (Tables 5.81-5.82) assumes a particular importance as a complementary source of evidence. However, the sample size of age-able cattle mandibles is small (NISP: 18), probably as a result of cattle crania being detached from the rest of the carcass and being deposited elsewhere. In addition, the protocol decision of reconstructing the mortality profiles by using only the mandibles with at least two teeth with recordable wear in the dP_4 / $P_4 - M_3$ row, obviously affected the already small size of the sample. This is particularly true for the deposits of Phase III, from which, no cattle

Table 5.81 Mandible wear stages for *Bos taurus* (cattle). Only Phases I-II are considered. Phase III is excluded due to small sample size. NISP counts.

Bos taurus	Mandible wear stages					
	P_4	dP_4	M_1	M_2	M_3	MWS
Phase I				k	g	Adult
			k	j	e	Adult
			m	k	h	Adult
		k	f	H		Immature
			m	l	k	Adult
		j	H			Juvenile
			o	n		Sub adult
	f		k	k		Sub adult
			d	E	C	Sub adult
	f		k			Immature
			j	k		Sub adult
		n	g	g	H	Sub adult
			m	l		Sub adult
Phase II		j	f	H		Immature
	f		n			Immature
			f	H		Juvenile
			j	g		Sub adult
		k	f			Immature

Table 5.82 Summary of mandible wear stages for *Bos taurus* (cattle). Only Phases I-II are considered. Phase III is excluded due to small sample size. Data for Figure 5.19. NISP counts.

Bos taurus	Phases I-II		
	NISP	% Attribution	% Cumulative loss
Neonatal		0%	100%
Juvenile	2	11%	89%
Immature	5	28%	61%
Sub adult	7	39%	22%
Adult	4	22%	0%
Elderly		0%	0%
TOTAL	**18**	**100%**	

mandibles with more than one tooth with recordable wear were recovered. In order, therefore, to deal with the bias created by the small sample size, Phases I and II are of necessity treated together. Although the integration of the two phases does not entirely eliminate the aforementioned bias, we can still draw some basic conclusions:

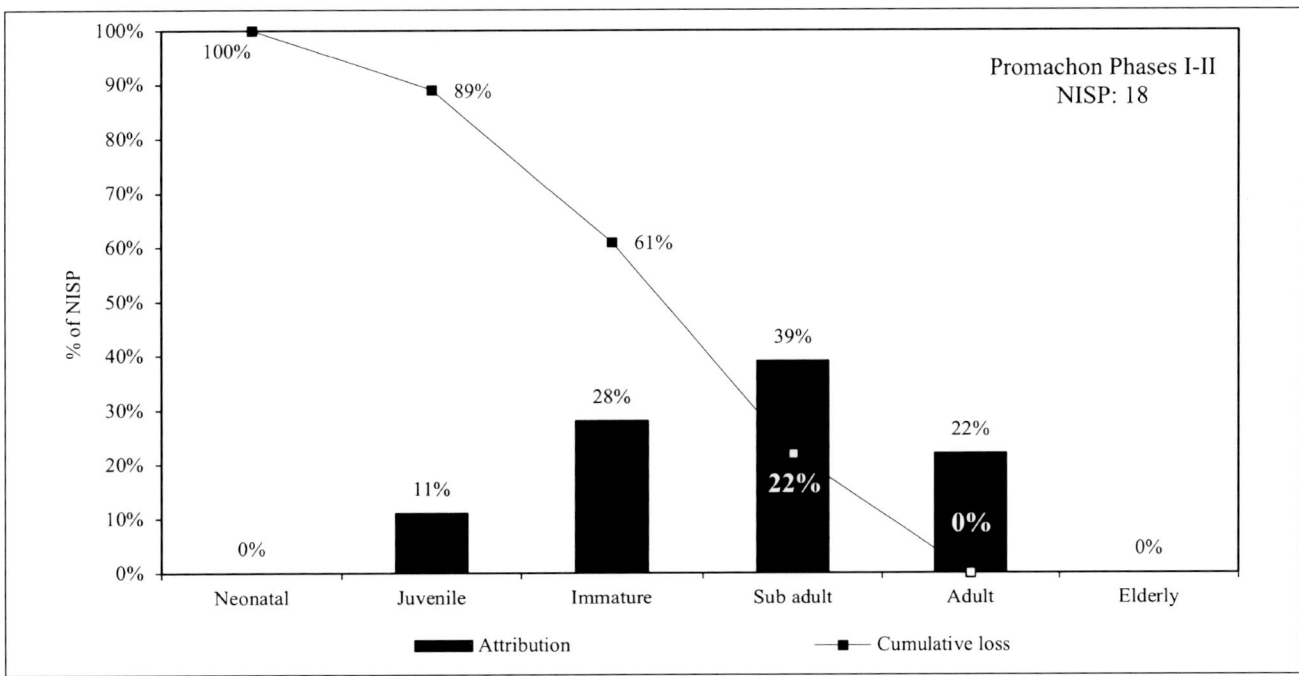

Figure 5.19 Mandible wear stages for *Bos taurus*. Only Phases I-II are considered. Data in Table 5.82. NISP counts.

The age-at-death profile of cattle (Figure 5.19) exhibits three mortality peaks: the first and most prominent at 'sub adult' stage (39 per cent), the second at 'immature' stage (28 per cent) and the third at 'adult' stage (22 per cent). About 11 per cent of the mandibles were also attributed to the 'juvenile' stage.

Of interest is the complete absence of 'neonatal' mandibles; this contrasts with the occurrence of a small number (NISP: 7) of neonatal postcranial remains (suggesting that some animals at least were reared on-site). Preservation will bias the neonatal (as well as the very juvenile) individuals, as the teeth are more likely to fall out of the mandibles. For this reason, cattle isolated teeth were also examined in order to see if there was any evidence of the very young individuals being biased against in the mandible data. Table 5.83 shows that a small number of unworn isolated mandibular first / second molars ($M_{1/2}$) are present, indicating that some mandibles of very young individuals were particularly affected by fragmentation factors.

The mortality profile of cattle indicates a considerable potential for the production of meat, with most animals being slaughtered when their maximum body weight had been reached. However, a diversified strategy for secondary products cannot be precluded, since the apparent frequency of juvenile and adult deaths is consistent with small-scale exploitation for milk (Halstead 1998; Payne 1973).

While the interpretation of Neolithic milk exploitation was initially challenged (*c.f.* Clutton-Brock 1981; Halstead 1998; McCormick 1992), it is now widely accepted due to mounting evidence for widespread dairy husbandry in this period (Evershed *et al.* 2008; Legge and Moore 2011).

This form of combined meat and milk husbandry is rather difficult to be identified by means of the slaughter pattern alone, without independent corroboration[2]. However, mortality profiles approximating to the 'meat model' are compatible with the exploitation of a mixture of products. Thus, the 'meat model' does not necessarily preclude the exploitation of cattle for milk, but rather implies that any such use was most likely of low intensity and limited in scale (Halstead and Isaakidou 2013).

As in the case of prehistoric milking, the use of cattle for labour during the late stage of the Neolithic has been subjected to many speculations (Bartosiewicz *et al.* 1997; Halstead 1995; Johanssen 2005). Pathological conditions (*e.g.* exostosis, lipping, osteoarthritis) in cattle limb joints (*c.f.* Baker and Brothwell 1980; Bartosiewicz *et al.* 1993; 1997) are considered strong evidence of heavy stress, such as that involved in pulling an ard or a plough (Halstead 1998). However, we should also keep in mind that the osteological effects of the use of cattle for traction may be hard to disentangle from other factors such as, the nature of the terrain that cattle lived and, in particular, old age (Baker and Brothwell 1980; Halstead 1998; Johanssen 2005). In any case, no cattle bones with pathological conditions were recorded from Promachon.

Returning to the kill-off pattern highlighted in Figure 5.19, of particular interest is the absence of mandibles belonging to 'elderly' individuals. This is consistent with previous suggestions that some of the skeletally mature (older) cattle might have been killed off-site, and that

---

[2] The likelihood of cattle management for milking would be increased by the discovery of milk residues in ceramics, but such analyses have not as yet been carried out in Promachon-Topolniča.

Table 5.83 *Bos taurus* (cattle) eruption stage and wear stage data from mandibular isolated teeth and teeth attached to mandibles. C= Crypt, V= Visible, E= Erupting, H= Half erupted. Teeth recorded in wear stage "a" are considered fully erupted, yet still unworn (U). NISP counts.

Individual mandibular teeth (attached & loose)

Bos taurus	Phases	C	V	E	H	a	b	c	d	e	f	g	h	i	j	k	l	m	n	o	p
dP4	Phase I						1		1				1		1	3		1	1		
dP4	Phase II										3		3	1	1		1				
dP4	Phase III								2		1					1					
dP4	**TOTAL**	0	0	0	0	0	1	0	3	0	4	0	4	0	2	4	1	2	1	0	0
P4	Phase I							1			4										
P4	Phase II			1	1				1		1		1								
P4	Phase III										5										
P4	**TOTAL**	0	0	1	1	0	0	1	1	0	10	0	1	0	0	0	0	0	0	0	0
M1	Phase I				3				1		2	1			1	4		3		1	
M1	Phase II				1		1			1	2				1	1			1		
M1	Phase III			2									1			1					
M1	**TOTAL**	0	0	2	4	0	1	0	1	1	4	1	1	0	2	6	0	3	1	1	0
M2	Phase I			1	2							2			1	5	2		1		
M2	Phase II				1							1					1				
M2	Phase III																				
M2	**TOTAL**	0	0	1	3	0	0	0	0	0	0	3	0	0	1	5	3	0	1	0	0
M1/2	Phase I					2	4	4	1	1	5	6	2		1	10	1		2		
M1/2	Phase II					1	3	2	4	1	3	11	2		3	10	2	1		2	
M1/2	Phase III						1	2			2	8	4			7					
M1/2	**TOTAL**	0	0	0	0	3	8	8	5	2	10	25	8	0	4	27	3	1	2	2	0
M3	Phase I	1		1	1	1					1	9	2			3		1			
M3	Phase II	1						1	2	2	2	5	2		1	3	3				
M3	Phase III							1			2	1	1		1	2					
M3	**TOTAL**	2	0	1	1	1	0	2	2	2	5	15	5	0	2	8	3	1	0	0	0

only some parts of their carcasses were introduced at the settlement. It is quite possible, therefore, that the absence of 'elderly' individuals in the observed kill-off pattern is the result of a selectivity of body parts brought on-site. Metrical examination on cattle horncores is too sparse to provide any information on the sexual composition of the cattle population at Promachon. However, we can assume that some of these 'elderly' individuals, which were killed off-site, were females used for breeding.

All in all, the evidence suggests that cattle in Promachon were used primarily for their meat. On the other hand, only tentative considerations can be made regarding the use of cattle for secondary products (milk and labour).

5.7.2 Caprinae age-at-death

Compared to sheep postcranial bones (NISP: 349), the sample size of goat postcranial bones is very small (NISP: 64), and therefore insufficient for independent ageing analysis. To increase sample size, sheep and goat postcranial bones as well as the three phases of occupation have been combined for this analysis. Figure 5.20 (Table 5.84) presents the frequency of the fused early, middle and late fusing caprine postcranial bones. Epiphyseal fusion evidence for caprines shows that 79 per cent of the early fusing bones (3-18 months) were fused. The frequency of fused middle fusing bones (18-36 months) drops to 77 per cent, while in the late fusing stage (older than 36 months),

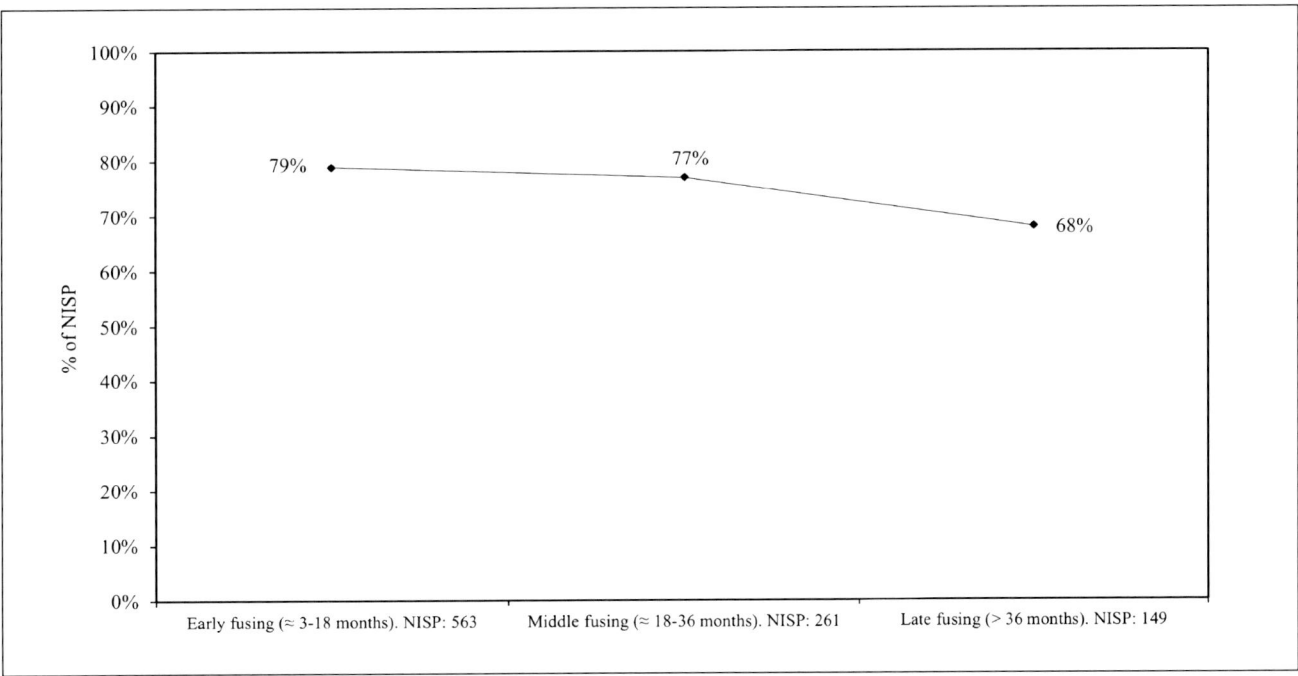

Figure 5.20 Epiphyseal fusion data for Caprinae. All phases are considered. Data in Table 5.84. NISP counts.

68 per cent of bones were fused. The fusion data indicates that a significant number of caprines survived to skeletal maturity, and that only a limited amount of slaughter occurred between the time the earliest and the latest fusing epiphyses fused. However, we need to look at the dental evidence too in order to draw a more accurate picture of the caprine kill-off pattern.

Tooth wear stages were analysed using the categories of Payne (1973; 1987) and the raw data are presented in Tables 5.85-5.87. Figure 5.21 (Table 5.88) present the percentage of attribution of mandible wear stages for caprines (sheep/goat, sheep and goat), considering all three phases. One of the main issues of the ageing analysis is whether the fusion evidence could be combined with the data obtained from the mandible wear stages. In the case of cattle, we were unable to look into detail whether there is a real consistency between the two methods, since a rather unusual pattern was observed between the fused middle and late fusing bones. Since such an unusual pattern does not apply for caprines, we can explore the issue of the compatibility of the two methods in the case of the caprine population. For instance, as previously noted, fusion data indicate that 68 per cent of the late fusing caprine bones were fused, thus suggesting that the bulk of the caprine population survived beyond their third year. On the other hand, mandible wear data indicate that almost 61 per cent of the caprine population survived beyond the third year [mandible wear stages F to I *sensu* Payne (1973); roughly equivalent to 3-10 years]. The fusion data is therefore consistent with the mandible wear data since the two methods present roughly the same frequencies with regard to the part of the caprine population that survived beyond the third year.

In more detail, the mandible wear data for caprines exhibit an almost even distribution of wear stages, though the

greatest amount of slaughtering (almost 60 per cent of the population) occurred between stages E and G (2-6 years). In overall therefore, the combined evidence of fusion and wear data is suggestive of the fact that caprines in Promachon were used for both primary (meat) and secondary (milk?) products. The culling of caprines between the age of six months and three years reflects an exploitation strategy particularly tuned towards the production of meat (Payne 1973). The mortality peak in stage E (2-3 years; 17 per cent) indicates a decision of an increase in profitability of the meat (Helmer *et al.* 2007), since a number of caprines were slaughtered when they reached their maximum body sizes. However, part of the caprine population was slaughtered before they reached the optimum body size, as indicated by the 22 per cent of animals represented in stages B to D. According to Helmer *et al.* (2007) and Vigne and Helmer (2007) a mortality peak between the first and second year suggests that a number of caprines might had been culled when the tender meat was at maximum weight.

High infant mortality – characteristic of dairying exploitation (Payne 1973) – is likely to be obscured by taphonomic processes (Isaakidou 2006; Munson and Garniewisz 2003). As in the case of cattle, caprine loose teeth were examined to see if there was any evidence of very young individuals being biased against in the mandible data (Table 5.89). Since this did not appear to be the case, we can assume that the observed pattern indicates a 'genuine' dearth of very young individuals (wear stages A and B; 0-2 and 2-6 months respectively; one per cent in total).

One would argue that the scarcity of very young caprines in Promachon does not conform to Payne's (1973) idealized model of dairy husbandry. Halstead (1998), however, argues

Table 5.84 Epiphyseal fusion data for Caprinae (caprines). Caprinae subfamily includes *Ovis/Capra* (sheep/goat), *Ovis aries* (sheep) and *Capra hircus* (goat). Fused (F) column includes fused, fusing and fusing/fused specimens. Unfused (UD) column includes unfused diaphyses. Unfused epiphyses are not counted. Data for Figure 5.20. NISP counts.

| Caprinae | | Late Neolithic I | | | | | | | | | | Late Neolithic II | | | | | TOTAL | | | | |
| | | Phase I | | | | | Phase II | | | | | Phase III | | | | | | | | | |
		NISP	F	%	UD	%	NISP	F	%	UD	%	NISP	F	%	UD	%	NISP	F	%	UD	%
Early Fusing	Scapula	21	12	57%	9	43%	27	19	70%	8	30%	6	5	83%	1	17%	54	36	67%	18	33%
	Humerus distal	72	50	69%	22	31%	52	43	83%	9	17%	47	35	74%	12	26%	171	128	75%	43	25%
	Radius proximal	43	39	91%	4	9%	46	43	93%	3	7%	30	27	90%	3	10%	119	109	92%	10	8%
	Pelvis acetabulum	61	47	77%	14	23%	70	52	74%	18	26%	36	28	78%	8	22%	167	127	76%	40	24%
	Phalanx 1	10	9	90%	1	10%	20	17	85%	3	15%	13	12	92%	1	8%	43	38	88%	5	12%
	Phalanx 2			0%		0%	4	4	100%		0%	5	5	100%		0%	9	9	100%	0	0%
	TOTAL	207	157	76%	50	24%	219	178	81%	41	19%	137	112	82%	25	18%	563	447	79%	116	21%
Middle Fusing	Metacarpal distal	5	3	60%	2	40%	10	4	40%	6	60%	8	6	75%	2	25%	23	13	57%	10	43%
	Tibia distal	57	51	89%	6	11%	65	59	91%	6	9%	45	44	98%	1	2%	167	154	92%	13	8%
	Calcaneum	15	9	60%	6	40%	26	11	42%	15	58%	10	5	50%	5	50%	51	25	49%	26	51%
	Metatarsal distal	7	4	57%	3	43%	8	4	50%	4	50%	5	4	80%	1	20%	20	12	60%	8	40%
	TOTAL	84	67	80%	17	20%	109	78	72%	31	28%	68	59	87%	9	13%	261	204	77%	57	23%
Late Fusing	Humerus proximal	6	5	83%	1	17%	3	2	67%	1	33%	2	1	50%	1	50%	11	8	73%	3	27%
	Radius distal	9	8	89%	1	11%	15	12	80%	3	20%	6	4	67%	2	33%	30	24	80%	6	20%
	Ulna proximal	23	12	52%	11	48%	20	9	45%	11	55%	18	9	50%	9	50%	61	30	49%	31	51%
	Femur proximal	8	7	88%	1	12%	9	8	89%	1	11%	2	2	100%		0%	19	17	89%	2	11%
	Femur distal	5	5	100%		0%	4	4	100%		0%	2	2	100%		0%	11	11	100%	0	0%
	Tibia proximal	6	5	83%	1	17%	7	5	71%	2	29%	4	2	50%	2	50%	17	12	71%	5	29%
	TOTAL	57	42	74%	15	26%	58	40	69%	18	31%	34	20	59%	14	41%	149	102	68%	47	32%
TOTAL		348	266	76%	82	24%	386	296	77%	90	23%	239	191	80%	48	20%	973	753	77%	220	23%

Table 5.85 Mandible wear stages for Caprinae (caprines) for Phase I. NISP counts.

Phase I		P₄	dP₄	M₁	M₂	M₃	MWS

	P₄	dP₄	M₁	M₂	M₃	MWS
Ovis/Capra				15A	17G	I
	P		15A	15A	17G	I
		23L	9A	8A		D
			15A	10A	12G	I
			10A	9A	6G	E
			4A	5A		C
				5A	E	C
		16L	7A	C		C
	12S		10A	9A		F
	H		9A	7A		C
			14A	9A		F
	P		9A	9A	P	D-E
			12A	9A		F
	15A		15A			G-H
			15A	15A	14G	I
			15A	12A	11G	H
				9A	8G	E
				12A	12G	I
			9A	9A		D-E
			15A	15A		G-H
Ovis aries	H		9A	9A	V	D
			15A	11A	11G	H
	0		9A	8A		D
				13A	11G	H
	12S		14A	9A	11G	G
		16L	7A	7A		C
	15A		15A	14A	11G	H
	15A		15A	15A	13G	I
	9A		9A	9A		D-E
	15A			15A	12A	I
	15A		15A	15A	17G	I
	12S		15A	9A		F-G
		16L	7A			C
	15A		15A			G-H
	H		9A	6A		C-D
	12S		15A	9A		F-G

	P₄	dP₄	M₁	M₂	M₃	MWS
Ovis aries (cont.)	12S		15A	9A	11G	G
	12S		15A	11A		F-G
	15A		15A	P		G-H
	0		14A	9A		F
	8A		9A	9A		E
		16L	7A			C
			15A	15A	12G	I
				10A	11G	H
	12S		12A	9A	11G	G
			11A	9A	7G	E
			15A	9A	9A	F
			9A	9A	6A	E
	15A		15A			G-H
	12S		15A	10A	11G	H
	15A		15A	11A		G-H
	12S		12A			F-G
		16L	H			C-D
	12S		10A			F-G
		16L	6A	C		C
	9A		9A	9A	9G	F
	H		9A	5A		C-D
Capra hircus			15A	15A	17G	I
	12S		12A	9A		F
	12S		15A	9A	11G	G
	12S		12A			F-G
	12S		12A	9A	8G	E
	15A		15A	9A		G
				10A	12G	I
	12S		15A		11G	G
	12S		10A	9A	5A	E
	12S		15A	10A	11G	H
	8A		9A	8A		D-E
	12S		12A	10A	11G	H
			9A	9A	8A	E
	12S		10A	9A	12G	I

Table 5.86 Mandible wear stages for Caprinae (caprines) for Phase II. NISP counts.

Phase II						
	P$_4$	dP$_4$	M$_1$	M$_2$	M$_3$	MWS
Ovis/Capra			15A	15A	12G	I
				11A	11G	H
				9A	10G	F
			15A	15A	16G	I
			12A	9A	6G	E
	H		9A	9A		D-E
			H	E		B
				9A	7G	E
			15A	15A	17G	I
	15A		15A	15A	P	G-H
Ovis aries	12S		11A			F
	P		9A	8A		D
	7A		9A	9A	7G	E
	12S		10A	9A	10G	F
	15A		15A			G
	4A		9A	9A	6G	E
		22L	8A			D
	12S		15A			G
	15A		15A			G
		20L	9A			D
	12S		12A	9A	5A	E
	12S		10A			F-G
		16L	5A	C		C

	P$_4$	dP$_4$	M$_1$	M$_2$	M$_3$	MWS
Ovis aries (cont.)	15A		15A			G
		18L	8A			D
			9A	8A	C	D
	15A		15A	15A	12G	I
	12S		13A	9A		E-F
	H		10A	9A		F
		14L	C			C
	15A		15A		11G	G
	12S		11A	9A	11G	G
		23L	9A			D
	12S		9A	9A	10G	F
		20L	5A			C
	12S		15A			G
	15A		15A	13A		F
	15A		15A	13A	12G	I
	12S		15A	10A		G
		23L	9A	6A		D
Capra hircus	C		9A	6A		D-E
	9A			9A	5A	E
	12S		12A	9A	9G	F
	12S		10A	9A		F
	12S		P	P	4A	E

that the culling of lambs and kids (two to three months old or less) is characteristic of a specialized economy seeking a surplus production intended for trade and commerce. On the other hand, herders with a mixed economy and a small number of animals not seeking to maximise but to produce a consistent return, extend the culling age up to six months (*cf.* Rowley-Conwy 2000). The latter model is more appropriate to Promachon, where during the Late Neolithic about 11 per cent of the caprine population was slaughtered before the first year (wear stages A, B and C). It is therefore probable that the management of the caprine population at Promachon included – in addition to the exploitation of meat – a small-scale exploitation of milk. As in the case of cattle, the exploitation of caprines for dairy products should be corroborated by other lines of evidence such as traces of milk residues and lipids in ceramics. However, as previously noted, such analyses have not as yet been carried out at Promachon.

The apparent frequency of older individuals (wear stages G, H and I; 4-10 years; 45 per cent in total) indicates that a number of (probably) female caprines were used for breeding, and also milk. One would argue however, that the high frequency of old individuals, combined with the presence of loom weights, clay spindle whorls and bone needles, which were found in the Late Neolithic deposits of Promachon (Koukouli-Chrysanthaki *et al.* 2007), might indicate that other secondary products – besides milk – were used, the most likely of which would have been fleece[3]. However, spindle whorls, loom weights and bone needles do not necessarily indicate the use of animal fibres, as implied by Bailey (2000). Woven flax is well known to have been used in the Near East as early as the

---

[3] The term fleece is intended in its larger sense, whatever the nature of animal fibres.

Table 5.87 Mandible wear stages for Caprinae (caprines) for Phase III. NISP counts.

Phase III		P₄	dP₄	M₁	M₂	M₃	MWS
Ovis/Capra				8A	9A	5A	E
					9A	5A	E
				10A	8A		C-D
		15A		15A			G
Ovis aries		15A		15A			G
		12S		10A	9A	8G	E
		12S		15A	11A	11G	G
				15A	10A	12G	I
			16L	6A			C
			23L	9A	7A		E
		12S		14A			F
		15A		15A	15A	12G	I
		12S		14A	10A	11G	H
		12S		15A	10A	12G	I
		15A		15A			G
Capra hircus		9A		11A	9A	4A	E
		12S		10A			F-G
		9A		P	9A		E-F
		12S			10A		F-G
		15A		15A			G

Table 5.88 Summary of mandible wear stages for Caprinae (caprines). Caprinae subfamily includes *Ovis/Capra* (sheep/goat), *Ovis aries* (sheep) and *Capra hircus* (goat). All phases are considered. Data for Figure 5.21. NISP counts.

Caprinae	Promachon I-II-III		
	NISP	% Attribution	% Cumulative loss
A (0-2 months)		0%	100%
B (2-6 months)	1	1%	99%
C (6-12 months)	14	10%	89%
D (1-2 years)	15	11%	78%
E (2-3 years)	24	17%	61%
F (3-4 years)	21.5	16%	45%
G (4-6 years)	27	20%	25%
H (6-8 years)	13.5	10%	15%
I (8-10 years)	20	15%	0%
TOTAL	**136**	**100%**	

eighth millennium BC (Perlès 2001), while in the Balkan Peninsula the use of the same organic material has been reported in Late Neolithic deposits of the Vinča culture in Serbia (Borojević 2006). In any case, the appearance of fine hairs – characteristic of wool – result from a long-term process of selection for particular reproductive traits (Halstead 1998), which do not seem to have occurred until the Bronze Age (*cf.* Helmer *et al.* 2007; Perlès 2001; Ryder 1969; 1982; 1993).

The preceding analysis took into consideration the information provided by the wear data of all caprine (sheep,

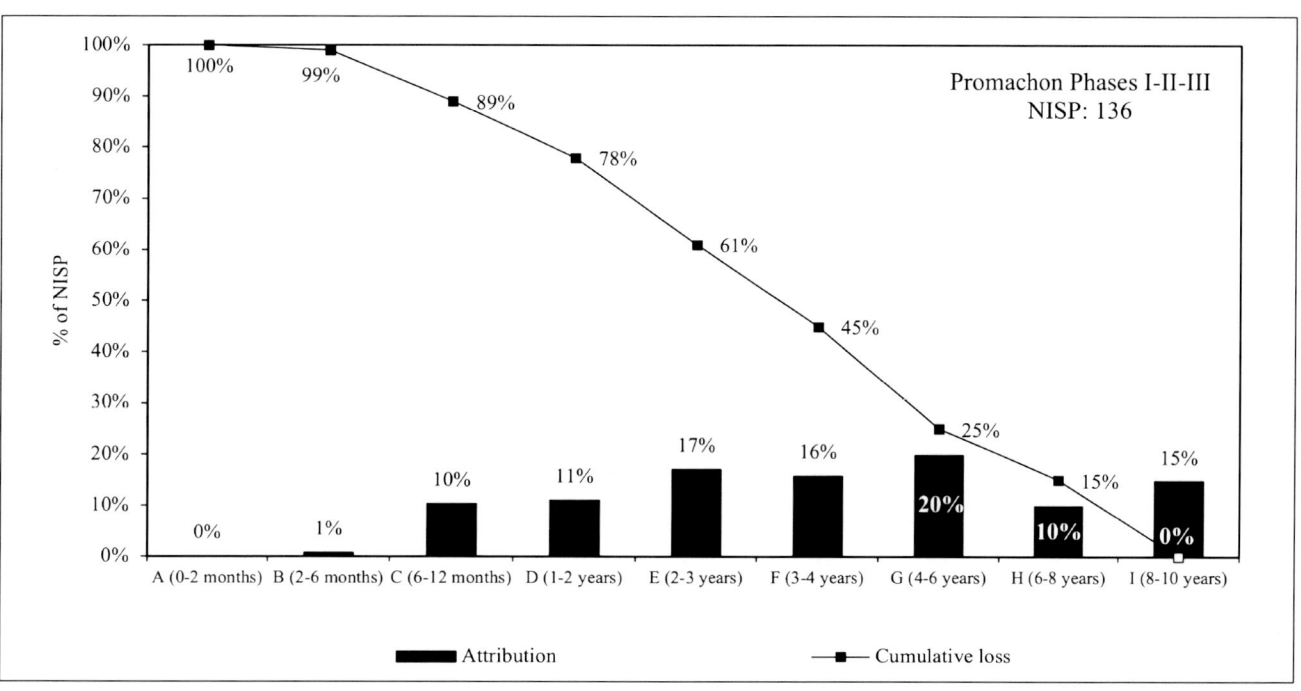

Figure 5.21 Mandible wear stages for Caprinae. All phases are considered. Data in Table 5.88. NISP counts.

Table 5.89 Caprinae (caprines) eruption stage and wear stage data from mandibular isolated teeth and teeth attached to mandibles. Caprinae subfamily includes *Ovis/Capra* (sheep/goat), *Ovis aries* (sheep) and *Capra hircus* (goat). C= Crypt, V= Visible, E= Erupting, H= Half erupted. NISP counts.

Individual mandibular teeth (attached & loose)

Caprinae	Phases	C	V	E	H	0	1	2	3	4	5	6	7	8	9	10	11	12	13	14	15	16	17	18	19	20	21	22	23
dP4	Phase I																		1	2		9	4	3					
	Phase II																			7		6	3	2		2		1	3
	Phase III																		1	1		8	3						1
	TOTAL	0	0	0	0	0	0	0	0	0	0	0	0	0	0	0	0	0	3	10	0	23	10	5	0	2	0	1	4
P4	Phase I			2	4	3		1					3	1	5			21			11								
	Phase II	1		2	2	5		1		1	1		2	1	6			28			15								
	Phase III			2				1		1	2				4			17			6								
	TOTAL	1	0	6	6	8	0	3	0	2	3	0	5	2	15	0	0	66	0	0	32	0	0	0	0	0	0	0	0
M1	Phase I	3		1	4							1	2	1	13	5	1	4	1	2	23								
	Phase II	1			1						2	1		2	12	4	2	3		1	14								
	Phase III					1						1		1	2	3	1			2	6								
	TOTAL	4	0	1	5	1	0	0	0	0	2	3	2	4	27	12	4	7	1	5	43	0	0	0	0	0	0	0	0
M2	Phase I	3									3	2	1	2	22	6	1	2	1	1	5								
	Phase II	1		1	2							2	2	2	17	2	2		2		5								
	Phase III													1	5	4	1				2								
	TOTAL	4	0	1	2	0	0	0	0	0	3	4	3	5	44	12	4	2	3	1	12	0	0	0	0	0	0	0	0
M1/2	Phase I									1	2	6	2	3	17	5	3	2			5								
	Phase II					2		2		2	5	7	15	10	62	12	3	5			4	1							
	Phase III					2		4		3	6	4	2	12	43	13	1			1	6								
	TOTAL	0	0	0	0	4	0	6	0	6	13	17	19	25	122	30	7	7	0	1	15	1	0	0	0	0	0	0	0
M3	Phase I									1	3	4		1	2	1	25	9	2	1		3	4						
	Phase II	1		1		5		5		1	4	3	3	2	3	2	22	6	2			1	1						
	Phase III					1		2		1	3	2	2	1	2	2	30	5		1		1	1						
	TOTAL	1	0	1	0	6	0	7	0	3	10	9	5	4	7	5	77	20	4	2	0	5	6	0	0	0	0	0	0

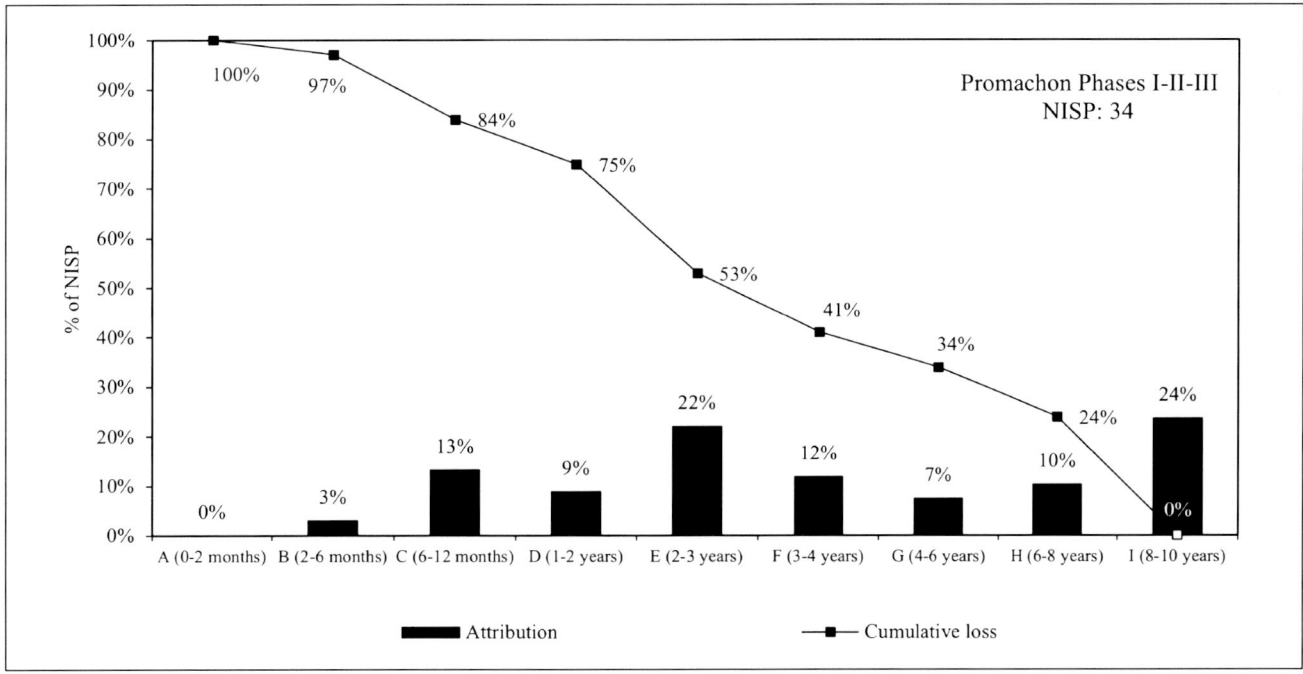

Figure 5.22 Mandible wear stages for *Ovis/Capra*. All phases are considered. Data in Table 5.90. NISP counts.

goat and sheep/goat) mandibles. However, in order to find whether the two closely related species were subject to different exploitation strategies, we have to look at the wear data from the mandibles of sheep/goat, sheep and goat respectively.

Figure 5.22 (Table 5.90), presents the percentage of attribution of wear stages only for the mandibles that were identified to the level of sheep/goat. The wear data for sheep/goat function as a control sample. We can see two mortality peaks: the first at stage E (2-3 years; 22 per cent) and the second, more prominent, at stage I (8-10 years; 24 per cent). About 16 per cent of the mandibles were attributed to wear stages B and C (2-6 months and 6-12 months respectively) indicating that a number of individuals were killed before the first year. This confirms previous claims that both species were utilized for both primary (meat) and secondary products (milk).

Figure 5.23 (Table 5.91) indicates that 41 per cent of sheep were killed-off between the first and the fourth year (wear stages D, E, F). This suggests that these animals were slaughtered for meat. About 47 per cent of the sheep population were killed-off between their fourth and tenth year (wear stages G, H, I). Of these, about 24 per cent were killed between the age of four and six (wear stage G). We can therefore assume that sheep – probably female individuals – were kept until they had lambed at least once, and hence produced milk and offspring.

Harvest profiles for goat (Figure 5.24; Table 5.92) suggest that animals less than two years old (wear stages A to D), account for less than four per cent of the mortality profile. The dearth of very young individuals (wear stages A, B and C; 0-2 months, 2-6 months and 6-12 months respectively) indicates that goats in Promachon were not particularly

Table 5.90 Summary of mandible wear stages for *Ovis/Capra* (sheep/goat). All phases are considered. Data for Figure 5.22. NISP counts.

Ovis/Capra	Promachon I-II-III		
	NISP	% Attribution	% Cumulative loss
A (0-2 months)		0%	100%
B (2-6 months)	1	3%	97%
C (6-12 months)	4.5	13%	84%
D (1-2 years)	3	9%	75%
E (2-3 years)	7.5	22%	53%
F (3-4 years)	4	12%	41%
G (4-6 years)	2.5	7%	34%
H (6-8 years)	3.5	10%	24%
I (8-10 years)	8	24%	0%
TOTAL	**34**	**100%**	

exploited for milk. This may be surprising considering that goats are known to be more prolific milk yielders than sheep (Halstead 1998; Ryder 1982). About 33 per cent of the goat population were killed-off at stage E (2-3 years), while 45 per cent were killed-off at stages F and G (3-4 years and 4-6 years respectively) suggesting that goats in Promachon were killed primarily for their meat. However, the apparent frequency of older individuals (wear stages H and I; 9 per cent respectively) indicates that some goats might have been kept until the end of their lives for breeding.

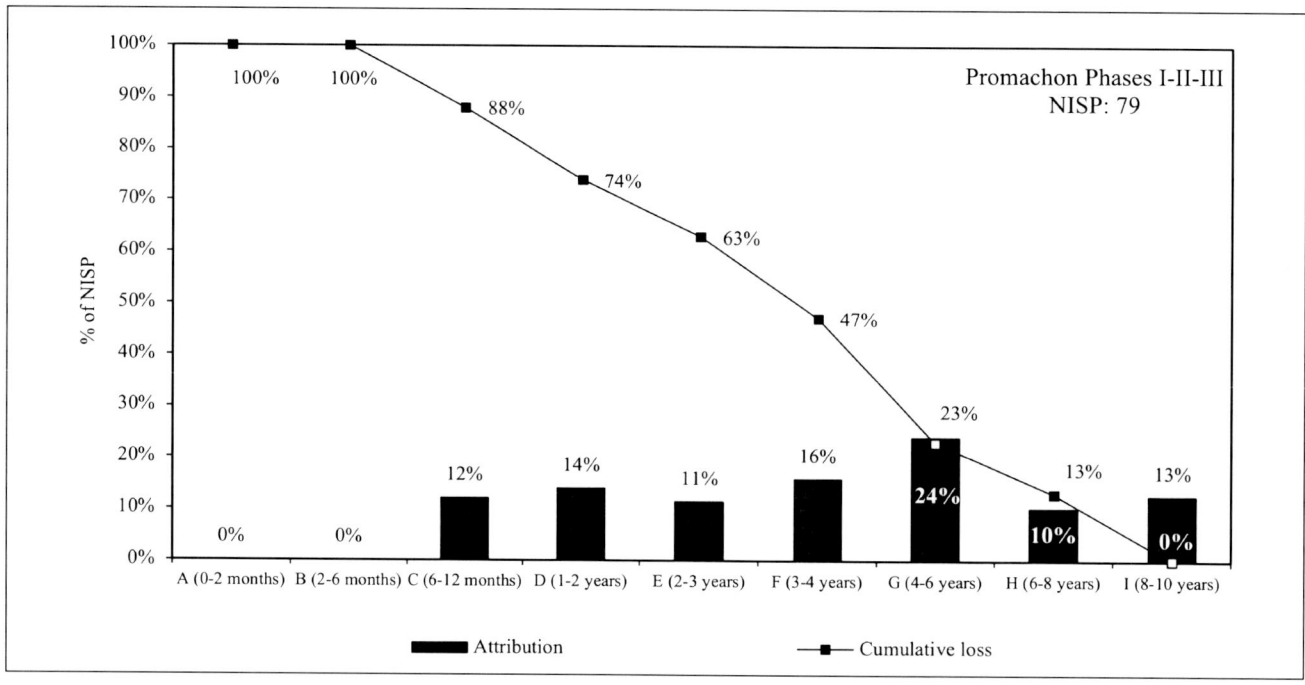

Figure 5.23 Mandible wear stages for *Ovis aries*. All phases are considered. Data in Table 5.91. NISP counts.

All in all, mortality profiles from Promachon indicate that caprines were used for meat. With regard to the presence of secondary products, it is more likely that the use of caprines included a small-scale exploitation for milk, rather than fleece. Sheep were subject to different exploitation strategies than goats. The evidence seems to suggest that sheep were used for meat and milk, while goats were used mainly for meat. In addition, a number of individuals from both species might have been kept until the end of their lives for breeding.

5.7.3 Sus *age-at-death*

Epiphyseal fusion data (Table 5.93) indicate that pigs were slaughtered before they reached their skeletal maturity. Figure 5.25 shows that 65 per cent of the early fusing (1 – 2 years) postcranial bones were fused. The frequency of fused bones in the middle fusing category (2 – 2½ years) drops to 56 per cent, while in the late fusing category (3 – 3½ years) only 21 per cent of the postcranial bones were fused. The data indicate that a substantial number of pigs

Table 5.91 Summary of mandible wear stages for *Ovis aries* (sheep). All phases are considered. Data for Figure 5.23. NISP counts.

Ovis aries	Promachon I-II-III		
	NISP	% Attribution	% Cumulative loss
A (0-2 months)		0%	100%
B (2-6 months)		0%	100%
C (6-12 months)	9.5	12%	88%
D (1-2 years)	11	14%	74%
E (2-3 years)	9	11%	63%
F (3-4 years)	12.5	16%	47%
G (4-6 years)	19	24%	23%
H (6-8 years)	8	10%	13%
I (8-10 years)	10	13%	0%
TOTAL	**79**	**100%**	

Table 5.92 Summary of mandible wear stages for *Capra hircus* (goat). All phases are considered. Data for Figure 5.24. NISP counts.

Capra hircus	Promachon I-II-III		
	NISP	% Attribution	% Cumulative loss
A (0-2 months)		0%	100%
B (2-6 months)		0%	100%
C (6-12 months)		0%	100%
D (1-2 years)	1	4%	96%
E (2-3 years)	7.5	33%	63%
F (3-4 years)	5	22%	41%
G (4-6 years)	5.5	23%	18%
H (6-8 years)	2	9%	9%
I (8-10 years)	2	9%	0%
TOTAL	**23**	**100%**	

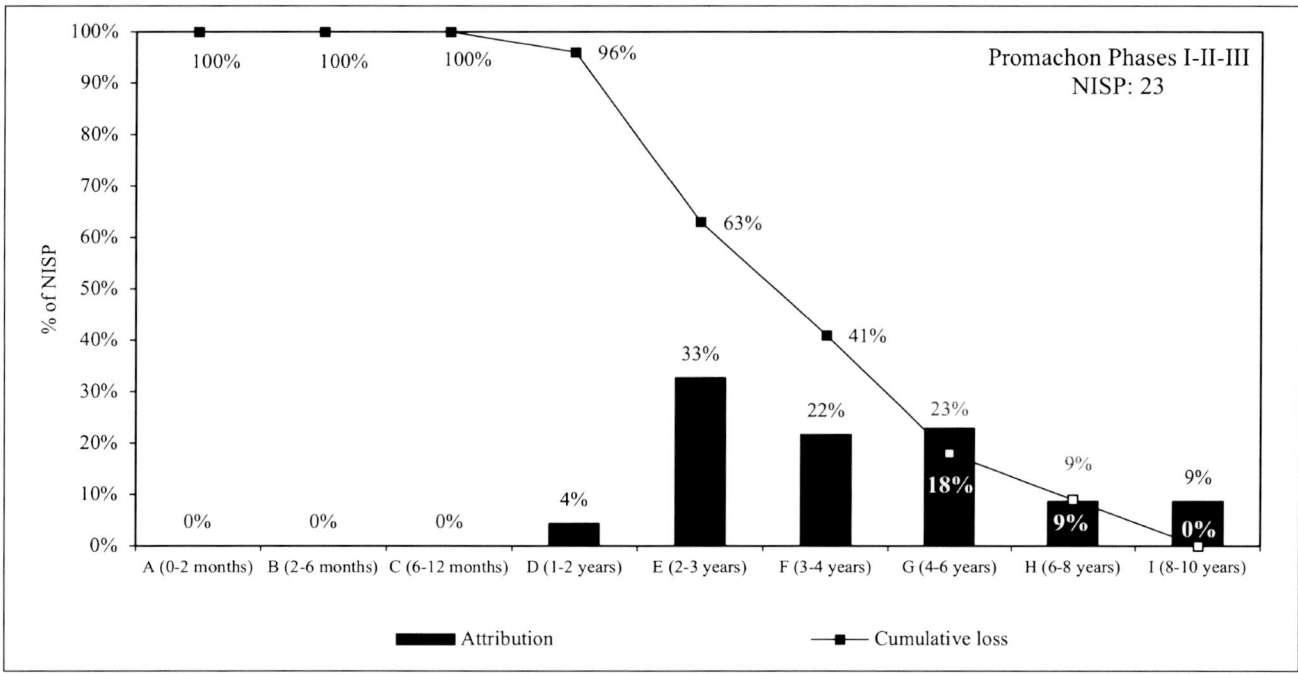

Figure 5.24 Mandible wear stages for *Capra hircus*. All phases are considered. Data in Table 5.92. NISP counts.

were killed during the first and second year and that the majority of the pig population did not survive their third year. The presence of a few neonatal postcranial bones (NISP: 5) shows that breeding of pigs may have taken place on-site, as these are most likely to be new born casualties.

Estimates of age-at-death, based on tooth wear, are probably subject to greater bias in pigs than in the case of ruminants, since the degree to which the former dig for food (a major source of dental attrition) is highly variable (Halstead and Isaakidou 2013). However, the striking similarity in the data between epiphyseal fusion and tooth wear (Tables 5.93-5.96), suggests that the observed trend is probably valid. Dental eruption and wear data for pigs reveal two mortality peaks (Figure 5.26): the first and most prominent at 'immature' stage (44 per cent) and the second at 'sub adult' stage (41 per cent). About 11 per cent of individuals were killed at 'juvenile' stage, while only 4 per cent of the individuals survived into the 'adult' stage.

All in all, mortality profiles for pigs in Promachon indicate that these animals were used for their meat. In addition, some of adult and sub adult individuals (females) might have been used for breeding. However, estimates on the sexual composition of the pig population in Promachon will be provided in the next part of this analysis.

5.8 Sexing

It was only possible to separate the sexes using morphological characteristics in pigs. For other taxa, any attempts to detect the sexual composition of the assemblage had to rely on metrical analysis, which will be presented later in this study. Pig isolated canines, as

well as those in jaws and their alveoli, were used for the analysis. Figure 5.27 (Table 5.97) presents the frequency of each sex category in the assemblage. When only isolated canines are considered, males and females are represented with similar frequencies, females being only slightly more frequent than males (45 per cent for males and 55 per cent for females). The ratio between male and female pigs in this case is 1 : 1.3. However, since the smaller isolated female canines may be biased against due to differential retrieval, the frequency is also calculated for canines in jaws and their alveoli, as these should only be negligibly affected by a recovery bias. The pattern shows that females predominate with a much higher frequency, which is probably closer to reality: 73 per cent of the sexed canines attached to jaws and their respective alveoli derive from females, while 27 per cent derive from males. The ratio between male and female pigs in this case is 1 : 2.6.

The higher frequency of female pig canines probably reflects the practice of keeping more mature female pigs for breeding. If this is the case, then we must assume that a high number of pigs, which were culled at a young age for their meat – as previously suggested – were mainly males. It is also highly likely that the very young animals, which could not be sexed due to the non-diagnostic shape of the deciduous canine, were also predominately males. The occurrence of a substantial proportion of older females confirms the evidence of neonatal bones that at Promachon there was an emphasis on pork production and the pigs were not merely imported from elsewhere.

Information on the sexual composition of pig populations from a number of contemporary settlements in Greek Macedonia is rather scarce, yet consistent with that from Promachon. For instance, in the Late Neolithic settlements

Table 5.93 Epiphyseal fusion data for *Sus* (pig). Fused (F) column includes fused, fusing and fusing/fused specimens. Unfused (UD) column includes unfused diaphyses. Unfused epiphyses are not counted. Data for Figure 5.25. NISP counts.

Sus	Late Neolithic I										Late Neolithic II					TOTAL				
	Phase I					Phase II					Phase III									
	NISP	F	%	UD	%	NISP	F	%	UD	%	NISP	F	%	UD	%	NISP	F	%	UD	%
Early Fusing																				
Scapula	30	18	60%	12	40%	34	25	74%	9	26%	12	7	58%	5	42%	76	50	66%	26	34%
Humerus distal	23	7	30%	16	70%	21	11	52%	10	48%	7	2	29%	5	71%	51	20	39%	31	61%
Radius proximal	17	15	88%	2	12%	12	9	75%	3	25%	8	8	100%		0%	37	32	86%	5	14%
Pelvis acetabulum	21	15	71%	6	29%	18	13	72%	5	28%	14	7	50%	7	50%	53	35	66%	18	34%
Phalanx 1	11	9	82%	2	8%	8	6	75%	2	25%	9	6	67%	3	33%	28	21	75%	7	25%
Phalanx 2						3	2	67%	1	33%	7	6	86%	1	14%	10	8	80%	2	20%
TOTAL	102	64	63%	38	37%	96	66	69%	30	31%	57	36	63%	21	37%	255	166	65%	89	35%
Middle Fusing																				
Metacarpal 3 distal	5	2	40%	3	60%	4	4	100%		0%	1	1	100%		0%	10	7	70%	3	30%
Metacarpal 4 distal	7	4	57%	3	43%	5	5	100%		0%	7	4	57%	3	43%	19	13	68%	6	32%
Tibia distal	12	8	67%	4	33%	14	8	57%	6	43%	11	8	73%	3	27%	37	24	65%	13	35%
Calcaneum	11	4	36%	7	64%	14	8	57%	6	43%	8		0%	8	100%	33	12	36%	21	64%
Metatarsal 3 distal	3	2	67%	1	33%	7	5	71%	2	29%	2	2	100%		0%	12	9	75%	3	25%
Metatarsal 4 distal	4	1	25%	3	75%	5	3	60%	2	40%	3		0%	3	100%	12	4	33%	8	67%
TOTAL	42	21	50%	21	50%	49	33	67%	16	33%	32	15	47%	17	53%	123	69	56%	54	44%
Late Fusing																				
Humerus proximal	2		0%	2	100%	3		0%	3	100%	3		0%	3	100%	8		0%	8	100%
Radius distal	14	1	7%	13	93%	15	6	40%	9	60%	3		0%	3	100%	32	7	22%	25	78%
Ulna proximal	30	8	27%	22	73%	20	6	30%	14	70%	14	4	29%	10	81%	64	18	28%	46	72%
Femur proximal	1		0%	1	100%	2	1	50%	1	50%						3	1	33%	2	67%
Femur distal	5		0%	5	100%	10	2	20%	8	80%	4		0%	4	100%	19	2	11%	17	89%
Tibia proximal	3		0%	3	100%	1		0%	1	100%	1		0%	1	100%	5		0%	5	100%
TOTAL	55	9	16%	46	84%	51	15	29%	36	71%	25	4	16%	21	84%	131	28	21%	103	79%
TOTAL	199	94	47%	105	53%	196	114	58%	82	42%	114	55	48%	59	52%	509	263	52%	246	48%

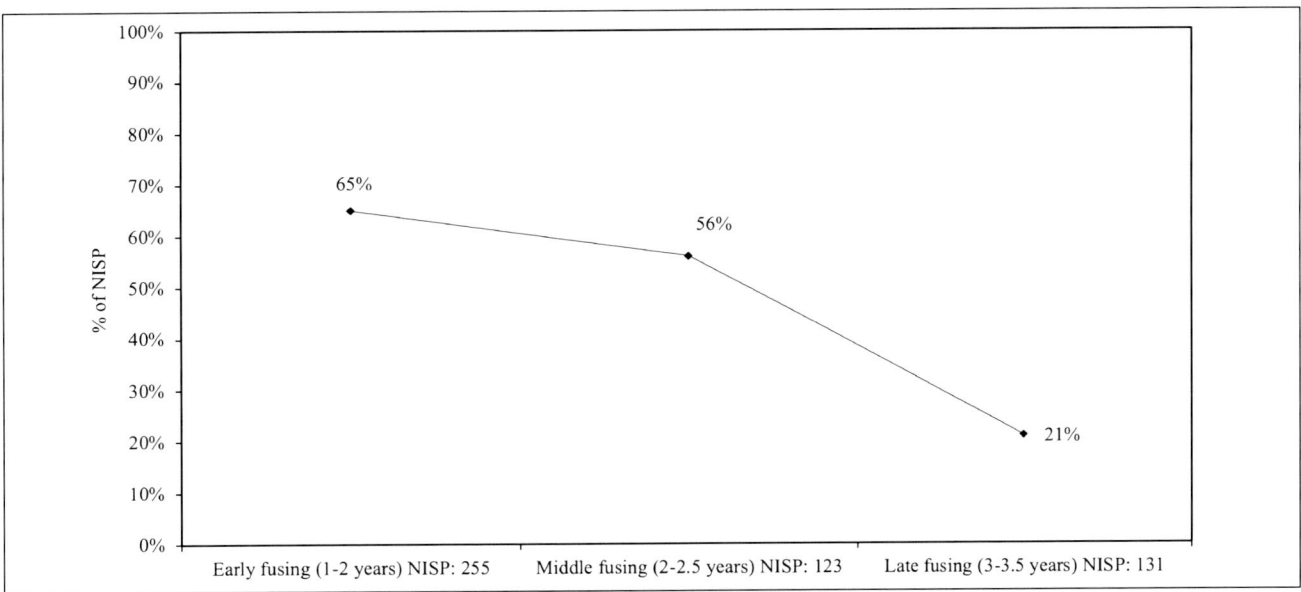

Figure 5.25 Epiphyseal fusion data for *Sus*. All phases are considered. Data in Table 5.93. NISP counts.

Table 5.94 *Sus* (pig) eruption stage and wear stage data from mandibular isolated teeth and teeth attached to mandibles. C= Crypt, V= Visible, E= Erupting, H= Half erupted. Teeth recorded in wear stage "a" are considered fully erupted, yet still unworn (U). NISP counts.

Sus		Phases	Eruption and wear stages																		
			C	V	E	H	a	b	c	d	e	f	g	h	i	j	k	l	m	n	o	p
Individual mandibular teeth (attached & loose)	dP4	Phase I					1	1		1	1	1	1			1		1			
		Phase II					1	1		1	1	1	1		1		2					
		Phase III									2											
		TOTAL	**0**	**0**	**0**	**0**	**2**	**2**	**0**	**1**	**4**	**2**	**2**	**1**	**1**	**0**	**3**	**0**	**1**	**0**	**0**	**0**
	P4	Phase I					1	1														
		Phase II		1							1			1								
		Phase III								2												
		TOTAL	**0**	**1**	**0**	**0**	**1**	**1**	**0**	**2**	**1**	**0**	**0**	**1**	**0**	**0**	**0**	**0**	**0**	**0**	**0**	**0**
	M1	Phase I	1				2	2	1		3											
		Phase II	1		1			3	3	2	2					1						
		Phase III		1			2			2		1	1									
		TOTAL	**2**	**1**	**1**	**0**	**4**	**5**	**4**	**4**	**5**	**1**	**1**	**0**	**0**	**1**	**0**	**0**	**0**	**0**	**0**	**0**
	M2	Phase I	4	1			1	1	3		2											
		Phase II	2		2		1	1	2	1	1							1				
		Phase III					1	1	1		2											
		TOTAL	**6**	**1**	**2**	**0**	**3**	**3**	**6**	**1**	**5**	**0**	**0**	**0**	**0**	**0**	**1**	**0**	**0**	**0**	**0**	**0**
	M1/2	Phase I									1											
		Phase II					4		1													
		Phase III					1		1	1		1										
		TOTAL	**0**	**0**	**0**	**0**	**5**	**0**	**2**	**2**	**0**	**1**	**0**	**0**	**0**	**0**	**0**	**0**	**0**	**0**	**0**	**0**
	M3	Phase I	2	1	2	1			2													
		Phase II	1	1		2		1	2													
		Phase III	1				2	1	1							1						
		TOTAL	**4**	**2**	**2**	**3**	**2**	**2**	**5**	**0**	**0**	**0**	**0**	**0**	**0**	**1**	**0**	**0**	**0**	**0**	**0**	**0**

Table 5.95 Mandible wear stages for *Sus* (pig) on the temporal level. NISP counts.

Sus	Mandible wear stages					
	P_4	dP_4	M_1	M_2	M_3	MWS
Phase I			k	b	C		Immature
					a	E	Immature
			m	b	V		Immature
			m	c	C		Immature
			f	a	C		Immature
				e	c		Sub adult
			g	a	C		Immature
				e	c		Sub adult
	b			e	c		Sub adult
					e	H	Sub adult
			k	d	b		Sub adult
Phase II			k	c			Immature
	V			b			Immature
				d	b		Adult
				c	V		Sub adult
				e	c		Sub adult
			b	C			Juvenile
			g	E	C		Juvenile
				c	a	C	Sub adult
				j	l		Sub adult
				e	b		Immature
				d	E		Immature
Phase III				d	b		Sub adult
	d			d			Immature
			e	a			Immature
				f	c		Sub adult
			e	V			Juvenile

Table 5.96 Summary of mandible wear stages for *Sus* (pig). All phases are considered. Data for Figure 5.26. NISP counts.

Sus	Phases I-II-III		
	NISP	% Attribution	% Cumulative loss
Neonatal		0%	100%
Juvenile	3	11%	89%
Immature	12	44%	45%
Sub adult	11	41%	4%
Adult	1	4%	0%
Elderly		0%	0%
TOTAL	**27**	**100%**	

2007). Unfortunately, no information about the excavation contexts and different phases from which the animal bone assemblage derives is provided for Topolniča. Consequently, the three phases had to be considered together under the broad cultural sequence of the Late Neolithic. A further complication concerns the fact that the report is written in Bulgarian, thus limiting the possibilities of understanding fully the adopted methodological approach, and therefore the nature of the evidence to be compared with Promachon.

The faunal material from the deposits associated with the first Phase of occupation in Promachon sector is compared also to the faunal material from the deposits of structure n. 4 (which, as previously noted is used only during Phase I) of the same sector. The faunal material from structure n. 4 was studied by O. Theodorogianni as part of her doctoral thesis and the results were published in the form of a preliminary report (Theodorogianni and Trantalidou 2013). The methodology employed by both researchers with regard to the recording and the quantification of the faunal material, as well as the assessment of the age-at-death of the main domesticated species, is inconsistent with the methodology used in this study. This reflects the fact that both researchers adjusted their methodological protocols to their research questions, which were related to their specific area of study. In addition to the aforementioned publication, two more zooarchaeological publications regarding the latter structural feature exist. Both of them deal with the bucrania recovered from the successive levels of structure n. 4 (Trantalidou 2010; Trantalidou and Gkioni 2008). The results from the analyses of the bucrania are also considered in the comparison between structure n. 4 and the rest of the deposits of Phase I.

5.9.1 *Promachon sector* versus *Topolniča sector*

Due to the aforementioned limitations, the faunal material from the sector of Topolniča could be compared with that of Promachon only on the basis of species composition and frequency. In total, 2502 animal bones and teeth were recorded in the Bulgarian sector of Topolniča (Iliev

of Kryoneri (Mylona 1997) and Stavroupoli (Yiannouli 2002a), the ratio between male and female pigs is 1 : 2 and 1 : 4 respectively. However, in order to sufficiently evaluate the sexual composition of the pig populations from the latter sites, we have to assess the significance of recovery bias for each site.

5.9 Intra-site analysis

This section compares the Promachon faunal assemblage with that recovered through excavations of the Bulgarian sector (Topolniča) of the same site (Iliev and Spassov

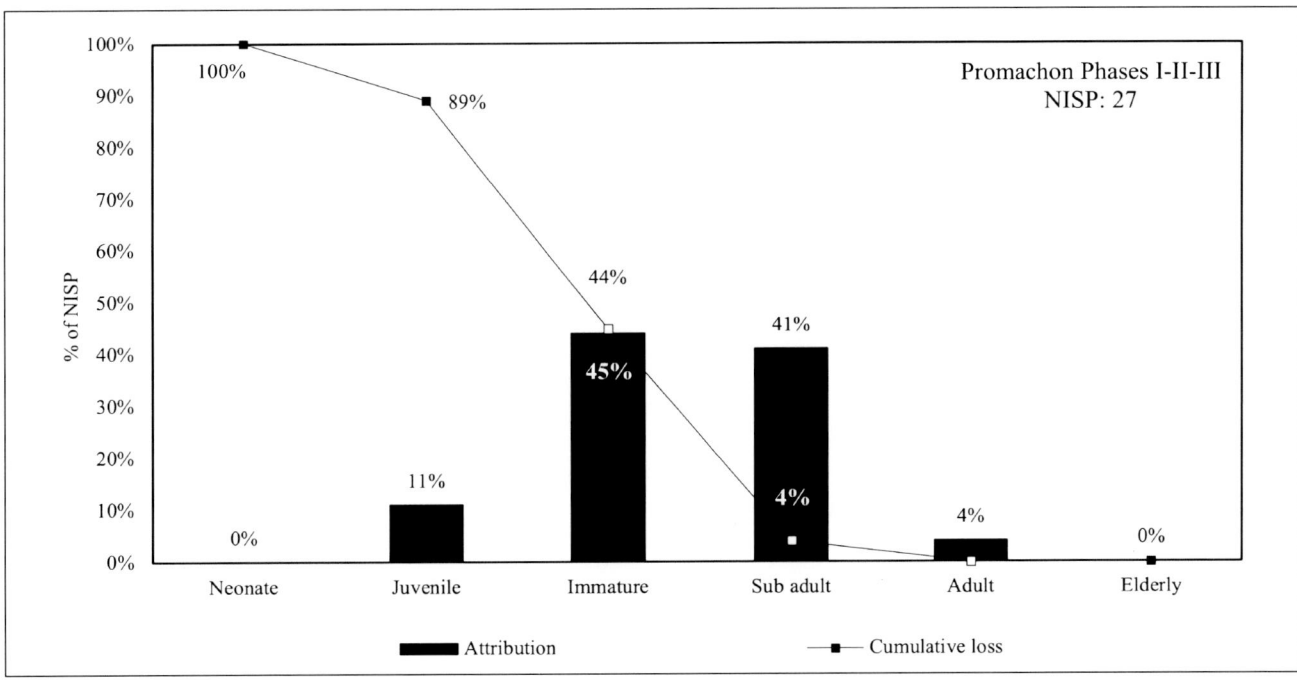

Figure 5.26 Mandible wear stages for *Sus*. All phases are considered. Data in Table 5.96. NISP counts.

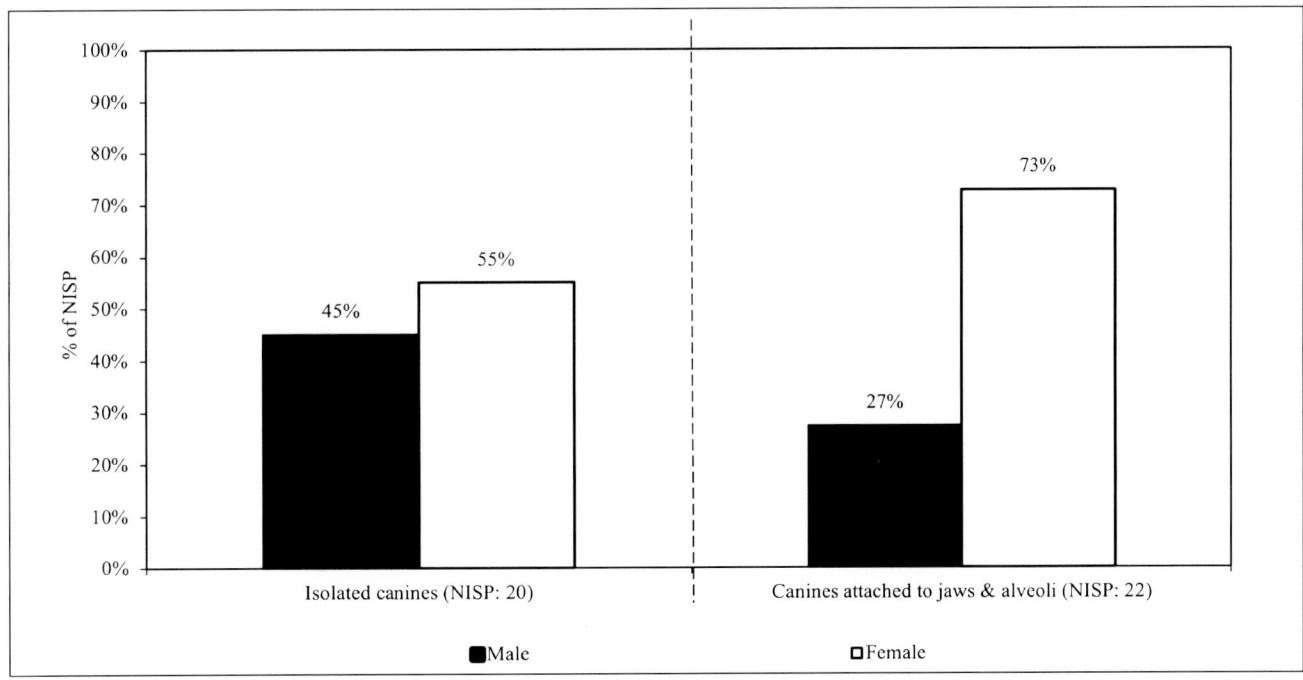

Figure 5.27 Frequency of male and female *Sus* isolated and attached to jaw canines and alveoli. All phases are considered. Data in Table 5.97. NISP counts.

and Spassov 2007). Of these, 2001 (79 per cent) were identified to the level of species. Overall, 15 species were identified from Topolniča. This number is lower than that of Promachon, where almost 27 species (including human) were eventually identified, but this is likely to be the result of differences in sample sizes between the two sectors. Table 5.98 presents the composition – in terms of NISP – of all the species identified from the Bulgarian sector of Topolniča and compares with those from Promachon. Most of the species identified from Topolniča were also found at Promachon: cattle, sheep, goat, pig, dog, red deer,

roe deer, red fox, hare and bear are present in both sectors. The absence of the fallow deer from Topolniča may be due to the lower chance to find such uncommon species in a much smaller sample size. There are however, some differences between the two sectors. Iliev and Spassov (2007) report the presence of wild horse (*Equus ferus*; a single calcaneum). The occurrence of the wild horse at Topolniča is noteworthy, especially if we consider that the species is not documented at other contemporary sites in Greek Macedonia. To be confident regarding the actual chronology of this horse specimen we would, however,

Table 5.97 Frequency of male and female *Sus* (pig) isolated and attached to jaw canines and alveoli. Both maxillary and mandibular canines and alveoli are considered. All phases are considered. Data for Figure 5.27. NISP counts.

Sus	Canines			
	Isolated		Attached to jaws and alveoli	
	NISP	%	NISP	%
Male	9	45%	6	27%
Female	11	55%	16	73%
TOTAL	**20**	**100%**	**22**	**100%**

need more information regarding its context of origin. Of additional interest is the identification of the aurochs (*Bos primigenius*; a single humerus and five phalanges) from Topolniča. No aurochs bones could be positively identified from Promachon. In addition, the number of wild boar specimens at Topolniča is relatively high (NISP: 140), while only one wild boar specimen was identified at Promachon. The identification was based on the large size of a single mandible of a male individual containing the tusk and the first, second, third and fourth premolars, but in general the evaluation of wild forms of cattle and pig was based on biometrical analysis and will be discussed later. Figure 5.28 (Table 5.99) presents the frequencies of the three main domesticated species between the two sectors in terms of NISP. Pig representation is roughly the same in both sectors (12 per cent in Topolniča and 15 per cent in Promachon), but there are substantial differences in the frequencies of cattle and caprines. Cattle at Topolniča are substantially better represented than caprines (58 per cent and 30 per cent respectively), whereas the opposite is the case at Promachon (45 per cent caprines and 40 per cent cattle).

Differences in the NISP frequencies of cattle and caprines between the two sectors are most likely due to variation in the approaches to counting and quantification. Body part distributions for all species identified at Topolniča (Iliev and Spassov 2007), suggest that – unlike Promachon – all parts of the skeleton (including parts of the cranium as well as vertebrae and ribs) were recorded and eventually used for the calculation of NISP. However, as already noted, recovery bias is likely to have played a significant role in the formation of the faunal assemblage, with large anatomical parts, and consequently, large taxa (such as cattle) being substantially better represented – in terms of NISP – than small anatomical parts deriving from small taxa (such as caprines and pigs).

We do not know whether the faunal material from Topolniča was hand-collected or sieved, yet, it is worth noticing that Iliev and Spassov (2007) do not assess the extent of recovery bias on site. In addition, the effect of fragmentation on large bones of large animals such as cattle, results in elements being counted more than once,

Table 5.98 Composition of domesticated and wild species identified in Promachon and Topolniča sectors. All phases are considered from Promachon sector. NISP counts.

Species	Late Neolithic	
	Topolniča Iliev and Spassov (2007)	Promachon (current study)
	NISP	NISP
Bos taurus	998	2444
Ovis/Capra	451	2075
Ovis aries	39	554
Capra hircus	22	129
Sus	201	879
Canis familiaris	14	124
Cervus elaphus	115	88
Dama dama		9
Capreolus capreolus	2	34
Bos primigenius	6	
Equus ferus	1	
Lepus europaeus	5	21
Vulpes vulpes	4	31
Rupicapra rupicapra		1
Canis lupus	2	
Sus scrofa	140	1
Lynx lynx		1
Ursus arctos	1	3
Meles meles		2
Mustela putorius		1
Mustela erminea		1
Martes foina		1
Buteo lagopus		2
Anser anser		3
Grus grus		1
Corvus corax		2
TOTAL	**2001**	**6407**
Aves	1	1
Testudinidae	2	Present but non-countable
Pisces	2	Present but non-countable
Murex trunculus		Present but non-countable
Homo sapiens		3
TOTAL	**2006**	**6411**

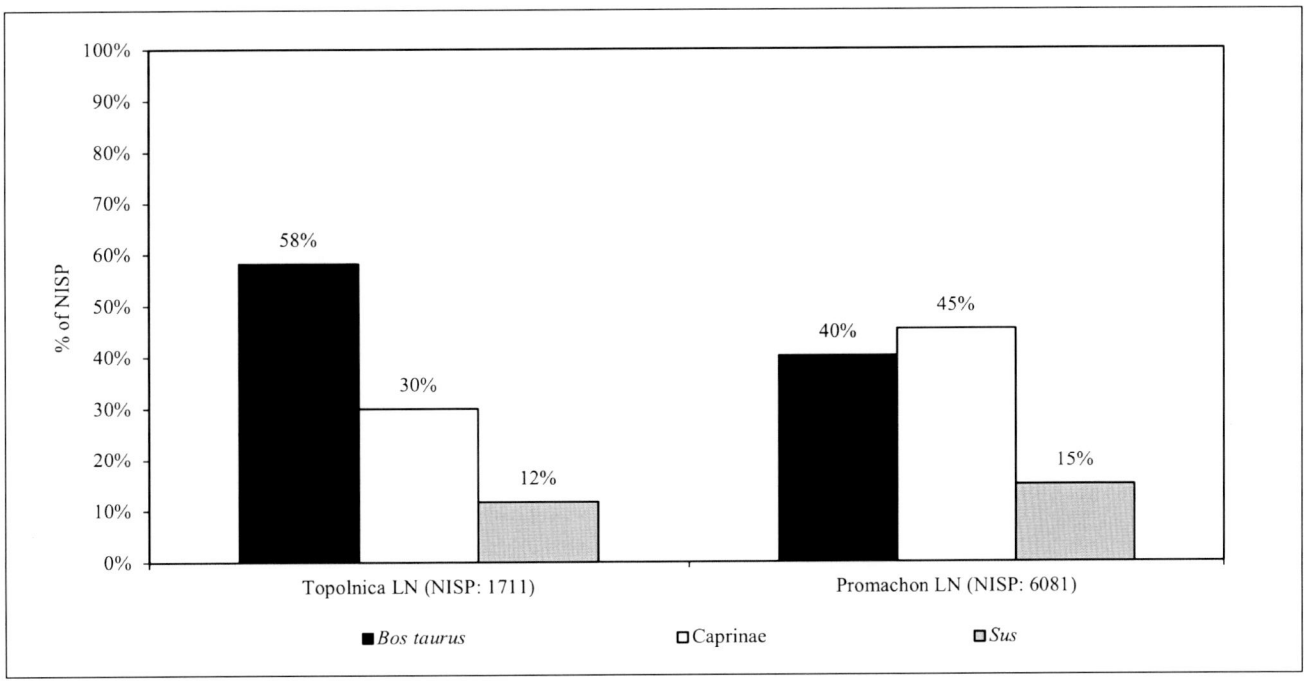

Figure 5.28 Three main domesticates between Promachon and Topolniča. Data in Table 5.99. NISP counts.

thus inflating the total NISP for this species. Unlike Topolniča, the system of Diagnostic Zones employed in the study of Promachon prevented any single zone from being counted twice: inter-taxon anatomical differences were partly circumvented by counting only certain key parts of the skeleton, and fragmentation bias was potentially reduced since zones were counted only if more than half was present.

One possible way to tackle the biases created by the different methodological approaches in the two sectors, would be to compare the frequencies of the three main domesticated species using the MNI – rather than NISP – as the main predictor of taxonomic frequency. Regardless of the fact that we do not know the exact method with which, Iliev and Spassov (2007) calculated the MNI for

the three main domesticates in Topolniča, we can see that caprines are represented with a higher frequency than cattle when MNI's are considered (50 per cent and 39 per cent respectively) (Iliev and Spassov 2007). This is consistent with the frequency – in terms of MNI – of the three main domesticated species in Promachon, which also points to the predominance of caprines over cattle (61 per cent and 24 per cent respectively) (Table 5.100; Figure 5.29). Therefore, the predominance of caprines in both sectors – in terms of MNI – possibly reflects the reality of the situation in Promachon-Topolniča. To be more specific, the results from both sectors indicate that caprines in Promachon-Topolniča are represented with higher frequencies than any other main domesticate during the whole cultural sequence of the Late Neolithic.

Table 5.99 Three main domesticates between the two sectors. All phases are considered for Promachon. Caprinae subfamily includes *Ovis/Capra* (sheep/goat), *Ovis aries* (sheep) and *Capra hircus* (goat). Data for Figure 5.28. NISP counts.

Species	Late Neolithic			
	Topolniča Iliev and Spassov (2007)		Promachon (current study)	
	NISP	%	NISP	%
Bos taurus	998	58%	2444	40%
Caprinae	512	30%	2758	45%
Sus	201	12%	879	15%
TOTAL	**1711**	**100%**	**6081**	**100%**

Table 5.100 Three main domesticates between the two sectors. All phases are considered for Promachon. Caprinae subfamily includes *Ovis/Capra* (sheep/goat), *Ovis aries* (sheep) and *Capra hircus* (goat). Data for Figure 5.29. MNI counts.

Species	Late Neolithic			
	Topolniča Iliev and Spassov (2007)		Promachon (current study)	
	MNI	%	MNI	%
Bos taurus	24	39%	61	24%
Caprinae	30	50%	159	61%
Sus	7	11%	39	15%
TOTAL	**61**	**100%**	**259**	**100%**

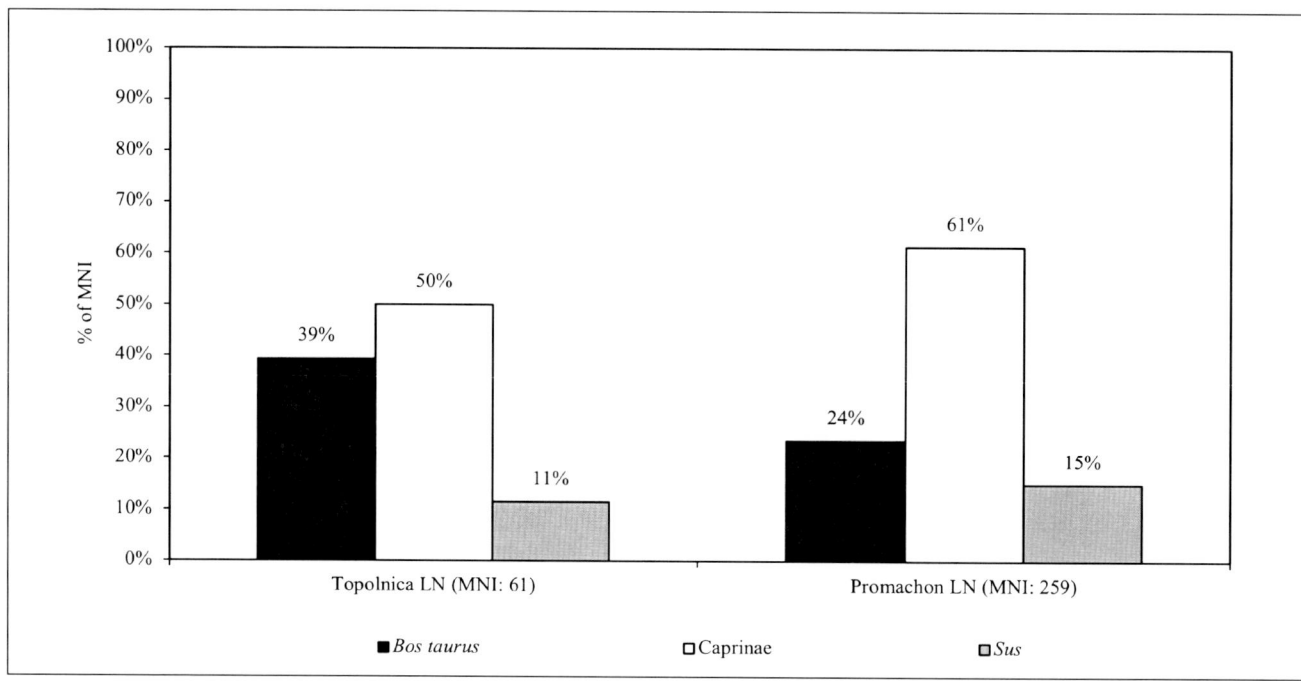

Figure 5.29 Three main domesticates between Promachon and Topolniča. Data in Table 5.100. MNI counts.

The information on the relative frequency of sheep and goat from Topolniča is approximately consistent with that of Promachon (Figure 5.30; Table 5.101) as it indicates a predominance of sheep. Nevertheless, sheep are better represented at Promachon than Topolniča (81 per cent and 64 per cent respectively). We do not, however, know which anatomical elements were used at Topolniča for the identification of the two species and it is therefore difficult to evaluate the factors that may have cause the discrepancy.

5.9.2 Structure n. 4 and the rest of deposits of Phase I

Despite differences in methodological protocols (which must be considered in the interpretation), it was possible to conduct comparisons between structure n. 4 and the rest of the deposits of Phase I on the basis of species composition and frequency, as well as ageing analysis.

Table 5.102 presents the composition – in terms of NISP – of all species identified in structure n. 4, and compares

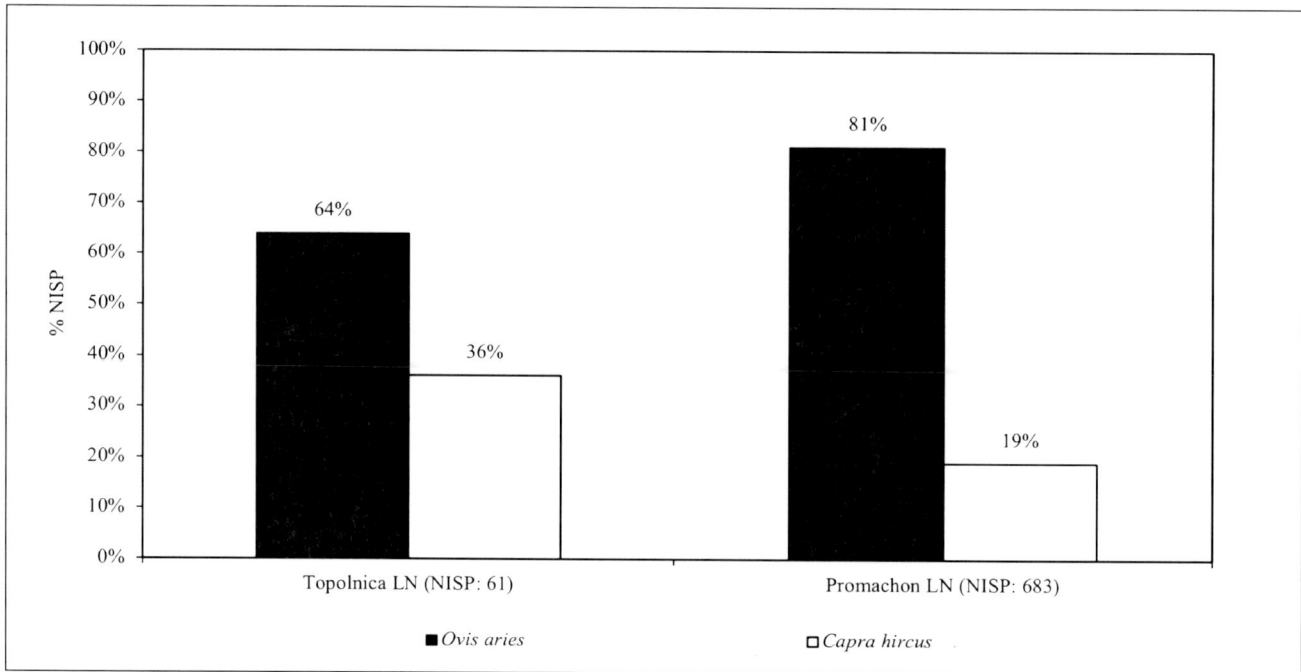

Figure 5.30 *Ovis aries versus Capra hircus* between Promachon and Topolniča. Data in Table 5.101. NISP counts.

Table 5.101 *Ovis aries* (sheep) *versus Capra hircus* (goat) between the two sectors. All phases are considered for Promachon. Data for Figure 5.30. NISP counts.

Species	Late Neolithic			
	Topolniča Iliev and Spassov (2007)		Promachon (current study)	
	NISP	%	NISP	%
Ovis aries	39	64%	554	81%
Capra hircus	22	36%	129	19%
TOTAL	61	100%	683	100%

it with that from the rest of the deposits of Phase I. In total, 8842 animal bones and teeth from the deposits of structure n. 4 (Phase I) were recorded (Theodorogianni and Trantalidou 2013). This number is higher than that from the rest of the deposits of Phase I, from which, 2263 bones and teeth were recorded in total[4]. It must, however, be considered that the dataset from the rest of the site derives from a selective, diagnostic-zone approach, and is therefore not directly comparable in quantity to that from structure n. 4. Out of a total of 8842 bones and teeth from structure n. 4, 8839 (more than 99 per cent) were identified down to the level of species. The rest of the faunal material consists of one specimen belonging to the family of Mustelidae (mustelids) and two indeterminate fish bones. In total, 12 species were identified in structure n. 4 (including human). This number is lower than the number of species identified from the rest of the deposits in Phase I (20 species, including human). Considering the much larger assemblage from structure n. 4, this indicates a much lesser taxonomic variability in the assemblage from this context. Cattle, sheep, goat, pig, dog, red deer, fallow deer, hare, wild boar and mustelids are present in both study areas. Roe deer, red fox and bird remains are, however, absent from structure n. 4 but were recorded in the rest of the deposits of Phase I. On the other hand, Theodorogianni and Trantalidou (2013) argue for the presence of aurochs and wild boar remains in structure n. 4 (NISP: 174 and 66 respectively). As previously noted, the significance of both the aurochs and the wild boar from the rest of the deposits will be assessed in a separate part of the analysis (biometry).

Table 5.103 presents the frequency – in terms of NISP – of domesticated and wild species between the two study areas. No difference can be seen between structure n. 4 and the rest the deposits of Phase I, since in both cases domesticates predominate with roughly the same frequencies (96 per cent in structure n. 4 and 94 per cent in the rest of the deposits of Phase I). A Chi^2 test was conducted to test whether the differences between the two research areas in domesticated and wild animal representation were statistically significant. The test

Table 5.102 Composition of domesticated and wild species identified in structure n. 4 and the rest of the deposits of Phase I in Promachon sector. NISP counts.

Species	Phase I in Promachon sector	
	Structure n. 4 (Theodorogianni and Trantalidou 2013)	Rest of deposits (current study)
	NISP	NISP
Bos taurus	7031	918
Ovis/Capra	322	659
Ovis aries	293	181
Capra hircus	175	48
Sus	610	329
Canis familiaris	86	48
Total domesticated	**8517**	**2183**
Cervus elaphus	73	30
Dama dama	1	2
Capreolus capreolus		10
Bos primigenius	174	
Lepus europaeus	6	8
Vulpes vulpes		16
Rupicapra rupicapra		1
Sus scrofa	66	1
Lynx lynx		1
Ursus arctos		3
Meles meles	Mustelidae: 1	1
Mustela putorius		1
Anser anser		3
Grus grus		1
Total wild	**321**	**78**
Total domesticated and wild	**8838**	**2261**
Pisces	2	Present but non-countable
Murex trunculus		Present but non-countable
Homo sapiens	2	2
TOTAL	**8842**	**2263**

---

[4] Excluding specimens, which were only roughly attributed to taxa (*i.e.* cattle/red deer; red deer/fallow deer; sheep/goat/roe deer; dog/red fox) and non-countable specimens.

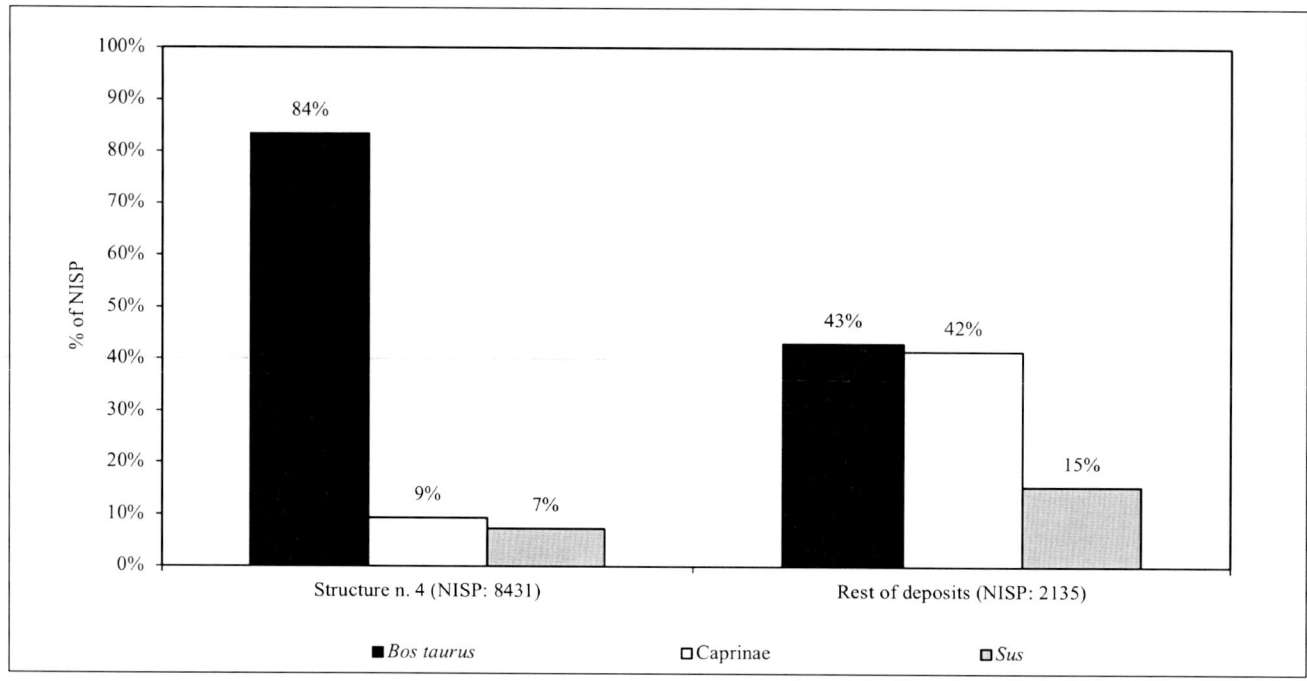

Figure 5.31 Three main domesticates between structure n. 4 and the rest of the deposits of Phase I. Data in Table 5.104. NISP counts.

Table 5.103 Domesticated *versus* wild taxa between structure n. 4 and the rest of the deposits of Phase I in Promachon sector. NISP counts.

Species	Phase I in Promachon sector			
	Structure n. 4 (Theodorogianni and Trantalidou 2013)		Rest of deposits (current study)	
	NISP	%	NISP	%
Domesticated	8517	96%	2183	94%
Wild	321	4%	78	6%
TOTAL	**8838**	**100%**	**2261**	**100%**

indicated that the two taxa representation does not differ significantly between structure n. 4 and the rest of the deposits of Phase I (p= 0.67).

Figure 5.31 (Table 5.104) compares the frequency of the three main domesticated species between structure n. 4 and the rest of the deposits of Phase I in terms of NISP. Pigs are represented with lower frequencies than any other domesticate in both study areas (seven per cent in structure n. 4 and 15 per cent in the rest of the deposits). There is, however, a great difference in the frequencies between cattle and caprines. Cattle are substantially better represented than caprines in structure n. 4 (83 per cent and nine per cent respectively), while the two species are almost equally represented in the rest of the deposits of Phase I (43 per cent for cattle and 42 per cent for caprines).

A Chi² test was conducted to test whether the differences between the two research areas in cattle and caprine

representation were statistically significant. The test indicated that the two taxa representation is highly different between structure n. 4 and the rest of the deposits of Phase I (p= 0.0001).

It could be argued that the differences in the NISP frequencies of cattle and caprines between the two study areas are due to methodological differences between the two studies, as in the case of the differences between Promachon and Topolniča. Fragmentation of the bucrania, which were found in structure n. 4[5], enhances the possibility of cattle cranial elements (*i.e.* horn cores, maxillae, mandibles) being counted more than once. In addition, isolated cattle teeth would also be likely candidates for multiple recording of the same specimen, thus inflating the total NISP of the species. Nevertheless, a glance at the table providing the body part distribution for cattle from structure n. 4 (Theodorogianni and Trantalidou 2013; 413, Table 4), indicates that postcranial elements are very well represented as well. This suggests that the pattern is most likely 'genuine' and that the fragmented bucrania cannot be the only reason for the overall high frequency of cattle in structure n. 4. The possibility that the high frequency of cattle postcranial elements in structure n. 4 is the result of a recovery bias should also be considered, but the deposits of structure n. 4 were sieved through a one-millimetre mesh (Koukouli-Chrysanthaki *et al.* 2007; Theodorogianni and Trantalidou 2013), thus ruling out the possibility that smaller animals such as caprines (and pigs) were biased against. Methodological, taphonomic and recovery differences between the two study areas are unlikely

---

[5] In total, 35 bucrania were found in the successive floor levels of structure n. 4 during Phase I (Trantalidou 2010; Theodorogianni and Trantalidou 2013; Trantalidou and Gkioni 2008).

Table 5.104 Three main domesticates between structure n. 4 and the rest of the deposits of Phase I in Promachon sector. Caprinae subfamily includes *Ovis/Capra* (sheep/goat), *Ovis aries* (sheep) and *Capra hircus* (goat). Data for Figure 5.31. NISP counts.

| Species | Phase I in Promachon sector | | | |
| | Structure n. 4 (Theodorogianni and Trantalidou 2013) | | Rest of deposits (current study) | |
	NISP	%	NISP	%
Bos taurus	7031	84%	918	43%
Caprinae	790	9%	888	42%
Sus	610	7%	329	15%
TOTAL	**8431**	**100%**	**2135**	**100%**

Species	NISP	MNI
Ovis aries	293	25
Ovis/Capra	322	? MNI

'Rule of three'	? MNI = (322 / 293) * 25
Ovis/Capra	MNI = 27

to account for the substantially better representation of cattle in structure n. 4. There is another issue that must be considered, however. As in the case of the comparison between the Bulgarian sector of Topolniča and the Greek sector of Promachon, one possible way to mitigate the biases created by the different methodological protocols in the two study areas, would be to calculate the frequency of the three main domesticated species in terms of MNI rather than NISP. However, unlike the Bulgarian sector of Topolniča, Theodorogianni and Trantalidou (2013) do not provide the MNI for the caprine assemblage that was generically identified as sheep/goat. In addition, there is no discussion of the method used for the calculation of the MNI's from the deposits of structure n. 4. The authors, however, suggest that, in the deposits of structure n. 4, out of a total of 110 domesticated individuals (excluding dogs), cattle are represented with 54, sheep with 25, goats with 16, and pigs with 15 individuals respectively (Theodorogianni and Trantalidou 2013; 410, Table 2). Therefore, according to Theodorogianni and Trantalidou (2013) caprines from structure n. 4 are represented by 41 individuals, without counting the number of individuals identified to the generic level of sheep/goat. In terms of MNI percentages, therefore, caprines account for 37 per cent (excluding sheep/goat), cattle for 49 per cent, and pig for 14 per cent of the total MNI for the three main domesticates. Undoubtedly, had Theodorogianni and Trantalidou (2013) calculated also the MNI for the part of the caprine assemblage that was identified to the level of sheep/goat, we would have expected the frequency – in terms of MNI – of the whole caprine population (that is sheep, goat and sheep/goat) to be very close – if not higher – to the frequency of cattle. In particular we must consider that in structure n. 4, sheep are represented with a NISP of 293, while sheep/goat are represented with a NISP of 322. Theodorogianni and Trantalidou argue that, 293 remains of sheep (in terms of NISP) account for 25 sheep (in terms of MNI). Therefore, by using the 'rule of three' we can roughly estimate what would probably be the MNI for sheep/goat:

With very rough estimates therefore, 322 sheep/goat remains (in terms of NISP), would account for 27 sheep/goats (in terms of MNI) in structure n. 4. This number, added to 25 sheep and 16 goats, would give a total MNI of 68 caprines (sheep, goat, sheep/goat). Therefore, the total MNI for the three main domesticates would reach 137 individuals (instead of 110) including cattle, sheep, goat, sheep/goat and pigs. Therefore, out of a total of 137 domesticated animals, cattle, which are represented with 54 individuals would account for 39 per cent (instead of 49 per cent), caprines (sheep, goat and sheep/goat), which would be represented with 68 individuals (instead of 41) would account for 49 per cent (instead of 37 per cent), and pigs, which are represented with 15 individuals would account for 12 per cent (instead of 14 per cent) of the total frequency for the three main domesticated species in terms of MNI.

The previous calculations indicate that, if the sheep/goat MNI was taken into consideration, caprines would – in overall – be represented with a higher frequency than cattle in the deposits of structure n. 4. More specifically, since MNI is less affected by recovery biases, it would be a much more reliable tool – than NISP – for the calculation of the frequency of the three main domesticates, and it would also demonstrate that the caprine population is represented with higher frequencies than any other domesticate in structure n. 4. There is, however, one further issue that should also be considered. It is peculiar that 7031 cattle remains account for 54 individuals only, while 293 sheep remains give an MNI as high as 25. This high number of sheep in terms of MNI could potentially be explained if the calculation of the MNI in structure n. 4 was based on the most common element, and that element in turn, was represented with the highest proportions than any other element in the body part distribution. However, according to the body part distribution of sheep from the latter structural feature, this is not the case: all anatomical parts are very well represented. This indicates therefore, that cattle MNI was either calculated wrongly, or simply reported wrongly in the faunal report. In any case, since the MNI for sheep/goat is not reported in the faunal report, only tentative considerations can be made with regard to the frequencies of the three main domesticates between the two study areas in terms of MNI. This obviously implies that the most useful predictor of taxonomic frequency for the three main domesticates between the two study areas, is NISP. It would have been more appropriate, however, to calculate the frequency of the three main domesticates between structure n. 4 and the rest of the deposits – except for NISP – also in terms of MNI.

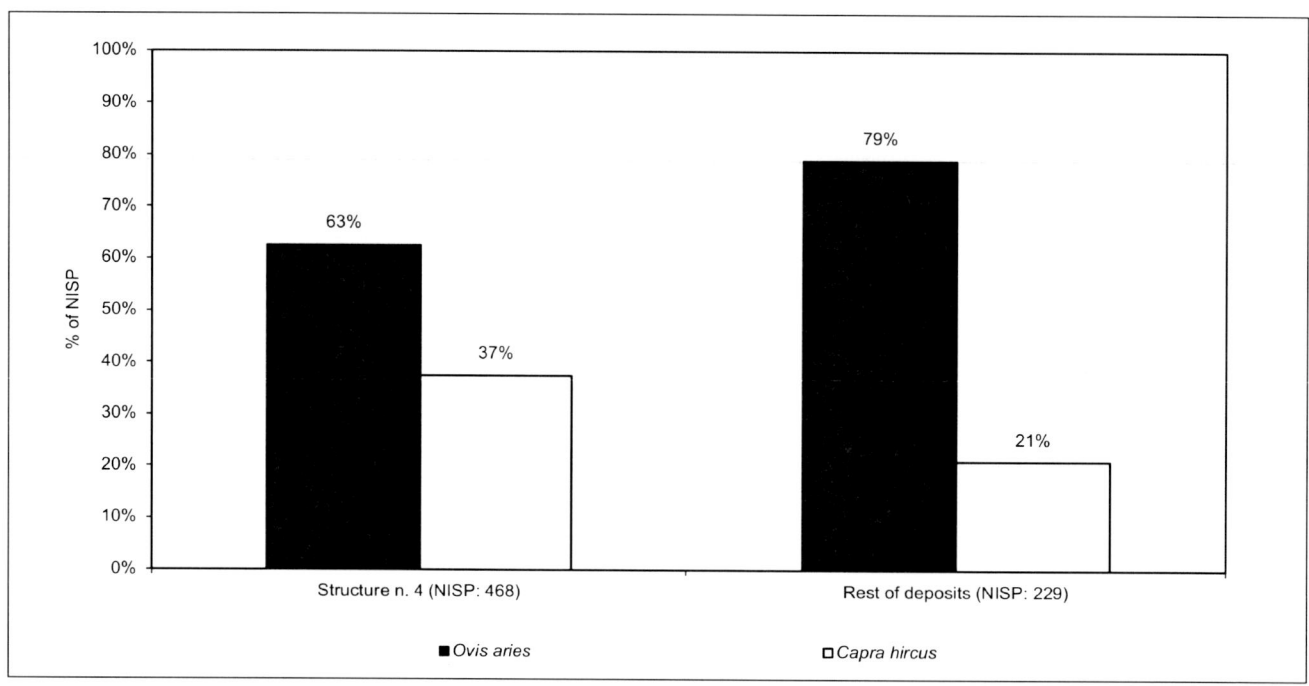

Figure 5.32 *Ovis aries versus Capra hircus* **between structure n. 4 and the rest of the deposits of Phase I. Data in Table 5.105. NISP counts.**

As previously argued, the deposits of structure n. 4 were completely sieved, whereas the faunal material from the rest of the deposits was hand-collected. Since the faunal material from the deposits not associated with structure n. 4 was hand collected, caprines are likely to be seriously underrepresented in terms of NISP. On the other hand, since the deposits of structure n. 4 were completely sieved, it is likely that – in terms of NISP – caprines are not underrepresented and cattle remains dominate structure n. 4. It can be therefore concluded that in terms of NISP, the remains of cattle dominate structure n. 4, whereas no particular emphasis on a single species can be detected in the rest of the deposits (although there are hints that due to recovery biases, caprines are seriously underrepresented in comparison to cattle).

Although we do not know which anatomical elements Theodorogianni and Trantalidou (2013) used for the identification of the caprine population to the finest taxonomical level, it seems that sheep are represented with higher frequencies than goat in structure n. 4 in terms of NISP. This is consistent with the data from the rest of the deposits of Phase I (Figure 5.32; Table 5.105). However, the frequency of sheep from structure n. 4 is higher than that in the rest of the deposits of Phase I. A Chi^2 test was also conducted to test whether the differences between the two research areas in sheep and goat representation were statistically significant. The test indicated that the two taxa representation is highly different between structure n. 4 and the rest of the deposits of Phase I (p= 0.00001).

As previously argued the assessment of the age-at-death for the main domesticates in Promachon was based on O' Connor's (1988) mandible wear stages for cattle and pigs, as well as Payne's (1973) mandible wear stages for caprines. On the other hand, Theodorogianni and Trantalidou (2013)

do not provide information on the methodology that they have used for assessing the age-at-death of the same species from structure n. 4. In overall, they use six mandible wear stages for assessing the age-at-death for cattle and sheep and five for assessing the age-at-death for goats.[6] Due therefore to the incompatibility of the methodology followed in the two study areas, we should be cautious with our interpretations. Figure 5.33 (Table 5.106) presents the comparison of cattle age-at-death between structure n. 4 and the rest of the deposits. Due to small sample size of Phase I from the deposits not associated with structure n. 4, this phase is considered together with Phase II. As previously seen (Figure 5.19; Table 5.82), neonate and senile individuals were completely absent from Phases I and II. On the other hand, senile individuals (beyond 3 years) are also absent from structure n. 4. Of interest however, is the fact that neonate individuals (calves, less than 6 months old) are represented in structure n. 4 with 18 per cent.

It could be argued that the differences in the frequency of calves between the two study areas are the result of recovery biases. The deposits of structure n. 4 were sieved through one-millimetre mesh (Koukouli-Chrysanthaki *et al.* 2007; Theodorogianni and Trantalidou 2013), whereas the bulk of the faunal material from the rest of the deposits was hand-picked. Indeed, as previously noted, a small number of cattle unworn isolated mandibular first / second molars ($M_{1/2}$) from our area of study, indicates that a number of calf mandibles were particularly affected by fragmentation mechanisms and, ultimately, poor recovery procedures. However, the frequency of calves from structure n. 4 is considerably high (18 per cent), and it cannot be explained only on the basis of differential retrieval between structure

---

[6] Only the frequencies of cattle and sheep and goat mandible wear stages (%NISP) are provided. No information on pig wear stages is provided.

Table 5.105 *Ovis aries* (sheep) *versus Capra hircus* (goat) between structure n. 4 and the rest of the deposits of Phase I in Promachon sector. Data for Figure 5.32. NISP counts.

Species	Phase I in Promachon sector			
	Structure n. 4 (Theodorogianni and Trantalidou 2013)		Rest of deposits (current study)	
	NISP	%	NISP	%
Ovis aries	293	63%	181	79%
Capra hircus	175	37%	48	21%
TOTAL	**468**	**100%**	**229**	**100%**

n. 4 and the rest of the deposits. It is rather suggested that the overall pattern indicates a genuine difference, and that structure n. 4 was favoured regarding the disposal of the remains of calves.

A possible explanation for this phenomenon is that this age group could represent young casualties, such as animals, which died immediately or relatively soon after birth, due to disease, weakness, difficult adaptation in the local environment *etc.* Given, however, the exceptional and distinctive function and nature of structure n. 4 (Koukouli-Chrysanthaki *et al.* 2007), it would be highly unlikely that ailing animals were killed and/or simply disposed of into the latter structural feature. It is rather suggested that the

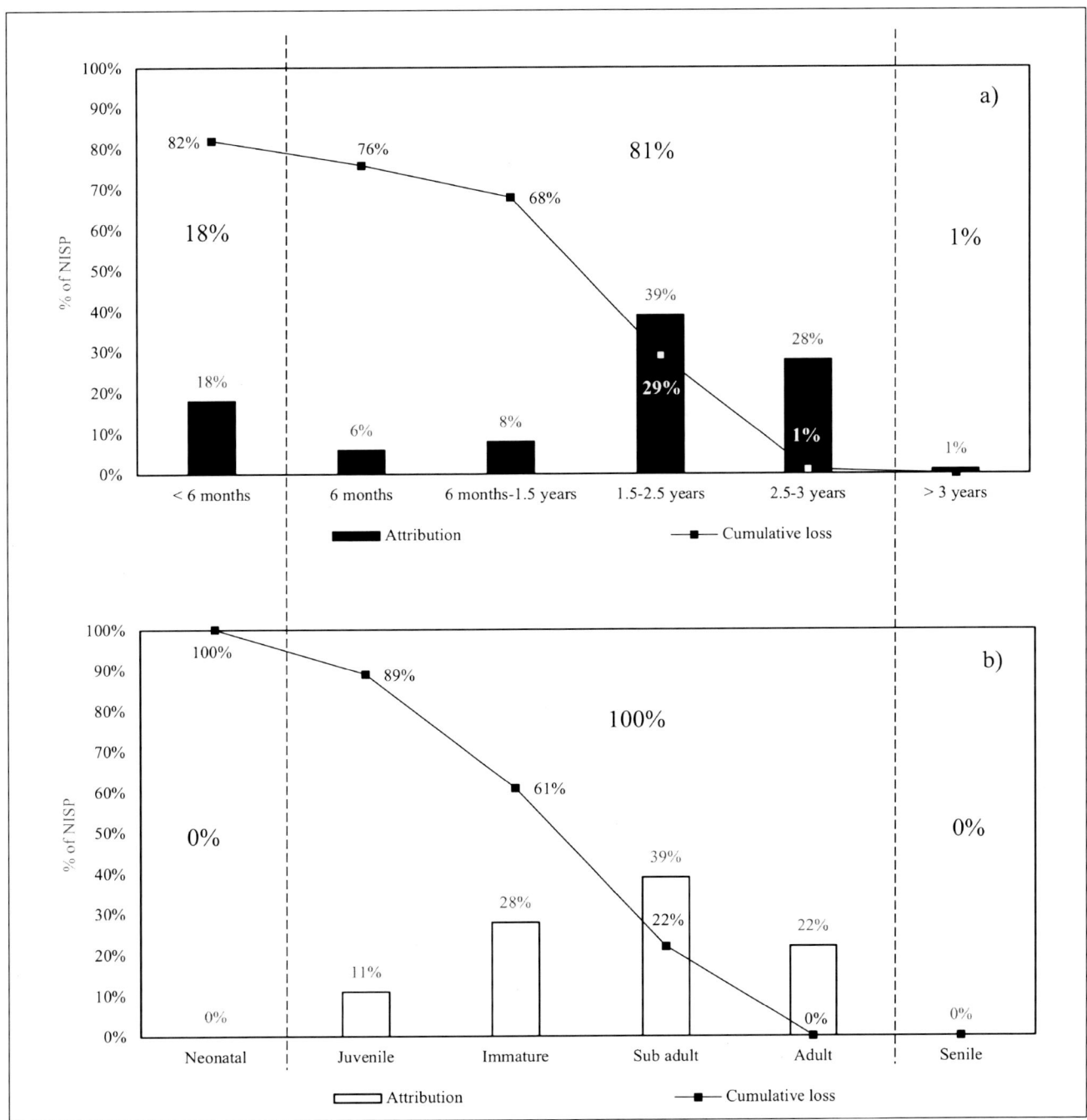

Figure 5.33 *Bos taurus* kill-off pattern between: a) structure n. 4 and b) Phases I-II in Promachon sector. Data in Table 5.106. NISP counts.

Table 5.106 *Bos taurus* (cattle) kill-off pattern between structure n. 4 and the rest of the deposits of Phase I in Promachon sector. Only the frequencies of cattle mandible wear stages are provided from structure n. 4. Phases I-II from our area of study are treated together, due to the small sample size of Phase I. Data for Figure 5.33. NISP counts.

Phase I in Promachon sector						
Structure n. 4 (Theodorogianni and Trantalidou 2013)			Rest of deposits (current study)			
Stages (unknown)	% Attribution	% Cumulative loss	Stages (O' Connor 1988)	Attribution	% Attribution	% Cumulative loss
< 6 months	18%	82%	Neonatal		0%	100%
6 months	6%	76%	Juvenile	2	11%	89%
6 months – 1½ years	8%	68%	Immature	5	28%	61%
1½ years – 2½ years	39%	29%	Sub adult	7	39%	22%
2½ years – 3 years	28%	1%	Adult	4	22%	0%
> 3 years	1%	0%	Senile		0%	0%
TOTAL	**100%**		**TOTAL**	**18**	**100%**	

preferential disposal of calves in structure n. 4 possibly reflects a purely economic perspective: calves were part of the cattle population that had to be slaughtered for the production of milk. Indeed, as previously noted, the frequency of calves is considerably high and therefore, largely conforms to Payne's (1973) idealized model of dairy husbandry. However, the economic perspective cannot be entirely disentangled from the symbolic perspective. In other words, the need for milk does not preclude the possibility that calves might have been considered as a species with a symbolic significance. To be more specific, the presence of luxurious material culture evidence (Koukouli-Chrysanthaki *et al.* 2007), packed with the presence of a characteristic age group, such as calves, is largely consistent with the distinctive and symbolic nature of structure n. 4. Overall, the pattern indicates differential disposal of calves between structure n. 4 and the rest of the deposits. In addition, older individuals, do not seem to have been disposed of in different ways. Before proceeding to the comparison of the age-at-death of sheep and goat between structure n. 4 and the rest of the deposits of Phase I, it should be noted that, as in the case of postcranial elements, Theodorogianni and Trantalidou (2013) do not state which teeth they used for the identification of the caprine population to the finest taxonomical level. Figure 5.34 (Table 5.107) presents the age-at-death of sheep between structure n. 4 (Theodorogianni and Trantalidou 2013) and the rest of the deposits of Phase I.

Lambs (0-6 months) are represented with three per cent in structure n. 4, while they are completely absent from the rest of the deposits of Phase I [stages A and B *sensu* Payne (1973): 0-6 months]. Despite the fact that this trend is similar to the one identified for cattle, the proportion of sheep neonates is too small to give us any confidence in the occurrence of deliberate disposal pattern. Other factors, such as differential recovery bias, may play a

role. However, a much larger discrepancy can be seen with regard to the rest of the sheep population. More specifically, structure n. 4, has a higher frequency of younger sheep (6 months to 3 years: 62 per cent in overall), while older sheep predominate in the rest of the deposits of Phase I [stages F-G-H-I *sensu* Payne (1973): 66 per cent]. In other words, it seems that sheep from structure n. 4 have a younger age profile than their counterparts from the rest of the deposits of Phase I. This appears to be a 'genuine' trend and, although it is difficult to pinpoint the reasons why such age differences occur, it does confirm the peculiarity of structure n. 4 in comparison to the rest of the site.

Comparison of the age-at-death of goats between the two study areas is presented in Figure 5.35 (Table 5.108). The pattern for goats is similar to that observed for sheep. Although, the small difference in the frequency of kids (0-6 months) between the two areas could be attributed to recovery bias or other taphonomic factor, structure n. 4 also has a high frequency of younger individuals (6 months to 3 years: 84 per cent in overall), while individuals being killed between 3 to 10 years [stages F-G-H-I *sensu* Payne (1973)] dominate in the rest of the deposits (69 per cent). Therefore, the results indicate a younger profile of goats in structure n. 4 and an older profile of the same species from the rest of the area in Phase I. This should be interpreted cautiously due to the very small sample size for goats, but the similarity to the sheep pattern gives some confidence in the reliability of the results.

Overall, there seems to be a differential disposal of caprines – on the basis of age – between structure n. 4 and the rest of deposits. The information thus, enhances previous suggestions regarding the different use of space, with the disposal of younger sheep and goats in structure n. 4 and the disposal of their older counterparts in the rest of the deposits of Phase I.

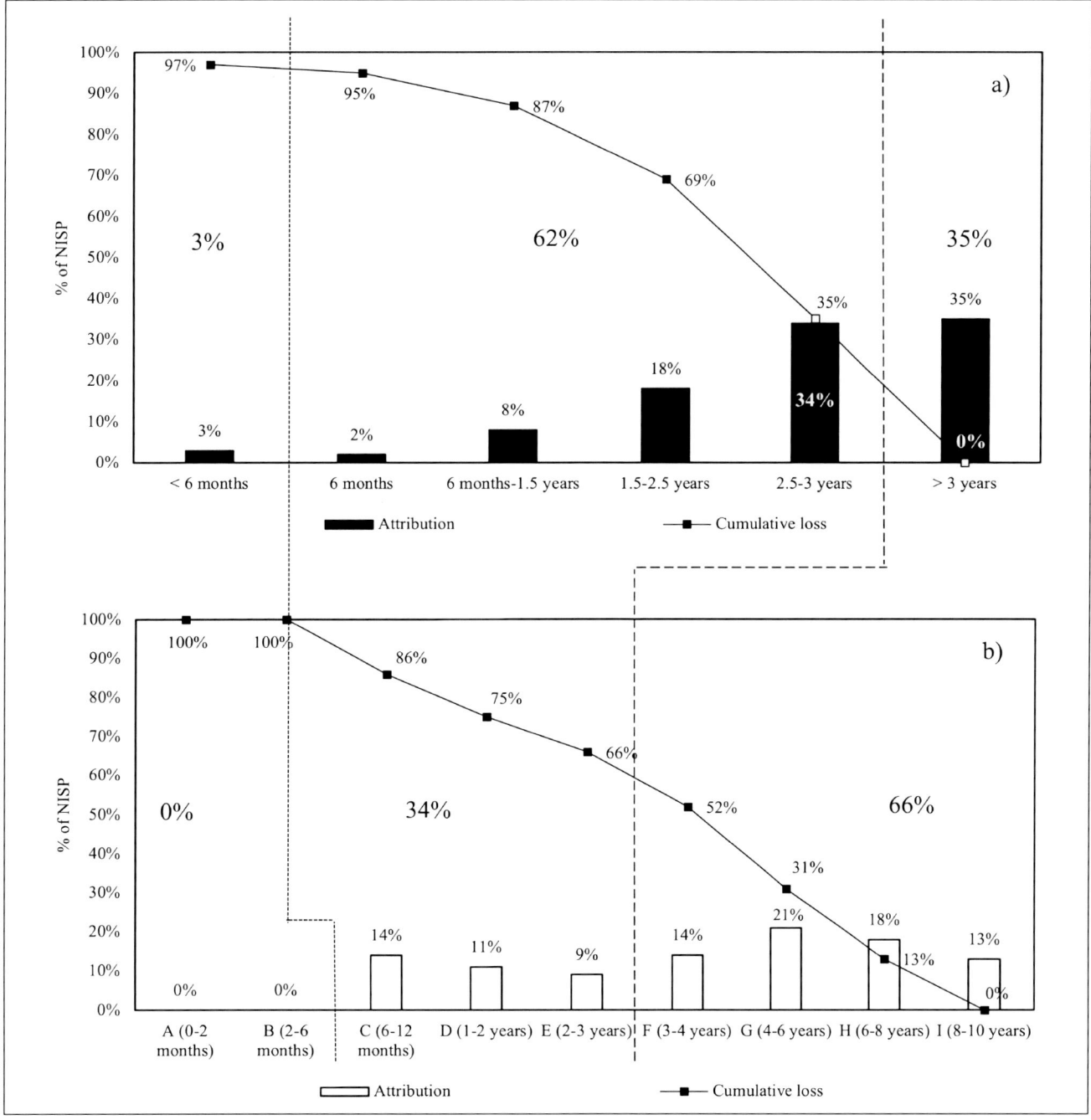

Figure 5.34 *Ovis aries* **kill-off pattern between: a) structure n. 4 and b) the rest of the deposits of Phase I in Promachon sector. Data in Table 5.107. NISP counts.**

As previously noted, there is no published information on tooth age stages of pigs from structure n. 4. However, Theodorogianni and Trantalidou (2013) argue that pigs from the latter structural feature were slaughtered between their first and second year. This information is thus consistent with the evidence from our area of study, in which immature and sub adult individuals predominate with an overall 85 per cent (Figure 5.26; Table 5.96).

5.10 Pathologies

Only two pathological bones were observed on the faunal assemblage from Promachon sector. These were

a broken and healed cattle rib and a caprine metatarsal that exhibited a slightly abnormal distal end. The fused distal end appeared to have extra bone growth around the condyles, while the whole bone appeared to be rather short and flattened. No other postcranial bones exhibited any abnormalities. Of interest is the fact that lower cattle limb bones (carpals, tarsals, metapodials, phalanges) did not exhibit any pathology, which support the hypothesis raised on the basis of the ageing evidence that there was no emphasis in the use of cattle for traction.

Oral pathologies were more common than the pathologies of the postcranial bones, but only affected caprines. The

Table 5.107 *Ovis aries* (sheep) kill-off pattern between structure n. 4 and the rest of the deposits of Phase I in Promachon sector. Only the frequencies of sheep mandible wear stages are provided from structure n. 4. Data for Figure 5.34. NISP counts.

Phase I in Promachon sector						
Structure n. 4 (Theodorogianni and Trantalidou 2013)			Rest of deposits (current study)			
Stages (unknown)	% Attribution	% Cumulative loss	Stages (Payne 1973)	Attribution	% Attribution	% Cumulative loss
< 6 months	3%	97%	A (0-2 months)		0%	100%
6 months	2%	95%	B (2-6 months)		0%	100%
6 months – 1½ years	8%	87%	C (6-12 months)	5.5	14%	86%
1½ years – 2½ years	18%	69%	D (1-2 years)	4	11%	75%
2½ years – 3 years	34%	35%	E (2-3 years)	3.5	9%	66%
> 3 years	35%	0%	F (3-4 years)	5.5	14%	52%
			G (4-6 years)	7.5	21%	31%
			H (6-8 years)	7	18%	13%
			I (8-10 years)	5	13%	0%
TOTAL	**100%**		**TOTAL**	**38**	**100%**	

most common oral pathologies were coral-like outgrowths at the root apices, probably caused by alveolar infection (Siegel 1976; Baker and Brothwell 1980). Bearing in mind that a high proportion of caprines survived beyond their ninth-tenth year, these oral infections presumably gradually developed with age. The condition was present in nine (eight of sheep, one of goat) loose fourth mandibular premolars (P_4), four loose either first or second mandibular molars ($M_{1/2}$) and two loose third mandibular molars (M_3). Another common pathological condition was abscess development, which was present in ten cases. There were only two pathological cases with both root infection and abscess development.

Two types of non-metric traits were recorded at Promachon, both of which were only observed in caprines. The first was the absence of the second mandibular premolar (P_2). Out of 27 caprine second mandibular premolars, two (seven per cent) were missing. The second non-metric trait was the absence of the hypoconulid of the third mandibular molar (M_3). Out of 145 caprine third mandibular molars, only two (two per cent) had missing hypoconulids. The two recorded non-metric traits seem to bear no relation to each other in terms of their frequency. This is not surprising, as there is no reason why they should be related. No cases of non-metric traits on domesticated populations from Greek Macedonia have been reported. Generally, we still know very little about their variation. It is possible, however, that the pattern observed in Promachon might reflect the genetic character of the local caprine population.

All in all, the scarcity of pathological conditions suggests that the domestic population at Promachon was in a generally healthy state throughout the period of the site's

occupation. Having said that, it is possible that many conditions, which would have not affected the bones and teeth and therefore are invisible to zooarchaeological research, might have occurred. Despite these limitations the observed pathologies are still very few, possibly due to the relatively young age of the animals (cattle and pigs mainly), but probably due also to the fact that animal husbandry was not under severe stress.

Finally, no pathological conditions were detected on the postcranial bones and teeth of wild species, but the sample sizes are too few to draw firm conclusions about the meaning of this.

5.11 Metrical analysis

The purpose of this part of the analysis is:

1. To find if there are differences in the size of the three main domesticated species between phases
2. To find if the wild progenitors of cattle (*Bos primigenius*), pig (*Sus scrofa*) and dog (*Canis lupus*) are present at Promachon during the Late Neolithic

Summary statistics [ranges ($x_{(1)}$= minimum; $x_{(n)}$= maximum), means (μ), standard deviation (σ) and coefficient of variation (CV)] for cattle, caprine, pig and dog teeth and postcranial measurements with ten or more cases are given in Tables 5.109-5.141 along with the results of the t-tests, which were also conducted for assessing the significance (p= probability) of the size differences between individual phases. Individual measurements were analyzed in order to study the relative sizes of teeth and bones between phases, before proceeding to more elaborate analysis (such as log

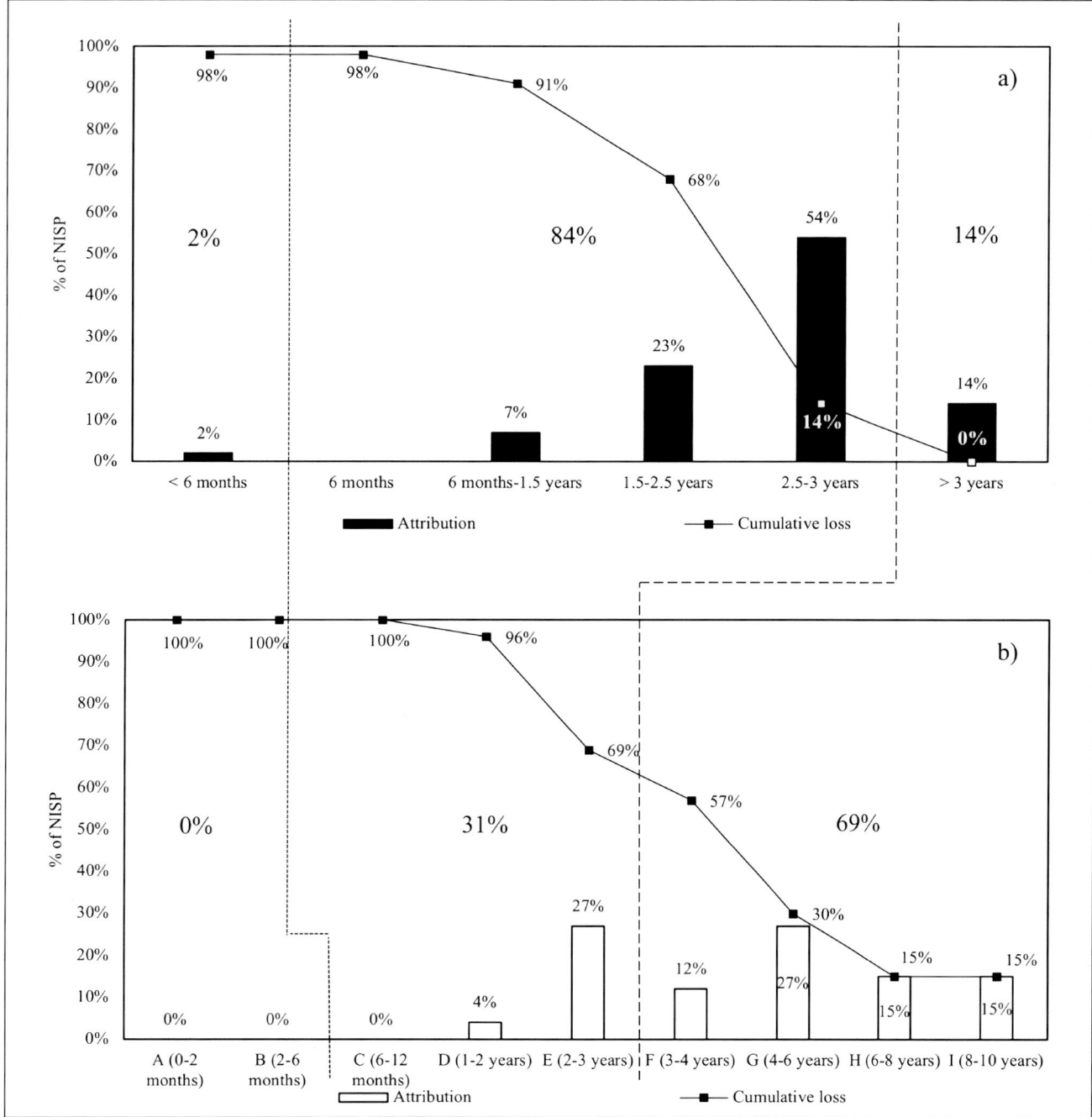

Figure 5.35 *Capra hircus* **kill-off pattern between: a) structure n. 4 and b) the rest of the deposits of Phase I in Promachon sector. Data in Table 5.108. NISP counts.**

ratios) and comparing the results with other contemporary Macedonian and Thessalian sites (chapter 6).

5.11.1 Bos taurus *size*

As a result of the volume of cattle bones recovered from Promachon, a large body of metrical data was collected. Summary statistics for cattle teeth and postcranial measurements with ten or more cases are given in Tables 5.109-5.119. The most numerous cattle tooth measurements were the lengths and the widths of the third mandibular molar (M_3). In general, teeth tend to be more conservative than postcranial bones since they are less affected by environmental factors as well as sex

and age (Albarella 2002; Payne and Bull 1988). They are therefore a useful tool for exploring if changes in the size of animals occur with time. In Figure 5.36 we plot the length of the third mandibular molar (M_3L) against the width of the same tooth (M_3W). The diagram shows some variation in cattle M_3, but no obvious differences in size between individual phases seem to occur (the latter is also confirmed by a t-test in Table 5.110).

One of the main characteristics of teeth is that they respond considerably more slowly than postcranial elements to environmental pressures that may cause size change (Johnstone and Albarella 2015). Bearing in mind that, since the chronological gap between the three phases under

Table 5.108 *Capra hircus* (goat) kill-off pattern between structure n. 4 and the rest of the deposits of Phase I in Promachon sector. Only the frequencies of goat mandible wear stages are provided from structure n. 4. Data for Figure 5.35. NISP counts.

Phase I in Promachon sector						
Structure n. 4 (Theodorogianni and Trantalidou 2013)			Rest of deposits (current study)			
Stages (unknown)	% Attribution	% Cumulative loss	Stages (Payne 1973)	Attribution	% Attribution	% Cumulative loss
< 6 months	2%	98%	A (0-2 months)		0%	100%
6 months		98%	B (2-6 months)		0%	100%
6 months – 1½ years	7%	91%	C (6-12 months)		0%	100%
1½ years – 2½ years	23%	68%	D (1-2 years)	0.5	4%	96%
2½ years – 3 years	54%	14%	E (2-3 years)	3.5	27%	69%
> 3 years	14%	0%	F (3-4 years)	1.5	12%	57%
			G (4-6 years)	3.5	27%	30%
			H (6-8 years)	2	15%	15%
			I (8-10 years)	2	15%	15%
TOTAL	100%		TOTAL	13	100%	

Table 5.109 *Bos taurus* (cattle) maxillary tooth measurements. Sample sizes (n.), ranges [x(1)= minimum; x(n)= maximum], means (μ), standard deviations (σ) and coefficients of variation (CV). Only sample sizes with a minimum of ten cases are considered. All measurements are in millimeters.

Measurements	*Bos taurus* maxillary teeth						
	Period	n.	x(1)	x(n)	μ	σ	CV
M¹ Width	LN	14	14.2	23.5	20.1	3	14.9
M³ Width	Phase I	17	17.7	24	19.7	1.68	8.5
	LN	34	16.3	24.9	20.1	1.98	9.8

study is relatively small, the diachronic analysis will focus on those cattle postcranial bones that produced the most measurements (tibia, humerus and astragalus). In Figure 5.37 we plot the distal breadth of cattle tibia against the distal depth. The scatterplot shows two or possible three apparent clusters. The smallest group is likely to be made of females, while the five largest specimens are likely to be from males. The intermediate group is closer to the 'males' but it is likely to be mixed in terms of sex distribution. The potential occurrence of castrates and cattle of different size types may of course contribute to confuse the pattern. To evaluate this better it is necessary to look at other postcranial bones.

Figure 5.38 presents the scatterplot of the measurements of the distal humerus. Here we compare the width of the trochlea (BT) against the diameter of the trochlea (HTC). This diagram is not very useful for detecting differences in cattle size between individual phases due to the very small sample size of Phases II and III.

The scatterplot indicates that the two measurements are poorly correlated, which is not surprising as they are

aligned on different axes (Davis 1996).[7] As for tibia, there appears to be some clustering of measurements, though the sample is smaller and invites caution. This is most likely due to sex differences, bearing also in mind that in artiodactyls, forelimb bones appear to be particularly sex dimorphic (Payne and Bull 1988).

The astragalus rapidly reaches adult size and thereafter exhibits limited size change once is fully ossified, also because it is constrained in an articulation and has limited room for growth (Rowley-Conwy *et al.* 2012; Payne and Bull 1988; Albarella and Payne 2005). Nonetheless, some age-related variability obviously also affects this bone (and this must be considered for all size comparisons where astragalus measurements are involved), but it should represent a minor factor, once porous or unusually light (*i.e.* not fully ossified) astragali have been excluded from biometrical analysis. The size of the astragalus is directly related to its weight-bearing role and it is therefore closely

---

[7] As Davis (1996) argues, there is better correlation between measurements taken on the same axis than between those on different axes.

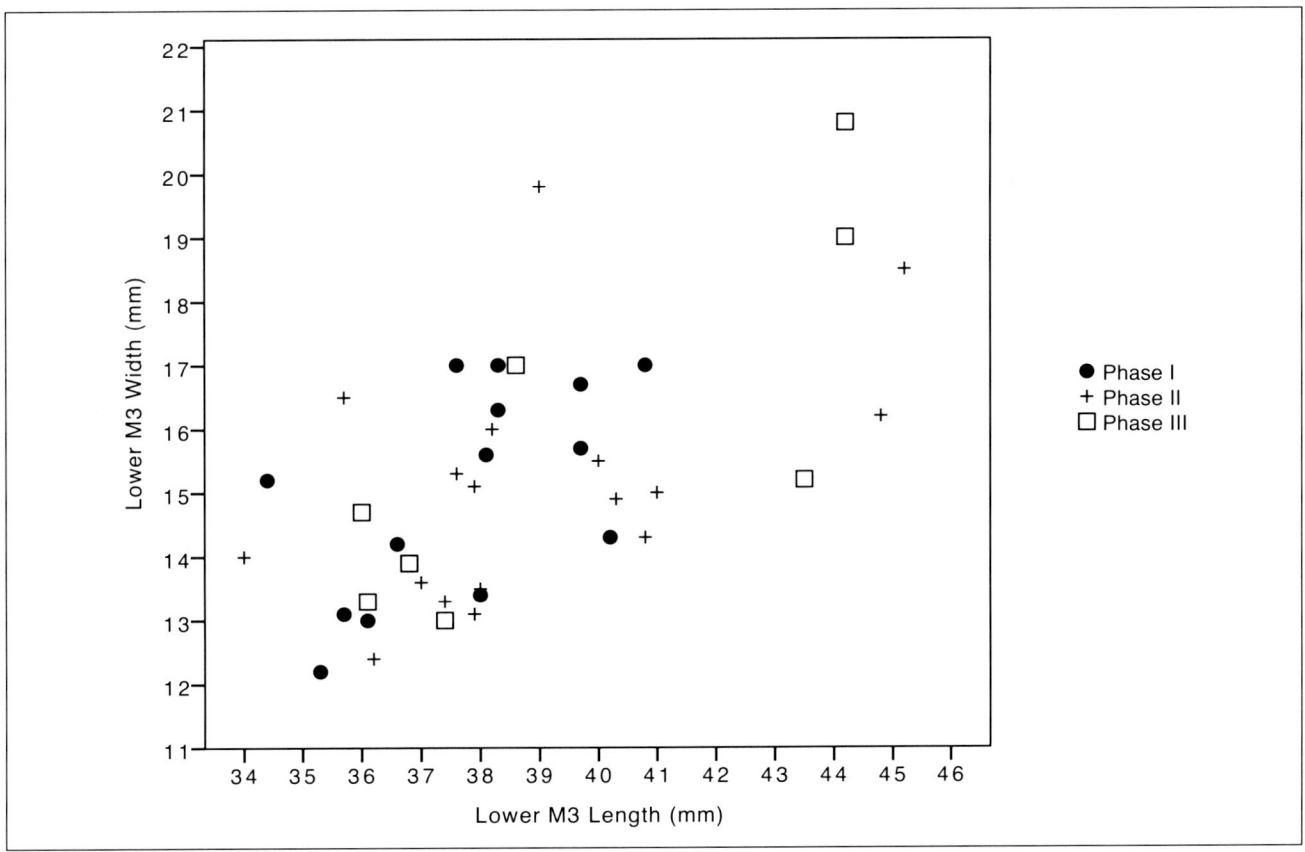

Figure 5.36 *Bos taurus* **mandibular third molar length** *versus* **width. Comparison between phases.**

Table 5.110 *Bos taurus* **(cattle) mandibular tooth measurements. Sample sizes (n.), ranges [x(1)= minimum; x(n)= maximum], means (μ), standard deviations (σ), coefficients of variation (CV), and statistical comparison (using a t-test) for assessing the significance (p. = probability) of the size differences between individual phases. Only sample sizes with a minimum of ten cases are considered. All measurements are in millimeters.**

Measurements	*Bos taurus* mandibular teeth							Comparison (t-test)	
								Phases I *vs.* II	Phases II *vs.* III
	Period	n.	x(1)	x(n)	μ	σ	CV	p.	p.
dP$_4$ Width	LN	22	10.5	14.8	12.6	1.24	9.8		
M$_1$ Width	Phase I	13	11.7	16.9	14.9	1.57	10.5		
	LN	21	11	16.9	14.4	1.79	12.4		
M$_2$ Width	Phase I	11	12.7	17.2	15.7	1.33	8.4		
	LN	13	12.4	18.9	15.7	1.80	11.4		
M$_3$ Length	Phase I	14	34.4	40.8	37.7	1.94	5.1	.280	
	Phase II	18	34	45.2	38.7	2.92	7.5		
	LN	39	34	45.2	38.5	2.81	7.3		
M$_3$ Width	Phase I	19	12.2	17	15.1	1.5	9.9	.911	
	Phase II	19	12.4	19.8	15.1	1.9	12.5		
	LN	46	12.2	20.8	15.2	1.92	12.6		

p. = .001-.01: Difference is highly significant (less than 1% probability that is due to chance)
p. = .01-.05: Difference is significant (less than 5% probability that is due to chance)
p. = > .05: No significant difference (more than 5% probability that is due to chance)

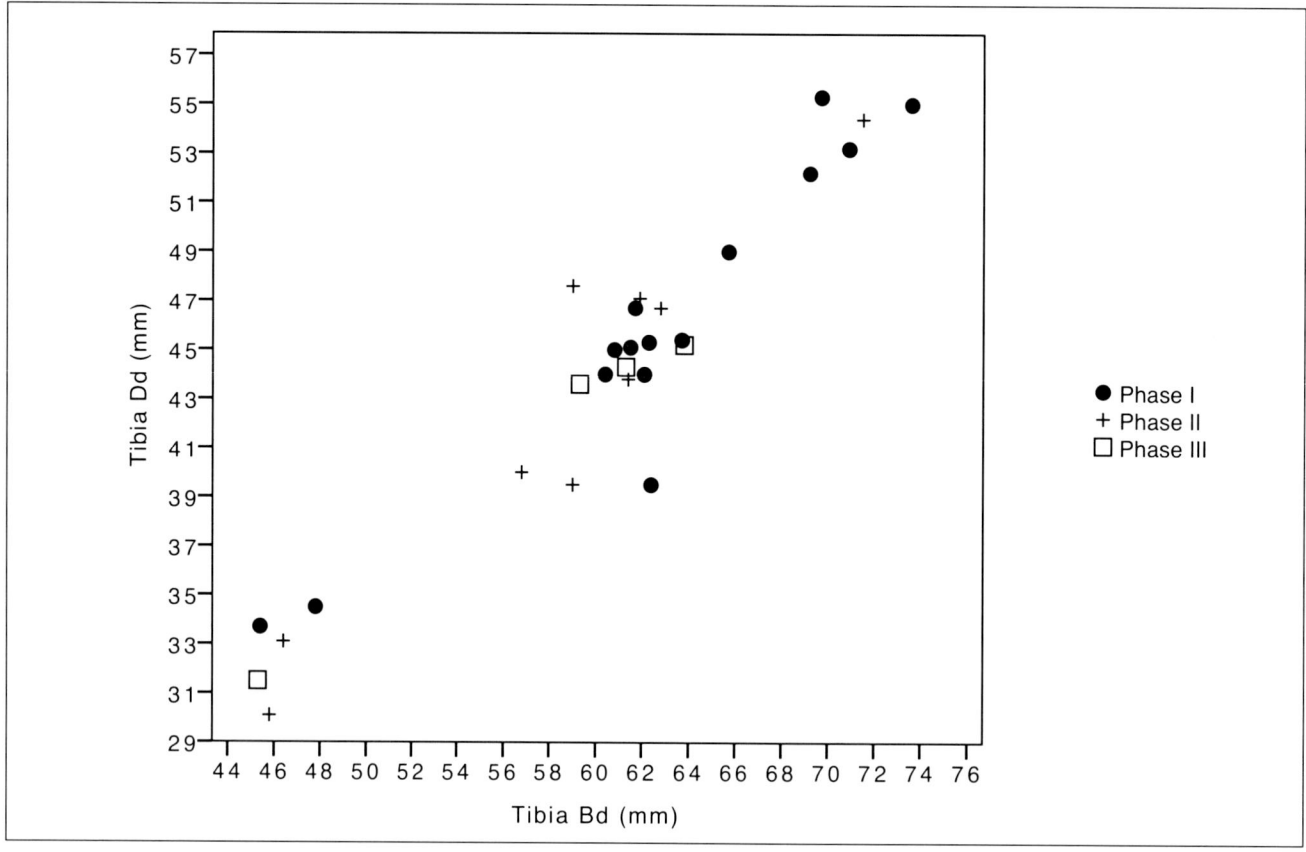

Figure 5.37 *Bos taurus* **tibia distal breadth (Bd)** *versus* **distal depth (Dd). Comparison between phases.**

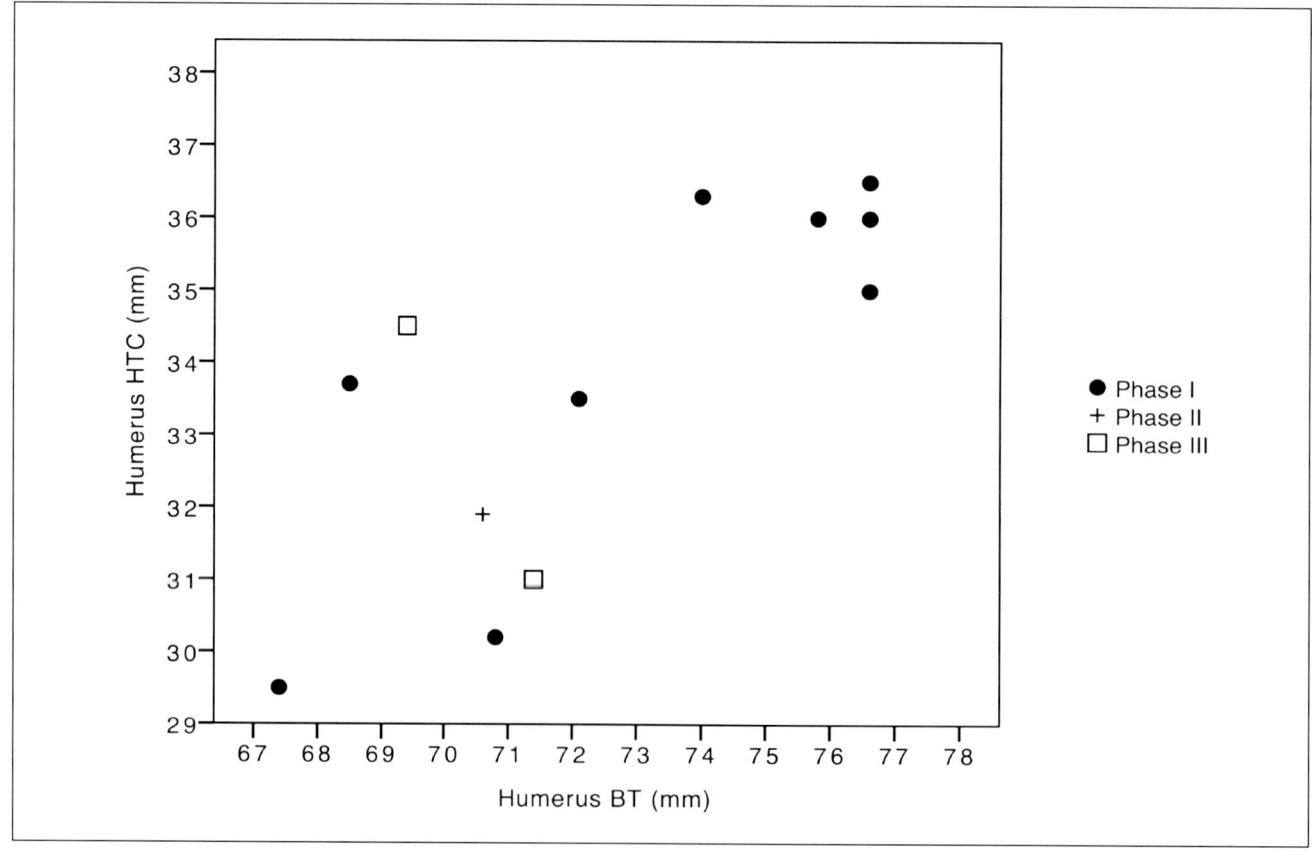

Figure 5.38 *Bos taurus* **humerus width of the trochlea (BT)** *versus* **diameter of the trochlea (HTC). Comparison between phases.**

Table 5.111 *Bos taurus* (cattle) scapula measurements. Sample sizes (n.), ranges [x(1)= minimum; x(n)= maximum], means (μ), standard deviations (σ) and coefficients of variation (CV). Only sample sizes with a minimum of ten cases are considered. All measurements are in millimeters (mm). Only fully fused specimens are considered.

Measurements	*Bos taurus* scapula						
	Period	n	x(1)	x(n)	μ	σ	CV
SLC	LN	12	38	58	50.9	5.19	10.2

Table 5.112 *Bos taurus* (cattle) humerus measurements. Sample sizes (n.), ranges [x(1)= minimum; x(n)= maximum], means (μ), standard deviations (σ) and coefficients of variation (CV). Only sample sizes with a minimum of ten cases are considered. All measurements are in millimeters (mm). Only fully fused specimens are considered.

Measurements	*Bos taurus* humerus						
	Period	n	x(1)	x(n)	μ	σ	CV
BT	LN	13	67.4	80.3	73	3.86	5.2
HTC	Phase I	13	29.5	36.5	33.6	2.28	6.8
	LN	23	23.0	37.9	32.9	3.77	11.4

Table 5.113 *Bos taurus* (cattle) metacarpal measurements. Sample sizes (n.), ranges [x(1)= minimum; x(n)= maximum], means (μ), standard deviations (σ), coefficients of variation (CV), and statistical comparison (using a t-test) for assessing the significance (p. = probability) of the size differences between individual phases. Only sample sizes with a minimum of ten cases are considered. All measurements are in millimeters (mm). Only fully fused specimens are considered.

Measurements	*Bos taurus* metacarpal							Comparison (t-test)	
								Phases I *vs.* II	Phases II *vs.* III
	Period	n	x(1)	x(n)	μ	σ	CV	p.	p.
Bd	Phase I	12	54.5	68.1	60.9	5.21	8.5	.149	
	Phase II	11	52.6	65.0	58.1	3.84	6.6		
	LN	29	52.6	71.2	60.3	5.28	8.7		
BatF	Phase I	11	50.6	61.5	55.9	4.27	7.6	.253	
	Phase II	11	45.7	60.0	53.7	4.33	8		
	LN	28	45.7	63.5	55.3	4.60	8.3		
a	Phase I	13	25.3	31.1	28.4	2.05	7.2	.160	
	Phase II	13	23.9	30.1	27.2	2.11	7.7		
	LN	33	23.9	34.5	28.3	2.61	9.2		
b	Phase I	14	24.5	33.0	29.3	2.52	8.6	.031	
	Phase II	11	24.2	31.0	27.2	2.02	7.4		
	LN	31	24.2	33.6	28.6	2.60	9		
3	Phase I	14	26.4	33.1	30.6	2.16	7	.775	
	Phase II	11	27.9	33.7	30.3	1.85	6		
	LN	31	26.4	34.0	30.5	2.05	6.7		
6	Phase I	14	25.3	33.1	30.4	2.31	7.6	.705	
	Phase II	11	27.4	33.0	30	1.90	6.3		
	LN	31	25.3	34.1	30.4	2.14	7		

p. = .001-.01: Difference is highly significant (less than 1% probability that is due to chance)
p. = .01-.05: Difference is significant (less than 5% probability that is due to chance)
p. = > .05: No significant difference (more than 5% probability that is due to chance)

Table 5.114 *Bos taurus* (cattle) pelvis measurements. Sample sizes (n.), ranges [x(1)= minimum; x(n)= maximum], means (μ), standard deviations (σ) and coefficients of variation (CV). Only sample sizes with a minimum of ten cases are considered. All measurements are in millimeters (mm). Only fully fused specimens are considered.

Measurements	*Bos taurus* pelvis						
	Period	n	x(1)	x(n)	μ	σ	CV
LAR	LN	10	50.5	71.5	64.7	6.75	10.4

Table 5.115 *Bos taurus* (cattle) femur measurements. Sample sizes (n.), ranges [x(1)= minimum; x(n)= maximum], means (μ), standard deviations (σ) and coefficients of variation (CV). Only sample sizes with a minimum of ten cases are considered. All measurements are in millimeters (mm). Only fully fused specimens are considered.

Measurements	*Bos taurus* femur						
	Period	n	x(1)	x(n)	μ	σ	CV
DC	LN	13	41.4	49.0	45.5	2.25	4.9

Table 5.116 *Bos taurus* (cattle) tibia measurements. Sample sizes (n.), ranges [x(1)= minimum; x(n)= maximum], means (μ), standard deviations (σ), coefficients of variation (CV), and statistical comparison (using a t-test) for assessing the significance (p. = probability) of the size differences between individual phases. Only sample sizes with a minimum of ten cases are considered. All measurements are in millimeters (mm). Only fully fused specimens are considered.

Measurements	*Bos taurus* tibia							Comparison (t-test)	
								Phases I *vs.* II	Phases II *vs.* III
	Period	n	x(1)	x(n)	μ	σ	CV	p.	p.
Bd	Phase I	15	45.4	73.6	62.4	7.65	12.2		
	LN	29	45.3	73.6	60.5	7.77	12.8		
Dd	Phase I	15	33.7	55.3	45.8	6.56	14.3	.288	
	Phase II	10	30.1	54.4	42.7	7.23	16.9		
	LN	29	30.1	55.3	44.1	6.81	15.4		

p. = .001-.01: Difference is highly significant (less than 1% probability that is due to chance)
p. = .01-.05: Difference is significant (less than 5% probability that is due to chance)
p. = > .05: No significant difference (more than 5% probability that is due to chance)

related to the overall size of the animal. Another great advantage for its use in biometric studies as a measure of the robustness of the individuals is the fact that – in most cases – it survives well, thus, permitting valuable metric data to be collected.

In Figure 5.39 we plot the greatest length of the lateral half of the astragalus (GLl) against the greatest length of the medial half of the astragalus (GLm). Unlike the previous elements there is high correlation between the two measurements, which make sense since they are both lengths. Consistently with the other measurements there are no differences in the size of cattle astragalus between individual phases, as also supported by the results of t-tests (Table 5.117). The clustering that had been identified in other bones is not apparent in the astragalus, which may be a consequence of the fact that this bone is less sexually dimorphic. If the separation in groups discussed above had been a consequence of the simultaneous occurrence at Promachon of different cattle morphotypes we would have expected this to show up in the astragalus measurements too.

A common method for detecting sexual dimorphism in cattle is the use of metapodial (metacarpal and metatarsal) measurements. This was not possible at Promachon since very few intact cattle metapodials were eventually recovered, and hence, very few length measurements could be taken. Since shape analysis could not be conducted on metapodials, as insufficient measurements were available, shape indices were calculated on cattle astragali (Albarella 2002). Diagrams based on metric ratios [*i.e.* Bd/GLl and Dl/GLl *sensu* von den Driesch (1976) for the astragalus] are relatively size-independent and are a useful tool for detecting potential variations in sex, breeds or regional types (*c.f.* Albarella 1997; 2002), although some authorities have expressed doubts about using such ratio values in the evaluation of statistical differences (Atchley *et al.* 1976).

Figure 5.40 presents the shape indices for cattle astragali. As for size, there is no detectable change between individual phases. They also show that there is no linear relationship between the two indices, thus indicating quite a lot of variation in the shape of the cattle astragalus. There

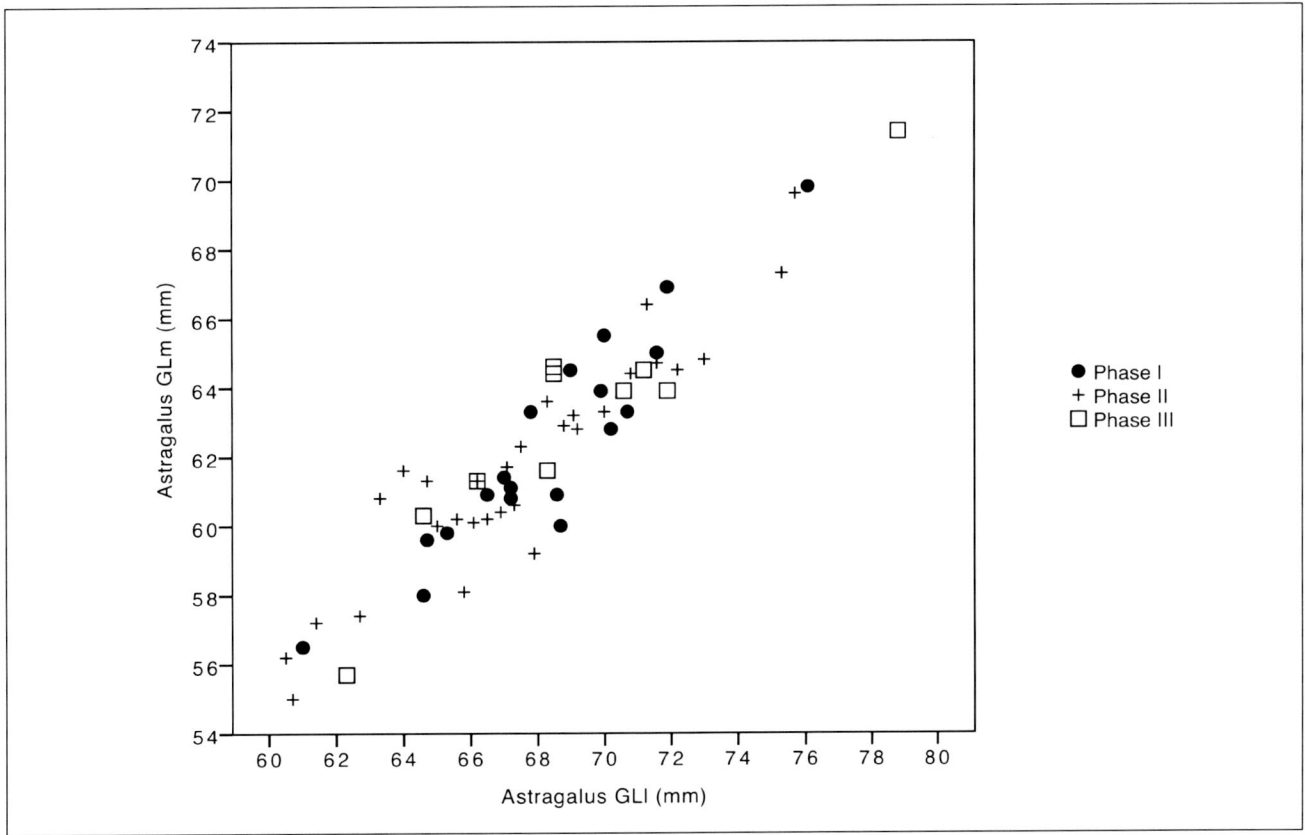

Figure 5.39 *Bos taurus* **astragalus greatest length of the lateral half (GLl)** *versus* **greatest length of the medial half (GLm). Comparison between phases.**

are however, no clear groupings, which would indicate that most cattle at Promachon – even in different phases – were of similar builds. This is rather interesting, as we would have expected that males, females and perhaps also castrates would be slightly different. However, it is possible that the differences are too slight to stand out visually.

The presence of the wild progenitor of cattle (*Bos primigenius*) has been reported at a number of Macedonian sites, contemporary to Promachon, such as Sitagroi (Bökönyi 1986), Stavroupoli (Yiannouli 2002a; 2004), Pigi athinas (Cantuel 2013) and Makriyalos (Halstead pers. comm.). The species' presence has also been reported in the Early Neolithic Thessalian sites of Achilleion (Bökönyi 1989) and Argissa (Boessneck 1962). Metrical data of aurochs' astragali (GLl) from a number of sites in Macedonia and Thessaly have been reported in some cases and are presented below[8]:

The identification of the aurochs in these sites was based on the observation of the largest specimens (in this case, the astragali), which showed up as the largest outliers in each sample. The major drawback, however, is the extremely small sample size for each case. However, we can still see that the aurochs astragali from these sites are larger than the largest cattle astragalus from Promachon (GLl: 79.1 mm). If we combine this observation with the lack of obvious outliers in the Promachon distribution, we can argue against the presence of the aurochs in the case of Promachon.

As already noted, the presence of the aurochs has been reported in structure n. 4 at Promachon (Theodorogianni and Trantalidou 2013), where 174 remains of this species – consisting mainly of lower forelimbs and lower hindlimbs (mainly metapodials and phalanges) – were identified. However, the authors do not provide any metrical data.

Sites	*Bos primigenius* astragalus: greatest length of the lateral half				
	Locale	Cultural sequence	N	GLl (in millimetres)	Sources
Achilleion IIb	Thessaly	Early Neolithic	1	82 mm	Bökönyi (1989)
Pigi Athinas	Macedonia	Late Neolithic	1	84.8 mm	Cantuel (2013)
Sitagroi IV	Macedonia	Early Bronze Age	1	86 mm	Bökönyi (1986)
Stavroupoli I-II	Macedonia	Late Neolithic	2	82.3 mm & 87.8 mm	Yiannouli (2002a)

[8] However, it is possible that aurochs might also be present in other sites contemporary to Promachon, but this is difficult to know, due to the dearth of available metrical data.

Table 5.117 *Bos taurus* (cattle) astragalus measurements. Sample sizes (n.), ranges [x(1)= minimum; x(n)= maximum], means (μ), standard deviations (σ) coefficients of variation (CV), and statistical comparison (using a t-test) for assessing the significance (p. = probability) of the size differences between individual phases. Only sample sizes with a minimum of ten cases are considered. All measurements are in millimeters (mm). Only fully fused specimens are considered.

Measurements	*Bos taurus* astragalus							Comparison (t-test)	
								Phases I vs. II	Phases II vs. III
	Period	n	x(1)	x(n)	μ	σ	CV	p.	p.
GLl	Phase I	21	61	76	68.2	3.15	4.6	.715	
	Phase II	37	61	76	67.9	3.7	5.5		.459
	Phase III	10	62	79	69	4.53	6.5		
	LN	68	61	79	68.1	3.67	5.3		
Glm	Phase I	22	56.1	69.8	62.3	3.34	5.3	.494	
	Phase II	31	55	69.6	61.7	3.2	5.1		.320
	Phase III	10	55.7	71.4	63.1	4	6.3		
	LN	63	55.0	71.4	62.1	3.37	5.4		
Bd	Phase I	24	36.8	49.3	43.7	2.96	6.7	.095	
	Phase II	33	36.5	48.5	42.4	2.93	6.9		.158
	Phase III	10	39.7	48.9	44.1	3.3	7.4		
	LN	67	36.5	49.3	43.1	3.04	7		
Dl	Phase I	22	33.5	45.3	39.3	2.59	6.6	.338	
	Phase II	36	33.2	44.4	38.6	2.62	6.8		.176
	Phase III	10	36.0	47.3	40.2	3.29	8.1		
	LN	68	33.2	47.3	39	2.74	7		

p. = .001-.01: Difference is highly significant (less than 1% probability that is due to chance)
p. = .01-.05: Difference is significant (less than 5% probability that is due to chance)
p. = > .05: No significant difference (more than 5% probability that is due to chance)

Table 5.118 *Bos taurus* (cattle) calcaneum measurements. Sample sizes (n.), ranges [x(1)= minimum; x(n)= maximum], means (μ), standard deviations (σ) and coefficients of variation (CV). Only sample sizes with a minimum of ten cases are considered. All measurements are in millimeters (mm). Only fully fused specimens are considered.

Measurements	*Bos taurus* calcaneum						
	Period	n	x(1)	x(n)	μ	σ	CV
GD	LN	12	34.4	56.2	51.14	5.6	10.9

In order to explore the possibility of the presence of the aurochs in our assemblage, we use the scale index technique (log ratio), which provides us with the advantage of observing how the distributions of different measurements compare with each other. The length, the width and the depth measurements were kept separate, as there is better correlation between measurements taken on the same axis than between those on different axes (Albarella 2002; Davis 1996). Unfortunatelly, metrical data of *Bos primigenius* is generally extremely scarce. In addition, since there is no published Greek standard of aurochs to calculate the log ratios, we use the standard from a known sample of aurochs from the Mesolithic site of Cabeço da Arruda in Portugal (Wright 2013). Regardless of the fact that the standard sample derives from a site distant from Promachon, we can still use the Cabeço da Arruda material since the geographical location of the site (Portugal) is similar to Greece in terms of latitude. When the data are plotted, the Cabeço da Arruda material will always be centered on zero (.00), thus giving an easy reference point to indicate whether the cattle material from Promachon is larger or smaller than Cabeço da Arruda. Figure 5.41 shows the log ratio diagrams for the three dimensions – the lengths, the widths and the depths respectively. These show that the bulk of the material from Promachon plots on the left side of the standard, indicating

Table 5.119 *Bos taurus* (cattle) metatarsal measurements. Sample sizes (n.), ranges [x(1)= minimum; x(n)= maximum], means (μ), standard deviations (σ) and coefficients of variation (CV). Only sample sizes with a minimum of ten cases are considered. All measurements are in millimeters (mm). Only fully fused specimens are considered.

Measurements	*Bos taurus* metatarsal						
	Period	n	x(1)	x(n)	μ	σ	CV
Bd	Phase II	12	41	62.5	52.5	7.47	14.2
	LN	17	41	62.5	53.4	6.57	12.2
BatF	Phase II	10	37.6	57	46.7	5.98	12.8
	LN	15	37.6	57	47.9	5.45	11.3
a	Phase II	11	17.9	28.8	23.7	3.44	14.5
	LN	17	17.9	28.8	24.5	3.14	12.8
b	Phase II	13	17.8	30.5	24.9	4.37	17.5
	LN	21	17.8	30.5	25.1	3.75	14.9
3	Phase II	12	22	33.9	28.4	3.51	12.3
	LN	17	22	33.9	28.7	3.16	10.9
6	Phase II	15	22.8	32.8	28.6	2.81	9.8
	LN	23	22.8	32.8	29	2.54	8.7

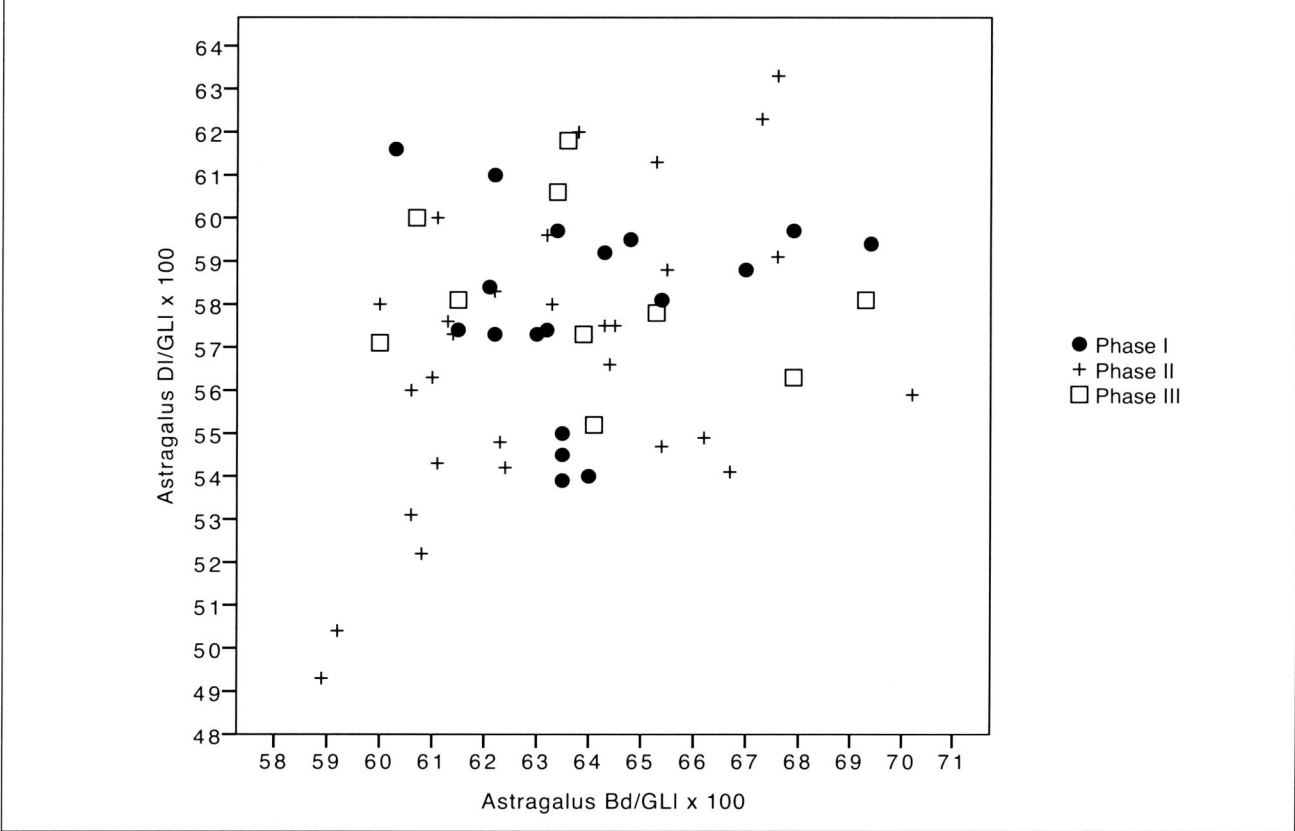

Figure 5.40 *Bos taurus* astragali shape indices. Comparison between phases.

that the overwhelming majority of *Bos* are smaller than the average aurochs from Cabeço da Arruda. All distributions confirm the metrical analysis provided above, with no clear large outliers. There are only a length and a depth that pull away slightly on the right-hand size of the distribution and also represent the only specimens that are larger than the standard. They are, however, still fairly close to the rest of the distribution and, although they could belong to the aurochs, the evidence is insufficient to be confident about it. Since the aurochs from Cabeço da Arruda is smaller

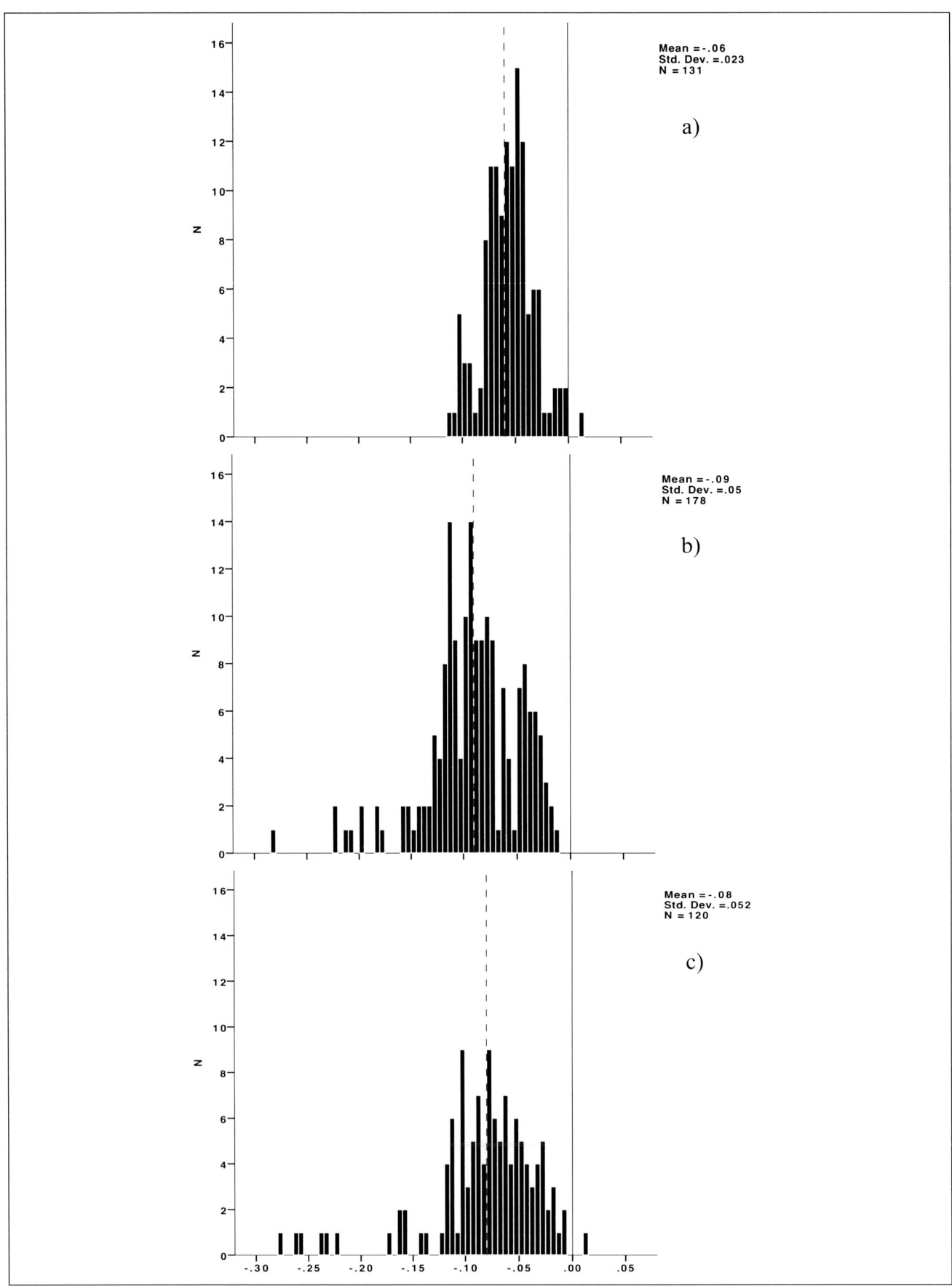

Figure 5.41 Comparison of the *Bos* size from Promachon sector with a standard *Bos primigenius* sample from the Mesolithic site of Cabeço da Arruda in Portugal (Wright 2013) using the log ratio technique (Simpson *et al.* 1960). Only fully fused postcranial bones were considered. Only compatible measurements, were considered: a) length measurements, b) width measurements, c) depth measurements. The mean is marked by a black dashed vertical line, and the standard measurement by a black vertical line at .00. The scale of the vertical axis is fixed to emphasize differences in sample sizes.

than those from northwest Europe (*e.g.* Denmark, Britain and Germany), then the cattle material from Promachon – being even smaller than Cabeço da Arruda – is unlikely to belong to the aurochs.

Of interest is the fact that on average widths and depths appear to be relatively smaller than the standard in comparison to lengths. They also have a tail of small specimens that is absent in the lengths. This is a consequence of the greater robustness of the aurochs in comparison to domestic cattle as demonstrated by Wright (2013).

All in all, we can say that the results of the biometry do not show any size differences in cattle between individual phases. Perhaps the time difference between phases of occupation is too small for any changes to be obvious. In addition, the biometrical evidence does not provide any support to the suggestion for the occurrence of the aurochs.

5.11.2 Caprinae size

Caprine measurements are more numerous than those of cattle – as expected – due to their overall higher frequency in the assemblage. Tables 5.120-5.126, Tables 5.127-5.129 and Tables 5.130-5.132 give a summary of the bone and tooth measurements with more than ten cases, for sheep, goat and sheep/goat respectively. Tooth measurements are the most numerous, which is unsurprising given the high proportion of teeth in the assemblage. In Figure 5.42 we plot the length of the third mandibular molar (M_3L) against the width of the same tooth (M_3W) for sheep, goat and sheep/goat on a temporal level. The sample size of goat teeth (especially in Phases II and III) is too small for any conclusions to be drawn. However, a comparison of the sheep and the sheep/goat M_3's shows that no obvious differences in the size of the caprines between individual phases occur. This result is also confirmed by a t-test (Table 5.120 and Table 5.130).

Humerus, tibia, astragalus, metapodials and calcaneum were the postcranial elements that were regularly used

Table 5.120 *Ovis aries* **(sheep) mandibular tooth measurements. Sample sizes (n.), ranges [x(1)= minimum; x(n)= maximum], means (μ), standard deviations (σ), coefficients of variation (CV), and statistical comparison (using a t-test) for assessing the significance (p. = probability) of the size differences between individual phases. Only sample sizes with a minimum of ten cases are considered. All measurements are in millimeters.**

Measurements	*Ovis aries* mandibular teeth							Comparison (t-test)	
								Phases I *vs.* II	Phases II *vs.* III
	Period	n.	x(1)	x(n)	μ	σ	CV	p.	p.
dP₄ Width	Phase I	19	5.6	6.6	6.1	.3	4.9	.188	
	Phase II	25	5.7	7	6.2	.32	5.1		.186
	Phase III	14	5.7	6.6	6.1	.24	3.9		
	LN	58	5.6	7	6.1	.3	4.9		
M₁ Width	Phase I	33	5.9	8.2	6.9	.55	7.9	.931	
	Phase II	28	6.3	8	6.9	.41	5.9		.322
	Phase III	10	6.3	7.6	7	.42	6		
	LN	71	5.9	8.2	6.9	.48	6.9		
M₂ Width	Phase I	29	6.9	8.5	7.8	.42	5.3	.069	
	Phase II	15	6.9	8.3	7.5	.4	5.3		
	LN	51	6.9	8.7	7.7	.46	5.9		
M₃ Length	Phase I	16	19.1	22.5	20.8	1.02	4.9		
	LN	31	15.9	22.8	20.5	1.5	7.3		
M₃ Width	Phase I	17	7.1	9.1	8.1	.59	7.2		
	LN	32	6.7	9.1	8	.64	8		

p. = .001-.01: Difference is highly significant (less than 1% probability that is due to chance)
p. = .01-.05: Difference is significant (less than 5% probability that is due to chance)
p. = > .05: No significant difference (more than 5% probability that is due to chance)

Table 5.121 *Ovis aries* (sheep) humerus measurements. Sample sizes (n.), ranges [x(1)= minimum; x(n)= maximum], means (μ), standard deviations (σ), coefficients of variation (CV), and statistical comparison (using a t-test) for assessing the significance (p. = probability) of the size differences between individual phases. Only sample sizes with a minimum of ten cases are considered. All measurements are in millimeters (mm). Only fully fused specimens are considered.

Measurements	*Ovis aries* humerus							Comparison (t-test)	
								Phases I *vs.* II	Phases II *vs.* III
	Period	n	x(1)	x(n)	μ	σ	CV	p.	p.
BT	Phase I	21	23.1	30.4	26.2	1.81	6.9	.687	
	Phase II	20	23.7	30.1	26.4	1.6	6		.937
	Phase III	14	22.9	37.3	26.3	3.53	13.4		
	LN	55	22.9	37.3	26.3	2.26	8.6		
HTC	Phase I	24	12.1	15.7	13.3	.97	7.3	.562	
	Phase II	23	11.7	14.8	13.2	.72	5.4		.922
	Phase III	13	11.5	15.7	13.2	1.24	9.3		
	LN	60	11.5	15.7	13.2	.94	7		

p. = .001-.01: Difference is highly significant (less than 1% probability that is due to chance)
p. = .01-.05: Difference is significant (less than 5% probability that is due to chance)
p. = > .05: No significant difference (more than 5% probability that is due to chance)

Table 5.122 *Ovis aries* (sheep) metacarpal measurements. Sample sizes (n.), ranges [x(1)= minimum; x(n)= maximum], means (μ), standard deviations (σ) and coefficients of variation (CV). Only sample sizes with a minimum of ten cases are considered. All measurements are in millimeters (mm). Only fully fused specimens are considered.

Measurements	*Ovis aries* metacarpal						
	Period	n	x(1)	x(n)	μ	σ	CV
b	LN	12	8.5	11.4	10.4	1	9
4	LN	12	8	11.4	9.8	1.1	9.7
6	LN	12	10	13.7	12.3	1.1	7.9

Table 5.123 *Ovis aries* (sheep) tibia measurements. Sample sizes (n.), ranges [x(1)= minimum; x(n)= maximum], means (μ), standard deviations (σ), coefficients of variation (CV), and statistical comparison (using a t-test) for assessing the significance (p. = probability) of the size differences between individual phases. Only sample sizes with a minimum of ten cases are considered. All measurements are in millimeters (mm). Only fully fused specimens are considered.

Measurements	*Ovis aries* tibia							Comparison (t-test)	
								Phases I *vs.* II	Phases II *vs.* III
	Period	n	x(1)	x(n)	μ	σ	CV	p.	p.
Bd	Phase I	44	21.0	27.8	23.3	1.52	6.5	.149	
	Phase II	46	20.0	26.8	22.9	1.27	5.5		.542
	Phase III	32	21.6	25.8	23	1.13	4.9		
	LN	122	20.0	27.8	23.1	1.34	5.8		
Dd	Phase I	44	15.8	20.2	17.7	1.12	6.3	.235	
	Phase II	46	16.3	20.5	18	.96	5.3		.265
	Phase III	32	14.9	20.9	17.7	1.22	6.9		
	LN	122	14.9	20.9	17.8	1.09	6.1		

p. = .001-.01: Difference is highly significant (less than 1% probability that is due to chance)
p. = .01-.05: Difference is significant (less than 5% probability that is due to chance)
p. = > .05: No significant difference (more than 5% probability that is due to chance)

Table 5.124 *Ovis aries* (sheep) astragalus measurements. Sample sizes (n.), ranges [x(1)= minimum; x(n)= maximum], means (μ), standard deviations (σ), coefficients of variation (CV), and statistical comparison (using a t-test) for assessing the significance (p. = probability) of the size differences between individual phases. Only sample sizes with a minimum of ten cases are considered. All measurements are in millimeters (mm). Only fully fused specimens are considered.

| Measurements | *Ovis aries* astragalus | | | | | | | Comparison (t-test) | |
| | | | | | | | | Phases I *vs.* II | Phases II *vs.* III |
	Period	n	x(1)	x(n)	μ	σ	CV	p.	p.
GLl	Phase II	23	23	32	25.1	1.79	7.1		.132
	Phase III	13	23	31	26.4	2.58	9.7		
	LN	44	23	32	25.4	2.21	8.7		
Glm	Phase II	24	21.7	30.0	23.9	1.63	6.8		.149
	Phase III	13	22.3	28.6	24.8	2.05	8.2		
	LN	45	21.7	30.0	24.1	1.87	7.7		
Bd	Phase II	23	14.4	18.6	16	.99	6.1		.052
	Phase III	13	14.7	21.7	17.3	2.01	11.6		
	LN	44	14.1	21.7	16.4	1.56	9.5		
Dl	Phase II	21	13.1	18.5	14.5	1.15	7.9		.224
	Phase III	13	13.5	16.9	15	1.17	7.8		
	LN	42	13.0	18.5	14.6	1.21	8.2		

p. = .001-.01: Difference is highly significant (less than 1% probability that is due to chance)
p. = .01-.05: Difference is significant (less than 5% probability that is due to chance)
p. = > .05: No significant difference (more than 5% probability that is due to chance)

Table 5.125 *Ovis aries* (sheep) calcaneum measurements. Sample sizes (n.), ranges [x(1)= minimum; x(n)= maximum], means (μ), standard deviations (σ) and coefficients of variation (CV). Only sample sizes with a minimum of ten cases are considered. All measurements are in millimeters (mm). Only fully fused specimens are considered.

| Measurements | *Ovis aries* calcaneum | | | | | | |
	Period	n	x(1)	x(n)	μ	σ	CV
GD	LN	10	17.9	21.7	20.1	1.21	6

Table 5.126 *Ovis aries* (sheep) metatarsal measurements. Sample sizes (n.), ranges [x(1)= minimum; x(n)= maximum], means (μ), standard deviations (σ) and coefficients of variation (CV). Only sample sizes with a minimum of ten cases are considered. All measurements are in millimeters (mm). Only fully fused specimens are considered.

| Measurements | *Ovis aries* metatarsal | | | | | | |
	Period	n	x(1)	x(n)	μ	σ	CV
3	LN	11	11.6	13.6	12.3	.61	4.9
6	LN	11	11.6	13.1	12.1	.49	4

Table 5.127 *Capra hircus* (goat) mandibular tooth measurements. Sample sizes (n.), ranges [x(1)= minimum; x(n)= maximum], means (μ), standard deviations (σ) and coefficients of variation (CV). Only sample sizes with a minimum of ten cases are considered. All measurements are in millimeters.

| Measurements | *Capra hircus* mandibular teeth | | | | | | |
	Period	n	x(1)	x(n)	μ	σ	CV
M_1 Width	Phase I	12	6.2	7.5	6.9	.4	5.8
	LN	18	6.2	7.6	7	.41	5.8
M_2 Width	Phase I	12	6.7	8.5	7.7	.63	8.1
	LN	19	6.7	8.5	7.8	.54	6.9
M_3 Length	LN	11	18.6	22.6	20.1	1.4	6.9
M_3 Width	LN	12	6.7	8.8	7.7	.55	7.1

Table 5.128 *Capra hircus* (goat) humerus measurements. Sample sizes (n.), ranges [x(1)= minimum; x(n)= maximum], means (μ), standard deviations (σ) and coefficients of variation (CV). Only sample sizes with a minimum of ten cases are considered. All measurements are in millimeters (mm). Only fully fused specimens are considered.

Measurements	*Capra hircus* humerus						
	Period	n	x(1)	x(n)	μ	σ	CV
BT	Phase I	11	23.2	25.8	24.7	.75	3.03
	LN	25	20.4	25.8	23.8	1.3	5.46
HTC	Phase I	11	11.8	13.1	12.5	.42	3.36
	LN	25	11.1	13.1	12.2	.52	4.26

Table 5.129 *Capra hircus* (goat) tibia measurements. Sample sizes (n.), ranges [x(1)= minimum; x(n)= maximum], means (μ), standard deviations (σ) and coefficients of variation (CV). Only sample sizes with a minimum of ten cases are considered. All measurements are in millimeters (mm). Only fully fused specimens are considered.

Measurements	*Capra hircus* tibia						
	Period	n	x(1)	x(n)	μ	σ	CV
Bd	LN	11	21.5	24.8	22.6	1.06	4.7
Dd	LN	11	14.7	19.9	17.7	1.35	7.6

Table 5.130 *Ovis/Capra* (sheep/goat) mandibular tooth measurements. Sample sizes (n.), ranges [x(1)= minimum; x(n)= maximum], means (μ), standard deviations (σ), coefficients of variation (CV), and statistical comparison (using a t-test) for assessing the significance (p. = probability) of the size differences between individual phases. Only sample sizes with a minimum of ten cases are considered. All measurements are in millimeters (mm).

Measurements	*Ovis/Capra* mandibular teeth							Comparison (t-test)	
								Phases I *vs.* II	Phases II *vs.* III
	Period	n.	x(1)	x(n)	μ	σ	CV	p.	p.
M_1 Width	Phase I	19	6	8.6	7.1	.67	9.4	.338	
	Phase II	10	6.4	8.4	7.3	.62	8.5		
	LN	32	6	8.6	7.2	.65	9		
M_2 Width	Phase I	20	6.2	9.4	7.5	.88	11.7	.917	
	Phase II	13	7.2	9.7	8	.67	8.3		
	LN	36	6.2	9.7	7.7	.8	10.4		
M_3 Length	Phase I	37	16.8	23.2	20.9	1.51	7.2	.316	
	Phase II	41	16.5	24.2	20.5	1.83	8.9		.155
	Phase III	31	15.1	24.6	21	1.85	8.8		
	LN	111	15.1	24.6	20.8	1.74	8.3		
M_3 Width	Phase I	45	6.4	9	7.9	.59	7.4	.667	
	Phase II	48	6.4	9.2	7.9	.68	8.6		.975
	Phase III	44	6.5	8.9	7.9	.54	6.8		
	LN	136	6.4	9.2	7.9	.6	7.6		

p. = .001-.01: Difference is highly significant (less than 1% probability that is due to chance)
p. = .01-.05: Difference is significant (less than 5% probability that is due to chance)
p. = > .05: No significant difference (more than 5% probability that is due to chance)

Table 5.131 *Ovis/Capra* (sheep/goat) scapula measurements. Sample sizes (n.), ranges [x(1)= minimum; x(n)= maximum], means (μ), standard deviations (σ) and coefficients of variation (CV). Only sample sizes with a minimum of ten cases are considered. All measurements are in millimeters (mm). Only fully fused specimens are considered.

Measurements	*Ovis/Capra* scapula						
	Period	n	x(1)	x(n)	μ	σ	CV
SLC	LN	14	15	22	17.4	1.78	10.2

Table 5.132 *Ovis/Capra* (sheep/goat) pelvis measurements. Sample sizes (n.), ranges [x(1)= minimum; x(n)= maximum], means (μ), standard deviations (σ), coefficients of variation (CV), and statistical comparison (using a t-test) for assessing the significance (p. = probability) of the size differences between individual phases. Only sample sizes with a minimum of ten cases are considered. All measurements are in millimeters (mm). Only fully fused specimens are considered.

Measurements	*Ovis/Capra* pelvis							Comparison (t-test)	
								Phases I *vs.* II	Phases II *vs.* III
	Period	n	x(1)	x(n)	μ	σ	CV	p.	p.
LAR	Phase I	28	19.0	25.4	22.2	1.44	6.4	.852	
	Phase II	25	19.4	26.4	22.3	2.33	10.4		.821
	Phase III	10	20.5	26.3	22.2	1.95	8.8		
	LN	63	19.0	26.4	22.3	1.89	8.4		

p. = .001-.01: Difference is highly significant (less than 1% probability that is due to chance)
p. = .01-.05: Difference is significant (less than 5% probability that is due to chance)
p. = > .05: No significant difference (more than 5% probability that is due to chance)

for the distinction of sheep and goats. However, the most numerous postcranial measurements derive from the humerus, the tibia and the astragalus.

In Figure 5.43 we plot the width (BT) against the smallest diameter (HTC) of the trochlea of the distal humerus, for sheep, goat and sheep/goat on a temporal level. There is tantalizing evidence of a size decrease in goats (perhaps sex-related?) between Phases I and II but sample sizes are rather small for any definite conclusions to be drawn. No such difference was observed in the sheep humerus, but a single specimen from Phase III plots in the upper right corner of the diagram, probably indicating a particularly large male individual.

In Figure 5.44 we plot the distal breadth (Bd) against the distal depth (Dd) of the tibia. No differences in the size of goats between phases can be inferred from the diagram, but the sample is very small. The sheep sample is much more substantial but also did not produce any clear differences between phases.

In Figure 5.45 we plot the greatest length of the lateral half (GLl) against the greatest length of the medial half (GLm) of the astragalus, for sheep, goat and sheep/goat. Once again, the sample size of goat astragali is too small to allow any reliable conclusion. In sheep, it is possible to identify a large concentration of smaller specimens and a smaller group of larger-sized animals (four or seven according to where one decides to draw the line). It is possible that the group of smaller astragali represents females (ewes), while the smaller group of larger astragali is made of males (rams and/or wethers). The larger proportion of smaller animals is consistent with the argument that, in most sites, females predominate, as only a few males need to be kept for reproduction (Albarella 1997).

Whatever is the sex distribution of the sheep population and the main purpose of sheep breeding at Promachon, there is no evidence of any change in the size of the sheep during the period of occupation, and in goat only a very tentative suggestion can be made for a size decrease, which may, in fact, be due to a chance higher proportion of females in the later phase.

As for cattle, it was possible to calculate shape indices only for the astragalus, due to the small sample of available metapodial measurements. The analysis was limited to sheep as there were not enough goat astragali. As can be seen in Figure 5.46, the two indices are poorly correlated (note the cloud-like, rather than linear, distribution), which means that any greater robustness according to the width does not necessarily correspond to an equivalent enhanced robustness according to the depth. We can see that there are no changes in the shape of sheep astragali between Phases I and II, which indicates that sheep during these two phases were of similar builds. However, the ratio between the distal width and the greatest length of the lateral half of the astragalus (Bd/GLl) tends to be higher for sheep belonging to Phase III than those belonging to Phases I and

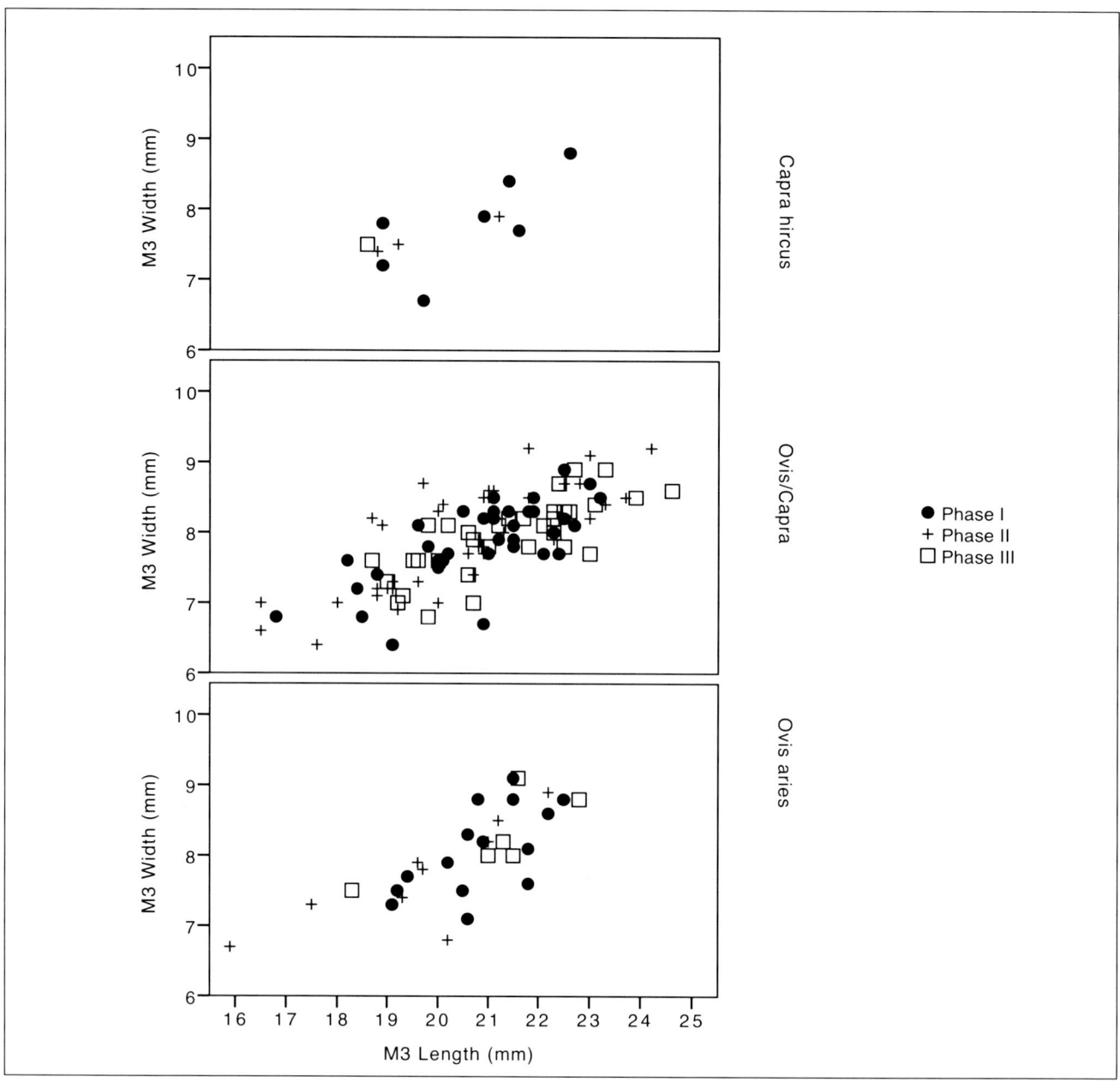

Figure 5.42 Caprinae mandibular third molar length *versus* width. Comparison between phases.

II. In other words, it seems that sheep astragali from Phase III are tentatively more robust than those from previous phases. This suggests the presence of slightly more robust sheep in Phase III.

In order to statistically test the significance of the differences in the shape indices of sheep astragalus between phases, an ANOVA test was conducted, although as previously noted, there are expressed doubts regarding the use of such ratios in the evaluation of statistical differences (Atchley *et al.* 1976). This took into account only the astragali of Phases II and III, since those of Phase I were too few to be tested. The test indicates that there is no significant difference in the ratio between the lateral depth and the greatest length of the lateral half of the astragalus (Dl/GLl) between the two phases (p= .553). However, a significant difference in the ratio between the distal width and the greatest length of

the lateral half of the astragalus (Bd/GLl) between Phases II and III was found (p= .035), with sheep from Phase III having a significantly higher Bd/GLl ratio (µ= 65.5 mm) than their counterparts from Phase II (µ= 63.7 mm). This confirms the previous suggestion of a slightly more robust sheep in Phase III than Phase II.

To extend the comparison between Phases II and III, it is useful to have larger samples of measurements, which can be obtained through the use of log ratios. Since a potential difference in the ratio between length and width has been highlighted by the analysis of the astragalus, measurements placed along these two axes were selected for the scaling index analysis. The standard used for the log ratio calculations is represented by the mean of a group of Shetland (UK) ewes (Davis 1996). By taking the Shetland ewes as a reference point, we can plot the length and the width measurements

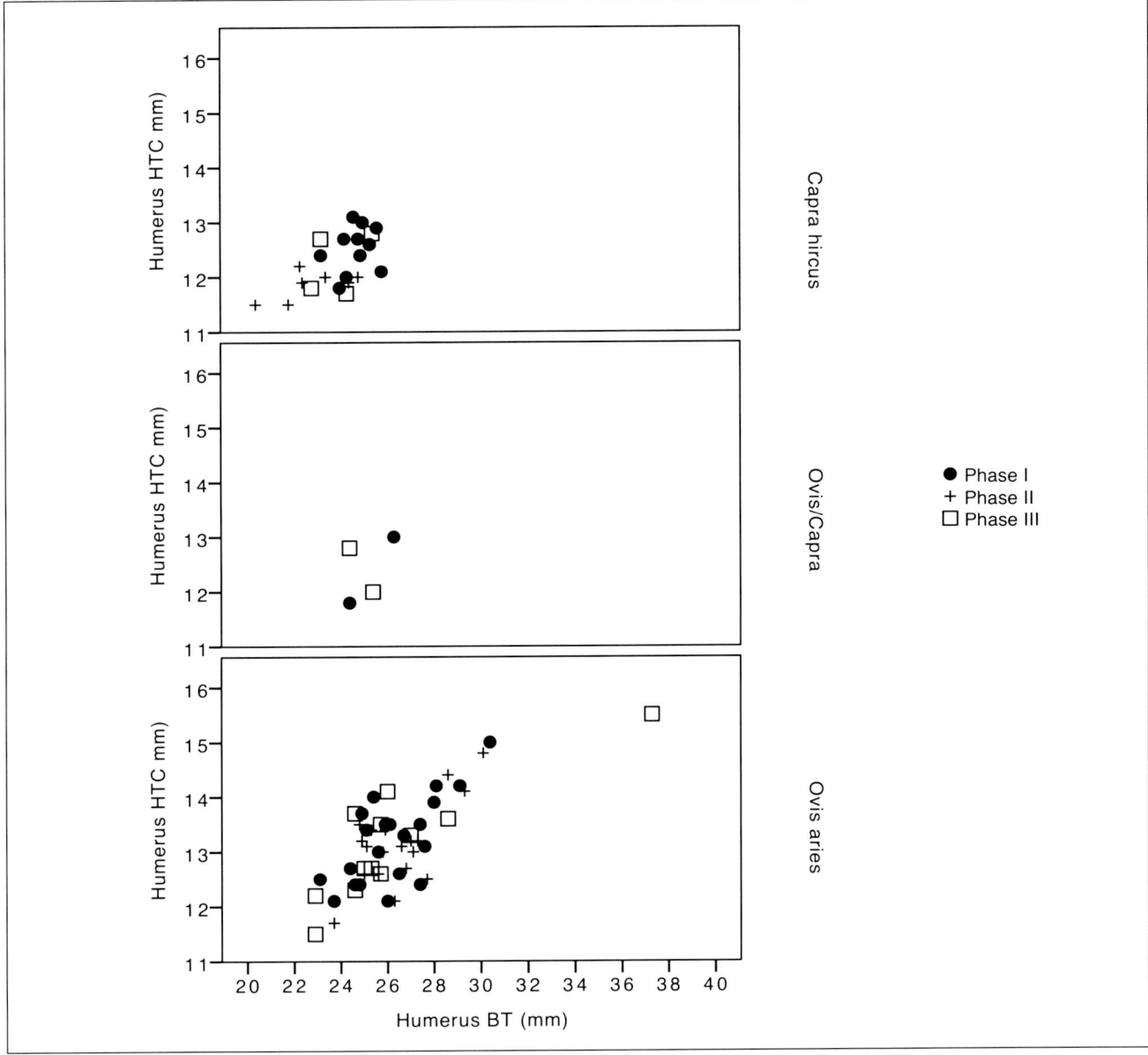

Figure 5.43 Caprinae humerus width of the trochlea (BT) *versus* diameter of the trochlea (HTC). Comparison between phases.

of sheep for Phases II and III respectively, in order to find if there are any differences in the distribution of measurements between the two phases. In other words, when the data are plotted, the Shetland material will always be centered on zero (.00), thus giving an easy reference point for comparison. The main aim however this time is, however, to compare phases with each other, rather than with the standard.

The results (Figure 5.47) show that during Phase II, there is a roughly unimodal distribution of length and width measurements from Promachon, with only one length measurement plotting as an outlier, indicating a particularly large individual, probably a male (ram). We can also notice that the means of both length and width measurements from Promachon plot on the left side of the standard, indicating that they are smaller than the standard. Length and width measurements are very similar in comparison to the standard, both plotting around a mean of -.04.

In Phase III, the mean of the length measurements is exactly the same as the standard, indicating that the length measurements of this phase are larger than the length measurements from Phase II. On the other hand, the mean of the width measurements plots on the left side of the standard, indicating that it is smaller than the standard and consistent with the values obtained for Phase II. There are, however, a few large outliers (right hand side of the histogram), which may, again, represent rams. The results of the log ratio diagrams are therefore indicating that the length measurements of Phase III are larger than those of Phase II, while the width measurements of Phase III remain roughly the same to those of Phase II. In other words, during Phase III the length measurements increase disproportionally to the width measurements. Thus, the results of the log ratio diagrams do not confirm previous suggestions regarding the more robust size of sheep during Phase III.

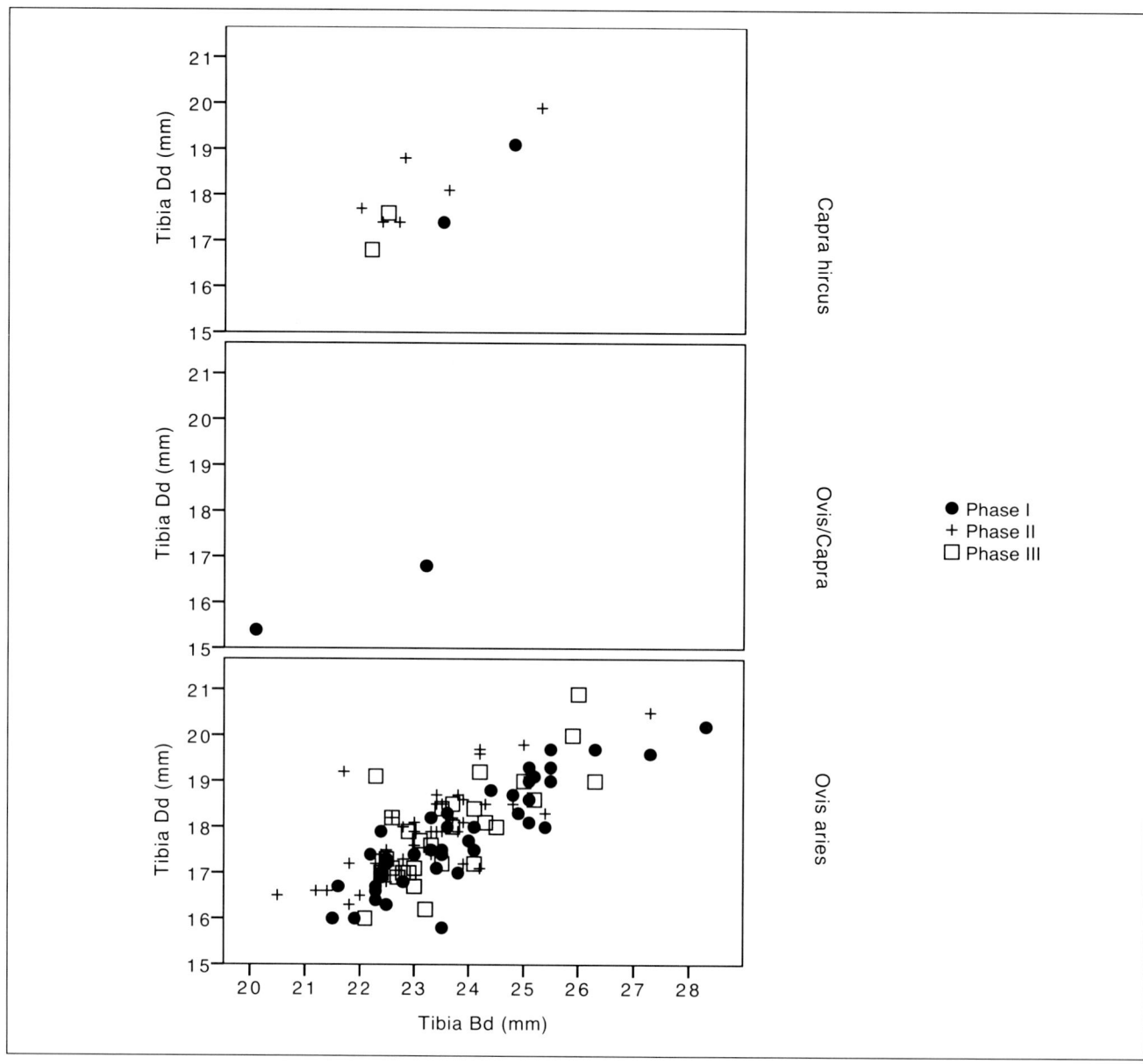

Figure 5.44 Caprinae tibia distal breadth (Bd) *versus* **distal depth (Dd). Comparison between phases.**

All in all, we can say that although the shape indices for sheep astragalus exhibit a more robust size of sheep in Phase III than earlier phases, the log ratio diagrams do not seem to support such hypothesis (at least in comparison to Phase II, since the small sample size of sheep measurements for Phase I did not permit the calculation of log ratios). There are hints that different body parts were subject to various changes between Phases II and III, but these did not all go in the same direction, which means that the sheep from Phase III are slightly different from those from Phase II, but such difference cannot be exemplified by concepts such as size and robustness. It is difficult to evaluate whether such difference is due to a change in the sex ratio or in the actual build of the sheep (due to a change in husbandry regime or the introduction of new animals) and future work will need to generate larger metric samples, so that such subtle differences can be explored in greater detail and become more informative about patterns of human life on site (or the wider region).

5.11.3 Sus *size*

Measurements of pig teeth and postcranial bones were fewer than those of the other food domesticates, which reflects the overall lower frequency of pig teeth and postcranial bones compared to those of cattle and caprines. Measurements of pig teeth were more numerous than those of postcranial bones. Tables 5.133-5.140 give a summary of tooth and postcranial measurements for which more than ten cases were recorded. The Pearson's coefficient of variation (CV) is very high for some teeth and postcranial measurements, probably as a consequence of the occurrence of some large outliers, here interpreted as likely to belong to wild boar (*Sus scrofa*). For this reason, the larger values of each measurement were excluded and the coefficients of variation were recalculated, as suggested by Albarella (2002).

Among teeth, the most numerous measurements were those of the third maxillary molar (M³). In Figure 5.48 we

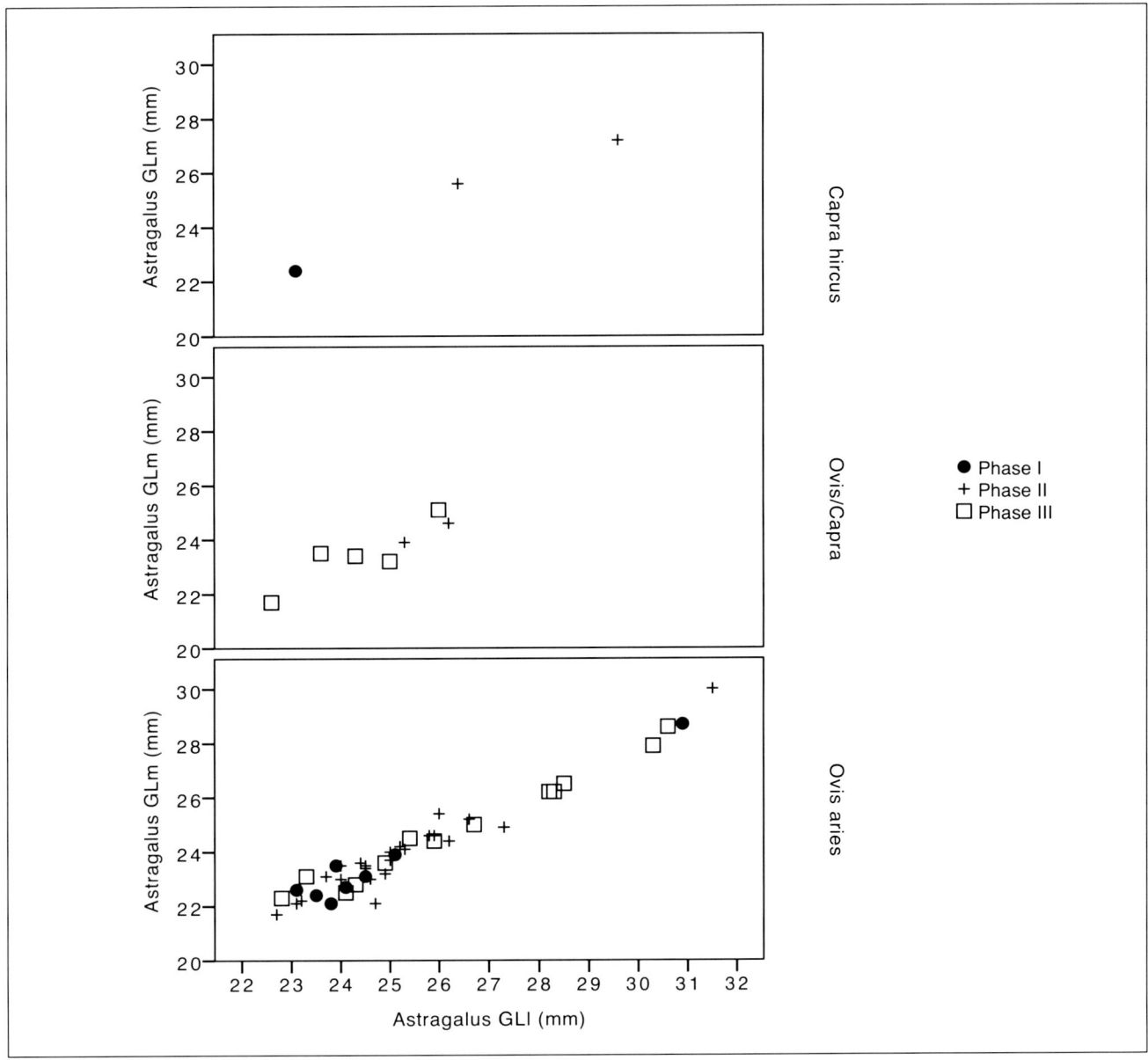

Figure 5.45 Caprinae astragalus greatest length of the lateral half (GLl) *versus* greatest length of the medial half (GLm). Comparison between phases.

plot the length against the width of the anterior cusp of the M³. The scatterplot indicates that most of the M³ 's are clustered together in the lower left part of the diagram, and they probably represent a domestic population. There is, however, one outlier plotting in the upper right corner of the diagram. This is a very large individual, probably a wild boar. No obvious differences in the size of domestic pigs between phases can be detected from this diagram. Measurements of the third mandibular molar (M₃) are unfortunately too few to verify the results of the upper M³.

Among pig postcranial elements, the most abundant measurements were provided by the humerus, the tibia and the astragalus. In Figure 5.49 we plot the width (BT) against the smallest diameter (HTC) of the trochlea of the distal humerus. The diagram shows that most measurements plot at the smaller end of the distribution, but there are three large outliers, one of which plots away at the very top of the distribution.

Pig forelimb bones tend to be fairly age dependent as they are subject to greater post-fusion growth than hindlimb bones (Albarella and Payne 2005; Albarella *et al.* 2006; Rowley-Conwy *et al.* 2012), but they are also much affected by sex variation (Payne and Bull 1988). Considering that BT and HTC are measurements that are much less affected by post-fusion growth than the commonly taken Bd (Payne and Bull 1988; Albarella and Payne 2005), the distribution is perhaps best explained as being characterized by a majority of domestic females, which would be consistent with the previous suggestion based on canine sexing that female pigs greatly outnumber males. The two smaller outliers are likely to represent domestic males – but could also be wild females – while the largest specimen is almost certainly a (male?) wild boar. The sample is too small to detect any potential difference between phases.

Distal tibia measurements can provide a good indication of differences between genetically distinct populations

127

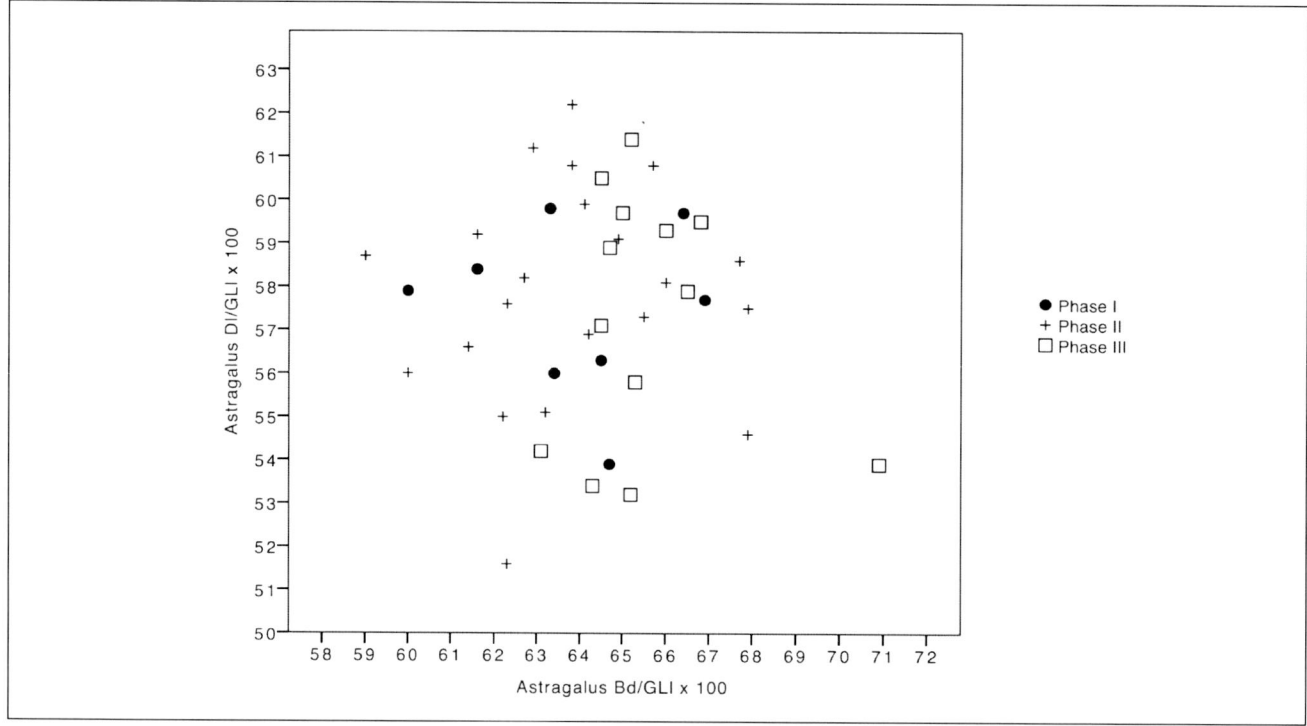

Figure 5.46 *Ovis aries* **astragali shape indices. Comparison between phases.**

(as in the case of domestic and wild populations), as this bone is not particularly affected by sex variation or post-fusion growth (Albarella and Payne 2005; Albarella *et al.* 2009; Payne and Bull 1988; Rowley-Conwy *et al.* 2012). In Figure 5.50 we plot the distal breadth against the distal depth of the pig tibia on a temporal level. The scatterplot shows two groups of tibiae. As in the case of humerus, there is no overlap between the two groups. It is likely the more numerous group of smaller measurements represents domestic pigs, while the two large outliers (both from Phase II) are wild boar.

Figure 5.51 presents the comparison of the pig astragalus between individual phases, by plotting the greatest length of the lateral half (GLl) against the greater length of the medial half (GLm) of the astragalus. As in the case of tibia, we can see two groups of pig astragali that do not present any overlap. The first group plots on the lower left part of the diagram and probably indicates the presence of domesticated individuals. The second group, which plots on the upper right part of the diagram is probably represented by wild individuals. Unlike the humerus and the tibia scatterplots, wild individuals from all three phases of occupation are present in the astragalus scatterplot, and they are only slightly less abundant than the domestic specimens.

All in all, the comparison of the pig teeth and postcranial measurements suggests the presence of a substantial number of wild individuals at Promachon. No changes in the size of domesticated pigs were detected between individual phases, but this may due to the limitations of small sample size. As for caprines and cattle the log ratio technique has been used to undertake an analysis based on a larger sample size. The standard that we use for the calculation of the log ratio is represented by the mean of a group of wild boar from Kizilcahaman in Turkey (Payne and Bull 1988). Both postcranial bones and teeth are used, as they can provide different types of information. In particular, cheek teeth do not grow after eruption and are only slightly – if at all – sex dependent (Albarella and Payne 2005; Payne and Bull 1988; Rowley-Conwy *et al.* 2012). They can therefore be useful indicators of the occurrence of distinct populations (*e.g.* domestic *vs.* wild). Since the collum of the scapula is heavily subject to post-fusion growth (Rowley-Conwy *et al.* 2012), the scapula SLC measurement is excluded from the calculation of the log ratios for postcranial measurements.

Figure 5.52 shows the log ratio diagrams for the tooth lengths, tooth widths and postcranial measurements respectively. By taking the Kizilcahaman wild pigs as a reference point, we can see how the tooth (length and width) as well as postcranial measurements of pigs from Promachon are compared to those of pigs from Kizilcahaman. In other words, when the data are plotted, the Kizilcahaman wild pig material will always be centered on zero (.00), thus giving an easy reference point to indicate whether the tooth and postcranial measurements of pigs from Promachon are larger or smaller than those of Kizilcahaman.

We can see that the log ratio diagrams for tooth lengths, tooth widths and postcranial measurements from Promachon have a broadly unimodal distribution (with a tail on the right-hand side). The mean of each log ratio diagram from Promachon plots on the left side of the standard, thus indicating that teeth and postcranial measurements from Promachon are smaller than those from Kizilcahaman.

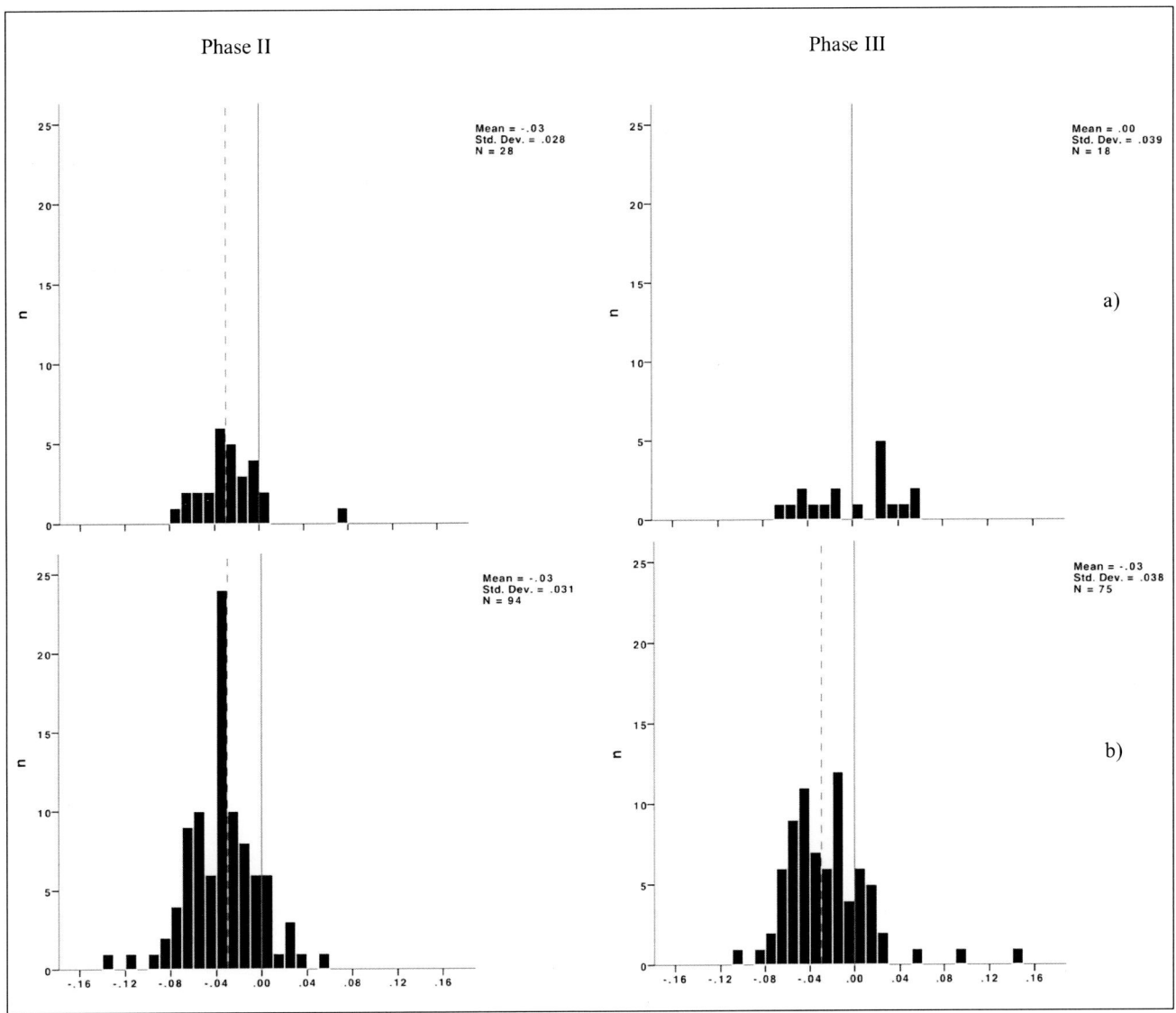

Figure 5.47 Comparison of the *Ovis aries* size between Phases II and III in Promachon sector with a standard sample of Shetland ewes (Davis 1996) using the log ratio technique (Simpson *et al.* 1960). Only fully fused postcranial bones were considered. Only compatible measurements were considered: a) length measurements and b) width measurements. The mean is marked by a black dashed vertical line, and the standard measurement by a black vertical line at .00. The scale of the vertical axis is fixed to emphasize differences in sample sizes.

This, in turn, indicates, that the bulk of the pig population at Promachon belongs to the domesticated form, a pattern that corroborates the results of the scatterplots. There are however, a number of outliers, which are plotted on the right side of the standard, thus confirming the presence of wild pigs in Promachon. Of interest, however, is the fact that postcranial bones plot bimodally far more than teeth, which may indicate that the wild boar is better represented by bones of the body than the head. So perhaps the pattern that we noticed earlier (in in the body part distribution) with regard to the higher representation of pig postcranial elements rather than teeth, applies in the case of wild boar rather than domestic pig. This would not be a surprising result as it has been reported elsewhere that wild boar heads may have in some cases been left at the kill-site rather than imported to the settlement (Albarella 1999). Alternative explanation is that the approximate bimodality of the pig postcranial bones is due to the confusing effect

of sex variation, with domestic, as well as wild, females and males all contributing to the distribution.

5.11.4 Canis familiaris *size*

No dog postcranial bones produced more than ten measurements within any phase or indeed within the entire Late Neolithic in Promachon. On the other hand, the only cranial elements that produced more than ten measurements within the entire Late Neolithic, were the first mandibular molar (length and width of M_1) and the mandible (height of the ramus mandibulae). A summary of these measurements is presented in Table 5.141.

In Figure 5.53 we plot the length against the width of the first mandibular molar. Most measurements plot in the lower left part of the diagram and are likely to belong to the domestic dog (*Canis familiaris*). A single outlier is much

Table 5.133 *Sus* (pig) maxillary tooth measurements. Sample sizes (n.), ranges [x(1)= minimum; x(n)= maximum], means (μ), standard deviations (σ), coefficients of variation (CV), and statistical comparison (using a t-test) for assessing the significance (p. = probability) of the size differences between individual phases. Only sample sizes with a minimum of ten cases are considered. All measurements are in millimeters (mm).

Measurements	*Sus* maxillary teeth											Comparison (t-test) [1]	
												Phases I vs. II	Phases II vs. III
	Period	n^1	$x(1)^1$	$x(n)^1$	μ^1	σ^1	CV^1	n^2	μ^2	σ^2	CV^2	p.	p.
$M^1 L$	Phase I	18	12.1	18.6	15.6	2	12.7	-	-	-	-		
	LN	33	11.9	19.8	15.4	2.02	13.1	30	15.3	1.8	11.7		
$M^1 WA$	Phase I	18	11.1	17.9	13.2	1.54	11.6	17	12.9	1	7.7		
	LN	31	11	17.9	12.9	1.40	10.8	28	12.7	1	8.2		
$M^1 WP$	Phase I	17	10.5	17.1	13.2	1.69	12.8	16	13	1.4	10.7	.073	
	Phase II	10	10.2	14.2	12	1.5	12.5						
	LN	33	10.2	17.1	12.8	1.64	12.8	30	12.6	1.4	11		
$M^2 L$	Phase I	17	15.7	27.4	20.2	2.81	13.8	16	19.7	2.18	11		
	LN	29	15.2	27.4	19.7	2.65	13.4	26	19.4	2.2	11.3		
$M^2 WA$	Phase I	17	12.1	23.1	15.7	2.49	15.8	16	15.3	1.7	11		
	LN	29	12.1	23.1	15.3	2.22	14.4	26	15	1.63	10.8		
$M^2 WP$	Phase I	18	12.8	22	15.4	2.13	13.8	17	15	1.4	9.3		
	LN	30	12.8	22	15.2	1.82	11.9	27	14.9	1.27	8.5		
$M^3 L$	LN	16	25.2	38.6	28.9	3.4	11.7	13	28.2	2	7.1		
$M^3 WA$	LN	15	16	23.1	17.6	1.92	10.9	13	17.2	1.17	6.8		
$M^3 WC$	LN	15	13	19.3	14.5	1.69	11.6	13	14.1	1	7.2		

[1]Including outliers (possibly wild individuals: wild boar)
[2]Excluding outliers (possibly wild individuals: wild boar)
p. = .001-.01: Difference is highly significant (less than 1% probability that is due to chance)
p. = .01-.05: Difference is significant (less than 5% probability that is due to chance)
p. = > .05: No significant difference (more than 5% probability that is due to chance)

larger than any other tooth and is likely to have belonged to a wolf (*Canis lupus*). There are no available metrical data of either postcranial bones or teeth of wolf from other sites in Macedonia, except for Sitagroi (Bökönyi 1986). The length of the first mandibular molar of wolf from Sitagroi is even larger (M_1 Length: 28.5 mm) than the one from Promachon (M_1 Length: 24.3 mm), but the clear separation between the Promachon outlier and the rest of the dataset should represent sufficient evidence to suggest that this outlier derives from a wild animal.

Table 5.134 *Sus* (pig) mandibular tooth measurements. Sample sizes (n.), ranges [x(1)= minimum; x(n)= maximum], means (μ), standard deviations (σ) and coefficients of variation (CV). Only sample sizes with a minimum of ten cases are considered. All measurements are in millimeters (mm).

Measurements	*Sus* mandibular teeth										
	Period	n^1	$x(1)^1$	$x(n)^1$	μ^1	σ^1	CV^1	n^2	μ^2	σ^2	CV^2
dP$_4$ L	LN	20	13.2	20.7	17.6	1.56	8.8				
dP$_4$ WP	LN	19	7.7	9.9	8.4	.65	7.7				
M$_1$ L	Phase II	10	14.5	24.1	16.8	2.85	16.9	9	16	1.35	8.4
	LN	25	14.5	24.1	16.8	2.21	13.1	21	16.5	1.56	9.4
M$_1$ WA	Phase II	10	8.4	16.3	10.4	2.21	21.1	9	9.8	.89	9.1
	LN	23	8.4	16.3	10.4	1.61	15.5	20	10.1	.92	9.1
M$_1$ WP	Phase II	11	9.5	16.6	11	1.97	17.9	10	10.5	.76	7.2
	LN	26	9.5	16.6	11	1.54	14	22	10.7	.96	8.9
M$_2$ L	LN	20	15.1	22.4	19.1	1.94	10.1				
M$_2$ WA	LN	20	10	13.7	12.2	.95	7.7				
M$_2$ WP	LN	20	10.6	14.1	12.8	.94	7.3				

[1]Including outliers (possibly wild individuals: wild boar)
[2]Excluding outliers (possibly wild individuals: wild boar)

Table 5.135 *Sus* (pig) atlas measurements. Sample sizes (n.), ranges [x(1)= minimum; x(n)= maximum], means (μ), standard deviations (σ) and coefficients of variation (CV). Only sample sizes with a minimum of ten cases are considered. All measurements are in millimeters (mm). Only fully fused specimens are considered.

Measurements	*Sus* atlas										
	Period	n^1	$x(1)^1$	$x(n)^1$	μ^1	σ^1	CV^1	n^2	μ^2	σ^2	CV^2
BFcr	LN	11	40.6	63.0	46.5	6.85	14.7	10	44.9	4.4	9.8

[1]Including outliers (possibly wild individuals: wild boar)
[2]Excluding outliers (possibly wild individuals: wild boar)

Table 5.136 *Sus* (pig) scapula measurements. Sample sizes (n.), ranges [x(1)= minimum; x(n)= maximum], means (μ), standard deviations (σ), coefficients of variation (CV), and statistical comparison (using a t-test) for assessing the significance (p. = probability) of the size differences between individual phases. Only sample sizes with a minimum of ten cases are considered. All measurements are in millimeters (mm). Only fully fused specimens are considered.

Measurements	*Sus* scapula											Comparison (t-test)[1]	
												Phases I *vs.* II	Phases II *vs.* III
	Period	n^1	$x(1)^1$	$x(n)^1$	μ^1	σ^1	CV^1	n^2	μ^2	σ^2	CV^2	p.	p.
SLC	Phase I	13	16	33	21.1	4.62	21.9	12	20.2	3.26	16.1	.994	
	Phase II	21	16	37	21.1	5.44	25.8	19	19.6	2.43	12.4		
	LN	37	16	37	21.1	4.86	23	34	20	2.66	13.3		

[1]Including outliers (possibly wild individuals: wild boar)
[2]Excluding outliers (possibly wild individuals: wild boar)
p. = .001-.01: Difference is highly significant (less than 1% probability that is due to chance)
p. = .01-.05: Difference is significant (less than 5% probability that is due to chance)
p. = > .05: No significant difference (more than 5% probability that is due to chance)

Table 5.137 *Sus* (pig) humerus measurements. Sample sizes (n.), ranges [x(1)= minimum; x(n)= maximum], means (μ), standard deviations (σ) and coefficients of variation (CV). Only sample sizes with a minimum of ten cases are considered. All measurements are in millimeters (mm). Only fully fused specimens are considered.

Measurements	*Sus* humerus										
	Period	n[1]	x(1)[1]	x(n)[1]	μ[1]	σ[1]	CV[1]	n[2]	μ[2]	σ[2]	CV[2]
BT	LN	13	26.7	42.7	31.7	5.02	15.8	12	30.8	3.9	12.8
HTC	LN	14	16.0	27.6	18.7	3.29	17.6	13	18	2.18	12

[1]Including outliers (possibly wild individuals: wild boar)
[2]Excluding outliers (possibly wild individuals: wild boar)

Table 5.138 *Sus* (pig) pelvis measurements. Sample sizes (n.), ranges [x(1)= minimum; x(n)= maximum], means (μ), standard deviations (σ), coefficients of variation (CV), and statistical comparison (using a t-test) for assessing the significance (p. = probability) of the size differences between individual phases. Only sample sizes with a minimum of ten cases are considered. All measurements are in millimeters (mm). Only fully fused specimens are considered.

Measurements	*Sus* pelvis											Comparison (t-test) [1]	
												Phases I *vs.* II	Phases II *vs.* III
	Period	n[1]	x(1)[1]	x(n)[1]	μ[1]	σ[1]	CV[1]	n[2]	μ[2]	σ[2]	CV[2]	p.	p.
LAR	Phase I	11	18.5	47.9	30.4	7.52	24.7	9	27.5	3.75	13.6	.842	
	Phase II	11	23.3	34.1	29.9	3.30	11	11	-	-	-		
	LN	27	18.5	47.9	29.5	5.47	18.5	24	28.3	3.53	12.5		

[1]Including outliers (possibly wild individuals: wild boar)
[2]Excluding outliers (possibly wild individuals: wild boar)
p. = .001-.01: Difference is highly significant (less than 1% probability that is due to chance)
p. = .01-.05: Difference is significant (less than 5% probability that is due to chance)
p. = > .05: No significant difference (more than 5% probability that is due to chance)

Table 5.139 *Sus* (pig) tibia measurements. Sample sizes (n.), ranges [x(1)= minimum; x(n)= maximum], means (μ), standard deviations (σ) and coefficients of variation (CV). Only sample sizes with a minimum of ten cases are considered. All measurements are in millimeters (mm). Only fully fused specimens are considered.

Measurements	*Sus* tibia										
	Period	n[1]	x(1)[1]	x(n)[1]	μ[1]	σ[1]	CV[1]	n[2]	μ[2]	σ[2]	CV[2]
Bd	LN	14	24.5	37.5	27.7	3.83	13.8	12	26.3	1.32	5
Dd	LN	16	18.4	33.0	24.1	4.48	18.6	13	22.2	1.66	7.4

[1]Including outliers (possibly wild individuals: wild boar)
[2]Excluding outliers (possibly wild individuals: wild boar)

Table 5.140 *Sus* (pig) astragalus measurements. Sample sizes (n.), ranges [x(1)= minimum; x(n)= maximum], means (μ), standard deviations (σ) and coefficients of variation (CV). Only sample sizes with a minimum of ten cases are considered. All measurements are in millimeters (mm). Only fully fused specimens are considered.

Measurements	*Sus* astragalus										
	Period	n[1]	x(1)[1]	x(n)[1]	μ[1]	σ[1]	CV[1]	n[2]	μ[2]	σ[2]	CV[2]
GLl	LN	17	34	50	40.7	5.97	14.6	14	38.9	4.84	12.4
GLm	LN	19	32.3	46.1	38.2	5.02	13.1	14	36.4	4.15	11.4
Bd	LN	11	20.5	31.2	26	3.98	15.3	8	24.6	3.74	15
Dl	LN	12	19.7	30.8	24.7	3.65	14.7	9	23.4	3	13

[1]Including outliers (possibly wild individuals: wild boar)
[2]Excluding outliers (possibly wild individuals: wild boar)

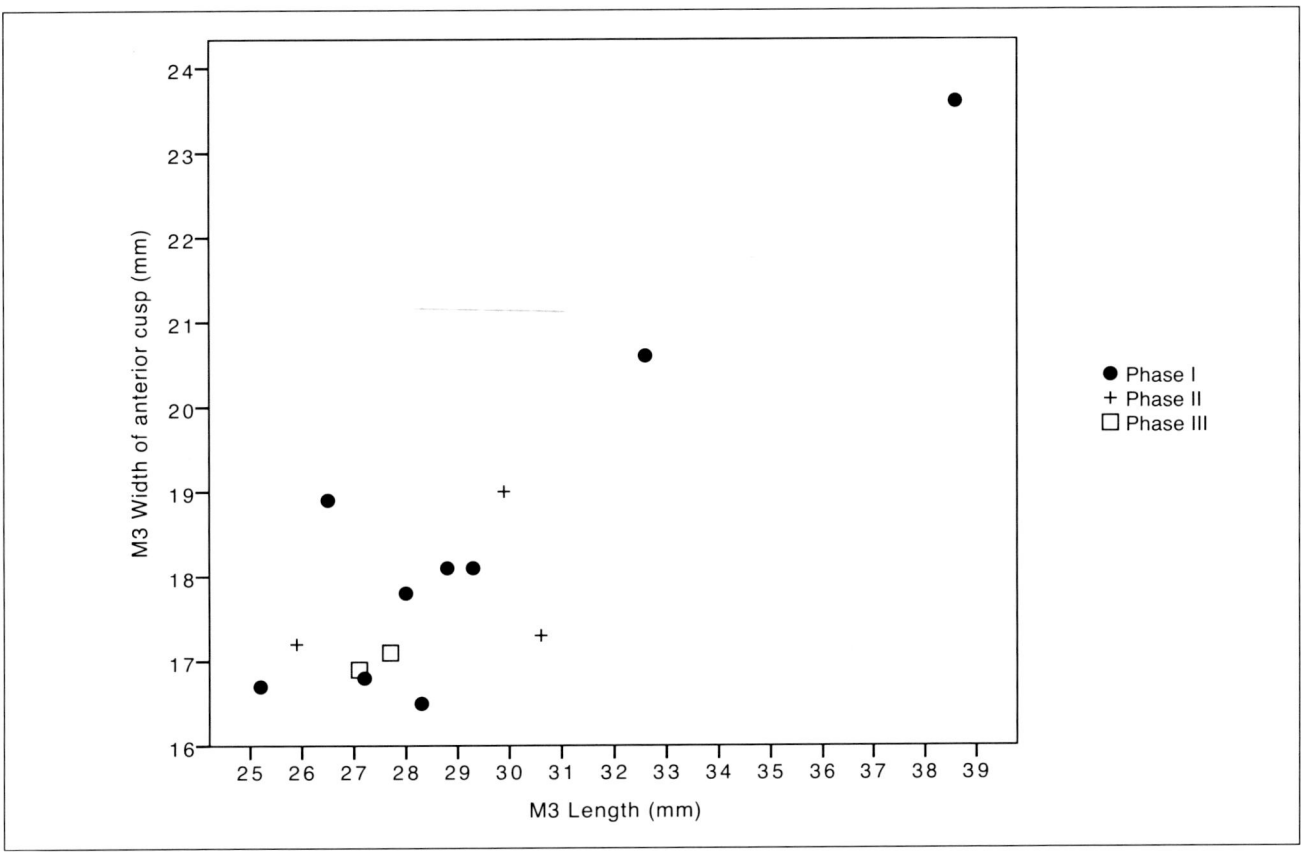

Figure 5.48 *Sus* **maxillary third molar length** *versus* **width. Comparison between phases.**

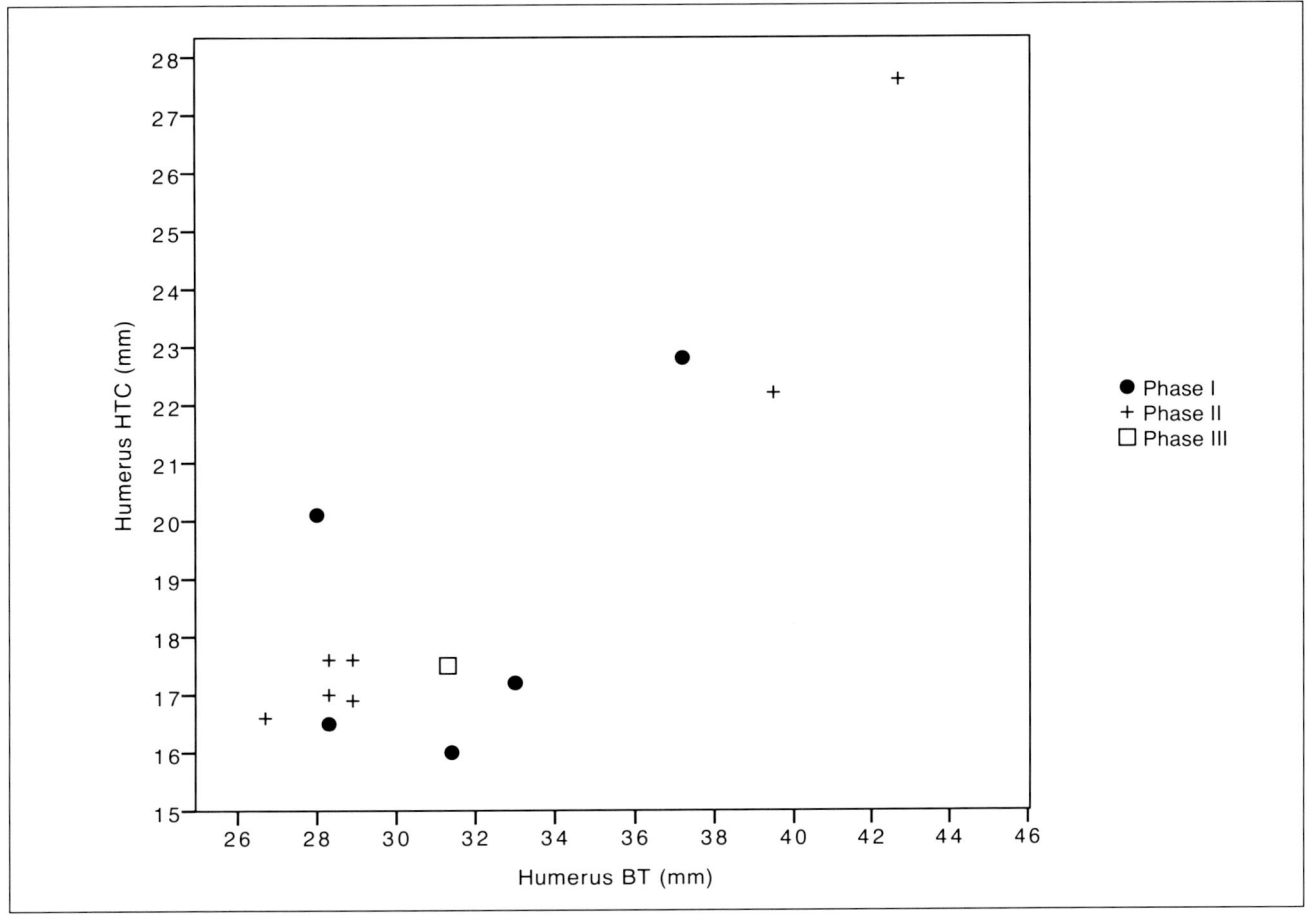

Figure 5.49 *Sus* **humerus width of the trochlea (BT)** *versus* **diameter of the trochlea (HTC). Comparison between phases.**

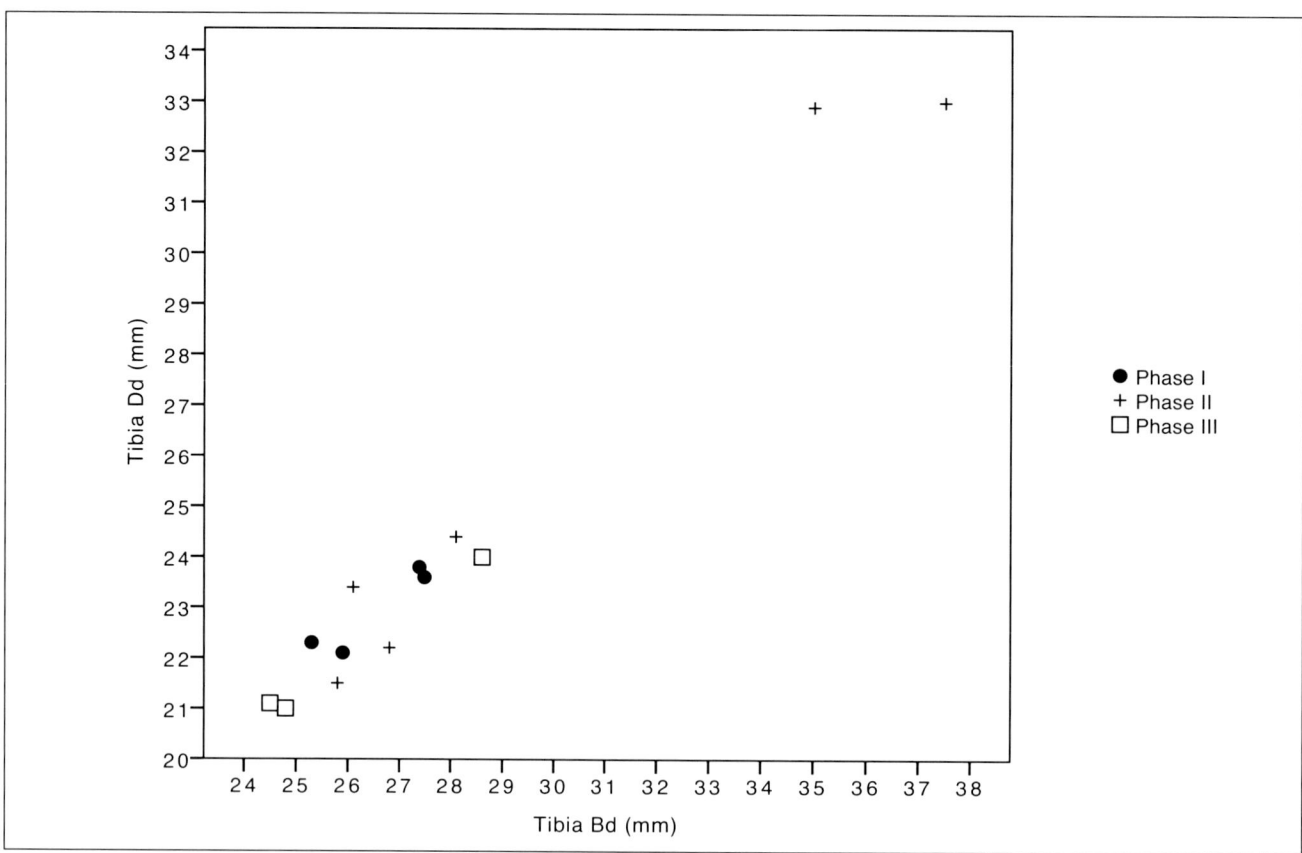

Figure 5.50 *Sus* **tibia distal breadth (Bd)** *versus* **distal depth (Dd). Comparison between phases.**

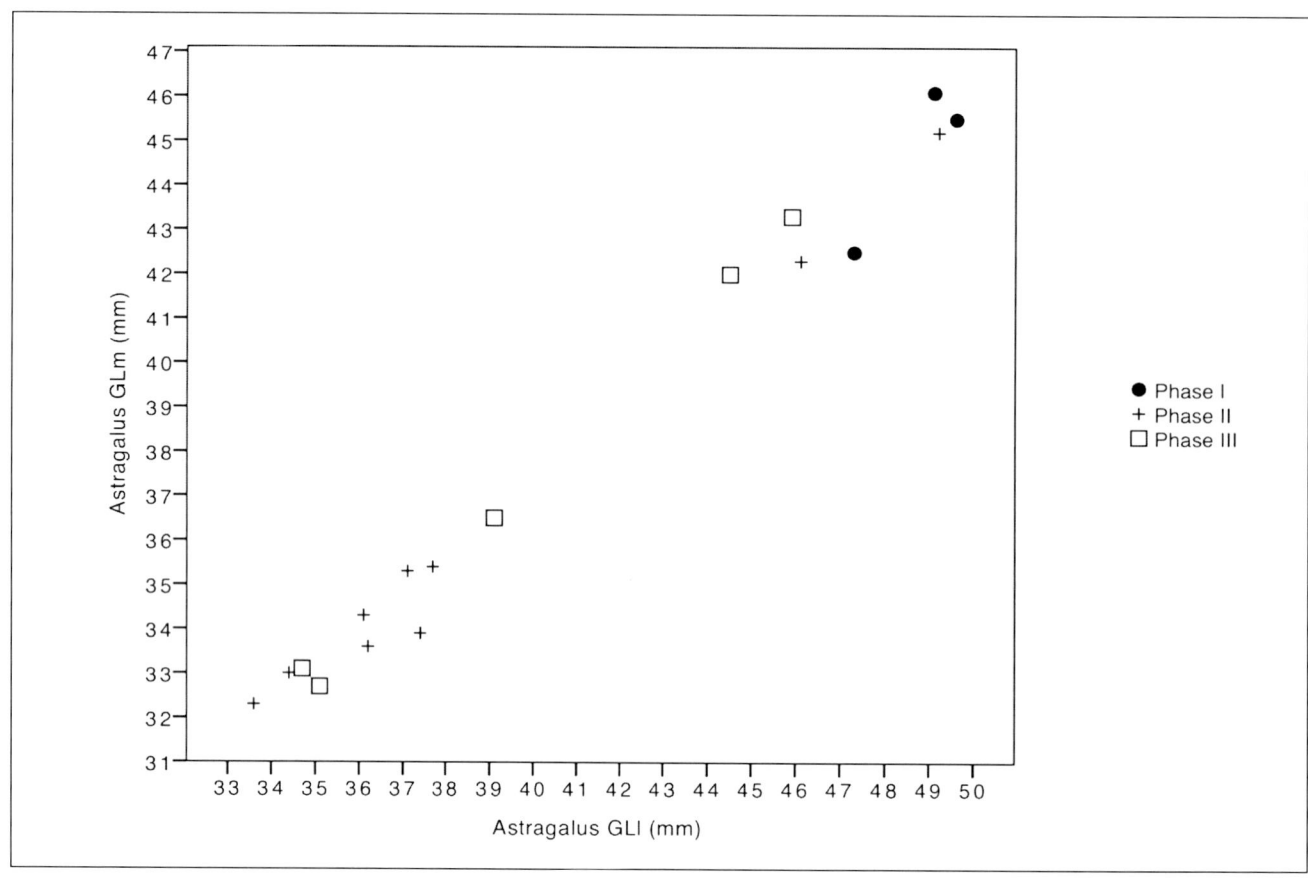

Figure 5.51 *Sus* **astragalus greatest length of the lateral half (GLl)** *versus* **greatest length of the medial half (GLm). Comparison between phases.**

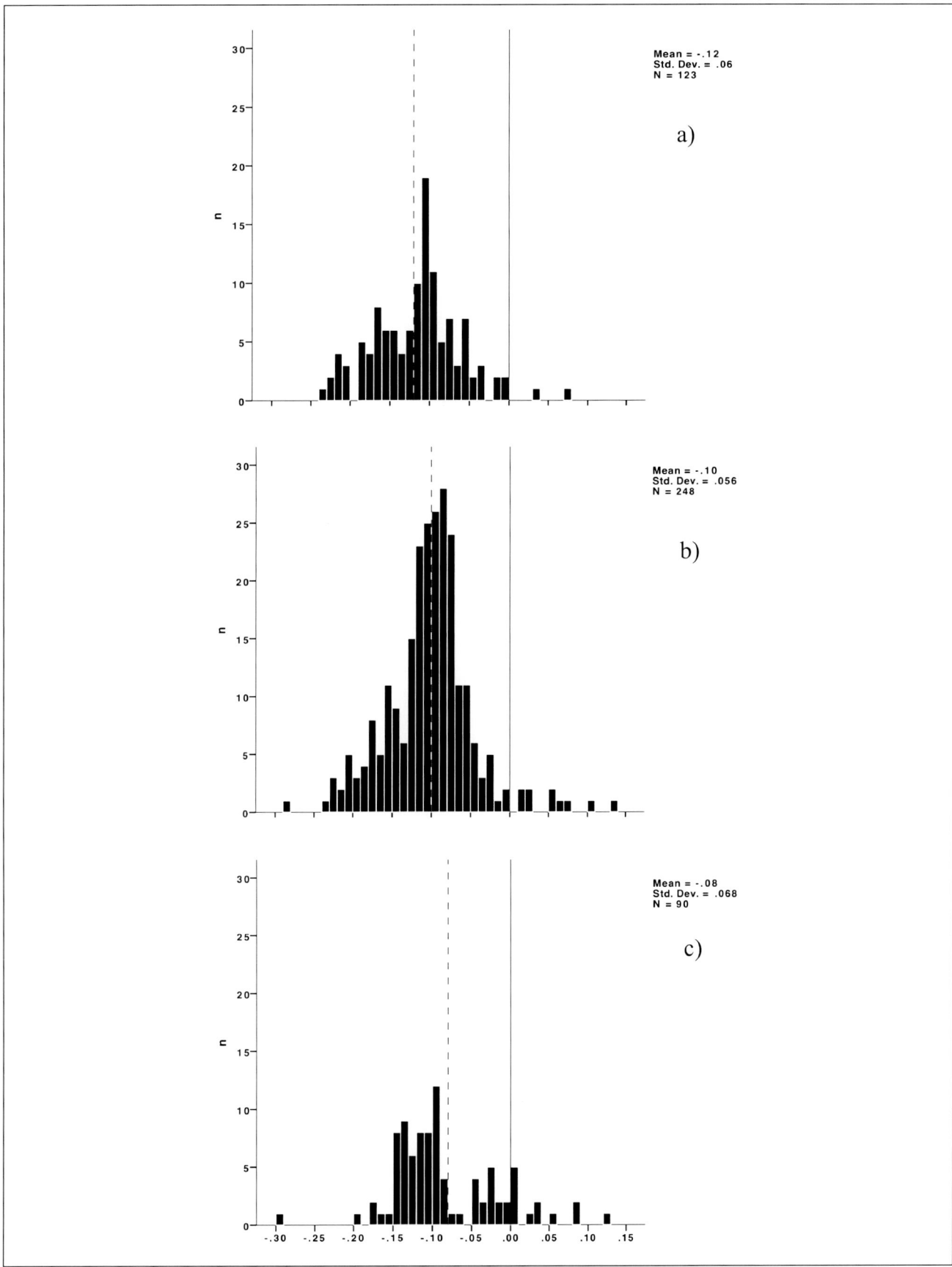

Figure 5.52 Comparison of the *Sus* size from Promachon sector with a standard *Sus scrofa* sample from Kizilcahaman in Turkey (Payne and Bull 1988) using the log ratio technique (Simpson *et al.* 1960). Maxillary and mandibular teeth were combined. Only fully fused postcranial bones were considered. Only compatible measurements were considered: a) tooth length measurements, b) tooth width measurements, c) postcranial measurements (lengths, widths and depths combined). The mean is marked by a black dashed vertical line and the standard measurement by a black vertical line at .00. The scale of the vertical axis is fixed to emphasize differences in sample sizes.

Table 5.141 *Canis familiaris* (dog) mandibular tooth measurements. Sample sizes (n.), ranges [x(1)= minimum; x(n)= maximum], means (μ), standard deviations (σ) and coefficients of variation (CV). Only sample sizes with a minimum of ten cases are considered. All measurements are in tenths of millimeters (mm).

Measurements	*Canis familiaris* mandibular teeth										
	Period	n^1	$x(1)^1$	$x(n)^1$	μ^1	σ^1	CV^1	n^2	μ^2	σ^2	CV^2
M1 Length	LN	14	14.5	24.3	18.6	2.05	11	13	18.2	1.31	7.2
M1 Width	LN	15	6.7	14.7	7.6	2.03	26.7	13	7.11	.23	3.3

[1]Including outliers (possibly wild individuals: wolf)
[2]Excluding outliers (possibly wild individuals: wolf)

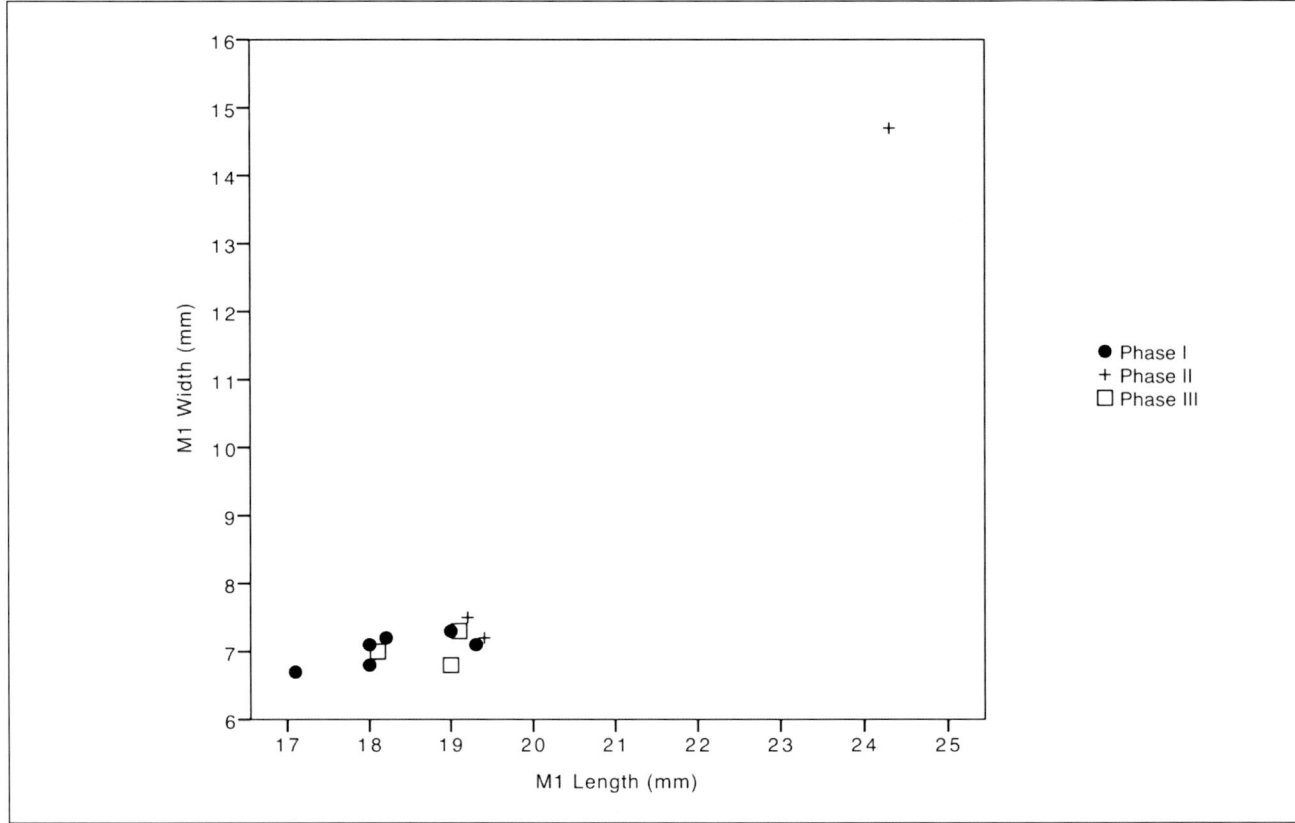

Figure 5.53 *Canis familiaris* mandibular first molar length *versus* width. Comparison between phases.

6

Contextualizing Promachon

6.1 From local to regional: assessing the risks and the incompatibilities

The preceding chapter presented the results of the analysis of the faunal assemblage from the Greek sector of Promachon. This chapter compares these results to those obtained from a number of northern Greek and other Balkan sites, which are contemporary to Promachon. The use of such a large body of faunal data fro   m contemporary northern Greek and Balkan sites (Figure 6.1) presents a number of challenges that should be articulated before proceeding to any comparisons. Adequate faunal data from a number of northern Greek sites were extracted from published sources. Comparisons between Promachon and northern Greek sites in terms of the frequency of the main domesticates were relatively straightforward, since most faunal researchers use NISP as the main predictor of taxonomic frequency. However, while in the 'diagnostic zone' approach discussed here it is clear which fragments have been counted, in cases of the northern Greek faunal reports this information is not so explicit. In addition, the extent of recovery bias has not been entirely assessed at each site. There are also a few cases where a number of researchers use quantification systems other than NISP (*i.e.* MNE, MinAU, MaxAU). These were obviously more difficult to compare with our quantifications and were naturally left out from the analysis. On the other hand, metrical comparisons between Promachon and northern Greek sites were also relatively straightforward, and any problems and/or incompatibilities encountered will be discussed separately for each site in the metrical analysis section of this chapter. Regardless of the fact that the age-at-death data from a number of northern Greek sites are based on quantification systems other than NISP (*i.e.* MNI), they are used here for purposes of comparison. This was decided since the age-at-death data are not affected by the same problems of taxonomic proportions as the frequency of taxa. There are cases of sites also, which have not yielded an adequate number of mandibles for ageing comparisons. This is mostly true for large species such as cattle, which in most of these sites are represented better by the bones of the main body rather than the head. Therefore, any comparisons of the age-at-death data of this species between Promachon and these sites are based on the epiphyseal fusion evidence with the inevitable limitations of the case. Lastly, there are also cases of sites where, due to the general scarcity of mandibles of all main domesticates, the researchers have chosen to combine mandible wear stages with wear stages from individual loose teeth. These sites were also excluded from any comparisons with Promachon. There are also a number of other issues that should be taken into consideration when conducting the comparison of Promachon to northern

Greek sites. However, these issues will be assessed for each site separately as we proceed with our analyses.

On the other hand, published faunal reports from Bulgarian sites are generally scarce. Moreover, the limited number of published Bulgarian faunal reports suffer from a number of drawbacks as well. For instance, the information included in these reports is limited only to the level of the frequency of the domestic taxa, while other aspects of analysis such as the age-at-death of the main domesticates and the metrical data are generally absent. In most cases, NISP is the main tool for calculating taxonomic frequency, which facilitates comparisons with Promachon. However, methodological problems such as, which fragments have been counted and which have been excluded apply – as in the case of the Greek faunal assemblages – in Bulgarian faunal assemblages as well. The extent of recovery bias is another problem that should also be considered, since it has not been vigorously assessed on Bulgarian faunal reports. All in all, the comparison between Promachon and contemporary Bulgarian sites is restricted only in terms of the frequency of the three main domesticated taxa. In order to enlarge the body of available data from the Balkans, the analysis includes also the frequencies of the main domesticates from a number of published and unpublished contemporary Serbian sites as well.

6.2 The domestic and the *agrion*

Faunal evidence dating as early as the fifth millennium BC indicates that domestic ruminants and pigs assume a leading role in the Neolithic economies of Greece (Halstead 1994; Perlès 2001; Valamoti 2004; Yiannouli 1997). Consistently with this notion, faunal data from Promachon indicated that cattle, caprines and pigs are represented with higher frequencies than wild species. As previously demonstrated however, a sizeable proportion of wild boar from Promachon was identified through metrical analysis. It is extremely difficult, however, to 'isolate' and quantify (in terms of NISP) this part of the pig population. Therefore, any comparison of the frequencies of the wild and the domesticated species between Promachon and other contemporary sites would be problematic as wild boar represent, numerically, an entity that is not completely known. A possible way to tackle this problem would be to compare the frequency of caprines and red deer. On one hand, red deer is definitely a wild species. On the other hand, caprines are definitely domestic and are preferred to cattle, as this latter may potentially include an aurochs element in the assemblage (though there is no real evidence of this at Promachon). This type of analysis may be crude but can be reasonably effective as caprines are common and widespread in all sites and red deer is often one of the

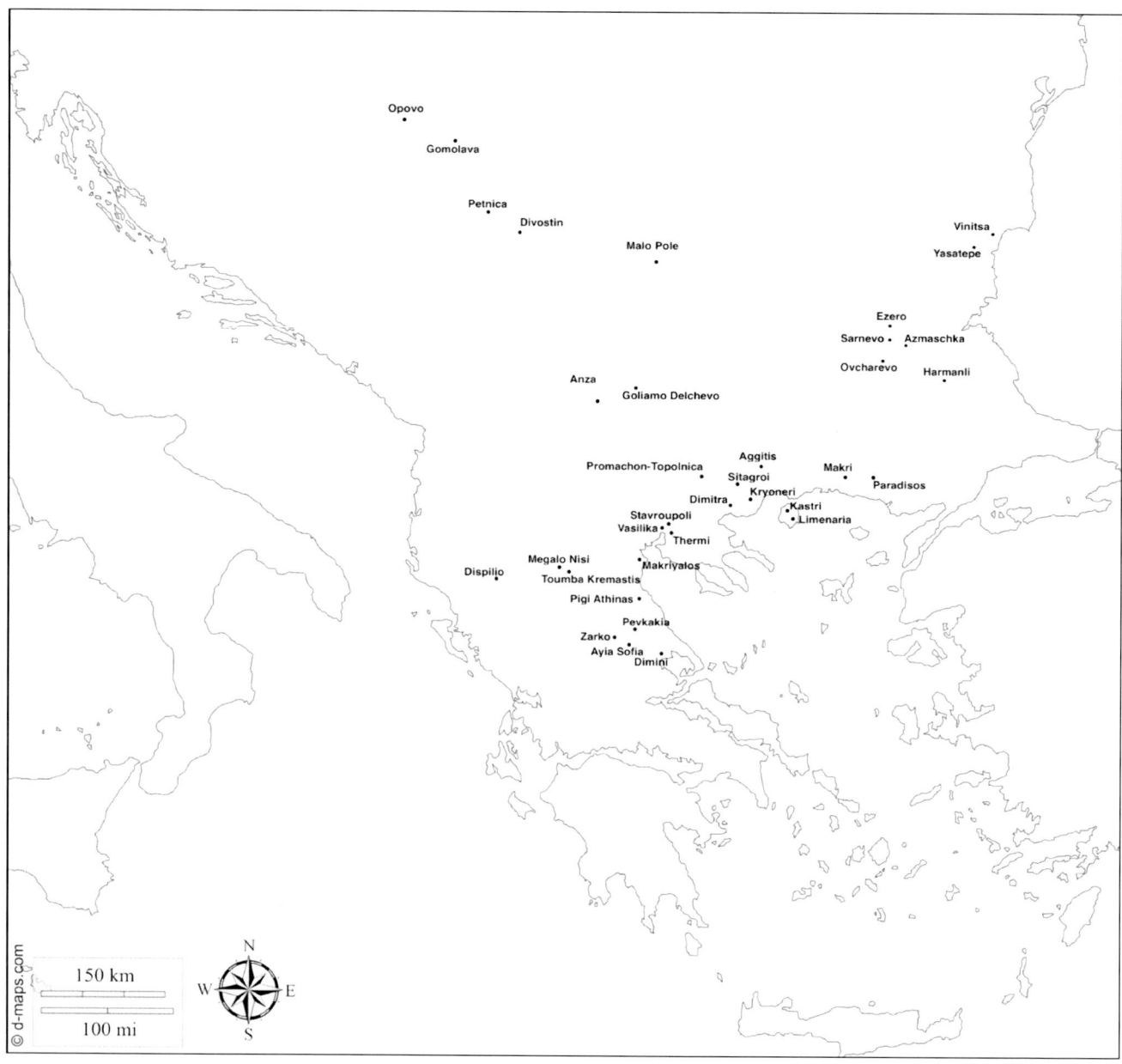

Figure 6.1 Map of Greek and Balkan sites used for comparisons with Promachon.

most (if not the most) hunted species. However, not all site reports from northern Greece provide the frequency of the red deer in terms of NISP. In some cases, the presence of this species is masked under the generic level of the family of Cervidae, which may also include roe deer and fallow deer. Secondly, there are cases, in which the authors of the faunal reports do not discuss which wild species were present on-site. Thirdly, there are cases, in which red deer is not particularly well represented among the wild fauna. Obviously, if we had taken into consideration these sites, they would have provided incorrect information on the significance of the wild species. Consequently, they were excluded from the following analysis (Figure 6.2; Table 6.1).

Faunal data from contemporary to Promachon settlements such as Dimitra (Yiannouli 1994; 1997), Megalo Nisi (Greenfield and Fowler 2005), Stavroupoli (Yiannouli

2002a; 2004), Sitagroi (Bökönyi 1986) and Paradisos (Larje 1987), suggest that caprines (and for the sake of this type of analysis, domesticated species) are of much higher economic importance than red deer (and thus, wild species). The Late Neolithic site of Promachon does not diverge from this pattern. Faunal data from sites such as Kryoneri (Mylona 1997) as well as the cave of Aggitis on the east bank of the river of Aggitis in the plain of Drama (Trantalidou *et al.* 2006) do, however, indicate that wild species are represented with higher percentages than any other settlement in Greek Macedonia, though domestic species still predominate.

Different strategies in animal exploitation may be associated to a number of factors. For instance, Helmer *et al.* (2005) argue that the variation in the proportions of domesticated and wild animals could plausibly be attributed to site function – for instance a difference

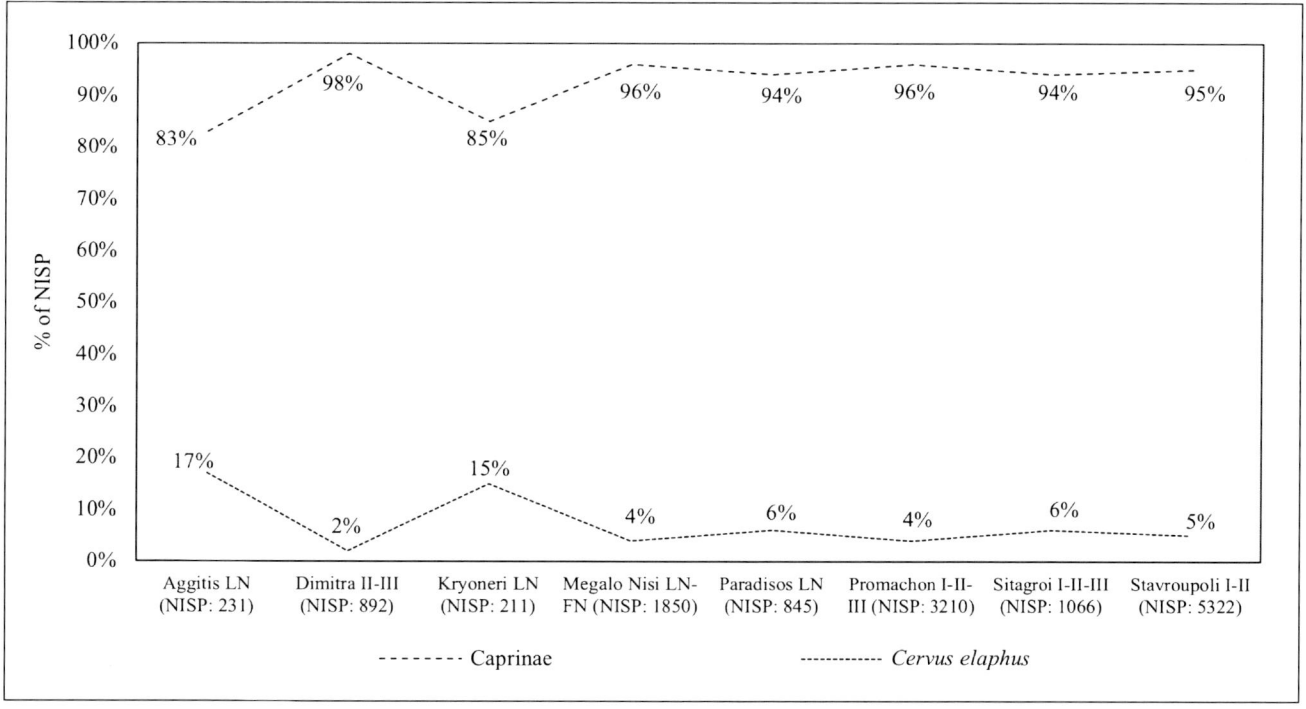

Figure 6.2 Frequency of Caprinae *versus Cervus elaphus* from Late/Final Neolithic Macedonia. Caprinae subfamily includes *Ovis aries*, *Capra hircus* and *Ovis/Capra*. Data in Table 6.1. NISP counts.

operating between open-air sites and caves. Helmer *et al.*'s argument could potentially explain the high frequency of wild animals in sites such as Aggitis, which is a cave-site. However, it cannot explain the high frequency of wild species in open-air sites such as Kryoneri. Therefore, the variations in the proportions between domesticated and wild species during the Late Neolithic should not be associated solely to the function of each site. To be more specific, the symbolic character that the wild animals might have had among Neolithic communities could have played a significant role in the decisions of Neolithic people regarding the more intensive exploitation of wild

Table 6.1 Frequency of domesticated [Caprinae (caprines)] *versus* wild [*Cervus elaphus* (red deer)] from Late/Final Neolithic Macedonia. Caprinae subfamily includes *Ovis aries* (sheep), *Capra hircus* (goat) and *Ovis/Capra* (sheep/ goat). Data for Figure 6.2. NISP counts.

Sites	Caprinae		*Cervus elaphus*	
	NISP	%	NISP	%
Aggitis LN	191	83%	40	17%
Dimitra II-III	874	98%	18	2%
Kryoneri LN	179	85%	32	15%
Megalo Nisi LN/FN	1779	96%	71	4%
Paradisos LN	794	94%	51	6%
Promachon I-II-III	3097	96%	113	4%
Sitagroi I-II-III	10043	94%	623	6%
Stavroupoli I-II	5082	95%	240	5%

resources (*cf.* Becker 1991; 1999; Hamilakis 2003; Perlés 2001, Trantalidou *et al.* 2006; Valamoti 2004).

In Greece, as elsewhere in temperate Europe, early famers relied on species of exotic origin: sheep and goats were non-native to Europe (Halstead and Isaakidou 2013). In addition, biometric evidence and ancient as well as modern DNA suggest that at least some the early domestic cattle and pigs were of southwest Asian descent (*cf.* Albarella *et al.* 2009; Larsson *et al.* 2007; Rowley-Conwy *et al.* 2012; Vigne 2011; Zeder 2005; Zeder *et al.* 2006). Figure 6.3 (Table 6.2) presents a tripolar diagram with the frequencies of cattle, caprines and pigs from a number of sites in Macedonia, Thrace and Thessaly during the Late Neolithic. This shows that the bulk of these sites are clustered in the lower right corner of the triangle, suggesting that caprines are represented with the highest frequencies than any other species in almost all sites, a pattern that is typical for the time-period.

The results from Promachon are on the edge of the distribution of contemporary settlements from Macedonia, Thrace and Thessaly, but by and large consistent with it. The high frequency of caprines in Promachon implies that the site was linked in terms of economic subsistence with the bulk of the northern Greek Late/Final Neolithic communities. In general, the predominance of caprines in Greece, has been subject to much discussion. To be more specific, this predominance has been attributed to the lack of expertise in the management of large species such as cattle (Cantuel *et al.* 2008), or as a failure of colonising farmers to adapt to alien environmental conditions due to 'cultural conservatism' (Whittle and Bartosiewicz

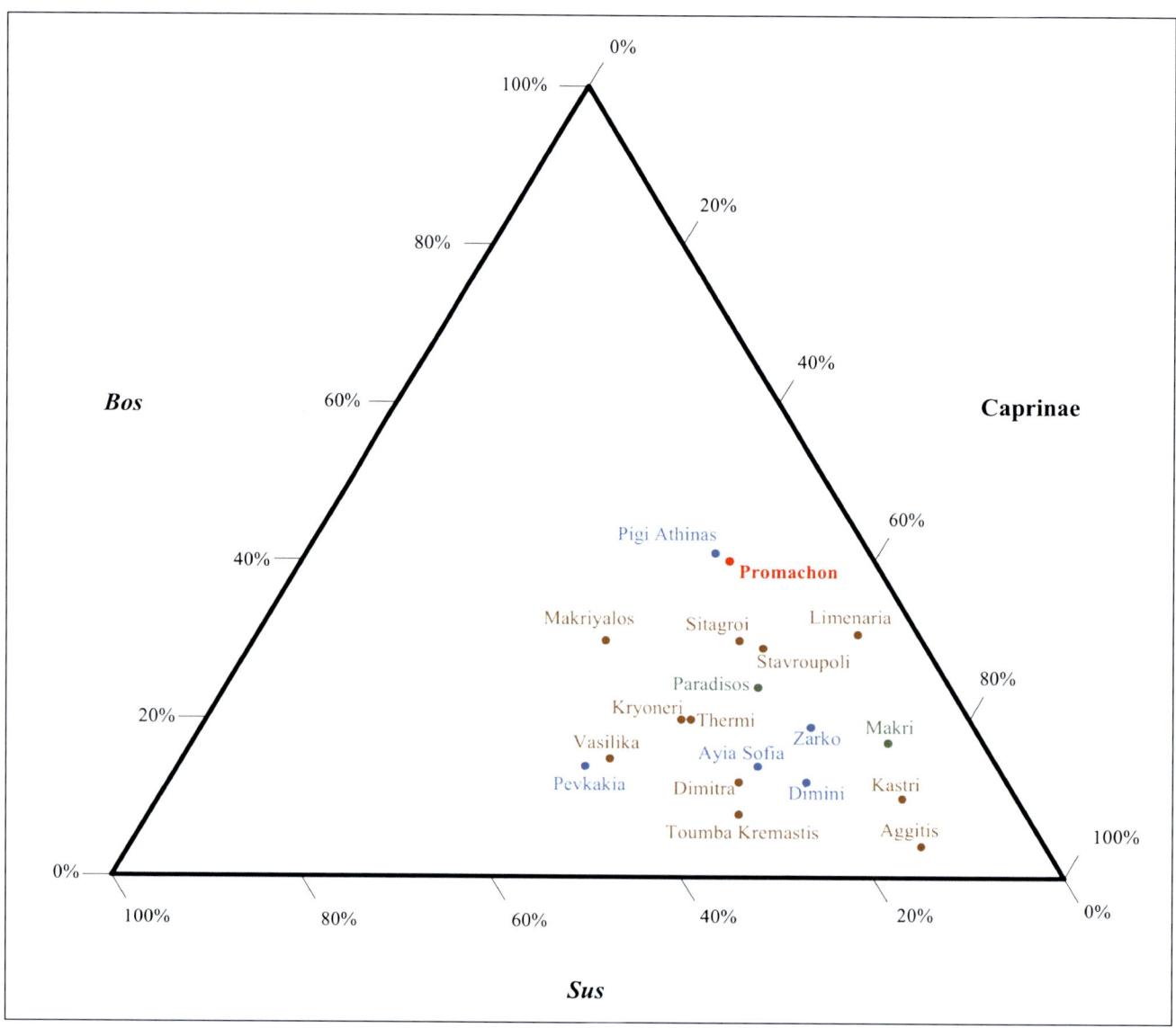

Figure 6.3 Corpus of Late Neolithic northern Greek sites: frequencies of the three main domesticated species. Brown: Macedonian sites; Green: Thracian sites; Blue: Thessalian sites. Caprinae subfamily includes *Ovis aries*, *Capra hircus* and *Ovis/Capra*. Data in Table 6.2. NISP counts.

2007). Alternatively, it has been suggested that the high frequency of caprines could plausibly be attributed to the slow reproduction of large livestock such as cattle (Bökönyi 1973), or to a purposeful choice by the Neolithic people, since sheep were closely integrated with crop cultivation (Halstead and Isaakidou 2013). Whatever the case, the evidence suggests that the keeping and breeding of caprines is characteristic of Neolithic farming, since it lasted for centuries. The climate and the environmental conditions in Greece might have played a decisive role in this choice: Greece has low winter precipitation the climate is warm and therefore caprines adapted well to climatic conditions that are substantially not unlike those of their area of origin (Barker 1985; Bailey 2000; Halstead 1989a; 2000).

Figure 6.4 (Table 6.3) presents a tripolar diagram with the frequencies of the three main domesticates from a number of sites in Bulgaria, Serbia and FYROM dating to the Late /Final Neolithic. In general, the frequency of these species

radically changes as one moves from the southern Balkans (Greece) into the Balkans proper (Halstead 1989a; Lazić 1988). What is interesting therefore, is the fact that the bulk of these sites are clustered on the upper triangle, indicating a predominance of cattle, which is in contrast with the information obtained from northern Greek sites.

A number of arguments have been proposed to explain the high frequency of cattle in northern Balkan regions. For instance, Bökönyi (1990) suggested that the high frequency of cattle at Vinča (Serbia) might be explained with the demand for large quantities of meat due to rapid demographic increase. A similar argument was put forward by Bökönyi to explain the high frequency of cattle in sites located in the Great Hungarian plain (Bökönyi 1974). Bökönyi argued that the Neolithic people of these regions invested in the keeping and breeding of cattle (and pigs), which would have produced larger quantities of meat than caprines. This would have been required

Table 6.2 Corpus of Late Neolithic northern Greek sites: frequencies of the three main domesticated species. Caprinae subfamily includes *Ovis aries* (sheep), *Capra hircus* (goat) and *Ovis/Capra* (sheep/goat). Data for Figure 6.3. NISP counts.

Site	Bos taurus		Caprinae		Sus		Sources
	NISP	%	NISP	%	NISP	%	
Aggitis LN	9	4%	191	83%	29	13%	Trantalidou *et al.* (2006)
Ayia Sofia LN	463	14%	1436	43%	1470	43%	Driesch and Enderle (1976)
Dimini LN	224	12%	1237	67%	399	21%	Halstead (1992)
Dimitra II-III	169	12%	874	60%	407	28%	Yiannouli (1994; 1997)
Kastri LN	-	10%	-	78%	-	12%	Halstead (1996)
Kryoneri LN	64	20%	179	50%	106	30%	Mylona (1997)
Limenaria LN	530	27%	1314	67%	105	6%	Webb (2012)
Makri I-II	78	17%	329	73%	41	10%	Curci and Tagliacozzo (2006)
Makriyalos I	6508	30%	8054	37%	7190	33%	Halstead (pers. comm.)
Megalo Nisi LN/FN	500	19%	1706	64%	466	17%	Greenfield and Fowler (2005)
Paradisos LN	346	24%	803	56%	294	20%	Larje (1987)
Pevkakia LN	69	14%	305	61%	126	25%	Jordan (1975)
Pigi athinas LN	590	41%	621	43%	217	16%	Cantuel (2013)
Sitagroi I-II-III	5583	30%	10043	51%	3555	18%	Bökönyi (1986)
Stavroupoli I-II	2788	29%	5082	54%	1607	17%	Yiannouli (2002a; 2004)
Thermi B	276	20%	741	51%	416	29%	Yiannouli (1989)
Toumba Kremastis LN	-	8%	-	62%	-	30%	Tzevelekidi *et al.* (2014)
Vasilika C	235	15%	758	45%	657	40%	Yiannouli (1994)
Zarko LN	198	19%	673	64%	182	17%	Becker (1991)

to meet the demands of an ever-growing population. If we accept Bökönyi's argument, then it would be normal to assume that meat in northern Balkan Late Neolithic communities was consumed on a more frequent basis than Greek Late Neolithic communities as implied by Halstead (*cf.* Halstead 2005; 2007; Halstead and Isaakidou 2013). This, ultimately, leads us to think that animals in northern Balkan regions (Bulgaria and mainly Serbia) were not subordinate to crops as it may have been the case in southern Balkan regions (Greece).

Putting aside Bökönyi's argument, other, more convincing arguments have been proposed to sufficiently explain cattle-dominated assemblages in the northern Balkan regions. Unlike the southern regions of the Balkans (Greece), which – as previously argued – has mainly winter precipitation, in the northern Balkans (Bulgaria and mainly Serbia) this is more evenly distributed year-round. This has important implications for cereal and pulse cultivations, which may have been disrupted by a shorter growing season, late frosts and potentially destructive wet summers (Halstead 1989a). In the case of domesticated animals from northern Balkan sites, Orton *et al.* (2016), noticed a shift from a subsistence economy

focused on the exploitation of caprines during the Early Neolithic, to an economy strongly dominated by cattle during the Middle/Late Neolithic. More importantly, this focus on cattle exploitation was rather persistent since it lasted for centuries. The pattern is interpreted by Orton and colleagues as an adaptation of the Balkan Neolithic communities to a climate and vegetation, which would have better-suited cattle (but also pigs) than sheep and goats (*c.f.* Bailey 2000; Barker 1985; Halstead 1989a; Orton *et al.* 2016). Indeed, the faunal data from the Late Neolithic northern Balkan regions indicate that cattle-dominated assemblages (in which red deer and pigs are also represented with high frequencies) ranged from southern Romania, to the western Balkans, and from south-central Bulgarian sites to the Gorges (Bailey 2000). Whatever the case, what can be inferred from both tripolar diagrams is that Promachon seems to have characteristics that are intermediate between the Aegean and Balkan Late and Final Neolithic communities. It is likely that Promachon was equally linked to Balkan and Aegean traditions. Cattle at Promachon are represented with the highest frequency than any other settlement in Macedonia, Thessaly or Thrace – as illustrated in Figure 6.3 – apart from Pigi Athinas, which has similar values (Cantuel 2013).

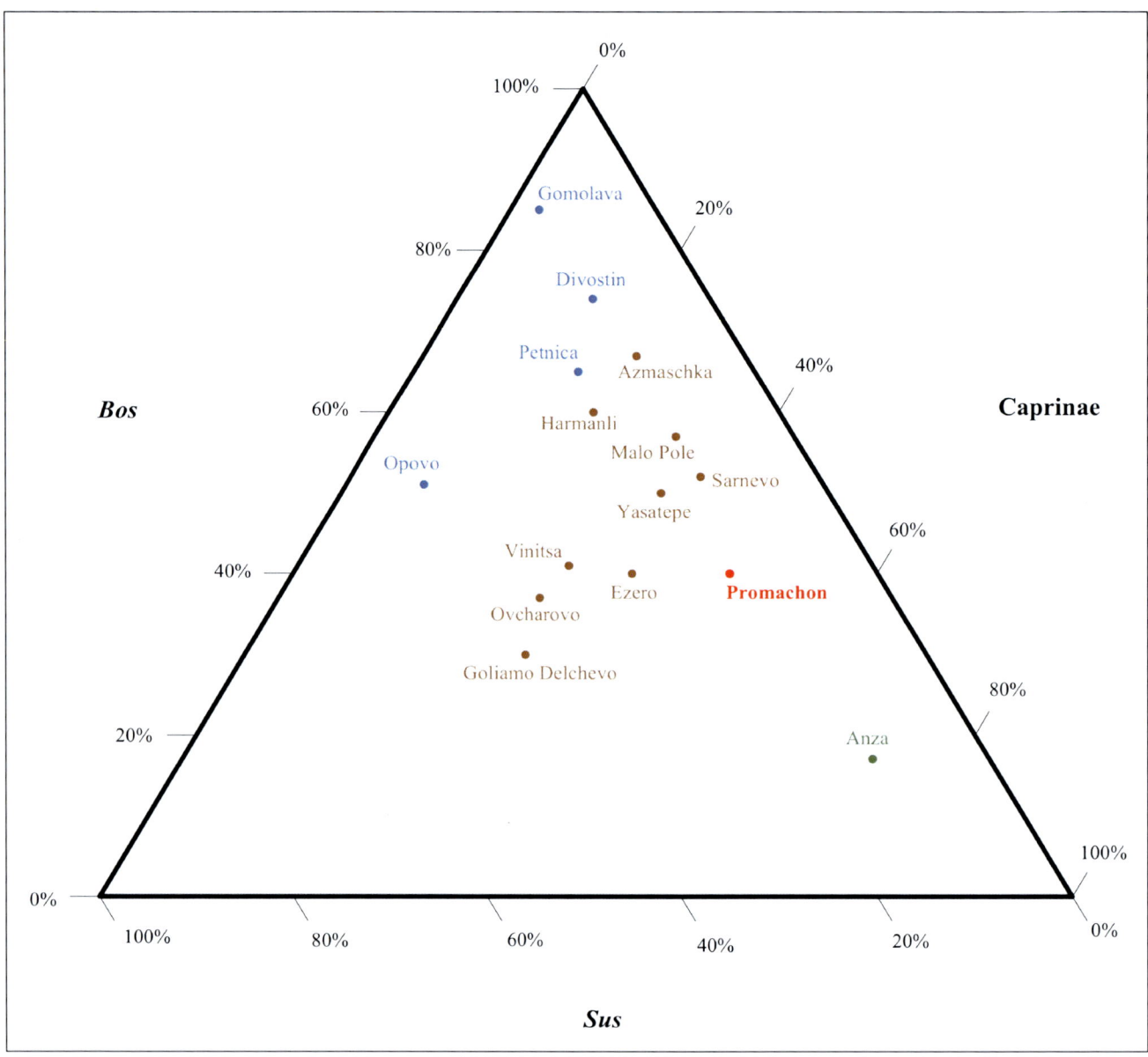

Figure 6.4 Corpus of Late/Final Neolithic Balkan sites: frequencies of the three main domesticated species. Brown: Bulgarian sites; Green: F.Y.R.O.M. sites; Blue: Serbian sites. Caprinae subfamily includes *Ovis aries*, *Capra hircus* and *Ovis/Capra*. Data in Table 6.3. NISP counts.

One could argue that the high frequency of cattle remains at Promachon could be the result of fragmentation bias, since the large cattle bones are likely to have been more fragmented than the bones of small animals such as caprines and pigs. However, as previously argued, the quantification system used for the faunal material form Promachon reduced the effects of fragmentation bias, since only certain, key-parts of the skeleton were recorded, thus preventing any bones from being counted twice. In any case, the frequency of fragmentation on cattle bones is close to that of caprines (98 per cent for cattle and 97 per cent for caprines). It has been previously argued that the extent of recovery bias at Promachon might have significantly affected the formation of the faunal assemblage. It can be therefore suggested, that the high frequency of cattle bones might be due to a particularly poor level of recovery. However, recovery bias would have also affected most of the other assemblages, perhaps even

more than at Promachon, where the use of a diagnostic zone approach to quantifications certainly reduced the effect of such bias. It can therefore not be the explanation for the high representation of cattle at Promachon. The environmental conditions in Promachon, the woodland environment, the strong vegetation cover, the slighter colder climatic conditions than other areas of Macedonia, could have significantly favoured the presence of a large number of cattle. The environmental conditions of the area probably played a significant role in the decision of the Neolithic people of Promachon to focus on cattle breeding.

The link of Promachon with the Balkan area is confirmed by evidence beyond that of animal economy and agriculture. Pottery decoration at Promachon is typical for contemporary settlements from the Balkans. For instance, Gradešnica as well as Marica incised decoration (Perniceva 1995; Vajsov 2007), along with bitumen type

Table 6.3 Corpus of Late/Final Neolithic Balkan sites: frequencies of the three main domesticated species. Caprinae subfamily includes *Ovis aries* (sheep), *Capra hircus* (goat) and *Ovis/Capra* (sheep/goat). Data for Figure 6.4. NISP counts.

Site	Bos taurus		Caprinae		Sus		Sources
	NISP	%	NISP	%	NISP	%	
Anza IV	496	17%	2067	71%	351	12%	Bökönyi 1976
Azmaschka LN	893	67%	295	22%	149	11%	Kostov 2006
Divostin II	6763	74%	1089	14%	1228	12%	Bökönyi 1988
Ezero LN	-	40%	-	35%	-	25%	Cited in Iliev and Spassov (2007)
Goliamo Delchevo FN	-	30%	-	29%	-	41%	Cited in Iliev and Spassov (2007)
Gomolava LN	1453	85%	55	3%	206	12%	Orton (2008)
Harmanli LN	381	60%	138	21%	124	19%	Bacvarov *et al.* 2010
Malo Pole LN	-	57%	-	31%	-	12%	Cited in Iliev and Spassov (2007)
Opovo LN	2955	51%	432	8%	2369	41%	Russel 1993
Ovcharovo LN	-	37%	-	27%	-	36%	Cited in Iliev and Spassov (2007)
Petnica LN	1324	65%	332	17%	371	18%	Orton (2008)
Sarnevo LN	991	52%	680	36%	231	12%	Gorczyk 2013
Vinitsa FN	-	41%	-	28%	-	31%	Cited in Iliev and Spassov (2007)
Yasatepe LN	-	50%	-	33%	-	17%	Cited in Iliev and Spassov (2007)

of decoration[1], and channeling type decoration[2], are found in the deposits of all habitation levels at Promachon. On the other hand, pit-houses, which are present during the first phase of occupation at Promachon, are the typical structural features of northern Balkan sites, in which, cattle play a dominant role. It can be argued therefore, that the high frequency of cattle remains, combined with the evidence from the ceramic repertoire as well as the evidence from the structural features, imply that the settlement of Promachon might had been culturally linked to Late and Final Neolithic communities from the northern regions of the Balkan Peninsula. This does not necessarily imply that Promachon was not culturally linked to northern Greek Late Neolithic communities as well. As far as the form of the chosen subsistence economy in Promachon is concerned, this was most likely to have been dictated by both environmental conditions and cultural ties that they shared with nearby Late/Final Neolithic communities.

6.3 Age-at-death of the main domesticates

As previously noted, age-at-death data for cattle, caprines and pigs from Bulgarian sites are extremely scarce. On the other hand, available age-at-death data from Serbian sites

could be obtained mainly through Greenfield's work (1986). However, these were not used for any comparisons with Promachon, mainly due to extremely small sample sizes.

This part of the analysis is therefore limited to comparisons of the age-at-death data for cattle, caprines and pigs between Promachon and other contemporary sites from Macedonia. However, these comparisons were not always straightforward. The main problem encountered was the incompatibility with regard to the methodological protocols that were employed by various researchers for the assessment of the age-at-death of the main domesticates. However, there were a number of other problems as well as biases. These will be further assessed for each species separately, as we proceed with our analyses.

6.3.1 Bos taurus *age-at-death*

The information on the age-at-death of cattle populations from a number of Late Neolithic sites in Macedonia is rather scarce. This is mainly due to the species' small sample size, since caprines and pigs significantly outnumber cattle in most Macedonian sites. As a result, zooarchaeologists working on Late Neolithic faunal assemblages from Macedonia provide a very crude and brief outline of cattle age-at-death, based solely on the fusion of postcranial bones. However, these results have limitations, since we can estimate the age of an animal before it is fully mature (*i.e.* before the bones are fully fused; after the bones are fully fused, we can estimate the age only by tooth wear

[1] Not an actual decoration, rather a gluing agent, upon which decorative elements from wood (mainly birch bark) were glued, typical of the Vinča-Turdaş period (Vajsov 2007).
[2] Typical of the Late Neolithic cultures of Hotnica and Podgorica in northern Bulgaria, Karanovo IV-Kalojanovec in Bulgarian Thrace and Vinča B₂ in Serbia (Vajsov 2007).

stages). Obviously, the estimation of the age-at-death by means of the fusion data alone poses additional limitations, since postcranial elements are subject to a number of post-depositional modifications (fragmentation, carnivore attrition, retrieval biases, *etc.*), which, have already been discussed. In some cases, however, the fusion data is corroborated by information regarding the presence (or the absence) of loose deciduous teeth.

With these *caveats* in mind, age-at-death data from a number of Macedonian sites contemporary to Promachon (*e.g.* Dimitra, Kryoneri, Sitagroi, Stavroupoli, Thermi) suggest a considerable variation regarding the exploitation of cattle. For instance, mortality profiles from the nearby sites of Dimitra (Yiannouli 1997) and Kryoneri (Mylona 1997) indicate an exploitation of cattle predominantly tuned to the production of meat. The ageing data suggest that the majority of the cattle population in Dimitra was culled between the ages of two and three. In addition, Yiannouli (1997) reports that only one individual from Dimitra was less than 18 months old. The pattern, thus, is not consistent with the exploitation of cattle for milk. Likewise, age-at-death data from Kryoneri (Mylona 1997) suggest that cattle – younger than the age of three – were completely absent in the faunal assemblage. The results, however, should be approached with extreme caution since they are based solely on the stage of fusion of postcranial bones. As already discussed, immature unfused bones are subject to severe fragmentation and/or obliteration by scavenger activity. Unlike Dimitra and Kryoneri, cattle ageing data from Sitagroi (Bökönyi 1986), Stavroupoli (Yiannouli 2002a;) and Thermi (Yiannouli 1989) are interpreted to reflect for the use of secondary products. The Late Neolithic deposits of Sitagroi and Stavroupoli yielded large samples of cattle mandibles. However, only in the case of Sitagroi we have sufficient information on the frequencies of different age stages. There is, however, one issue that should be considered in the case of the age-at-death data of cattle from Sitagroi. The age stages that Bökönyi (1986) uses ('Neonate', 'Juvenile', 'Sub adult', 'Adult', 'Mature/Senile') belong to a method that has been defined (and possibly used only) by him (Bökönyi 1970). The same problem, in fact, applies to caprines and pigs. This obviously creates a problem of compatibility for any attempted comparisons of the age-at-death of the domestic species between the two sites, since Bökönyi does not state the level of eruption and wear of teeth for each of the age stages that he uses. Nevertheless, comparisons between the two assemblages (Promachon and Sitagroi) are attempted in this chapter, but it is important to consider that the age stages used for the two sites are only roughly comparable (Figure 6.5; Table 6.4).

The bulk of the cattle population at Sitagroi was killed at the 'Adult' stage (57 per cent), whereas at Promachon the frequency of adult individuals is 22 per cent. This indicates that cattle from Sitagroi exhibit a slightly older age profile than those from Promachon. Of additional interest, is the fact that 'Neonate' and 'Mature/Senile' individuals are very scarce at Sitagroi, similarly to Promachon.

According to Bökönyi (1986), cattle mortality profiles at Sitagroi suggest that the species was used mainly for meat. However, he also argues that a diversified strategy for milk (presence of 'Juvenile' and 'Adult' individuals) cannot be excluded. On the other hand, a zoomorphic clay figurine (probably cattle; Bailey 2000) provides corroborating evidence for the use of cattle as pack animal at the Late Neolithic Sitagroi. Its presence, led Bökönyi to speculate that this was evidence for the use of cattle for traction as well. Nevertheless, pack animals are not the same as draught animals, and in any case, Bökönyi does not mention the presence of pathological conditions on cattle lower limbs, which may be associated with heavy stress, such as that involved in pulling an ard or a plough.

On the other hand, mandible wear data from Stavroupoli are consistent with those from Promachon, since almost half of the cattle population was slaughtered between the first and the third year, indicating an exploitation for meat. In addition, almost eight per cent of the cattle population was slaughtered before the first year, indicating – according to Yiannouli (2002a) – exploitation for milk. Cattle mortality profiles are conspicuously absent from the original faunal report on Thermi (Yiannouli 1989). The author however, suggests an exploitation of cattle both for primary (meat) and secondary products (milk).

All in all, the evidence from Macedonia indicates little evidence for specialization in terms of products and uses. At several sites the emphasis seems to have been on meat production but is also compatible with the additional exploitation of secondary products (milk).

6.3.2 Caprinae age-at-death

Sufficient information on the age-at-death data of caprines from contemporary to Promachon sites in Macedonia could be drawn from Dimitra (Yiannouli 1997), Thermi (Yiannouli 1989), Sitagroi (Bökönyi 1986), Makriyalos (Tzevelekidi *et al.* 2014) and Toumba Kremastis (Tzevelekidi *et al.* 2014). With the exception of Sitagroi, the methodology for the assessment of the age-at-death of caprines from the rest of the sites is identical to the one used from Promachon. While in the cases of Makriyalos, Toumba Kremastis and Sitagroi we have sufficient information regarding the culling practices of sheep and goat separately, in Dimitra and Thermi the author combines the overall caprine assemblage (sheep, goat and sheep/goat), without exploring whether the two species were subject to differential exploitation regimes. In addition, the author of these two reports used a different system to quantify the caprine mandibles from Dimitra and Thermi (*i.e.* MNI). However, as previously noted this did not constitute a significant problem, as the age-at-death data are not affected by the same problems of taxonomic proportions as the frequency of taxa. Therefore, the two sites are used here for comparative purposes.

Wear data of the caprine population from Promachon are more similar to those of Dimitra than Thermi (Figure 6.6;

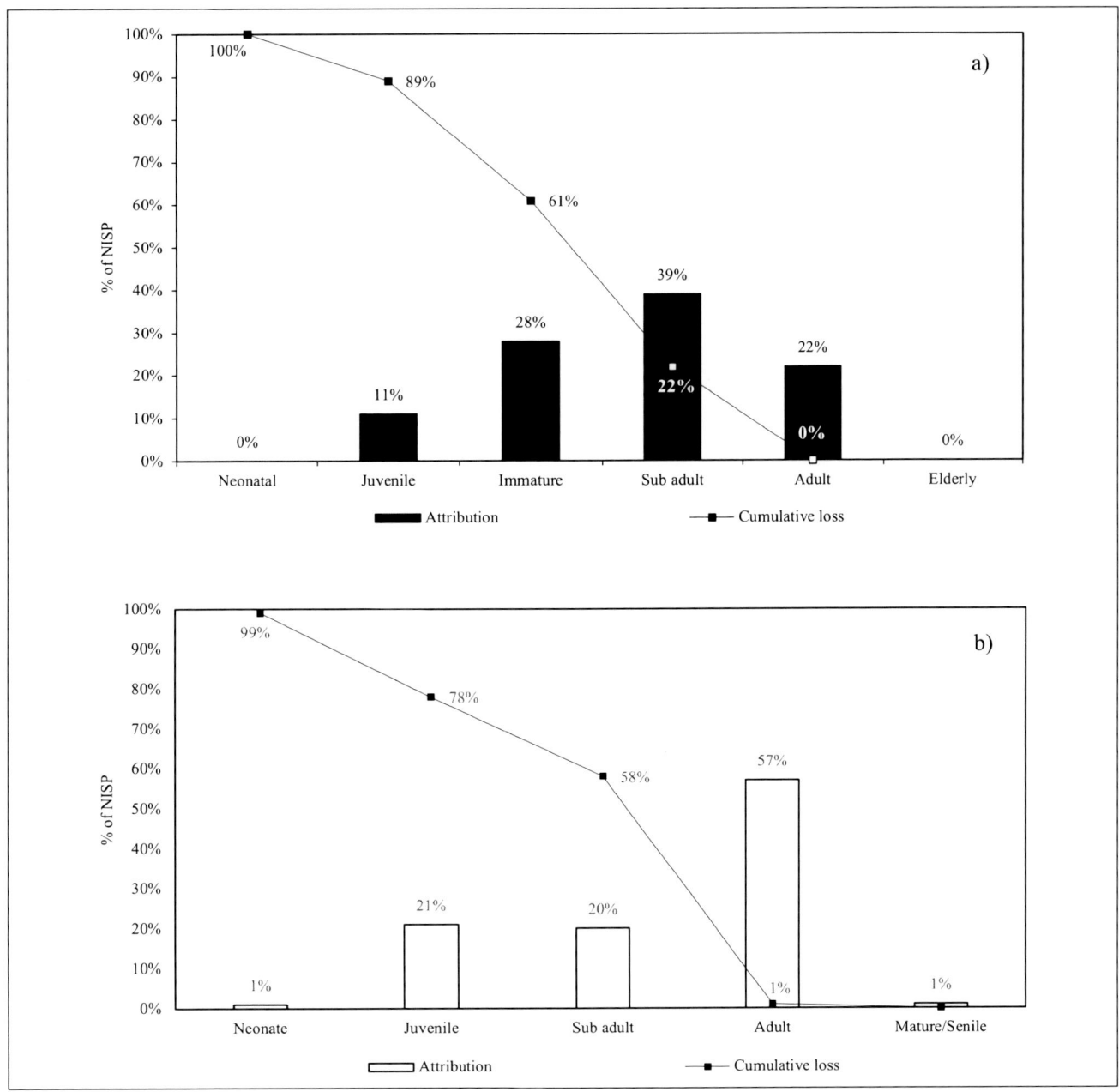

Figure 6.5 *Bos taurus* **kill-off pattern comparison between: a) LN Promachon (Promachon I-II-III) and b) LN Sitagroi (Sitagroi I-II-III). Data for Promachon in Table 5.82. Data for Sitagroi in Table 6.4. NISP counts.**

Table 6.4 *Bos taurus* **(cattle) kill-off pattern from LN Sitagroi (Bökönyi 1986). Data for Figure 6.5. NISP counts.**

Bos taurus	Sitagroi I-II-III		
	NISP	% Attribution	% Cumulative loss
Neonatal	5	1%	99%
Juvenile	139	21%	78%
Sub adult	132	20%	58%
Adult	371	57%	1%
Mature/Senile	4	1%	0%
TOTAL	**651**	**100%**	

Tables 6.5-6.6). As in the case of Promachon, an almost even distribution of wear stages can be detected at Dimitra. Almost 41 per cent of the caprine population were killed-off between their first and fourth year (wear stages D, E, F) suggesting exploitation for meat. In addition, 32 per cent of the individuals were killed between their fourth and tenth year (wear stages G, H, I). This according to Yiannouli (1997) indicates that – in addition to breeding – a number of caprines were also kept for milk and also fleece. Of interest is the fact that age-at-death data from Dimitra suggests a younger age profile than Promachon, since nine per cent of the caprine population was slaughtered between two and six months (wear stage B). In overall, almost 27 per cent of caprines were killed before the first year (wear stages A, B and C) suggesting that caprines were also exploited for milk (Yiannouli 1997).

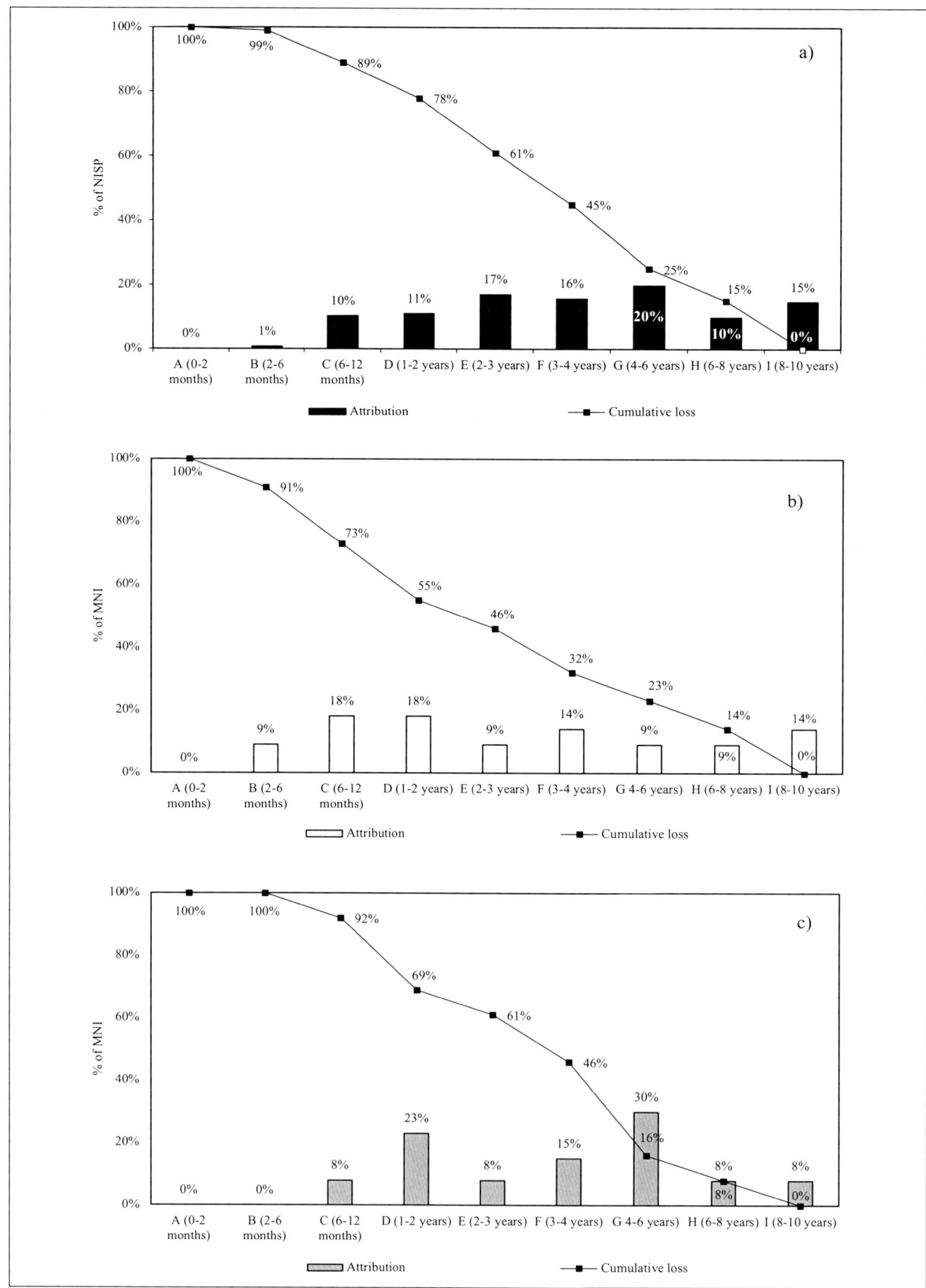

Figure 6.6 Caprinae kill-off pattern comparison between: a) LN Promachon (Promachon I-II-III), b) LN Dimitra (Dimitra II-III) and c) LN Thermi (Thermi B). Data for Promachon in Table 5.88. Data for Dimitra in Table 6.5 and data for Thermi in Table 6.6. NISP counts (Promachon) and MNI counts (Dimitra and Thermi).

Table 6.5 Caprinae (caprines) kill-off pattern from LN Dimitra (Yiannouli 1997). Data for Figure 6.6. MNI counts.

Caprinae	Dimitra II-III		
	MNI	% Attribution	% Cumulative loss
A (0-2 months)		0%	100%
B (2-6 months)	2	9%	91%
C (6-12 months)	4	18%	73%
D (1-2 years)	4	18%	55%
E (2-3 years)	2	9%	46%
F (3-4 years)	3	14%	32%
G (4-6 years)	2	9%	23%
H (6-8 years)	2	9%	14%
I (8-10 years)	3	14%	0%
TOTAL	22	100%	

Table 6.6 Caprinae (caprines) kill-off pattern from LN Thermi (Yiannouli 1989). Data for Figure 6.6. MNI counts.

Caprinae	Thermi B		
	MNI	% Attribution	% Cumulative loss
A (0-2 months)		0%	100%
B (2-6 months)		0%	100%
C (6-12 months)	1	8%	92%
D (1-2 years)	3	23%	69%
E (2-3 years)	1	8%	61%
F (3-4 years)	2	15%	46%
G (4-6 years)	4	30%	16%
H (6-8 years)	1	8%	8%
I (8-10 years)	1	8%	0%
TOTAL	13	100%	

Unlike Promachon and Dimitra, caprine wear data from Thermi indicate two mortality peaks: one at stage D (one to two years: 23 per cent) and a more prominent one at stage G (four to six years: 30 per cent). Yiannouli (1989) suggests that caprines at Thermi were most probably exploited for meat and fleece. On the other hand, there seems to be a dearth of very young individuals (wear stages A and B: zero to two months and two to six months respectively) as in the case of Promachon. However, since the author does not assess the effect of recovery bias, we cannot be entirely confident whether the absence of very young individuals represents a 'genuine' pattern. In any case, Yiannouli argues that a small-scale exploitation of caprines for milk is not entirely unlikely.

As previously noted, Sitagroi, Makriyalos and Toumba Kremastis are the only sites from Macedonia where sufficient data on the age-at-death of sheep and goat respectively are provided. The age stages used by Bökönyi (1986) for the assessment of the age-at-death of sheep and goats from Sitagroi are the same as in the case of the cattle example. An additional problem in the case of caprines, however, is represented by the fact that the age stages that we use in our caprine assemblage (following Payne 1973) are more numerous than those created by Bökönyi in his study of Sitagroi. Nevertheless, in the comparison of the mortality profiles for sheep and goats between the two sites, an attempt has been made to find equivalence between Payne's (1973) and Bökönyi's (1986) age stages. The age-at-death data based on the sheep mandibles from Sitagroi (Figure 6.7; Table 6.7) indicate a much younger age profile compared to Promachon. In Sitagroi, the sheep population did not survive beyond Bökönyi's 'Adult stage'; on the contrary, almost 45 per cent of individuals in Promachon survived beyond their fourth year (stages G-H-I). About 48 per cent of the individuals at Sitagroi were killed at 'Juvenile-Sub adult stages' [roughly equivalent to stages C-D (six months to two years: 26 per cent in Promachon)], which is consistent with the exploitation for milk and mainly meat. In addition, about 52 per cent of the sheep population at Sitagroi was killed at 'Adult stage' [roughly equivalent to stage E-F (two to four years: 27 per cent)] which, according to Bökönyi (1986) indicates the exploitation of sheep for secondary products, such as milk and fleece. This interpretation is, however, questionable, as one should expect a greater proportion of adults, and at least some elderly individuals, if the emphasis were on secondary products. Overall, the caprine kill-off pattern from Sitagroi seems to be mainly consistent with an emphasis on meat production.

Of interest is the fact that neonate sheep are missing from Sitagroi. This is consistent also with the information from the sheep assemblage from Promachon [stage A (zero to two months)]. One could argue that the absence of neonate sheep from Sitagroi could be the effect of recovery bias since unworn teeth are most likely to fall out of the young sheep mandibles, which are particularly affected by fragmentation. However, the presence of neonate goats does not support this hypothesis and we can therefore assume that the pattern for sheep is indicating a 'genuine' dearth of neonate individuals. Figure 6.8 (Table 6.8) provides age data for goat mandibles from Sitagroi. As for sheep, goats at Sitagroi present a much younger age profile than those from Promachon. Almost 10 per cent of the goats from Sitagroi were killed at the stage of 'Neonate' [roughly equivalent to stage A (zero to two months: zero per cent in Promachon)]. In addition, almost 45 per cent of goats from Sitagroi were killed at the stage of 'Juvenile-Sub adult', [roughly equivalent to stages C-D (six months to two years: four per cent in Promachon)], probably indicating the exploitation of these animals for meat (Bökönyi 1986). About 45 per cent of goats from Sitagroi were killed at the stage of 'Adult' [roughly equivalent to stages E-F (two to four years: 55 per cent in Promachon)]. This part of the

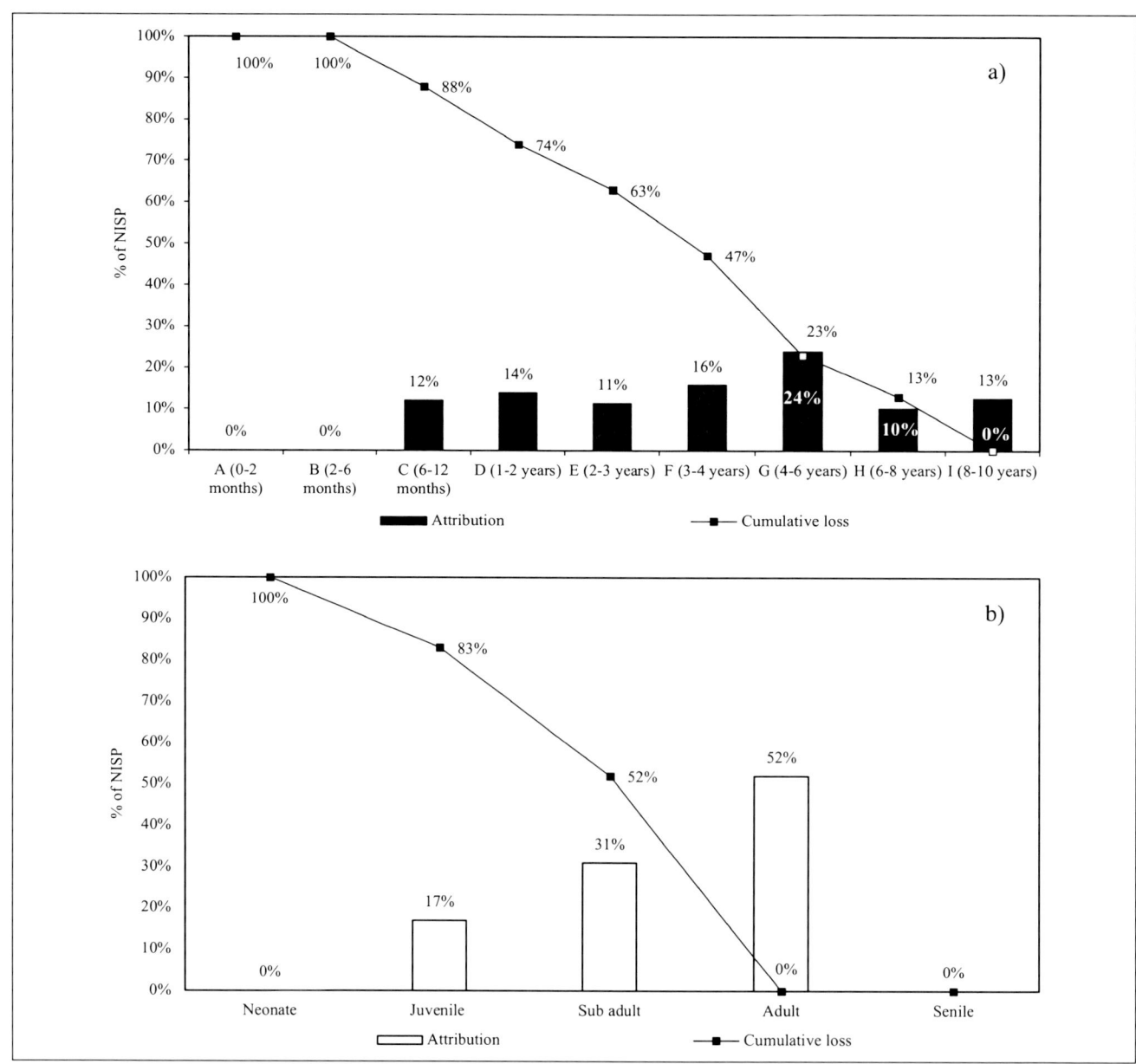

Figure 6.7 *Ovis aries* **kill-off pattern comparison between: a) LN Promachon (Promachon I-II-III) and b) LN Sitagroi (Sitagroi I-II-III). Data for Promachon in Table 5.91. Data for Sitagroi in Table 6.7. NISP counts.**

Table 6.7 *Ovis aries* **(sheep) kill-off pattern from LN Sitagroi (Bökönyi 1986). Data for Figure 6.7. NISP counts.**

Ovis aries	Sitagroi I-II-III		
	NISP	% Attribution	% Cumulative loss
Neonatal		0%	100%
Juvenile	36	15%	85%
Sub adult	73	31%	54%
Adult	125	53%	1%
Senile	2	1%	0%
TOTAL	**236**	**100%**	

population, combined with 'Neonate' individuals, may indicate the exploitation of goats for milk. Unlike sheep,

Bökönyi argues against the use of 'Adult' goats for fleece, since the sample size of goat mandibles with recordable wear is small for any definite conclusions. 'Senile' goats [roughly equivalent to stages G-H-I (four to ten years)] are completely missing from Sitagroi (zero per cent). They are however represented in Promachon with a high frequency (41 per cent), which supports Bökönyi's view that fleece production was not a major concern in goat breeding.

Figure 6.9 presents the kill-off pattern for sheep and goats respectively from Makriyalos and Toumba Kremastis and compares the data to Promachon. Age-at-death data for sheep and goat from these two sites were drawn from Tzevelekidi *et al.* (2014). In their publication, the authors present only the frequencies of the age survival for each age stage (according to Payne 1973) and the data can therefore be only roughly compared with Promachon.

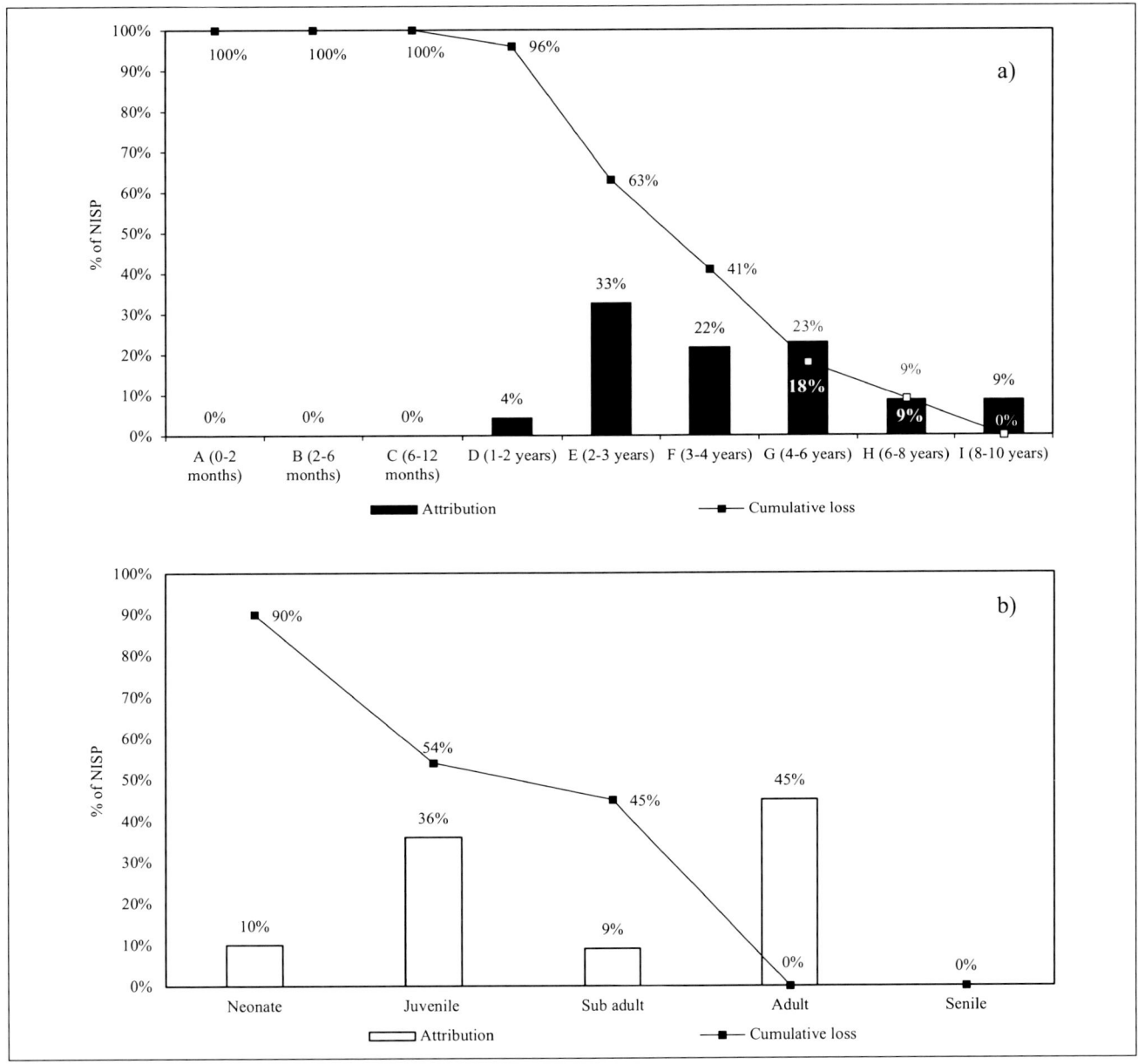

Figure 6.8 *Capra hircus* **kill-off pattern comparison between: a) LN Promachon (Promachon I-II-III) and b) LN Sitagroi (Sitagroi I-II-III). Data for Promachon in Table 5.92. Data for Sitagroi in Table 6.8. NISP counts.**

Table 6.8 *Capra hircus* **(goat) kill-off pattern from LN Sitagroi (Bökönyi 1986). Data for Figure 6.8. NISP counts.**

Capra hircus	Sitagroi I-II-III		
	NISP	% Attribution	% Cumulative loss
Neonatal	1	2%	98%
Juvenile	7	16%	82%
Sub adult	12	27%	55%
Adult	24	55%	0%
Senile		0%	0%
TOTAL	**44**	**100%**	

than with Promachon. In comparison to Promachon, there is a higher mortality of younger sheep at Makriyalos and Toumba Kremastis, since a large proportion of the sheep population was killed before their first year (stage C: six to twelve months). The evidence therefore for the use of sheep for their milk is stronger at Makriyalos and Toumba Kremastis than at Promachon. This however, does not imply that sheep milk was not exploited at the latter site, as previously noted (chapter 5). On the other hand, at all three sites nearly half of the sheep population was killed at stages E-F (two to four years), suggesting an exploitation tuned to the production of meat. With regard to the older sheep, the data between the three sites is roughly similar, since a small proportion of the sheep population survived well into adulthood (stages G-H and I: four to ten years).

With regard to sheep, the age-at-death data from Makriyalos and Toumba Kremastis are more similar with each other

As in the case of sheep, the age-at-death data of goats from Makriyalos and Toumba Kremastis are more similar

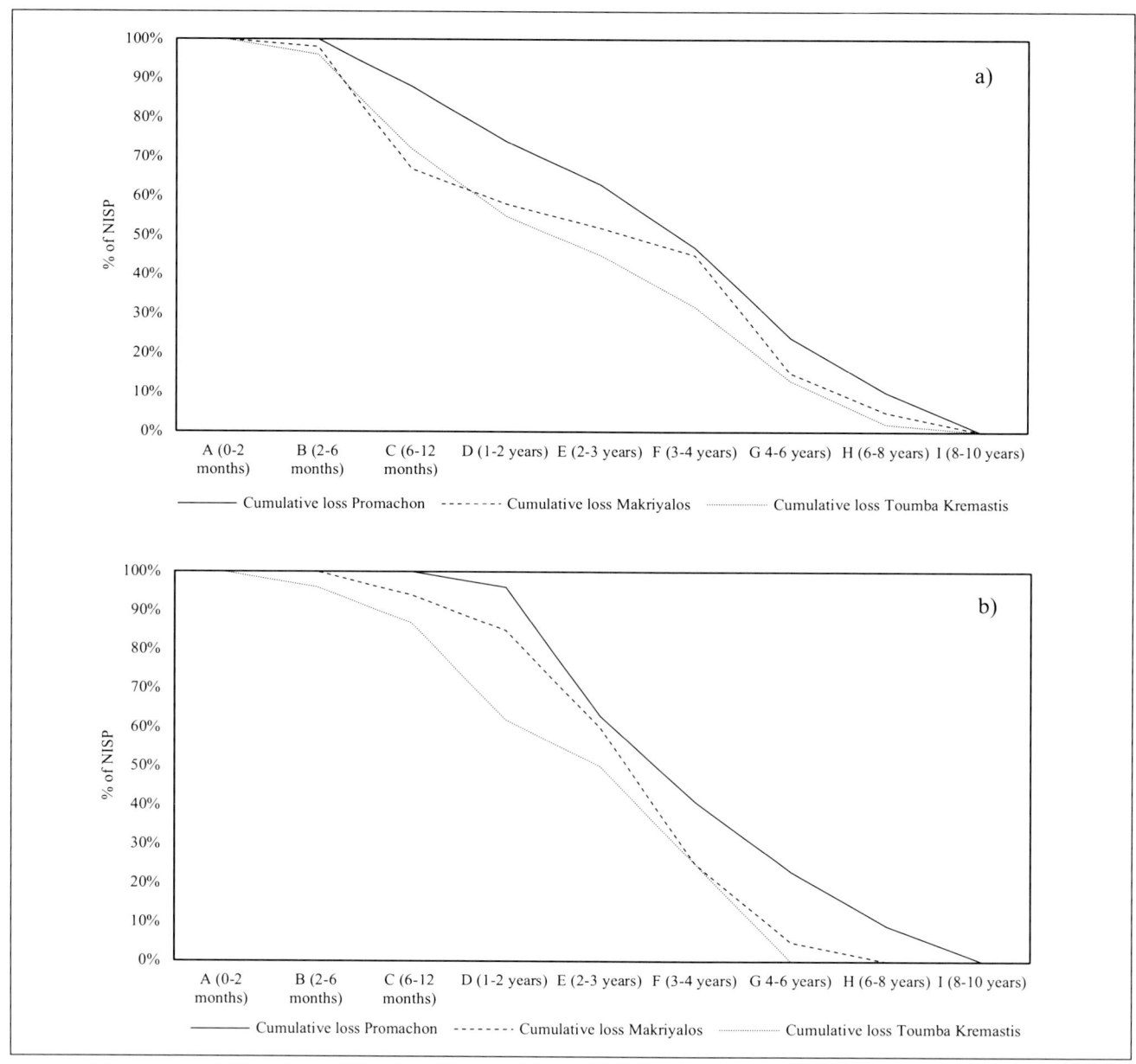

Figure 6.9 Kill-off pattern comparison of: a) *Ovis aries* **and b)** *Capra hircus* **between LN Promachon (Promachon I-II-III), LN Makriyalos (Makriyalos I) and LN Toumba Kremastis. Data for Promachon in Tables 5.91-5.92 for sheep and goat respectively. Data for Makriyalos were drawn from Tzevelekidi** *et al.* **(2014; Figure 8; percentage of age survival from habitation levels) and data for Toumba Kremastis were drawn from the same publication (Figure 9; percentage of age survival from pits). NISP counts.**

with each other than with Promachon. In general, there is a younger age profile of goats in Makriyalos and Toumba Kremastis and an older one in Promachon. At Makriyalos and Toumba Kremastis a small proportion of the very young goats (less than one year) was culled, whereas at Promachon the entire goat population survived their first year. There is also a large discrepancy between the three sites with regard to the older individuals (stages G-H and I: four to ten years). The data shows that goats did not survive beyond the sixth year at Toumba Kremastis, and beyond the eighth year at Makriyalos. At Promachon however, a large proportion of goats survived well into their elderly stage (stage I: eight to ten years). In general, one cannot argue against the use of goats at all three sites for their meat, since at all sites a large proportion of the goat population was culled between their first and fourth

year (stages E-F). However, the use of goats for milk seems more likely at Makriyalos and Toumba Kremastis than at Promachon.

As in the case of cattle, caprine ageing data from several sites in Macedonia indicate an emphasis on meat production. However, in almost all sites, caprine age-at-death data have also been interpreted to reflect for the use of secondary products, such as milk and fleece. In general, faunal researchers working in Late Neolithic faunal assemblages from northern Greece suggest the exploitation of caprines for secondary products. This is mainly due to the fact that milk and fleece have been considered as the products with which, the Neolithic people would 'balance' the loss from the small quantities of caprine meat (in comparison to that of cattle and pigs) (Trantalidou 1990).

On one hand, the evidence for the use of milk in Greek Macedonia has been attested through residue analyses of ceramic vessels from Stavroupoli (Evershed *et al.* 2008). On the other hand, the arguments for the use of caprine fleece heavily rely on a combination of evidence, between the high mortality of 'elderly' individuals, and the presence of clay spindle whorls, loom weights and bone needles with eyes, which appear in high quantities in various sites from Greek Macedonia during the late stage of the Neolithic. However, the presence of 'elderly' individuals does not necessarily indicate that these animals were kept for their fleece (these individuals might have been used for breeding and milking), and certainly, the latter material culture objects do not necessarily indicate the use of animal fibres. Obviously, a larger body of mandible wear data should allow clarification on issues regarding the use of caprines during the late stages of the Neolithic in northern Greece.

6.3.3 Sus *age-at-death*

The practice of killing off pigs at a young age has been observed at other sites from Greek Macedonia, contemporary to Promachon. This is not unusual, as pigs have been reared for meat since they were first domesticated and this kind of exploitation has never changed (Albarella *et al.* 1997). Age at death data for pigs from Sitagroi (Bökönyi 1986), Dimitra (Yiannouli 1997) and Thermi (Yiannouli 1989) are compared to those from Promachon. Before proceeding to the comparisons however, a note should be made with regard to the methodology used by the two researchers for the assessment of the age-at-death of this species from the three sites (Sitagroi, Dimitra and Thermi). On one hand, the age stages that Bökönyi uses are similar to the cattle and caprine example. On the other hand, Yiannouli argues that the assessment of the age-at-death of the domestic pigs from Dimitra and Thermi was based on Bull and Payne's (1982) age stages for pigs. However, the age stages that she provides in her faunal reports from both sites are not the ones that Bull and Payne (1982) have defined. In view of this inconsistency, therefore, we have to be cautious with our interpretations.

Comparison of the four sites is presented in Figure 6.10 (Tables 6.9-6.11). Age-at-death data from Sitagroi exhibit a striking similarity with that from Promachon and demonstrates that the overwhelming majority of pigs were killed before reaching their 'Adult' stage. At Dimitra (Yiannouli 1997) and Thermi (Yiannouli 1989), almost all age stages are well represented. In Promachon however, the bulk of the pig population was killed at the stages of 'Immature' and 'Sub adult', which are roughly equivalent to the first and the second year. In addition, unlike Promachon, almost six per cent of the pigs from Dimitra and seven per cent of the pigs from Thermi survived beyond the end of the third year, possibly reflecting the practice of keeping a number of elderly female pigs for breeding (Yiannouli 1989; 1997). On the other hand, the discussion with regard to the exploitation of very young

pigs between Promachon, Thermi and Dimitra would be problematic. This is because Yiannouli does not mention the extent of recovery bias in these sites and also because we do not have information about the proportion of neonatal individuals from Thermi and Dimitra, since these might be possibly included in the 'zero to six months' stage. All in all, Yiannouli argues that pigs in these sites were used for meat. In addition, a number of older female pigs might have been kept for breeding.

6.4 Metrical analysis

The purpose of this part of the analysis is to compare the size of the main domesticated species between Promachon and other contemporary sites in Macedonia and Thessaly. It should be noted that most of the metrical data used for comparisons with Promachon were provided by a number of (limited) published sources. However, a number of colleagues (Umberto Albarella, Keith Dobney and Paul Halstead) also provided unpublished metrical data as well: I am indebted to all of them. It should also be noted that the results of the metrical comparisons between Promachon and Macedonian as well as Thessalian sites were largely published in 2016 (Kazantzis and Albarella 2016). However, they are presented here as well, citing whenever appropriate this publication. Lastly, but also quite importantly, the comparison of the size of cattle and sheep between Promachon and Makriyalos was not possible to be included in current book. It is included, however, in the original thesis submitted in 2015 (Kazantzis 2015). In the discussion that follows the results of the biometry section of this chapter, notes are being made with regard to the observed differences in the size of these two domesticates between the two sites.

For the Neolithic of Greece, the use of biometry is linked with the intensity of zooarchaeological research in different regions, with Thessaly a greater focus of research than Macedonia (Kazantzis and Albarella 2016). This is the result of an archaeological perception of the Neolithic cultures of Macedonia as largely derivative from, and marginal to, those of Thessaly (Fotiadis 2001). Indeed, while faunal reports from Late/Final Neolithic Thessalian sites contain full ranges of measurements for all species identified, this is less so the case for contemporary Macedonian sites, which provide only summary statistics of measurements (Kazantzis and Albarella 2016). With regard to Macedonia, an exception is represented by the work of Bökönyi (1986) at the Late Neolithic site of Sitagroi, which provides a full range of tooth and postcranial measurements. On the other hand, measurements used by the zooarchaeologists who conducted faunal research in both Thessalian and Macedonian sites generally follow von den Driesch (1976). However, different researchers chose to take different measurements. Differences are mainly noticed between German zooarchaeologists, who primarily worked in Thessaly, and those who worked in Macedonia. For instance, most German zooarchaeologists did not measure the distal breadth (Bd) and the lateral depth (Dl) of the pig astragalus, both of which were

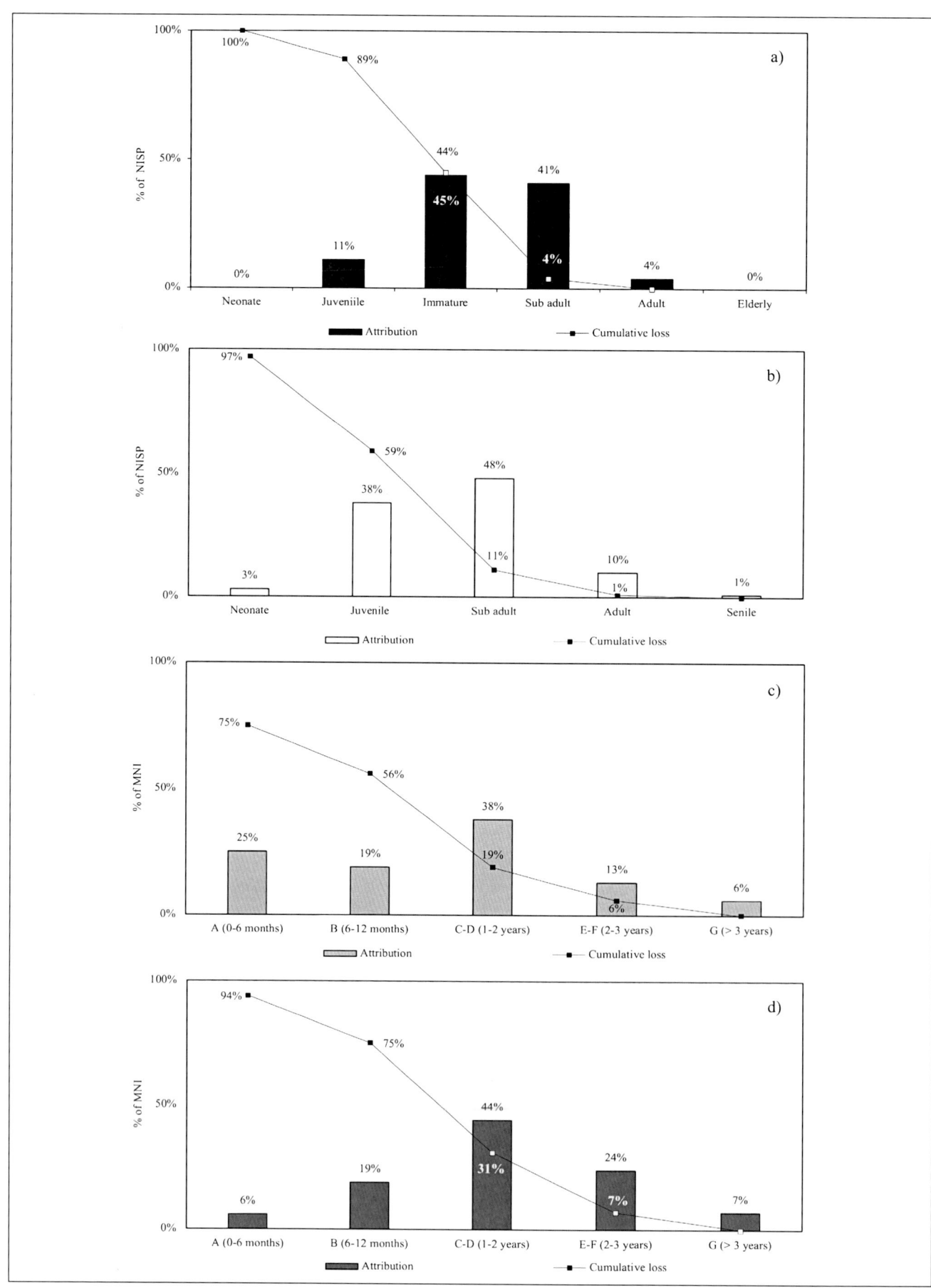

Figure 6.10 *Sus* **kill-off pattern comparison between: a) LN Promachon (Promachon I-II-III), b) LN Sitagroi (Sitagroi I-II-III), c) LN Dimitra (Dimitra II-III) and LN Thermi (Thermi B). Data for Promachon in Table 5.96. Data for Sitagroi in Table 6.9, data for Dimitra in Table 6.10 and data for Thermi in Table 6.11. NISP counts (Promachon and Sitagroi) and MNI counts (Dimitra and Thermi).**

Table 6.9 *Sus* (pig) kill-off pattern from LN Sitagroi (Bökönyi 1986). Data for Figure 6.10. NISP counts.

Sus	Sitagroi I-II-III		
	NISP	% Attribution	% Cumulative loss
Neonatal	17	3%	97%
Juvenile	236	38%	59%
Sub adult	306	48%	11%
Adult	61	10%	1%
Senile	5	1%	0%
TOTAL	**625**	**100%**	

Table 6.10 *Sus* (pig) kill-off pattern from LN Dimitra (Yiannouli 1997). Data for Figure 6.10. MNI counts.

Sus	Dimitra II-III		
	MNI	% Attribution	% Cumulative loss
A (0-6 months)	4	25%	75%
B (6-12 months)	3	19%	56%
C-D (1-2 years)	6	38%	19%
E-F (2-3 years)	2	13%	6%
G (> 3 years)	1	6%	0%
TOTAL	**16**	**100%**	

Table 6.11 *Sus* (pig) kill-off pattern from LN Thermi (Yiannouli 1989). Data for Figure 6.10. MNI counts.

Sus	Thermi B		
	MNI	% Attribution	% Cumulative loss
A (0-6 months)	1	6%	94%
B (6-12 months)	3	19%	75%
C-D (1-2 years)	7	44%	31%
E-F (2-3 years)	4	24%	7%
G (> 3 years)	1	7%	0%
TOTAL	**16**	**100%**	

commonly measured for Macedonian sites. Tooth measurements were also largely neglected by almost all German zooarchaeologists, since only the lengths of the third mandibular molars were measured (Kazantzis and Albarella 2016). Bökönyi, on the other hand, did not measure the depth of various postcranial elements (*e.g.* tibia Dd, astragalus Dl) of small ruminants (sheep/goats). Obviously, all of these issues represent serious problems, that somewhat limit comparability. However, and despite such problems, in the following lines a comparison of the size of the main domesticates will be attempted in order to

investigate the nature of human-animal relationships in the Late Neolithic of northern Greece.

In general, size comparisons are usually best interpreted by comparing data from various sites in order to investigate relative differences. Accordingly, measurements from Promachon are plotted on the same graphs with measurements from other sites. In cases in which, sample sizes are too small, we use the scaling index technique (through log ratios) in order to increase the effectiveness of size comparisons.

6.4.1 The size of the main domesticates in the wider Late Neolithic context of northern Greece

Unfortunately, cattle metrical data from Greek Macedonia are scarce. This is mainly a consequence of cattle not being particularly well represented at sites of this time and area. In addition, even when cattle are more abundant, metric data are not commonly reported. Fortunately, there is more available evidence from contemporary Thessalian sites, which can also be used for comparison. The problem with these sites is, however, that not always the measurements were comparable with those collected at Promachon. With these *caveats* in mind, the only sites from Greek Macedonia and Thessaly where a sufficient number of measured cattle bones could be used were Sitagroi (Bökönyi 1986), Ayia Sofia (von den Driesch and Enderle 1976), Pevkakia (Jordan 1975) and Zarkos (Becker 1991). In all cases, the most numerous measurements that could be used for comparisons were those of the astragalus. In Figure 6.11 we compare the size of cattle astragalus between Promachon and Sitagroi by plotting the greatest length of the lateral half of the astragalus (GLl) against the distal breadth of the astragalus (Bd). The diagram shows that cattle astragali at Promachon and Sitagroi have similar lengths, but those from Sitagroi have a relatively greater distal breadth (Bd). The distal breadth (Bd) is a measure of the width of the joint surface and it is therefore related to the weight-bearing ability of that particular joint (Johnstone and Albarella 2002). An increased Bd reflects the presence of more robust animals (Johnstone and Albarella 2015).

In order to statistically test the significance of the difference in the size of the cattle astragalus between the two sites, an ANOVA test was also conducted. This indicates that there is no significant difference in the greatest length of the lateral half (GLl) of the astragalus between Promachon and Sitagroi (p= .129) but there is a highly significant difference in the distal breadth (Bd) between the two groups (p= .000). The Sitagroi astragali have a much greater distal breadth (μ= 46 mm) than the Promachon astragali (μ= 43.4 mm) (Kazantzis and Albarella 2016). In order to obtain large enough samples of measurements to facilitate cattle size comparisons between Promachon and Sitagroi, log ratios were also calculated. Figure 6.12 shows the log ratio diagrams for all three dimensions (lengths, widths and depths respectively) of cattle postcranial bones from Promachon (top diagrams) and Sitagroi (bottom diagrams)

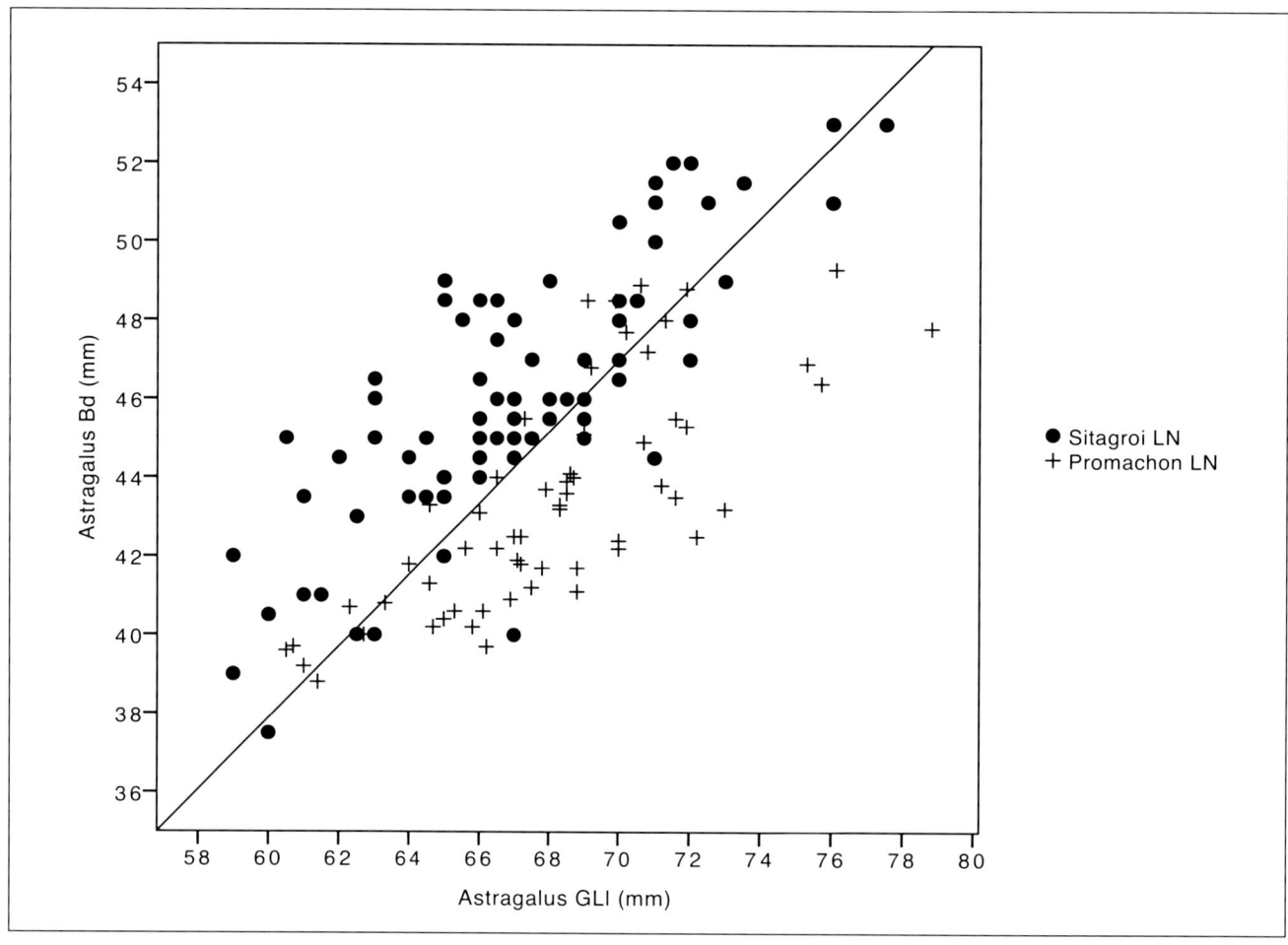

Figure 6.11 *Bos taurus* **astragalus greatest length of the lateral half (GLl)** *versus* **distal breadth (Bd). Comparison between LN Promachon (Promachon I-II-III) and LN Sitagroi (Sitagroi I-II-III).**

in order to see how different measurements are distributed according to the standard. The standard that we use for the calculation of the log ratio is the mean of the length, width and depth measurements of cattle postcranial bones from Promachon. Unlike the use of an articulated skeleton, a standard deriving from a commingled assemblage does not imply that the measurements will necessarily be related to each other (Meadow 1999). Chances that different anatomical elements from an archaeological assemblage derive from entirely different populations are, however, minimal, and the archaeological standard has the advantage of relying on a larger sample size (Albarella, 2002; Kazantzis and Albarella 2016). This is why archaeological standards are increasingly commonly used in the literature (e.g. Albarella and Payne 2005; Kazantzis and Albarella 2016; Wright and Viner-Daniels 2015). In terms of absolute size, the log ratio diagrams indicate that cattle bones from Sitagroi were of similar length to cattle bones from Promachon, but they were larger both in the width and the depth measurements (Kazantzis and Albarella 2016). In view of the fact that cattle metapodials are heavily sexually dimorphic – the metacarpals even more so than the metatarsals (Albarella 1997) – and that the log ratio diagrams for the widths and the depths might be affected by the presence of different sexes

(males, females and possibly castrates), we recalculated the log ratio for the width and depth measurements, excluding Promachon's metapodial measurements. Width measurements of cattle metapodials from Sitagroi were also excluded. The new log ratio diagrams for the width and the depth measurements (Figure 6.13) shows – once more – that cattle bones from Sitagroi have a greater width and depth than those from Promachon. It also indicates that the width of the metapodials slightly affected the results of the previous log ratio diagram, since – this time – fewer width measurements from Sitagroi plot on the left side of the standard, while the number of the width measurements plotted on the right side of the standard remains roughly the same. Altogether the log ratio analysis supports the results obtained from analysis of the astragalus, indicating that width and depth measurements at Sitagroi are relatively larger than lengths, in comparison to Promachon.

All in all, the results show that cattle from Sitagroi are more robust than cattle from Promachon. However, before moving to interpretations for the observed trend, we have to compare the size of the other domesticates (caprines and pigs) between the two sites in order to obtain a clearer picture. This will be further discussed in the next parts of this analysis.

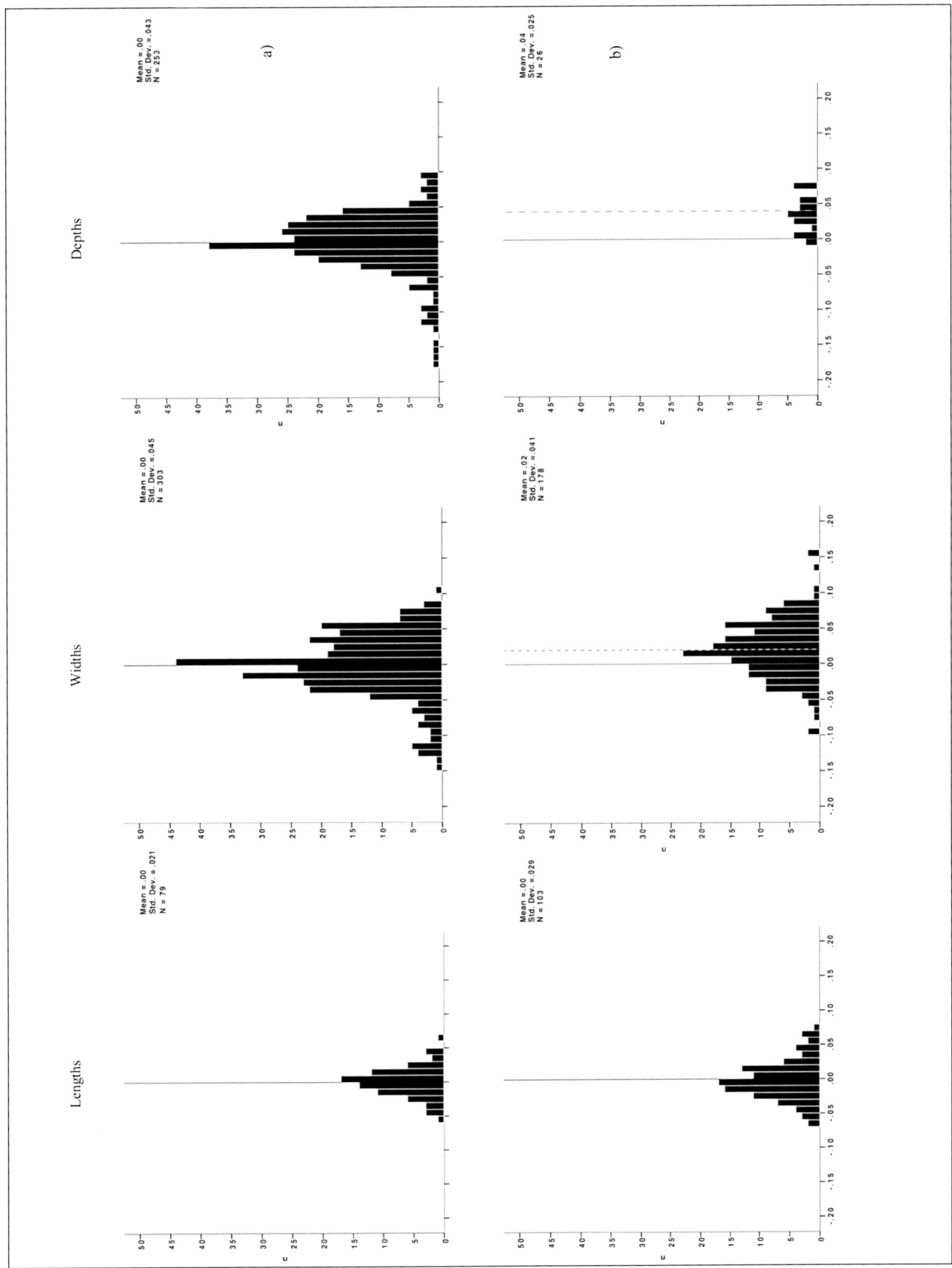

Figure 6.12 Distribution of: a) LN Promachon and b) LN Sitagroi *Bos taurus* postcranial length, width and depth measurements using the log ratio technique (Simpson *et al.* 1960). The standard is provided by the Promachon mean. Only fully fused postcranial bones from Promachon were considered. Only measurements from Sitagroi compatible to Promachon were considered. The mean of Sitagroi length, width and depth measurements is marked by a black dashed vertical line, and the standard measurement by a black vertical line at .00. The scale of the vertical axis is fixed to emphasize differences in sample sizes.

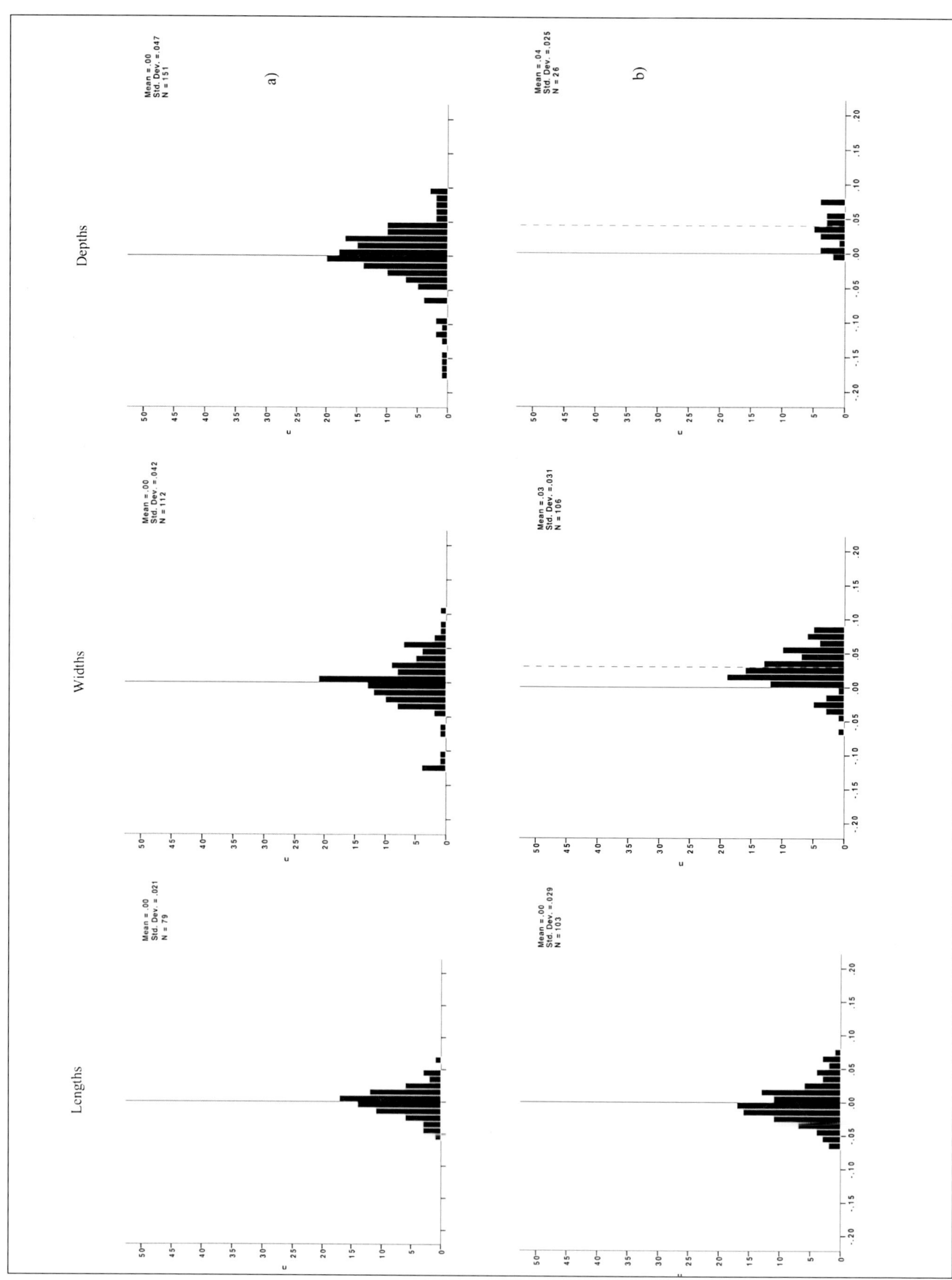

Figure 6.13 Distribution of: a) LN Promachon and b) LN Sitagroi *Bos taurus* postcranial length, width and depth measurements using the log ratio technique (Simpson *et al.* 1960). Metapodial measurements are excluded. The standard is provided by the Promachon mean. Only fully fused postcranial bones from Promachon were considered. Only measurements from Sitagroi compatible to Promachon were considered. The mean of Sitagroi length, width and depth measurements is marked by a black dashed vertical line, and the standard measurement by a black vertical line at .00. The scale of the vertical axis is fixed to emphasize differences in sample sizes.

Figure 6.14 presents the comparison of the cattle astragalus between Promachon, Ayia Sofia, Pevkakia and Zarkos by plotting the greatest length of the lateral half (GLl) against the greatest length of the medial half (GLm) of the astragalus. Cattle from Promachon are slightly larger than their counterparts from Thessaly, but some of the sample sizes from Thessaly are rather small (Ayia Sofia and especially Pevkakia). Cattle astragali from Zarkos are, however, definitely much smaller.

Comparing the size of goats between Promachon and contemporary Macedonian and Thessalian sites was not possible, since almost all sites produced too few goat measurements. On the other hand, enough biometric data for sheep were available from four sources for comparison. These are represented by the sites of Sitagroi (Bökönyi 1986) from Macedonia, and Ayia Sofia (Driesch von den and Enderle 1976), Pevkakia (Jordan 1975) and Zarkos (Becker 1991) from Thessaly. In all cases, the most numerous measurements that could be used for comparison were – once more – those of the astragalus.

In Figure 6.15 we compare the size of sheep astragalus between Promachon and Sitagroi. The scatterplot indicates the presence of two slightly overlapping groups. The lower group includes the astragali from Promachon, while the upper group includes the astragali from Sitagroi. What is inferred from the diagram is that sheep astragali from Promachon are smaller than those from Sitagroi

both in terms of length and width. There are, however, some astragali from Promachon that are similar in size to those from Sitagroi, but they are a minority. These larger Promachon astragali are also different in shape from those from Sitagroi as their width is relatively smaller in comparison to the length, which makes them slenderer in comparison.

An ANOVA test indicates that there is a highly significant difference in the greatest length of the lateral half (GLl) of the astragalus between Promachon and Sitagroi (p= .000), with Sitagroi astragali having a much greater length (μ= 28.7 mm) than Promachon astragali (μ= 25.5 mm). In addition, a highly significant difference in the distal breadth (Bd) between the two groups was also found (p= .000), with Sitagroi astragali having a much greater distal breadth (μ= 20.2 mm) than Promachon astragali (μ= 16.4 mm) (Kazantzis and Albarella 2016).

In order to obtain large enough samples of measurements to make further comparisons between Promachon and Sitagroi, we use the log ratio technique. In Figure 6.16 we plot Promachon (top diagrams) and Sitagroi (bottom diagrams) length and width measurements in order to see how these are distributed according to the standard. The standard that we use for the calculation of the log ratio is – as in the case of cattle – the mean of the length and width measurements of sheep postcranial elements from Promachon. Log ratios from depth measurements from

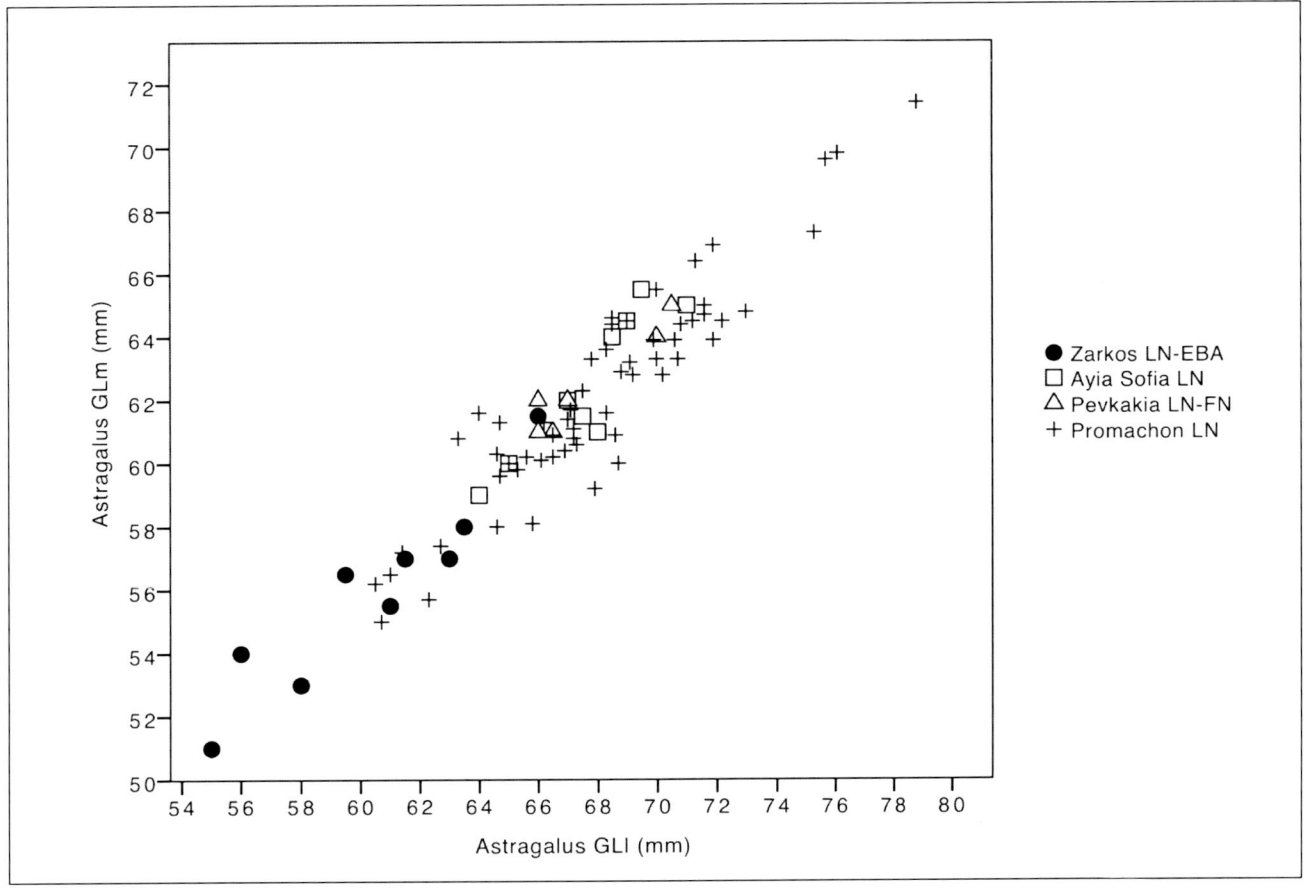

Figure 6.14 *Bos taurus* astragalus greatest length of the lateral half (GLl) *versus* greatest length of the medial half (GLm). Comparison between LN Promachon (Promachon I-II-III), LN/EBA Zarkos, LN Ayia Sofia and LN/FN Pevkakia.

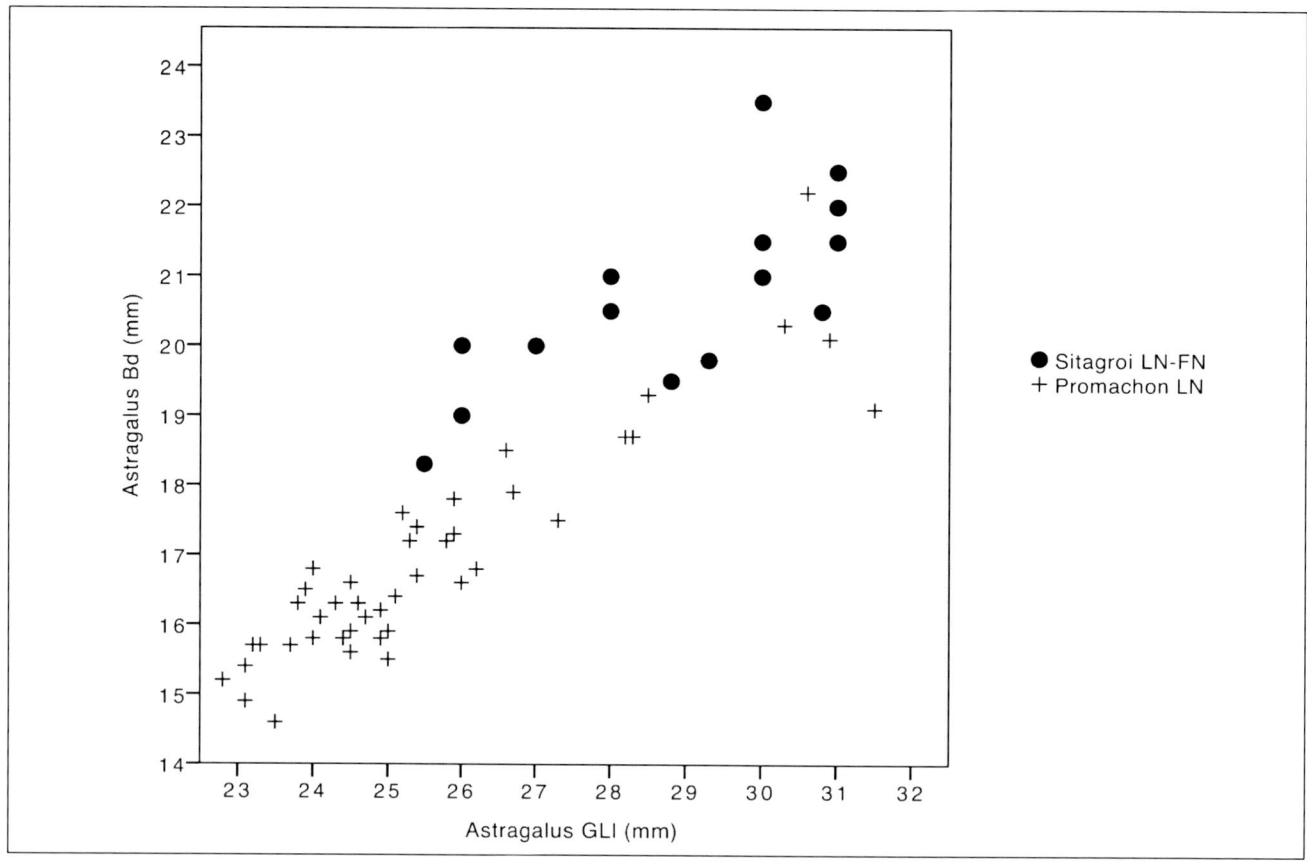

Figure 6.15 *Ovis aries* **astragalus greatest length of the lateral half (GLl)** *versus* **distal breadth (Bd). Comparison between LN Promachon (Promachon I-II-III) and LN/FN Sitagroi (Sitagroi I-II-III-IV).**

both sides were not calculated, since Bökönyi (1986) does not measure the depth of sheep postcranial elements.

The log ratio diagrams show that the mean of both length and width measurements from Sitagroi plots on the right side of the standard (Promachon mean) indicating that, in terms of absolute size, Sitagroi sheep bones have a greater length and a greater width than those from Promachon. Therefore, the log ratio diagrams are consistent with the astragalus scatterplot and the statistical test, which indicated that sheep from Sitagroi are taller and wider than their counterparts from Promachon. However, the log ratio analysis indicates that length measurements at Sitagroi are relatively larger than widths, in comparison to Promachon. This is not consistent with the evidence that we had from the larger group of Promachon sheep astragali (Figure 6.15) and confirms a trend that had been seen in cattle – namely that differences in the shape of different anatomical elements are variable between the two sites. Nonetheless, the greater relative length of the Sitagroi sheep may be due to the presence of a greater occurrence of castrates (Kazantzis and Albarella 2016), which are known to keep their epiphyses unfused for longer, therefore allowing greater length on their bones (Davis 1996; Hatting 1974). All in all, however, it has emerged that differences existed between both cattle and sheep kept at the two sites.

Figure 6.17 presents the comparison of sheep astragalus between Promachon and three Thessalian sites (Ayia

Sofia, Pevkakia and Zarkos). In this diagram we plot the length of the lateral half (GLl) against the length of the medial half (GLm) of the astragalus.

Promachon sheep astragali seem to have the widest range of all sites, but most of them plot in the lower part of the diagram. Sheep astragali from Pevkakia, and especially Zarkos, are on average substantially larger than those from Promachon, while those from Ayia Sofia are similar but the sample is too small to be relied on. The large size of the sheep from Zarkos is noteworthy, particularly in view of the entirely opposite trend showed by cattle (Figure 6.14).

As in the cases of cattle and sheep, an adequate number of comparative measurements of pigs could be obtained from Sitagroi (Bökönyi 1986), Ayia Sofia (von den Driesch and Enderle 1976), Pevkakia (Jordan 1975) and Zarkos (Becker 1991). In addition, unpublished metrical data for pigs from Makriyalos were also kindly provided by Umberto Albarella and Keith Dobney on material made available by Paul Halstead. In the cases of Ayia Sofia, Pevkakia and Zarkos, the most numerous measurements that could be used were those of the astragalus. In the case of Makriyalos, we plot measurements of the distal humerus, as there is sufficient sample size. Lastly, in the case of Sitagroi, apart from the measurements of the astragalus, we were also able to use those of the tibia.

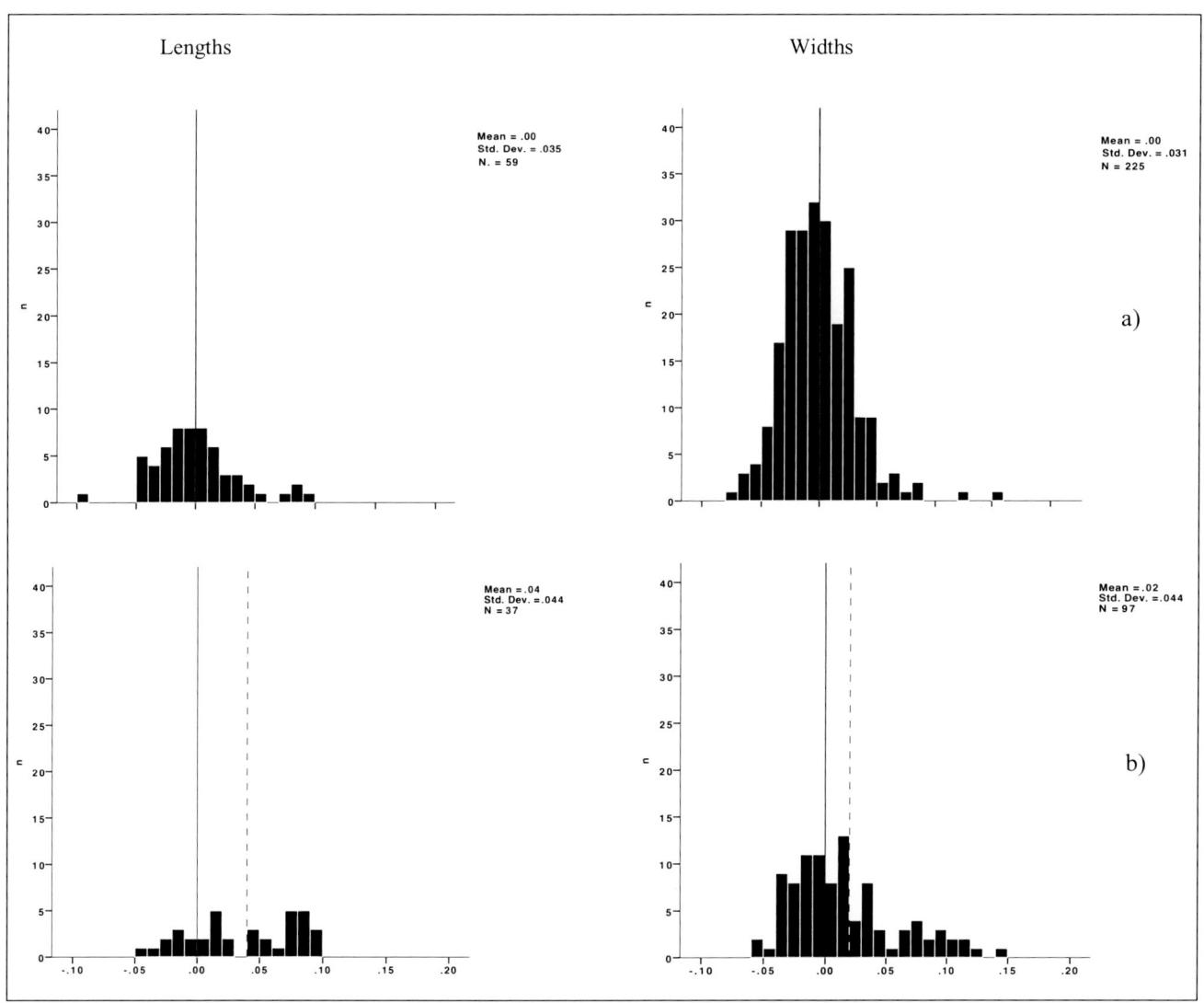

Figure 6.16 Distribution of: a) LN Promachon and b) LN/FN Sitagroi *Ovis aries* postcranial length and width measurements using the log ratio technique (Simpson *et al.* 1960). The standard is provided by the Promachon mean. Only fully fused postcranial bones from Promachon were considered. Only measurements from Sitagroi compatible to Promachon were considered. The mean of Sitagroi length and width measurements is marked by a black dashed vertical line, and the standard measurement by a black vertical line at .00. The scale of the vertical axis is fixed to emphasize differences in sample sizes.

Figures 6.18-6.19 present the comparison of the pig astragalus and the pig tibia between Sitagroi and Promachon. We also include the astragali and the tibiae from Sitagroi, which were identified by Bökönyi (1986) as belonging to the wild form (*Sus scrofa*). At both sites, there are two distinct metric groups, presumably domestic and wild. Both domestic and wild populations appear to be metrically consistent at the two sites (Kazantzis and Albarella 2016). The Sitagroi evidence supports the Promachon interpretation of the larger astragali and tibia specimens as belonging to the wild boar (Figures 5.50-5.51).

In Figure 6.20 we plot the width (BT) against the smallest diameter (HTC) of the trochlea of the distal humerus of pig between Promachon and Makriyalos (*cf.* Kazantzis and Albarella 2016). Most measurements plot at the smaller end of the distribution (lower left part of the scatterplot), but there are a number of large outliers from both sites. In general, pig forelimb bones tend to be fairly age dependent as they are subject to greater post-fusion growth than

hind limb bones (Albarella and Payne 2005; Albarella *et al.*, 2006; Rowley-Conwy *et al.* 2012); however, they are also much affected by sex variation (Payne and Bull 1988). Despite such variation and considering that BT and HTC are much less affected by post-fusion growth than the commonly taken distal breadth (Bd) (Payne and Bull 1988; Albarella and Payne 2005), the two main groups are best interpreted as representing domestic (the majority) and wild forms. Both domestic pigs and wild boar are similar in size at the two sites. The few points plotting in-between the two main clusters could equally represent large domestic males or small wild females. Nonetheless, the distinction between the domestic and wild forms is fairly pronounced (Kazantzis and Albarella 2016).

Figure 6.21 presents the comparison of the pig astragali between Promachon and three Thessalian sites (Zarkos, Ayia Sofia and Pevkakia). As in the case of Sitagroi, we include also the astragali that were originally identified as belonging to wild individuals, though there are only a few

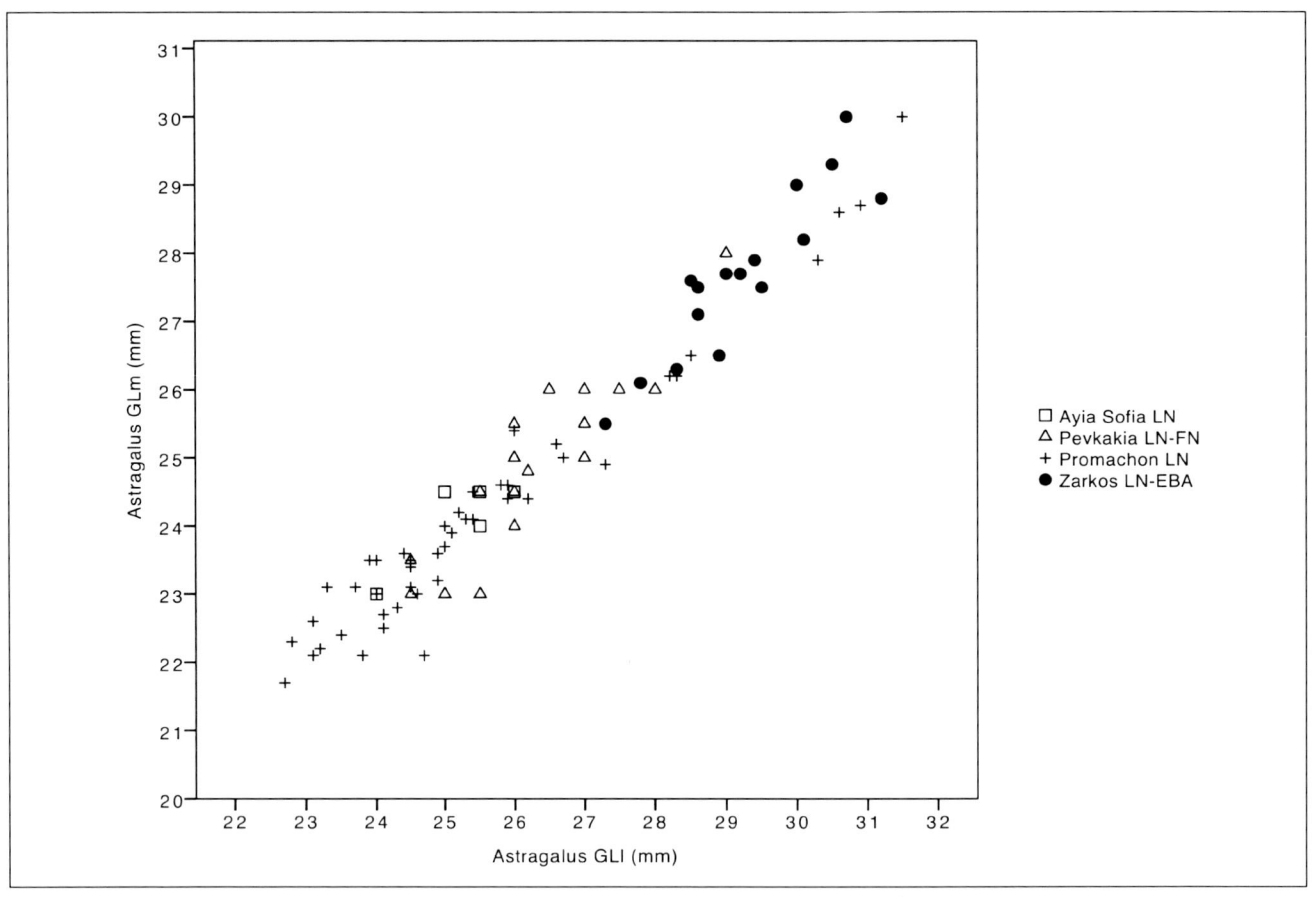

Figure 6.17 *Ovis aries* **astragalus greatest length of the lateral half (GLl)** *versus* **greatest length of the medial half (GLm). Comparison between LN Promachon (Promachon I-II-III), LN/EBA Zarkos, LN Ayia Sofia and LN/FN Pevkakia.**

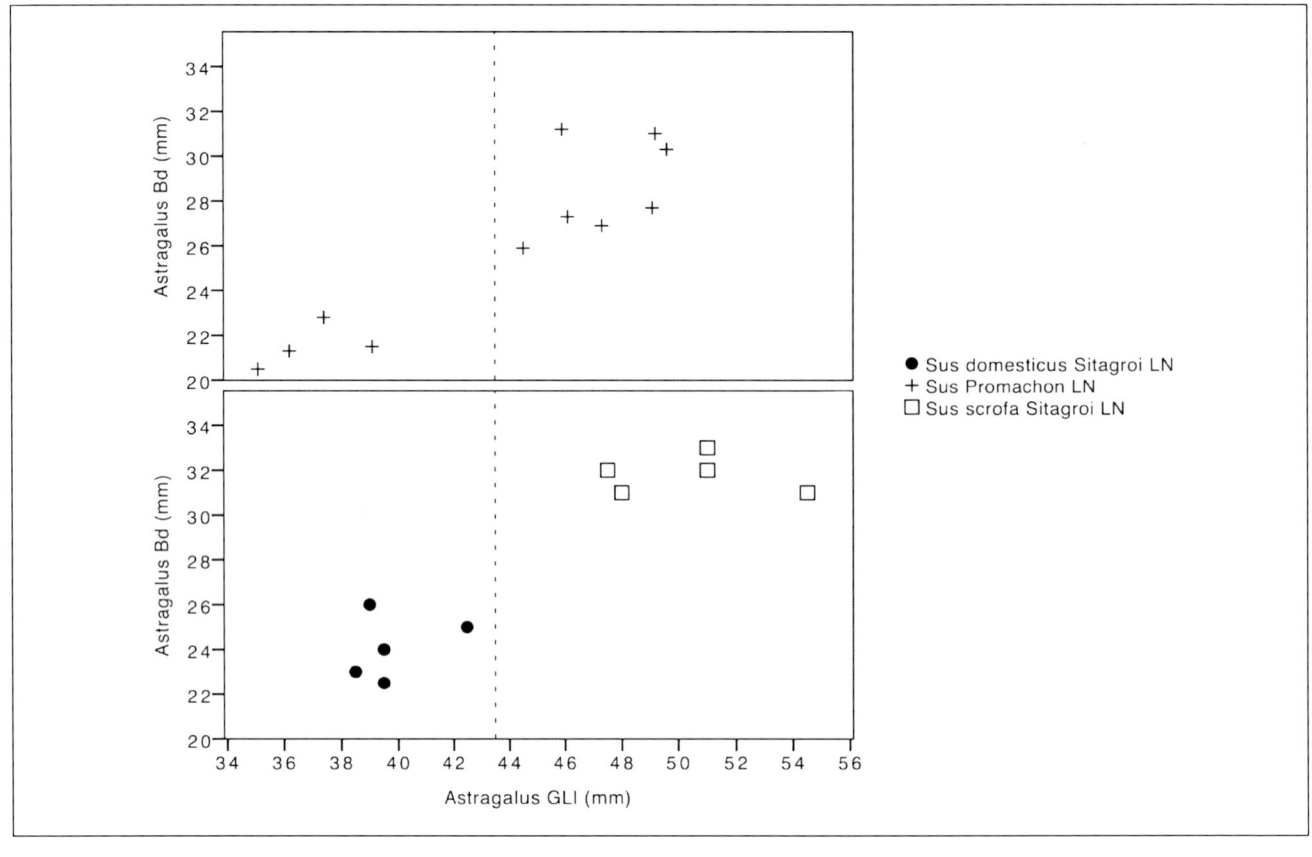

Figure 6.18 *Sus* **astragalus greatest length of the lateral half (GLl)** *versus* **distal breadth (Bd). Comparison between LN Promachon (Promachon I-II-III) and LN Sitagroi (Sitagroi I-II-III).**

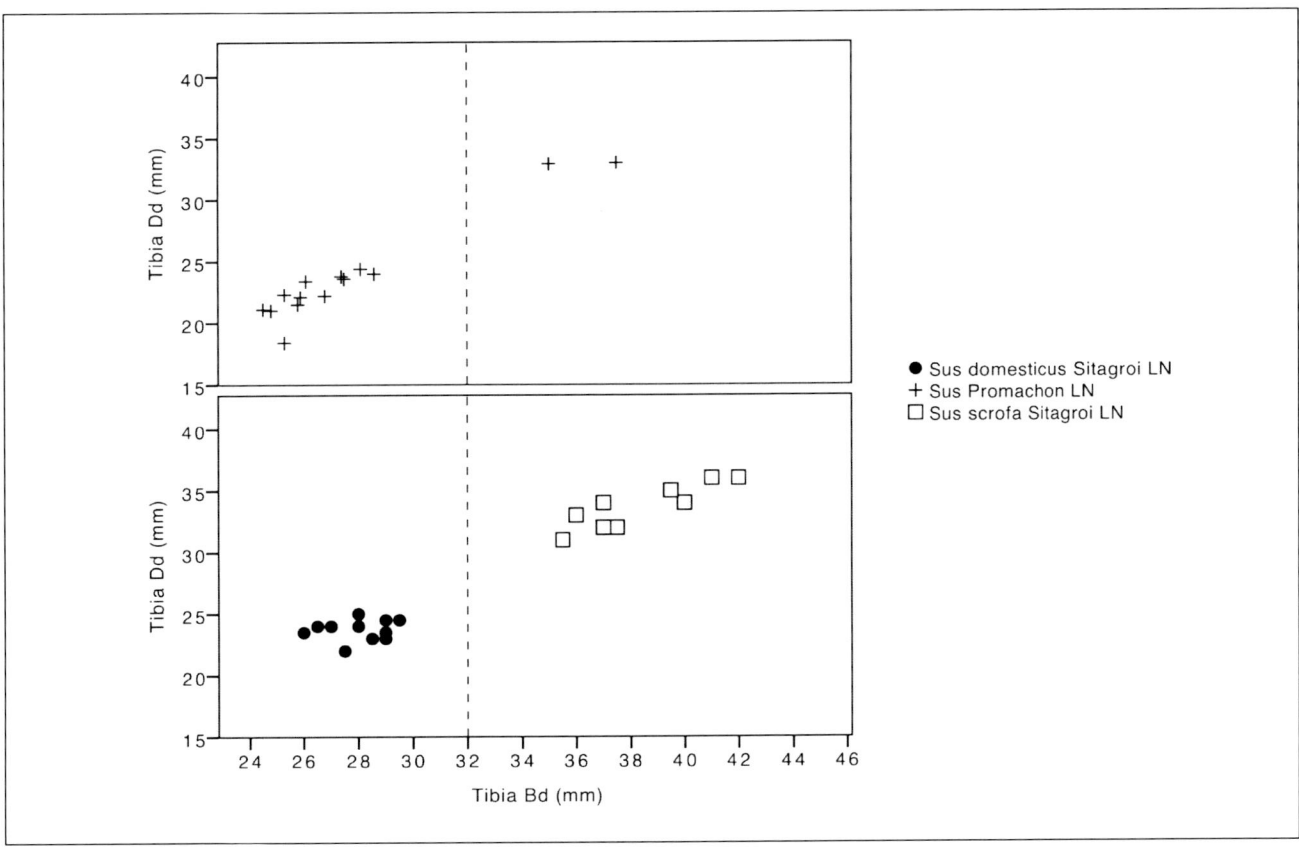

Figure 6.19 *Sus* **tibia distal breadth (Bd)** *versus* **distal depth (Dd). Comparison between LN Promachon (Promachon I-II-III) and LN Sitagroi (Sitagroi I-II-II).**

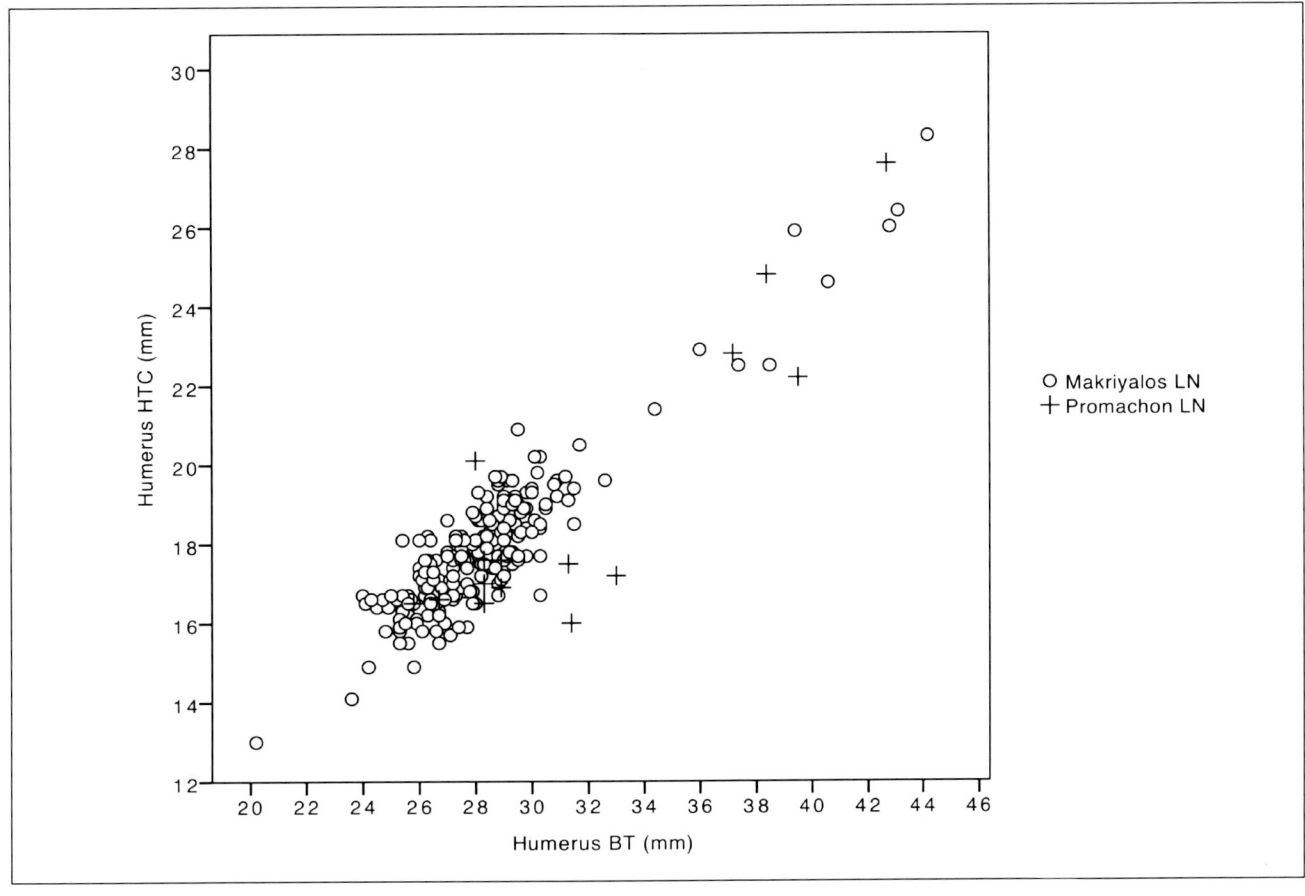

Figure 6.20 *Sus* **humerus width of the trochlea (BT)** *versus* **diameter of the trochlea (HTC). Comparison between LN Promachon (Promachon I-II-III) and LN Makriyalos (Makriyalos I).**

of them. The wild boar does not appear to have been hunted at these Thessalian sites as commonly as in the cases of Promachon and Sitagroi. Concerning the domesticated pigs, although the pattern shows that there is some overlap in terms of size between the four settlements, domestic pigs from Promachon are, in general, smaller than their counterparts from Thessaly. Domestic pigs from Ayia Sofia are particularly large, perhaps due to interbreeding with wild boar or the occurrence of some wild females within the 'domestic' group. On the other hand, there is no argument against the identification of domestic and wild pig astragali from EBA Zarkos (no LN specimens were recovered), since we can notice two distinct metric groups: one domestic and another one wild.

6.4.2 Contemplating the size of domestic ruminants and pigs during the Late Neolithic of Macedonia and Thessaly

The preceding analysis took into account the metrical data from Promachon and compared them with the metrical data from other contemporary Macedonian and Thessalian sites, in an attempt to find if size differences in domestic ruminants and pigs between Promachon and these sites occur. A number of interesting issues were detected. Probably, most remarkable were the differences in the overall size of cattle and sheep between Promachon and Sitagroi. Cattle and sheep from Sitagroi seem to have been more robust than their counterparts from Promachon. In the next few pages, we will try to point out possible factors that might have affected the overall size of the domestic

ruminants between the two sites. However, before proceeding with our interpretations, it is appropriate to present Bökönyi's (1986) arguments with regard to the large size of cattle and sheep from Sitagroi.

Bökönyi argues that the large size of cattle from Sitagroi is the result of the presence of a "transitional" form of cattle. According to Bökönyi, the "transitional" form of cattle is represented by the crossbreeding of aurochs and domesticated cattle, as well as by "newly domesticated cattle". Bökönyi's argument was based on the observation of a large group of intermediate-sized cattle metapodials (mainly belonging to Phases I-II-III from Sitagroi), which plotted between the smaller bones, assumed to have belonged to domestic cattle, and the larger bones, as sumed to have belonged to aurochs (Bökönyi 1986; Figures 5.2-5.4).

The question of whether crossbreeding between aurochs and domestic cattle occurred in Europe has been the subject of much debate (Bollongino *et al.* 2008; Edwards *et al.* 2007; Götherström *et al.* 2005; Troy *et al.* 2001). Its proponents (among them, also Bökönyi) have argued that crossbreeding might have been unavoidable – or even encouraged – by Neolithic pastoralists, in order to improve the breeding stock and increase the numbers of their domestic livestock. Studies of ancient cattle DNA resulted in the identification of repeated hybridization between domesticated cattle and aurochs (Götherström *et al.* 2005). However, more recent analyses based on the ancient DNA of 59 Neolithic skeletal samples from Central, Western, and south-eastern Europe do not support the hypothesis of introgression (*i.e.*

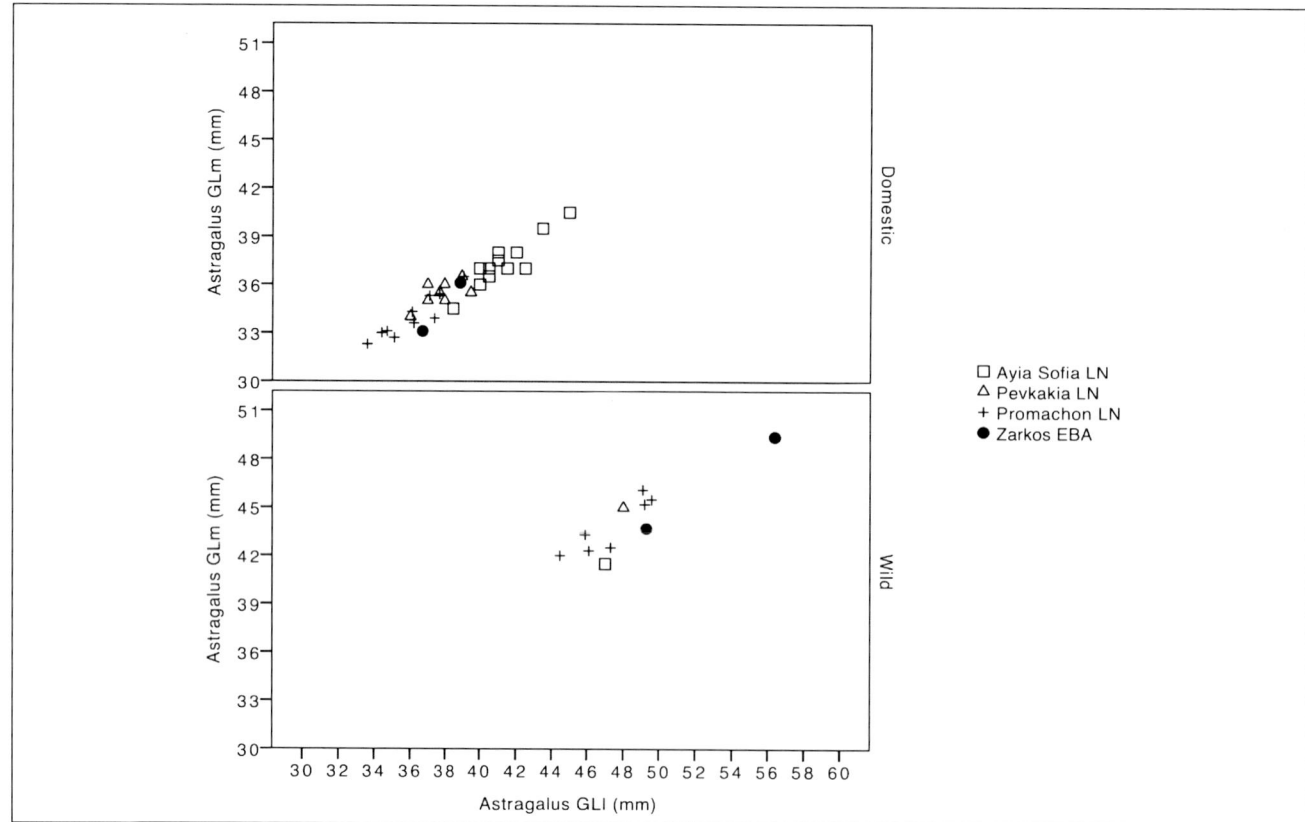

Figure 6.21 *Sus* **astragalus greatest length of the lateral half (GLl)** *versus* **greatest length of the medial half (GLm). Comparison between LN Promachon (Promachon I-II-III), LN Ayia Sofia, LN Pevkakia and EBA Zarkos.**

the transfer of genetic information from one species to another as a result of hybridization) between aurochs and domesticated cattle (Bollongino *et al.* 2008). Overall, the issue of crossbreeding of domestic cattle with aurochs still remains open, although by no means we should exclude the possibility of hybridization between wild and domestic types of cattle. In addition to crossbreeding, Bökönyi also argued in favor of "newly domesticated" cattle. In general, Bökönyi has been a proponent of the domestication of cattle in Europe, as a feature of local contributions to the farming economy (Bradley and Magee 2006). Due to a considerable number of mature aurochs individuals from Sitagroi, Bökönyi suggested that:

"...*man tried to capture the immature wild cattle – since only these could be tamed and domesticated – and killed the adults that were attempting to protect their young*" (Bökönyi 1986, 72).

The argument of local domestication of cattle has also been suggested by Boessneck (1962) in his study of the faunal material from EN Argissa in Thessaly, as well as Becker in her study of the faunal material from Middle Neolithic Zarko (1999). However, recent work in the Aegean area argues that domestication was introduced much earlier than previously thought, with the arrival of colonists, who, at *ca.* 9,000 to 8,000 Cal. BP carried many components of the Neolithic package with them (Zeder 2008). In other words, according to such view, the late stage of the Neolithic cannot be considered as a time-period during which cattle was still in the process of domestication. In addition, Bökönyi does not take into account the effects of sexual dimorphism (Rowley-Conwy 2003), which is highly pronounced in cattle metapodials (Albarella 1997; Bartosiewicz *et al.* 1993; 1997). Thus, it is possible that the intermediate-sized cattle metapodials, which Bökönyi had identified in his assemblage, could have been either female aurochsen or male domesticated cattle. All in all, the evidence does not really support the argument of a local domestication at Sitagroi (and Argissa and Zarko), and the large size of cattle at Sitagroi can be explained on the basis of other factors, such as sex or regional variation.

As concerns sheep, Bökönyi (1986) does not mention the possibility of local domestication at Sitagroi, since the presence of the wild progenitor of sheep (*Ovis orientalis*; mouflon) is not documented in the area. Bökönyi, however, does not elaborate on the large size of the domestic sheep during the Late Neolithic at Sitagroi, possibly due to the lack of available comparable metrical data from contemporary Macedonian sites. On the contrary, he argues for a size increase of the domestic sheep during the transition between the Final Neolithic and the Early Bronze Age (Phases IV-V at Sitagroi)[3]. According to Bökönyi, the increase in the size of sheep during this transitional period is most likely the result of a combination between the practice of penning, breeding and satisfactory feeding for

the production of fleece. What is interesting however, is the fact that – regardless of the time period (Late and Final Neolithic and Early Bronze Age) – sheep from Sitagroi seem to be larger than their counterparts from any other site in Macedonia (and also Thessaly).

Moving away from Bökönyi's arguments regarding the large size of cattle and sheep in Sitagroi, the observed differences in the overall size of domestic ruminants between the two sites may have other explanations. The practice of intensive rotation in grazing grounds is a key factor for the reduction of animal size (Hart *et al.* 1993), though, in the case of Promachon, the practice of transhumance (*i.e.* the action of moving livestock from one grazing ground to another in a seasonal cycle, typically to lowlands in winter and highlands in summer) is not supported by the archaeological evidence. However, by no means this should preclude the possibility of a considerable mobility of segments of the population of Promachon on a seasonal or other basis. For this reason, strontium analyses (^{87}Sr/^{86}Sr) for the assessment of the geological 'signature' of the enamel from the teeth of domesticates should be carried out in Promachon in the future[4]. The availability of pasture, and more specifically, the availability of food resources is another factor that could potentially explain the differences in the overall size of domestic ruminants between Promachon and Sitagroi. However, if we assume that there is a limitation in food resources in Promachon, which might have significantly affected the size of domestic ruminants, then, we might also assume that some kind of environmental degeneration might have taken place in the vicinity of the site sometime during the Late Neolithic. However, this assumption cannot be fully supported, since palynological analyses have not as yet been carried out in Promachon.

It is probable however, that the problem in the overall pattern is the unusually large size of cattle and sheep at Sitagroi, rather than the small size of the same species at Promachon. The reconstruction of the settlement pattern in the plain of Drama may provide some explanation. This suggests that during the Late Neolithic, there was a considerable expansion in the number of settlements in the plain of Drama (where the site of Sitagroi is located) with the utilization of a greater variety of locations. Overall, it seems that the expansion in the number of settlements in the plain of Drama might have resulted in a greater production of food resources, which in turn allowed population numbers to increase considerably (Blouet 1968). The evidence suggests higher yields and a far greater degree of control over cropping, with an agricultural system that attained a high degree of expertise. It is possible that the settlements in the plain of Drama progressed from habitation sites to being villages in the functional sense, and that they had moved to the point where they provided a number of services other than convenient places for families to group (Blouet 1968). To be more specific, the evidence

---

[3] Bökönyi (1986; Figures 5.7; 5.12-5.13).

[4] Note that this would work only if the underlying geology of highland and lowland were different in terms of the age of the rocks.

seems to suggest that Sitagroi was linked to a group of settlements in the plain of Drama, where opportunities of better responses to environmental constraints and/or food limitations (possibly through a system of exchange?) might have taken place. Of particular importance is the fact that one of the most dynamic settlements that thrived during this time-period in the plain of Drama – as indicated by the persistence and the density of occupation, the abundance of finds, the variety and quality of artifacts and a number of innovations in food-consuming procedures (such as wine-pressing; Valamoti *et al.* 2007) – was Dikili-Tash (Darcque *et al.* 2007; Koukouli-Chrysanthaki 2006). Promachon on the other hand, is not centralized in the plain of Serres; being located on the northernmost part of the plain of Serres, Promachon was most likely to have been isolated from the rest of the sites, thus having a slower response to environmental and/or economic constraints.

On the other hand, the size of domestic pigs between Promachon and Sitagroi is roughly the same. This similarity is in contrast with the greater size of both cattle and sheep at Sitagroi. If we accept the argument that the larger size of domestic ruminants at Sitagroi was the result of better-fed animals due to a more organized and centralized system of economy, it must follow that no equivalent attention was placed on pig husbandry. This may be consistent with the lower apparent importance of pig keeping for the economy of the site, as well as the partial reliance on wild boar.

The observed differences in the size of domestic ruminants and pigs between Promachon and Thessalian sites could plausibly be attributed to diverse husbandry strategies. Metrical examination indicated that sheep and pigs from Promachon were slightly smaller than their counterparts from Ayia Sofia, Zarkos and Pevkakia, whereas the exact opposite pattern was detected in the case of cattle. These size differences might be related to the economic importance of cattle, sheep and pigs between Macedonian and Thessalian sites. To be more specific, the relative proportions (in terms of NISP) of the three main domesticates from sites from Thessaly contemporary to Promachon, such as Dimini (Halstead 1992), Zarko (Becker 1991), Ayia Sofia (von den Driesch and Enderle 1976) and Pevkakia (Jordan 1975) suggest the predominance of sheep, followed in most cases by pigs (Cantuel *et al.* 2008). The pattern can plausibly be attributed to the fact that the geomorphology, environment and vegetation in Thessaly are different from those in Macedonia, thus favouring the keeping and breeding of small ruminants and pigs, rather than cattle. This obviously indicates that the former animals were the backbone of the economic subsistence for the Neolithic economies in Thessaly, in contrast with Promachon (and Macedonia in general) in which – although caprines still predominate – cattle certainly played a more important role than Thessaly. Therefore, the large size of small ruminants and pigs at sites such as Ayia Sofia, Zarkos and Pevkakia, might be the result of a particular emphasis in sheep and pig husbandry, possibly through the method of satisfactory feeding. In the case of pigs, however, we should by no means exclude the possibility of the interbreeding of

domestic pigs with wild animals, especially in the case of Ayia Sofia (Kazantzis and Albarella 2016). In any case, the large size of domestic pigs from Ayia Sofia, Zarkos and Pevkakia indicates the general importance of pig keeping for Thessalian Late Neolithic economies. Unlike Thessalian sites, pig metrical data from Macedonian sites, such as Promachon and Sitagroi, indicate that the Neolithic people from these sites commonly hunted wild pigs. In addition, the smaller size of domestic pigs from Promachon and Sitagroi in comparison to their counterparts from Thessaly, possibly suggests that there was not a particular emphasis on pig keeping in Macedonian sites and that no particular attention was placed on pig husbandry (through either interbreeding with wild boar, or satisfactory feeding).

Another interesting pattern that was observed in the metrical analysis were the differences in the size of domestic ruminants between Thessalian sites. More specifically, sheep from Zarkos seem to be larger than their counterparts from Pevkakia and Ayia Sofia, whereas the exact opposite pattern was detected in the case of cattle. We would probably be going too far to suggest that the pattern indicates different breeds of cattle and sheep in Zarkos than the rest of the settlements in Thessaly, but at least we can suggest the presence of different regional types. If this is the case, then it seems that these sites were fairly independent from each other and maintained their own types of livestock.

Promachon and Makriyalos appear to be different also. Metrical analyses (Kazantzis 2015) showed that cattle from Promachon were larger and more robust in comparison to Makriyalos, whereas sheep were of roughly similar size (Kazantzis 2015; Kazantzis and Albarella 2016). In addition, at both sites, both domestic pigs and their wild counterparts were of similar size as well.

Probably the most remarkable phenomenon that the evidence highlights is the great variation in livestock size between sites and regions – and how this may vary according to animal species (Kazantzis and Albarella 2016). It seems that the size of these animals may have been dependent on food availability and on the adequacy of Neolithic communities to respond to risk and uncertainty. It can also be argued that the economic importance of certain animals within each settlement might have played a significant role in the decisions of Neolithic people regarding the investment in their keeping. This evidence suggests that the sites operated rather independently from each other, and husbandry regimes needed to be adapted to local conditions, in terms of environment, organization of the society and cultural preferences. Sitagroi probably benefitted from the support of a network of local sites in the plain of Drama, in contrast with Promachon, which seems to have been rather isolated in the plain of Serres (Kazantzis and Albarella 2016). A larger body of metrical data from Late Neolithic Macedonian and Thessalian settlements should allow further clarification of some of these issues and should definitely represent a priority for future research.

7

Synthesis

7.1 Putting together the evidence

The preceding chapters presented the results of the analysis of the animal bone assemblage from Promachon and compared them to the results obtained from a number of contemporary settlements from northern Greece and the wider Balkan regions. The investigation has focused on how animals were managed at both local (Promachon and Strymon river valley) and regional (northern Greece and Balkan regions) levels. This chapter will move away from strict zooarchaeological narratives by taking into consideration other lines of archaeological evidence. This by no means implies that zooarchaeology will not be taken into account, but rather that zooarchaeology and other lines of archaeological evidence will be integrated in order to address broader archaeological questions regarding past patterns of human behavior at Promachon and in the wider region.

Three broad themes are discussed in this chapter. Each theme incorporates a number of key-points that are ultimately essential in our understanding of animal use and site function. Economic considerations will focus on the scale and the nature of animal husbandry at Promachon, assessing also the relative contribution of domestic and wild animals to subsistence. Social and symbolic considerations touch upon the issue of consumption[1], which has arguably received small attention in Greek zooarchaeology, before moving to the symbolic significance of domestic and wild species in Promachon. Finally, the attention turns to the function of the settlement, and the discussion moves to the understanding of the wide range of activities attested on-site.

7.2 Economic considerations

The economic aspects dealt with by the current research can be divided into three main subjects. These are:

1. Scale and nature of animal husbandry
2. The economic importance of cattle
3. The economic importance of wild resources

7.2.1 Scale and nature of animal husbandry

One of the key aims of the current research was to understand the scale of animal husbandry at Promachon. In

general, this is a contentious issue in Greek zooarchaeology (Halstead 2000). The debate is often polarized around two models, which are particularly relevant to the late stage of the Neolithic and the Early Bronze Age. In addition, both models heavily rely on circumstantial evidence, mainly due to the complexities of bone fragmentation and recovery (Halstead 1996; 2000; 2002).

Proponents of the first model argue that the Late Neolithic (and Early Bronze Age) pastoral economies of Greece were small-scale and relatively sedentary. In addition, these economies were based on a small number of animals, which were subordinate to crops (Halstead 2000; 2002). Due to the absence of a market economy, Late Neolithic communities were not able to invest in product specialization (Halstead 1989b). All in all, small-scale pastoralists – since they were not seeking to maximize the production, but to produce a consistent return – are characterized by a mixed composition of animals (Halstead 1996), and no heavy specialization in secondary products (*i.e.* milk, wool, traction).

Proponents of the second model argue in favor of extensive, large-scale herding (Cavanagh 1999). The argument of large-scale herding is based on the fact that certain regions and site locations in Greece were unsuitable for arable farming (it is interesting to note however, that areas unsuitable for farming activities are mainly located in southern Greece, for instance, Peloponnese. On the contrary, areas in Macedonia, where Promachon is located, are known to be more cultivable). Consequently, these areas offered more potential for grazing than cultivation (Johnson 1996). It has also been argued that large-scale herders might have been relatively mobile. However, this argument is based on ethnographic studies of contemporary ethnic groups residing in Greece, such as the Sarakatsani and the Vlachs (Halstead 1990). These economies are also characterized by their reliance on a single species and specialization in secondary products.

At Promachon, the faunal evidence exhibits a number of characteristics that are consistent with small-scale mixed economy, rather than extensive and specialized herding. First of all, the economy at Promachon is based on the exploitation of a highly mixed composition of livestock (cattle, caprines and pigs), rather than a strong focus on the exploitation of a single domestic species. The latter strategy is the norm among contemporary pastoralists, such as the ethnic group of the Sarakatsani (Halstead 1990), who are specialized in the exploitation of a number of caprine products (*i.e.* milk, cheese and wool).

The ageing evidence also supports the argument of small-scale herding at Promachon. The age-at-death data for

---

[1] The issue of consumption could also be discussed in the economic considerations of the current chapter. However, it will be discussed in the social and symbolic considerations, since the archaeological and the faunal evidence suggest that the consumption of animal carcasses was of high social and symbolic significance at Promachon. In any case, it should be noted that consumption is largely affected by economic as well as social factors.

the three main domesticated species do not indicate the pastoral specialism proposed by the secondary products revolution (SPR) model (Arnold and Greenfield 2006; Greenfield 2005). The use of cattle for traction, which constitutes a major capital intensification of arable farming (Gilman 1981), as well as the exploitation of caprines for their fleece seem rather unlikely, except for the very small scale. All in all, the ageing evidence from Promachon indicates that animals were bred and kept primarily for their meat.

Having said that, small-scale exploitation of milk is not impossible, even though the age-at-death data (at least for caprines, since the sample size of cattle mandibles is too small to provide any definite conclusions) does not conform to Payne's (1973) milk model. However, as previously argued, the evidence from the nearby site of Stavroupoli attested to the exploitation of milk in the area of Macedonia during the late stage of the Neolithic (Evershed *et al.* 2008). It is therefore possible that settlements that were contemporary and close to Stavroupoli – including Promachon – were aware of the utilization of milk.

Of particular interest is also the fact that the management of sheep is different from that of goats. The age-at-death data from Promachon indicate that both sheep and goats were bred primarily for their meat. However, while goat remains provided a kill-off pattern that is highly typical of a focus on meat exploitation, this is less so for sheep, which may therefore have, to some extent, also been used for secondary products. This is the first time that a distinction in the management of sheep and goats has been attempted at kill-off pattern level in the valley of the river Strymon. It is possible that sheep milk would have constituted a "welcome and nutritionally valuable variety" (Halstead 1989a; 30) into the crop and meat diet of the Neolithic people of Promachon.

Despite the lack of evidence for penned structures at Promachon, recent micromorphological analyses (Karkanas pers. comm.) indicate the presence of dung in almost all areas of the settlement. In general, herbivores can produce large quantities of dung. Modern sheep breeds can produce around one and a half kilogram per day, which amounts to between 500 and 900 kilograms per year per animal. Goats are even more productive (Mlekuz 2009). Cattle on the other hand, can produce up to ten tones of dung per year per animal (Mlekuz 2009). Dung might have been used by the Neolithic people of Promachon as fuel for cooking and heating fires (Valamoti 2007), or as a very durable material in flooring. Whatever the case, the dung evidence is important as it suggests that animals were kept on-site – or at least – in areas close to it. This does not necessarily suggest that transhumance was not practiced at Promachon. This practice does not imply that all animals will be moved away from the site. In addition, even the section of the animal population that is seasonally moved will spend part of the year locally. Thus, as previously argued, the possibility of the movement of segments of the animal population of Promachon on a seasonal or other basis should not be excluded. In any case, the dung evidence at Promachon is interesting in pointing out that animals were actually present in the habitation area. This means that domestic livestock were likely to have played an important part in people's everyday lives, thus representing a "more constant domestic sociality" in the sense that Whittle (2003; 94) implies.

7.2.2 The economic importance of cattle

The analysis of the faunal assemblage from Promachon indicates that caprines are represented with higher frequencies (both in terms of NISP and MNI) than any other domesticated species on-site. However, the abundance of a species in terms of the number of fragments (and/or the estimated number of individuals) does not necessarily indicate that this species had the highest economic importance. Although caprines at Promachon are represented with a higher frequency than cattle (both on a phase-by-phase level and also for the whole cultural sequence of the Late Neolithic), from an economic and symbolic point of view, cattle could have been more important than caprines.

Cattle are much larger than caprines and pigs, and therefore, they would have undoubtedly provided the largest quantity of meat than any other domesticated animal on-site. Hence, in terms of meat provision, cattle would have been far more important than caprines (and pigs). The economic importance of cattle was also attested through inter-site analyses. To be more specific, the comparison of the frequencies of the three main domesticates on a regional level, indicated that cattle in Promachon are represented with a higher frequency than most contemporary sites from Macedonia. Although – as previously argued – the abundance of a species should not be confused with its importance, the higher frequency of cattle at Promachon (in comparison to other contemporary Macedonian sites) provides an indication that cattle would have played a particularly significant role for the inhabitants of Promachon.

There is however, another issue, which should also be considered. We should bear in mind that the extent of recovery bias at a number of sites that have been compared to Promachon has not been entirely assessed, and therefore, some of our interpretations should be approached with caution. In this sense, it would have been more appropriate to compare the frequencies of the three main domesticated species (on a regional level) in terms of MNI rather than NISP, as the former is less affected by recovery bias. However, as previously argued, a large number of faunal researchers do not use MNIs, therefore, making a regional comparison based on MNIs was impossible.

Of additional interest were the results of biometry, which indicated that cattle from Promachon were larger than their counterparts from Macedonia (with the exception of Sitagroi) and Thessaly (Kazantzis 2015; Kazantzis and Albarella 2016). It is possible that the Neolithic people of

Promachon placed particular attention on cattle husbandry and provided them with ample and/or better-quality fodder in order to increase their size. A high quality-feeding regime could plausibly be attributed to the high economic importance that this species had for the Neolithic people of the site.

All in all, although the faunal evidence from Promachon indicates that caprines are represented with a higher frequency than cattle, the latter seems to have been the species with the highest economic importance.

7.2.3 The economic importance of wild resources

The economic importance of hunting in Neolithic economies of Macedonia has primarily been inferred by the presence of deer, which – in most cases – are represented with the highest frequencies among wild taxa. On the other hand, the importance of the aurochs and the importance of wild pig in the same region have not been adequately investigated. In most cases, aurochsen and wild pigs have been identified only through a visual assessment of shape and size. At most sites, cattle and pig bones are, by default, attributed to domesticated individuals, while the identification of their wild counterparts is limited to cases of particularly large specimens. This obviously represents a potential problem, since the significance of both species in Neolithic sites from Macedonia has not been properly evaluated.

Concerning Promachon, biometrical analysis has provided no evidence of the presence of the aurochs, although Theodorogianni and Trantalidou (2013) and Iliev and Spassov (2007) argue for its presence in the successive layers of structure n. 4 and the Bulgarian sector of Topolniča respectively. Conversely, biometrical analysis has confirmed the presence of a substantial number of wild pig remains. This mirrors Bökönyi's (1986) assessment of the situation at Sitagroi. Therefore, metrical analyses have indicated the general importance of wild pigs for the Neolithic people of Promachon and Sitagroi during the Late Neolithic. This does not necessarily mean that the Neolithic people of Promachon and Sitagroi hunted wild pigs more regularly than the inhabitants of other sites. There could be many reasons why at different sites wild pig hunting may have been practiced more or less extensively (*i.e.* regional differences in the environmental conditions and vegetation cover). The lack of in-depth biometrical analysis at other sites means, however, that the possibility of a similar level of hunting at other sites cannot be ruled out.

It is therefore possible that the hunting of wild boar was the norm among a considerable number of Late Neolithic communities in Macedonia. Perhaps, reliance on substantial wild pig hunting also meant that not particular attention was paid to intensify pig husbandry. Conversely, the low frequency of wild pigs in Thessaly could plausibly be attributed to the higher attention that was paid to pig husbandry. In the absence of clear evidence from other sites it cannot be ruled out that wild pigs in the whole

Macedonia were equally important to other wild species (mainly deer), and that Neolithic people in the region hunted them more regularly than previously thought. The evidence from Sitagroi and Promachon is, in this respect, tantalising.

A useful example, which demonstrates the importance of biometrical work for the understanding of past patterns of human behavior, was presented earlier in this study. More specifically, pig body part distribution indicated that during Phases I-II the highest MNI values were gained from pig postcranial elements rather than teeth. It was therefore suggested that pig heads might have been disposed off-site. However, log ratios indicated that pig postcranial bones plotted bimodally far more than teeth, suggesting that wild pigs were better-represented by bones of the body than the head. Therefore, it is likely that the disposal of pig heads off-site was practiced in the case of wild pigs rather than their domestic counterparts.

It has been repeatedly argued that recovery bias is the main reason for the underrepresentation of small animals, small anatomical parts and young age categories. One would argue that the scarcity of fish remains from Layers 1-6 in Promachon could plausibly be attributed to poor recovery procedures, since the faunal assemblage was hand-collected. However, it is interesting to note that a very small number of fish remains [24 fish remains out of a total NISP of 31377 (less than one per cent) (Theodorogianni and Trantalidou 2013)], was also recovered from structure n. 4, whose deposits were sieved. A general scarcity of fish remains was also detected in other sites: for instance, at the LN sites of Aggitis and Dimitra the frequency of fish remains is less than one per cent of the total NISP. More specifically, at Aggitis, out of a total NISP of 869, only one fish fragment was recovered, while in Dimitra, out of a total NISP of 2457, only 12 fish fragments were retrieved (Mylona 2003). In both cases, fish remains were not identified at any taxonomical level.

Therefore, the scarcity of fish remains at a number of sites from Greek Macedonia, which were located near water sources, cannot be entirely attributed to retrieval biases. It is probable that this scarcity is the result of a genuine pattern, which indicates a general reliance on terrestrial rather than fresh water resources. This should be viewed in the context of the vicinity of Promachon to the river Strymon, and Aggitis and Dimitra from the river Aggitis in the plain of Drama. Lack of fishing was therefore not due to a lack of opportunity to access appropriate environments.

7.3 Social and symbolic considerations

The social and symbolic considerations of the current research can be divided into three subjects as well. These are:

1. The social significance of meat consumption
2. The symbolic significance of cattle
3. The social and symbolic significance of wild resources

7.3.1 Contemplating the social significance of meat consumption in Promachon

Zooarchaeological studies in prehistoric sites from Greece have arguably neglected the issue of consumption and focused mainly on the process of production (Hamilakis 1999; 2003). The discussion has primarily been focused on how animals were managed (bred, raised and killed), rather than on the context and the possible special circumstances under which meat was consumed.

Concerning Promachon, the main question to be asked is in which cases, and under which particular circumstances, meat was consumed. It has been suggested that the consumption of meat in Neolithic of Greece was linked to particular social events. This model contrasts with what has been proposed for the northern Balkan Neolithic economies (Bulgaria and Serbia), in which the high frequencies of cattle and pigs (in comparison to caprines) have been regarded as an indication that meat was consumed more frequently than in the southern Balkans (*e.g.* Greece), due to a rapid demographic increase (Bökönyi 1974; 1990).

At Promachon, the large assemblage of animal bones, the evidence for unselective deposition of anatomical parts of domestic animals and the large number of standardized cooking and serving vessels suggest that the entire *chaîne opératoire*, from slaughter to consumption, took place mainly on-site. With regard to the consumption of meat in the Neolithic (and Early Bronze Age) Greece, two hypotheses have been made (Halstead 2007). The first is that, the consumption of meat may have taken place by individual households over an extended period of time. A problem that we need to consider in connection with this hypothesis concerns meat preservation. It is well known that meat spoils too quickly to be consumed over an extended period of time by individual households, if not preserved properly. Ethnographic evidence suggests that the preservation of meat with pre-modern technological implements could be achieved in a number of ways, the most common of which is salting (Halstead 2007; McGee 1988). However, the amount of salt needed for the preservation of large carcasses, is considerably high. Therefore, unless and until evidence for salt collection on a significant scale is found in prehistoric Greece, the hypothesis of the preservation of animal carcasses by salting should be approached with caution (Halstead 2007).

The second hypothesis is that the consumption of meat may have taken place collectively, at large-scale social events (Halstead 2007). It is likely that cattle played a significant role in large-scale social events. Strong evidence for the collective consumption of cattle carcasses is provided by the incidence of butchery on cattle postcranial bones, which is relatively low (six per cent), implying that cattle were butchered into large parcels, perhaps for consumption by large social groups. Conversely, caprines and pigs may have been small enough to have been consumed primarily

at the level of the household. However, as already seen, the frequency of butchery marks on the postcranial bones of caprines and pigs from Promachon is roughly similar to that of cattle (four per cent for caprines and five per cent for pigs). Although not as much as for cattle, pig and caprine carcasses would also be expected to be butchered fairly intensively for household consumption. It is therefore possible that, like beef, mutton and pork were consumed communally in Promachon.

A potential problem that must be considered is that the incidence of butchery marks on the bones of the three main domesticates from Promachon could be masked by taphonomic phenomena. As already argued however, the faunal material from Promachon is in a very good state of preservation. In addition, the incidence of carnivore gnawing at Promachon's faunal material is low, thus making it less likely that carnivore attrition resulted in the obliteration of butchery marks.

Therefore, the low frequency of butchery marks on the bones of the three main domesticates from Promachon is certainly genuine. This indicates that animal carcasses were not intensively butchered, in order to be consumed communally. It is likely that structure n. 4 was the main recipient of consumption residues, following large-scale feasting. The significance of this particular structure, however, will be assessed later in the current chapter. Possible reasons for the consumption of animal carcasses at large-scale social events could be related to a number of different possibilities: visitors from neighboring settlements, sealing of alliances or exchanges, responses to difficult environmental conditions, and generally village-based feasts in order to celebrate all kind of possible events.

The consumption of animal carcasses at large-scale events does not entirely preclude the possibility of meat consumption at the level of household. The contextual analysis indicated that the areas of everyday activities, such as use surfaces, floors and hearths were the recipients of high proportions of bone refuse. Thus, although the evidence indicates that the consumption of animal carcasses in Promachon took place mainly at a large social scale, it is also highly likely that some meat was consumed at a domestic level. It would be unrealistic to suggest that, if the opportunity arose, the Neolithic people of Promachon would not consume some meat as part of their everyday life.

There is however, a further issue, which should also be considered. The evidence from Phase III suggests an increase in the frequency of cut marks on the postcranial bones of the three main domesticates. This indicates that during Phase III animal carcasses were more intensively butchered, possibly for household consumption. If this was the case, then it can be assumed that there was an increase in household-based consumption during Phase III in Promachon. This issue will be further discussed later in the current chapter.

7.3.2 The symbolic significance of cattle

The economic significance of cattle at Promachon has been discussed earlier in this chapter. Cattle, however, like all other animals, but perhaps particularly so, has a symbolic significance as well. The universal idea that cattle is a beast of great strength and at the same time, the incarnation of nature's rebirth, may have been reflected in the ideology of many Neolithic groups (Cauvin 2004). The symbolic significance of cattle is cross-cultural and characterizes many periods in human history. For instance, cattle are considered to have been of particular symbolic significance in Minoan art, while in Hinduism, cattle is a symbol of wealth, strength, abundance, selfless giving, and a full earthly life (Shaffer and Lichtenstein 1995).

With regard to the Neolithic, the large number of cattle zoomorphic figurines from a number of sites such as Knossos, Itea, Sitagroi, Zarko (Toufexis 2003), indicates that cattle, was probably the most prized animal (Halstead and Isaakidou 2013). Due to its large size, Ingold (1980; 225) has also suggested that cattle are the only species to meet the requirements to act as a "store of wealth". According to Orton (2008) however, the word 'wealth' should not imply commodification, and should not be used in its strict materialistic sense. Rather, cattle might have been regarded and also used as exchangeable goods (Ray and Thomas 2003), for the creation and maintenance of social ties (Halstead 2007; Halstead and Isaakidou 2013; Orton 2008).

In view of the absence of cattle zoomorphic figurines at Promachon, the presence of almost 35 bucrania (Trantalidou 2010; Trantalidou and Gkioni 2008) from the deposits of structure n. 4 constitutes probably the most reliable source of evidence for highlighting the symbolic importance of cattle at Promachon. According to a number of scholars, bulls reflected a male entity in fertility rites, and the sacredness of the animal was expressed with the presence of horns (Gimbutas 1991).

In general, bucrania are powerful symbols and they can be found in sites from the Near East dating as early as the 10th millennium BC, as well as the Balkan (Vinča and Tisza cultures) regions. However, their use is not always clear and the archaeologists hold conflicting opinions. For instance, bucrania might be linked with the religious perception for the sacredness of cattle, manifested through the use of horncores (Trantalidou and Gioni 2008), but they could also have been used as decorative objects (Trantalidou and Gkioni 2008). The bucrania that have been found at Hallan Çemi in Turkey (Rosenberg 1999) and Kormadin in Croatia (Koukouli-Chrysanthaki *et al.* 2007) have been interpreted as such. A single bucranium, which was found in the deposits of a Phase I structure from Dikili Tash in eastern Macedonia, has been interpreted as a decorative object as well. Archaeologists of the site argue that the bucranium, which was covered in clay, could have been suspended on posts around the periphery of the structure (Darque and Treuil 1997; Treuil and Darque 1998). The

probable use of bucrania as decorative objects does not necessarily imply that these did not have a symbolic value as well (Trantalidou and Gkioni 2008). The use of the bucrania inside structures, under floors, or on walls, may – in the minds of the Neolithic people – have strengthened the power and the longevity of the building (Treuil and Darque 1998).

In this sense, it is possible that the inhabitants of Promachon suspended bucrania on posts or in visible parts of structure n. 4, in order to reassure the structure's durability against physical phenomena and potential environmental disasters. Corroborating evidence for the latter hypothesis is represented by a clay house model, which was found in the deposits of structure n. 4, with the decoration of plastered bucrania on its walls.

The occurrence of bucrania tends to increase at times when the economic importance of cattle is high (Orton 2008), as is also the case at Promachon. The bucrania at Promachon were found in the deposits of structure n. 4, which belongs to the first phase of occupation, when cattle are represented with the highest frequencies. It can be suggested therefore, that there is a link between the economic and the symbolic significance of cattle, and that the two variables should not be entirely disentangled. For instance, as suggested, the large size of cattle at Promachon (in comparison to sites from Makriyalos and Thessaly) could be the result of the economic importance of the species for the Neolithic people of Promachon. However, it may also be the result of the symbolic significance of the species. If we accept the argument that cattle carcasses were consumed in large-scale social events, then it is highly likely that cattle were subject to special treatment by the Neolithic people at Promachon, possibly being fed in a privileged way in comparison to other livestock.

7.3.3 The social and symbolic significance of hunting

Arguably, the issue of hunting in farming societies has received small attention in European zooarchaeology (Hamilakis 2003). Zvelebil (1992) notes that this is mainly the result of the evolutionary thought in archaeology, which perceived hunting as a remnant of a backward and outdated stage in human evolution. The information from single, as well as multi-period, sites from mainland Greece indicates a marked increase in the percentage of wild animals during the late stages of the Neolithic and the Early Bronze Age (Halstead 1992; 1999; Hamilakis 2003). One of the main questions in Greek zooarchaeology therefore, is why people during these time-periods hunted and consumed wild animals given that fact that they had plenty of access to meat that could be produced by domesticated animals (Hamilakis 2003).

In the case of the Greek Neolithic, a number of hypotheses regarding the importance of hunting in farming economies have been suggested. For instance, Halstead and O'Shea (1989) argue that hunting constituted a risk-buffering choice by the Neolithic people in cases of crop failures and livestock diseases. Conversely, Hamilakis (2003) suggests that hunting in farming societies was linked with the development of an institutionalized authority and that wild animals may have been regarded as 'trophies' by an emerging elite group of people. The argument for the presence of elite groups during the Late Neolithic of Greece is based on archaeological evidence, such as the presence of large structures and monumental buildings in Thessaly (*i.e.* Dimini, Sesklo, Magoula Visviki), which denote delineation and separation from the rest of the structures.

The presence of monumental buildings also applies in the case of Promachon. For instance, structure n. 4 is a particularly large structure in Promachon, and in this respect, it is a distinct feature from the rest of the structures of Phase I (pit-houses). However, structure n. 4 should not be taken as an indication for the presence of a hierarchical and socially stratified society at Promachon. It is possible that it was not used to strengthen the authority of an elite group of people, but rather as a public building, where activities of symbolic nature took place. These probably involved the consumption of meat (and perhaps other stimulants) aimed to strengthen bonds and social relations in the community.

Returning to the issue of Neolithic hunting, the relatively high frequency of wild animals at a number of sites in Greek Macedonia could be linked to the symbolic significance that these animals had among Neolithic communities. Like the meat of the domestic animals, the meat of the wild animals could have been consumed primarily communally. Unfortunately, this cannot be firmly demonstrated at

from Promachon might be an indication for the disposal of deer crania in workshop areas for the production of antler tools and objects. This is also corroborated by the presence of two tine antlers with polished surfaces in Promachon. However, we should not also exclude the possibility that, as in the case of wild pig, deer heads might have been disposed off-site due to their heavy weight and limited meat content. The use of antlers as a source of raw materials is attested elsewhere as well. For instance, antlers are known to have been used as picks and digging implements in various Neolithic sites of Europe (Clutton-Brock 1984). However, the use of bone as raw material is likely to have represented just a useful by-product of hunting.

7.4 Use of space and chronological development

This part of the discussion will combine zooarchaeological and archaeological information in order to discuss settlement patterns at Promachon. It will also discuss the most interesting patterns that emerged from the comparison of Promachon with other Macedonian, Thessalian and Balkan settlements.

7.4.1 Phase I and structure n. 4

The comparison of the faunal material between structure n. 4 (Theodorogianni and Trantalidou 2013) and the rest of the deposits of Phase I provided some interesting insights. This faunal evidence is complementary to the evidence from the material culture and the structural features and in general support of the hypothesis of the different use of space during the first phase of occupation at Promachon (Kazantzis 2017):

Spatial differentiation in Phase I		
Evidence	**Structure n. 4 (Layers 7-11)**	**Rest of the deposits (Layers 4-6)**
Faunal	Emphasis on cattle (in terms of NISP)	No particular emphasis on a single species (in terms of NISP)
	Presence of calves	Absence of calves
	Younger caprines	Older caprines
	Presence of bucrania	Absence of bucrania, only fragments of crania present
Archaeological	Elaborate material culture objects	Everyday material culture objects
	Large structure (12 m diameter, 7 m in depth)	Pit-houses (each 8-10 m²)

Promachon due to the complexity of bone fragmentation and recovery, as well as sample size. In any case, it is highly possible that the consumption of the meat of wild animals might have had particular symbolic and social implications, which possibly outweighed its nutritional value as a source of protein. We should not forget also that the bones of wild animals represented a valuable source of raw materials, as the presence of a number of worked deer ulnae demonstrates. In general, the bones of wild animals constitute better working material than the bones of domestic animals, since they tend to be denser and more resilient. The absence of deer cranial elements

We should note, however that, due to the differences in the methods of study of the faunal material between the two areas, the results of this comparison should be approached with caution. The comparison of the frequencies of the three main domesticates (in terms of NISP) between the two areas indicated that the remains of cattle dominate the deposits of structure n. 4, whereas no particular emphasis on a single species could be detected in the rest of the deposits of Phase I. In addition, in structure n. 4 there is an emphasis on the disposal of calves, whereas the same age group is completely absent from the rest of the deposits. Of particular interest is also the fact that there is a higher proportion of younger caprines in structure n. 4, whereas the opposite pattern could be detected in the rest of the deposits of Phase I. The comparison of the faunal material between structure n. 4 and the rest of the deposits of Phase I supports the arguments of the excavation team regarding spatial differentiation during the first phase of occupation in Promachon. As previously noted, the low frequency of butchery marks on the bones of the three main domesticates indicates that animal carcasses were not intensively butchered, probably as a consequence of their communal consumption. It has also been argued that some meat was probably also consumed at the level of household. The contextual analysis from Phase I indicates that neither the pits of the pit-houses, nor the floors and the hearths of Phase I indicate the preferential disposal of the remains of a particular species. The higher frequency of older caprines from the deposits of Phase I (in comparison to the higher frequency of younger caprines from structure n. 4) suggests that these animals were not bred exclusively for meat, but secondary products were also used, though they may have been less important. It is possible that communal consumption of animal carcasses in the deposits of Phase I did not have a particular symbolic (and/or ritual) significance and that it did not involve large gatherings of people (Kazantzis 2017). There is nothing in the overall archaeological context that suggests social exclusivity. Therefore, the consumers are unlikely to have been particularly chosen people, but merely extended family groups or similar social gatherings. Unlike the majority of the deposits of Phase I, where the consumption of animal carcasses is likely to have been practiced both communally and to the household level, the deposits of structure n. 4 were the recipients of consumption residues associated exclusively with large-scale feasting (Kazantzis 2017). The mass disposal of this material in structure n. 4 could be interpreted "as a symbolic reinforcement of the importance of a series of major consumption events" as Halstead (2007; 39) implies in the case of Late Neolithic Makriyalos, Pieria, Greece. The high frequency of cattle remains from the deposits of structure n. 4 may be explained on the basis of the particular symbolic significance of this animal for the Neolithic people at Promachon. In addition, the presence of a characteristic age group such as calves, the presence of the bucrania and antlers, as well as other luxurious material culture objects, is consistent with the particular symbolic nature of structure n. 4[2]. The significance of the presence of younger caprines in the deposits of structure n. 4 is difficult to understand yet it is tempting to assume that this part of the caprine population was reserved particularly for large-scale feasting (Kazantzis 2017).

All in all, it can be suggested that there are differences in the use of space during the first phase of occupation in Promachon (Kazantzis 2017). The pit-houses, the use surfaces, the floors and the hearths were areas of everyday activities, where consumption took place primarily communally; however, we cannot also exclude the possibility of household consumption. On the other hand, structure n. 4 was exclusively used for large-scale consumption events. It is highly likely that the communal consumption of animal carcasses between the two areas of the settlement during Phase I did not have the same significance. Probably, the large-scale consumption events that took place in structure n. 4 were of higher symbolic (and/or ritual) significance than those from the rest of the settlement during Phase I (Kazantzis 2017).

7.4.2 Phase II

One may expect that the changes in the structural features (the replacement of the pit-houses of Phase I by the aboveground structures of Phase II) were also related to changes in the economy of the site and the husbandry regime. However, the study of the faunal material from Phase II does not indicate any substantial changes in the proportions of the three main domesticates in comparison to Phase I. In addition, metrical analyses do not indicate changes in the size of the animals between the two phases. The contextual analysis suggests that the use surfaces, the floors and the hearths were the recipients of the highest proportion of bone refuse during Phase II. Thus, it can be argued that the bones represent discarded material after some form of collective consumption took place. However, as in the case of Phase I, we cannot also exclude the possibility that domestic consumption took place.

On the other hand, it is highly likely that the large structure (structure n. 1), which was found at the Bulgarian sector of Topolniča during the second phase of occupation[3], was used as a public structure with a symbolic significance similar to that of structure n. 4 (Phase I) in the Greek sector of Promachon. It is therefore possible that in the second phase of occupation, large-scale social events took place in the Bulgarian sector of the site (Topolniča). It would have been interesting to find out whether the higher frequency of cattle postcranial elements during the second phase of occupation at Promachon were the result of the disposal of bucrania in structure n. 1 at Topolniča, as it had been the case for structure n. 4 from Promachon. Unfortunately, however, the absence of contextual detail from Topolniča (Iliev and Spassov 2007), limits the possibility of comparing the material between the two sectors beyond the level of the frequency of species.

7.4.3 Phase III: a time of change?

As previously noted, the excavators of the site have argued that the settlement of Promachon-Topolniča was abandoned

---

[2] However, as previously noted, we should not entirely disentangle the symbolic significance of cattle from its economic value. In this sense, there is a possibility that calves, as a characteristic age group, might have had a particular symbolic value for the people of Promachon. However, calves might also have been the part of the cattle population that had to be slaughtered to favour the production of milk for human consumption.

[3] As already noted, the conflagration event that took place in Phase I, may have forced the inhabitants of the settlement to move the 'public' building (structure n. 4) from the western plateau (Promachon sector) to the eastern plateau (Topolnica sector), by constructing a new aboveground structure (structure n. 1).

at the end of Phase II and it was reoccupied in Phase III for a short period of time (Koukouli-Chrysanthaki *et al.* 2007). This argument is based on the changes that were noticed in pottery decoration between Phases II and III. The material culture evidence from Promachon indicates that the pottery of Phase II is characterized by high quality decoration [*i.e.* thin and thick 'Strumsko' and 'Akropotamos' decorative lines, black-on-top and 'Bituminus' decoration, (Koukouli-Chrysanthaki *et al.* 2007; Vajsov 2007)], whereas that of Phase III is characterized by drab and incised decoration, which reveals "a dramatic reduction of stylistic variation and aesthetic brilliance" in the sense that Bailey (2000, 252) implies. In addition, absolute dating has indicated a habitation gap of almost two centuries between Phases II and III. In general, it is suggested that the habitation gap between Phase II and Phase III represents a time-period of cultural discontinuity (Koukouli-Chrysanthaki 2014).

The study of the faunal assemblage has highlighted a number of patterns that are consistent with the argument of changes at Promachon during this time-period. Perhaps most important is the decline in cattle frequency, which has in particular been highlighted by the MNI counts. The rise of caprines at the expense of cattle during Phase III probably indicates that there is indeed a change in the husbandry practices between Phases II and III in Promachon.

Of particular interest is also the fact that the study of the frequency of cut marks and chopping marks on the bones of the three main domesticates from Promachon, suggest differences in patterns of butchery between Phase III and the preceding Phases I and II. As previously noted, the frequency of chopping marks is higher than the frequency of cut marks on the bones of the three main domesticates during Phases I and II. The low frequency of cut marks in Phases I and II was interpreted as an indication that animal carcasses were processed in large chunks, possibly for consumption in large-scale social events. On the other hand, the study of the frequency of cut marks and chopping marks during Phase III indicates the exact opposite pattern. More specifically, cut marks are represented with a higher frequency than chopping marks on the bones of the three main domesticates during Phase III. The presence of a clay crucible that was found at the bottom of a small pit belonging to Phase III [which contained traces of copper smelting (Koukouli-Chrysanthaki *et al.* 2007)] might be suggestive of the use of metal tools and knives. However, there is also the possibility that stone tools and flints (rather than metal tools, which in any case were not found in Promachon) might have been used more intensively during Phase III than earlier phases. In any case, the identification of stone marks *versus* metal marks on site falls beyond the scope of this study: the study of the tool specialist (Rozalia Christidou pers. comm.) will provide valuable information with regard to this issue. What is really interesting however, is that the higher frequency of cut marks during the third phase of occupation in Promachon may indicate that animal carcasses were

butchered more intensively, which in turn, might indicate an increase in household-based consumption during Phase III at Promachon.

Metrical analyses tentatively suggest changes in the size of sheep between Phases II and III. More specifically, shape indices showed that sheep from Phase III were more robust than their counterparts from Phase II. Despite the use of the scaling technique did not firmly confirm the previous point, there are some hints that different body parts of sheep were subject to various changes between Phases II and III. It seems that sheep from Phase III were slightly different in comparison to those from Phase II, but such difference could not be exemplified by concepts such as size and robustness. It is difficult to evaluate the reasons behind such difference but considering the changes in the patterns of butchery as well as the changes in the frequency of caprines between Phases II and III, it is tempting to assume that such difference was the result of changes in the actual build of sheep, possibly due to the introduction of a new type of sheep during Phase III.

All in all, the faunal evidence is consistent with the suggestion that significant changes occurred during the third phase of occupation. We should also consider that this phase corresponds to the late stage of the Late Neolithic (LNII), which is a time-period during which significant changes in settlement patterns, burial practices, economy and material culture took place in the area of the Balkans (Bailey 2000; Greenfield 2005; Whittle 1996). Bailey (2000) argues that the changes in this time-period were similar to those that distinguished mobile hunter-gatherers from the early villagers of the mid-seventh millennium BC of the Balkans:

> "*However, whereas the mid-seventh millennium BC shift had been from flexibility and mobility to the physical demarcation and anchored residence of increasingly divided communities, the shift of this time period was from stable, but perhaps inflexible, village communities, in which the ideology of the household held sway, to mobile communities*" (Bailey 2000; 261).

It is possible therefore that the people who reoccupied Promachon during Phase III brought different ideas, new subsistence methods, and new methods in husbandry practices. In any case, the reoccupation of the site of Promachon did not last for a long period, since absolute dating indicates that the site was abandoned during the last quarter of the 5th millennium BC.

7.4.4 Human remains

As previously noted, modern human is represented in Phase I with a proximal scapula and a proximal radius and in Phase II with a proximal ulna. The mixed deposits have also yielded a human proximal scapula (glenoid cavity). The occurrence of human remains at Promachon is interesting but needs to be interpreted by considering the context of origin.

These human remains derive from a number of different contexts. The proximal scapula and proximal radius from Phase I derive from a ditch and a use surface (outdoor surface) respectively, while the Phase II proximal ulna derives from the floor of an aboveground structure. Of additional interest is the fact that a part of a human mandible and a fragment of a human skull were also found in the deposits of structure n. 4 at the time of the excavation (Koukouli-Chrysanthaki *et al.* 2007), while Theodorogianni and Trantalidou (2013) in their report on the faunal remains from the same structure argue for the presence of two human ulnae. On the other hand, no evidence of human remains was reported from the Bulgarian sector of Topolniča (Iliev and Spassov 2007).

In general, the evidence from the late 5th millennium BC in northern Greece, southern and western Bulgaria and Serbia, suggests that human bodies, whole or partial, were buried under the floors of buildings (Bailey 2000). For instance, in the western Thessalian plain at Ayia Sofia, two burials were associated with a mud-block mortuary structure, while at Pevkakia near Dimini people placed the burial beneath the floor of a structure (Andreou *et al.* 1996). There were also cases where burials were found in ditches or refuse pits (Bailey 2000). For instance, at the site of Makriyalos in Western Macedonia, primary or secondary burials were found in one of the site's three concentric ditches (Pappa 1993; Pappa and Besios 1998; Andreou *et al.* 1996).

The small number and scattered form of the human remains found at Promachon rules out the possibility that they may represent primary deposition, which leads to the following questions:

1. Why are only a few parts of the deceased skeleton found
2. Where is the primary deposition area located

Hourmouziadis (1973) suggested that, in Neolithic Greece, corpses could have been either cremated, or buried in cemeteries outside the settlements' limits. If we accept the assumption that cemeteries existed and were outside the limits of settlements, then it could be assumed – on the basis of the exemplified burial patterns from the Early Neolithic site of Prodromos (Hourmouziadis 1973) – that scattered bones might reflect exhumation and reburial of certain, selected parts of the deceased skeleton (Perlès 2001). In other words, it is possible that the deceased from Promachon were buried outside the settlement's limits and a number of certain parts of the skeletons were reintroduced to the site by being deposited in a number of different areas (*i.e.* beneath house floors or simply thrown inside pits and/or ditches). This entire process could be related to a change of status from deceased to ancestor, thus suggesting the existence of an ancestor cult (Perlès 2001), with the ultimate purpose of the protection of the world of the living.

Alternatively – if indeed a cemetery existed during the Late Neolithic at Promachon – this might as well have been located within the limits of the settlement, either in an unused part of the site, or in an area not affected by the excavation. For instance, the evidence from the site of Gomolava in Serbia (first half of the fifth millennium BC), suggests that the Neolithic people living there buried the deceased within the settlement's limits, but in an area of the site that was not intensively used. This eventually led some researchers to characterize this particular area as an "intramural necropolis" (Bailey 2000; Orton 2008). If the cemetery was located within the settlement of Promachon, then it is possible that digging activities may have easily disturbed the burials and led to the accidental scattering of human bones.

7.4.5 Beyond the site: Macedonia, Thessaly and the Balkans

One of the key aims of the study was to understand the economy, the scale of animal husbandry and the nature of human-animal relations at Promachon. In this respect, the analysis of the animal bone assemblage from Promachon indicated a number of interesting patterns, which have been discussed earlier in this chapter. Also important was to incorporate Promachon in the context of contemporary sites from northern Greece and the Balkan regions. For this reason, the results of the faunal analysis from Promachon were compared to those from Late Neolithic sites of this broader area. This comparison placed Promachon in a regional context, but it also provided interesting insights into the diverse husbandry practices practiced among Late Neolithic communities of northern Greece.

Of particular interest is the consideration that the subsistence economy of Promachon could have been dictated by the environmental conditions of the Strymon river valley, as well as the cultural bonds that the Neolithic people of Promachon had with contemporary communities in the Balkans. It has been repeatedly argued that cattle at Promachon are represented with the highest frequencies among Macedonian and Thessalian Late Neolithic sites. The high frequency of cattle from Promachon can plausibly be attributed to the geomorphology, the environment, the vegetation and the climate in the region, which may have significantly favored the keeping and breeding of these animals.

However, the high frequency of cattle in Promachon cannot be attributed solely to the favorable environmental conditions of the area. The evidence from the pottery decoration and the structural features from Promachon, indicate that the site was culturally linked with contemporary communities from the Balkan regions, in which cattle had an important role. In terms of the economy, Promachon could have been linked to Aegean Late Neolithic communities. However, it is also highly likely that Promachon was linked with Late and Final Neolithic communities of the Balkans. This is one of the most interesting aspects of the analysis of the faunal material from Promachon, since it confirms previous suggestions of the excavators of the site with regard to the cultural bonds between Promachon and contemporary Balkan sites.

There is however, an interesting issue, which should also be considered. A number of settlements contemporary to Promachon are located in the southern part of the plain of Serres (*i.e.* Toumba, Dimitra, Kryoneri). Promachon on the other hand, is the only Late Neolithic settlement in the northern part of the plain. It is possible therefore that, Promachon was rather isolated (although we should also note that the scarcity of settlements contemporary to Promachon in the northern part of the plain of Serres might also be the result of 'gaps' in the archaeological research). It is likely that other contemporary sites will eventually emerge, thus adding to the information currently available. Unlike Promachon, Sitagroi might have belonged to a group of sites in the plain of Drama, which had progressed from small villages to being highly interacting communities. It is likely that the particularly large size of cattle and sheep from Sitagroi was the result of an agricultural system that had attained a high degree of expertise, thus permitting the people of Sitagroi to provide ample and/or better-quality fodder to their livestock. Sitagroi would not have overcome difficult situations, without being part of a wider network of communities in the plain of Drama, which interacted with each other in order to respond to economic and/or environmental constraints. It is likely therefore that Sitagroi – unlike Promachon – was part of a group of settlements with a more organized and centralized system of economy in the plain of Drama.

Biometry gave also important insights into the diverse husbandry practices between Macedonian and Thessalian Late Neolithic sites. More specifically, metrical analyses indicated that cattle from Macedonia were larger than their counterparts from Thessaly, whereas the opposite pattern was suggested in the case for sheep and pigs. The large size of sheep and pigs in Thessaly could be the result of a particular emphasis on sheep and pig husbandry, whereas the large size of cattle in Macedonia might be the result of the particular attention on cattle husbandry. On the other hand, the comparison of the size of domestic ruminants and pigs between Thessalian sites indicates that each site possibly maintained their own types of livestock. If this was the case, then it could be argued that different sites in Thessaly were fairly independent from each other (Kazantzis and Albarella 2016).

The collection of a larger body of metrical data from Late Neolithic Macedonian and Thessalian settlements should represent a priority for future research in order to provide clarification to some of the aforementioned issues. However, this cannot be achieved without the inclusion of whole ranges of measurements of the main domesticates in faunal publications. The inclusion of metrical data – and not just the presentation of summary statistics of measurements – should represent a top priority for current and future faunal researchers working on Greek faunal assemblages.

8

Epilogue

In this chapter, a number of key issues that have emerged from the faunal study will be presented. The subsequent paragraphs elaborate on each of the key issues.

1. The faunal evidence exhibits a number of characteristics that are consistent with small-scale mixed economy rather than extensive and specialized herding

The economy of Promachon is based on the exploitation of a highly mixed composition of livestock (cattle, caprines and pigs), rather than a strong focus on the exploitation of a single domestic species. The ageing evidence indicates that animals were bred and kept primarily for their meat. However, a small-scale exploitation for milk could also be inferred: the ageing evidence suggests that sheep – unlike goats – were used for milk. This represents a rare occasion in Greek archaeology for the kill-off patterns of the two species to have been analysed independently. There is also tentative evidence for the use of cattle for milk, given the high proportion of calves in structure n. 4. On the other hand, the use of cattle for traction and the exploitation of caprines for their fleece seem rather unlikely.

2. Cattle were the species with the highest economic importance. In addition, they had a symbolic significance

The environmental conditions in the area of Promachon could have significantly affected the decision of the Neolithic people of the site to invest substantially on cattle. Due to their large size, cattle would have undoubtedly provided the largest quantities of meat than any other domesticate. Of particular interest is also the fact that, at Promachon, cattle are represented with the highest frequency among contemporary settlements in Macedonia and Thessaly. Metrical analysis indicated that cattle from Promachon were larger than their counterparts from Macedonia (with the exception of Sitagroi) and Thessaly. It is possible therefore that the Neolithic people of Promachon placed particular attention on cattle husbandry and provided them with ample and/or better-quality fodder in order to increase their size. However, the large size of cattle at Promachon may also be attributed to the likely symbolic role that the species probably had for the Neolithic people of the site. The presence of 35 bucrania from structure n. 4 constitutes the most substantial source of evidence for highlighting the symbolic importance of cattle at the site.

3. The faunal evidence suggests that the consumption of animal carcasses took place primarily communally. However, we cannot exclude also the possibility of some household consumption

The low frequency of butchery marks on the postcranial bones of the three main domesticates suggests that animal carcasses were not intensively butchered, in order to be consumed communally. In other words, it is highly likely that the consumption of meat at Late Neolithic Promachon was practiced at a large social scale. However, we cannot exclude the possibility of the consumption of some meat at the domestic level, too.

4. The comparison of the faunal material between structure n. 4 and the rest of the deposits of Phase I indicates spatial differentiation during the first phase of occupation in Promachon

Unlike the deposits of Phase I, where the consumption of animal carcasses was practiced (primarily) communally, and (to a lesser extent) at the level of household, the deposits of structure n. 4 were the recipients of consumption residues probably associated with large-scale feasting. It seems that the communal consumption of animal carcasses between the two areas of the settlement did not have the same significance. Probably, the large-scale consumption events that took place in structure n. 4 were of higher symbolic (and/or ritual) significance than those from the rest of the settlement during Phase I.

5. The study of the faunal assemblage has highlighted a number of patterns that are consistent with the argument of changes in Phase III

The rise of caprines at the expense of cattle (in terms of MNI) during Phase III probably indicates that there is a change in the husbandry practices between Phases II and III at Promachon. In addition, the higher frequency of cut marks than chopping marks on the bones of the three main domesticates during Phase III, may also indicate that animal carcasses were butchered more intensively in Phase III than the preceding phases. If this was the case, then it follows that there is an increase in household-based consumption during Phase III. Metrical analysis tentatively suggests changes in the size of sheep between Phases II and III; this could be the result of the introduction of a new 'type' of sheep during the third phase of occupation in Promachon.

6. Pig hunting was particularly important for the Neolithic people of Promachon and Sitagroi

Biometrical analysis has not confirmed the presence of the aurochs at Promachon, even though Theodorogianni and Trantalidou (2013) and Iliev and Spassov (2007) argue for the species' presence in structure n. 4 and the Bulgarian sector of Topolniča respectively. However, biometrical analysis has indicated the presence of a substantial number of wild pig remains. This mirrors Bökönyi's (1986) assessment for the situation at Sitagroi. The pattern does not necessarily imply that the Neolithic people from Promachon and Sitagroi were hunting wild pigs more regularly than the people from other contemporary settlements in Macedonia. Rather, the lack of in-depth biometrical analyses at other Neolithic sites from Macedonia resulted in the significance of wild pig hunting not being properly evaluated. In this respect, the possibility of a similar level of wild pig hunting at other sites – contemporary to Promachon and Sitagroi – cannot be entirely excluded. The importance of the use of biometry for the identification of wild pigs from Macedonian Late Neolithic settlements must be emphasized. Biometrical analysis also suggested that wild pig heads were disposed off-site and the Neolithic people of Promachon were transferring to the site the rest of their carcasses.

7. Promachon was probably isolated from the rest of the sites in the southern part of the plain of Serres

This argument is mainly based on the archaeological rather than zooarchaeological evidence. The absence of sites contemporary to Promachon from the northern part of the plain of Serres indicates that Promachon was probably a distant and isolated site. However, we should not exclude the possibility that the absence of Late Neolithic sites in the north part of the plain of Serres could be the result of gaps in the archaeological research.

8. Promachon was linked with Late and Final Neolithic communities of the Balkans

The substantially better representation of cattle at Promachon than any other settlement in Greek Macedonia, along with the evidence from pottery decoration and structural features, suggests that – to some extent – Promachon was linked to Balkan Late and Final Neolithic communities. This evidence is complementary to that obtained from other sources of archaeological data suggesting a link between Promachon and other contemporary sites in the Balkans.

9. The large size of cattle and sheep from Sitagroi (in comparison to other sites from Macedonia) may be the result of a highly proficient feeding regime at that site. This may indicate that settlements in the plain of Drama were part of a network of communities, which could overcome economic as well as environmental constraints through cooperation

It is likely that the large size of cattle and sheep from Sitagroi was the result of an agricultural system that had attained a high degree of expertise, thus permitting the Neolithic people of Sitagroi to provide ample and/or better-quality fodder to their livestock. The plain of Drama is characterized by a wide network of sites – among them also Dikili Tash – in relatively close proximity, which had possibly proceeded from small villages to being highly interacting communities. Sitagroi was probably one of the most important. Conversely, Promachon may have been isolated from the other contemporary sites in the plain of Serres.

10. Biometry gave important insights into the diverse husbandry practices between Macedonian and Thessalian Late Neolithic sites

Biometrical analyses indicated that cattle from Macedonia were larger than their counterparts from Thessaly, whereas the opposite was the case for sheep and pigs. The large size of the livestock may be indicative of the focus that husbandry in different regions had on different species. As concerns pigs from Thessaly, the possibility of the interbreeding of domestic and wild pigs must be considered. The comparison of the size of livestock between different Thessalian sites indicates that each of them possibly maintained their own types of livestock. If this was the case, then it can be assumed that different sites in Thessaly were fairly independent from each other. All in all, biometrical analyses provided important insights regarding husbandry practices at both local (Promachon and Strymon river valley) and regional (Macedonia and Thessaly) levels. Given the general scarcity of biometrical data from Macedonian settlements, this study has hopefully demonstrated the importance of biometry for the investigation of aspects of economy and animal use.

Lastly, a note about the Bulgarian sector of Topolniča and structure n. 4 from Promachon sector. Unfortunately, the lack of contextual information from Topolniča limited the possibility of comparing or at least combining the results between the two sectors. In addition, the comparison of the faunal assemblages between structure n. 4 and the rest of the deposits of Phase I has some inevitable limitations due to the differences in the methods of study of the faunal material between the two areas. However, and despite the differences in the methodology, such comparison has provided interesting insights, though the interpretation had to be kept at an inevitably approximate level.

Bibliography

Albarella, U. (1995). Problemi metodologici nelle correlazioni inter-sito: alcuni esempi da archeofaune dell'Italia meridionale. *Padusa Quaderni* 1, 15-28.

Albarella U. (1997). Shape variation of cattle metapodials: age, sex or breed? Some examples from Medieval and Postmedieval sites. *Anthropozoologica* 25, 37-47.

Albarella, U. (1999). The animal economy after the eruption of Avellino pumice: the case of La Starza (Avellino, Southern Italy). In Albore Livadie, C. (ed) *L'eruzione Vesuviana delle 'Pomici di Avellino' e la Facies Culturale di Palma Campania (bronzoantico)*, 317-330. Bari, Edipuglia.

Albarella, U. (2002). 'Size matters': how and why biometry is still important in zooarchaeology. In Dobney, K. O'Connor, T. (eds) *Bones and the Man: Studies in honor of Don Brothwell*, 51-62. Oxford, Oxbow.

Albarella, U. and Davis, S.J.M. (1994). *The Saxon and Medieval animal bones excavated 1985-1989 from West Cotton, Northamptonshire*. Ancient Monuments Laboratory Report 17/94.

Albarella, U. and Payne, S. (2005). Neolithic pigs from Durrington Walls, Wiltshire, England: a biometrical database. *Journal of Archaeological Science* 32, 589-99.

Albarella, U. and Serjeantson, D. (2002). A passion for pork: meat consumption at the British late Neolithic site of Durrington Walls. In Miracle, P. Milner, N. (eds) *Consuming Passions and Patterns of Consumption*, 33-49. Cambridge, McDonald Institute Monographs.

Albarella, U., Beech, M. and Mulville, J. (1997). *The Saxon, Medieval and post-Medieval mammal and bird bones excavated 1989-1991 from Castle Mall, Norwich (Norfolk)*. Ancient Monuments Laboratory Reports 72/97.

Albarella, U., Davis, S.J.M., Detry, C. and Rowley-Conwy, P. (2005). Pigs of the 'Far West': the biometry of *Sus* from archaeological sites in Portugal. *Anthropologica* 40, 27-54.

Albarella, U., Dobney, K. and Rowley-Conwy, P. (2006). The domestication of the pig (*Sus scrofa*): new challenges and approaches. In Zeder, M., Bradley, D., Emshwiller, E. and Smith, B. (eds) *Documenting Domestication: new genetic and archaeological paradigms*, 209-227. Berkeley, University of California Press.

Albarella, U., Dobney, K. and Rowley-Conwy, P. (2009). Size and shape of the Eurasian wild boar (*Sus scrofa*), with a view to the reconstruction of its Holocene history. *Environmental Archaeology* 14, 103-136.

Andreou, S., Fotiadis, M. and Kotsakis, K. (1996). Review of Aegean prehistory V: the Neolithic and Bronze Age of northern Greece. *American Journal of Archaeology* 100 (3), 537-597.

Andreou, S., Fotiadis, M. and Kotsakis, K. (2001). The Neolithic and Bronze Age of Northern Greece. In Cullen, T. (ed) *Aegean Prehistory: a review*, 259-327. American Journal of Archaeology, Supplement 1, Boston, Archaeological Institute of America.

Arnold, E.R. and Greenfield, H.J. (2006). *The Origins of Transhumant Pastoralism in temperate Southeastern Europe*. British Archaeological Reports International Series 1538. Oxford, BAR Publishing.

Atchley, W.R., Gaskins, C.T. and Anderson, D. (1976). Statistical properties of ratios. I. Empirical Results. *Systematic Zoology*, 137-148.

Bacvarov, K., Bozhilov, V. and Anastasova, E. (2010). The prehistoric site at Harmanli, southeast Bulgaria. In Nikolov, V., Gurova, M., Bacvarov, K., Sirakov, N., Boyadzhiev, Y. and Alexandrov, S. (eds) *Studia Praehistorica* 13, 135-168. Sofia, National Institute of Archaeology and Museum.

Bailey, W.D. (2000). *Balkan Prehistory: exclusion, incorporation and identity*. London, Routledge.

Bakalakis, G. and Sakellariou, A. (1981). *Paradimi*. Internationale interakademische kommission für die erforschung der vorgeschichte des Balkans, Monographien Band 2, 15-20. Mainz am Rhein, Heidelberger Akademie der Wissenschaften.

Baker, J. and Brothwell, D. (1980). *Animal Diseases in Archaeology*. London, Academic Press.

Barker, G. (1985). *Prehistoric Farming in Europe*. Cambridge, Cambridge University Press.

Bartosiewicz, L., Van Neer, W. and Lentacker, A. (1993). Metapodial asymmetry in draft cattle. *International Journal of Osteoarchaeology* 3, 69-75.

Bartosiewicz, L., Van Neer, W. and Lentacker, A. (1997). *Draught Cattle: Their Osteological Identification and History*. Musee Royal de L'Afrique Centrale Tervuren, Belgique, Annales Sciences Zoologiques, Vol. 281.

Becker, C. (1986). *Kastanas. Die Tierknochenfunde. Prähistorische archäologie in südesteuropa Band 5*. Berlin, Wissenschaftsverlag Volker Spiess.

Becker, C. (1991). Die tierknochenfunde von der Platia Magoula Zarkou: neue untersuchungen zu haustierhaltung, jagd und rohstoffverwendung im Neolithisch-Bronzezeitlichen Thessalien. *PZ* 66, 14-78.

Becker, C. (1999). The Middle Neolithic and the Platia Magoula Zarkou: A review of current archaeozoological research in Thessaly (Greece). *Anthropozoologica* 30, 3-22.

Binford, L.R. (1978). *Nunamiut Ethnoarchaeology.* New York, Academic Press.

Binford, L.R. (1981). *Bones: ancient man and modern myths.* New York, Academic Press.

Blouet, B. (1968). Development of the settlement pattern. In Renfrew, C., Gimbutas, M. and Elster, S. (eds) *Excavations at Sitagroi: a prehistoric village in northeastern Greece, Volume 1* (Monumenta Archaeologica 13), 133-143. Los Angeles, California, Institute of Archaeology, University of California.

Boessneck, J. (1962). Die Tierreste aus der Argissa Magula vom präkeramischen Neolithikum bis zur Mitteleren Bronzezeit. In Milojcic, V., Böessneck, J. and Hopf M. (eds) *Argissa-Magula 1*, 27-99. Bonn, Rudolf Habelt.

Boessneck, J. (1969). Osteological differences between sheep (*Ovis aries Linné*) and goat (*Capra hircus Linné*). In Brothwell, D. and Higgs, E.S. (eds) *Science in Archaeology*, 331-358. London, Thames and Hudson.

Bogdanović, M. (1988). Architecture and structural features at Divostin. In McPherron, A. and Srejović N. (eds) *Divostin and the Neolithic of central Serbia*, 35-141. Pittsburg, Department of Anthropology, University of Pittsburg.

Bökönyi, S. (1970). A new method for the determination of the number of individuals in animal bone material. *American Journal of Archaeology* 74 (3), 291-292.

Bökönyi, S. (1973). Stock breeding. In Theocharis, D.R. (ed), *Neolithic Greece*, 165-178. Athens, National Bank of Greece.

Bökönyi, S. (1974). *History of Domestic Mammals in Central and Eastern Europe.* Budapest, Akadémiai.

Bökönyi, S. (1976). The vertebrate fauna from Anza. In M. Gimbutas (ed) *Neolithic Macedonia, as reflected by excavation at Anza, Southeast Yugoslavia* (Monumenta Archaeologica 1), 313-316. Los Angeles, California, Institute of Archaeology, University of California.

Bökönyi, S. (1986). Faunal remains. In Renfrew, C., Gimbutas, M. and Elster, S. (eds) *Excavations at Sitagroi: a prehistoric village in northeastern Greece, Volume 1* (Monumenta Archaeologica 13), 63-132. Los Angeles, California, Institute of Archaeology, University of California.

Bökönyi, S. (1988). The Neolithic fauna of Divostin. In McPherron A. and Srejović, D. (eds) *Divostin and the Neolithic of Central Serbia*, 419-445. Pittsburgh: University of Pittsburgh.

Bökönyi, S. (1989). Animal remains. In Gimbutas, M., Winn, S. and Shimabuku, D. (eds) *Achilleion, a Neolithic Settlement in Thessaly, Greece, 6400-6500 BC*, 315-332. Los Angeles, California, Institute of Archaeology, University of California.

Bökönyi, S. (1990). Tierknochenfunde der Neuesten Ausgrabungen in Vinča. In Srejović, D. and Tasić N. (eds) *Vinča i njen svet. Proceedings of the International Symposium: The Danubian Region from 6000 to 3000 B.C.*, 155-165. Belgrade, Smederevska Palanka Yugoslavia.

Bollongino, R., Elsner, J., Vigne, J.D. and Burger, J. (2008). Y-SNPs do not indicate hybridization between European aurochs and domestic cattle, *PLoS ONE* 3 (10), e3418. doi:10.1371/journal. pone.0003418.

Borojević, K. (2006). *Terra and Silva in the Pannonian Plain: Opovo agro-gathering in the Late Neolithic.* British Archaeological Reports International Series 1563. Oxford, BAR Publishing.

Bosold, K. von (1968). Geschlechts und gattungsunterschiede an metapodien und phalangen mitteleuropäischer wildwiederkäuer. *Säugetierkundliche Mitteilungen* 2, 93-153.

Bradley, D. and Magee, D. (2006). Genetics and the origins of domestic cattle. In Zeder, M., Bradley, D., Emswiller, E. and Smith, B. (eds) *Documenting domestication: new genetic and archaeological paradigms*, 317-328. Berkeley and Los Angeles, California, University of California Press.

Brain, C.K. (1981). *The hunters or the hunted? An introduction to African cave taphonomy.* Chicago, University of Chicago Press.

Bull, G. and Payne, S. (1982). Tooth eruption and epiphysial fusion in pigs and wild boar. In Wilson, B., Grigson, C. and Payne, S. (eds) *Ageing and Sexing Animal Bones from Archaeological Sites*, 55-71. British Archaeological Reports British Series 109. Oxford, BAR Publishing.

Cantuel, J. (2013). Faunal remains from Pigi Athinas, a Late Neolithic settlement in Aegean (Thessaly, Greece). *Haemus Journal* 2, 43-51.

Cantuel, J., Gardeisen, A. and Renard, J. (2008). L'exploitation de la faune durant le Néolithique dans le bassin Égéen. In Vila, E. Gourichon L. Choyke, A. Buitenhuis H. (eds) *Archaeozoology of the Near East VIII*, 279-298. TMO 49, Lyon, Maison de l' orient et de la Méditerranée.

Cauvin, J. (2004). *Naissance des divinités naissance de l'agriculture. La revolution des symbols as Néolithique.* Paris, CNRS.

Cavanagh, W. (1999). Revenons à nos moutons: surface survey and the Peloponnese in the Late and Final Neolithic. In Renard, J. (ed) *Le Pélponnèse: archeologie et histoire*, 31-65. Rennes, Presses Universitaires Rennes.

Chapman, J. (1981). *The Vinča culture of South-East Europe.* British Archaeological Reports International Series 117. Oxford, BAR Publishing.

Chapman, J. (1989). The early Balkan village. *Varia Archaeologica Hungarica* 2, 33-53.

Chernych, E.N. (1978). Ai Bunar, a Balkan copper mine of the fourth Millennium BC. *Proceedings of the Prehistoric Society* 44, 203-217.

Childe, V.G. (1936). *Man Makes Himself*. London, Watts and Co.

Chochadziev, St. (1986). Frühaeneolithische keramik aus der praehistorischen siedlung bei Slatino. *Studia Praehistorica* 8, 185-202.

Christidou, R. (2012). A preliminary study of the bone industries of Limenaria. In Papadopoulos, S. and Malamidou, D. (eds) Δέκα χρόνια ανασκαφικής έρευνας στον προϊστορικό οικισμό Λιμεναρίων Θάσου, 225-274. Hellenic Ministry of Culture (ΥΠΠΟ)-18th Ephorate of Prehistoric and Classical Antiquities (18η ΕΠΚΑ).

Chrysostomou, P. 1991. Γιαννιτσά Β. ΑΕΜΘ 5, 111-125.

Çilingiroglu, Ç. (2005). The concept of 'Neolithic package': considering its meaning and applicability. *Documenta Praehistorica* 32, 1-13.

Clarke, D. (1973). Archaeology: the loss of innocence. *Antiquity* 47, 6-18.

Clutton-Brock, J. (1981). Contribution to discussion. In Mercer, R.J. (ed) *Farming practice in British prehistory*, 218-220. Edinburgh, Edinburgh University Press.

Clutton-Brock, J. (1984). *Excavations at Grimes Graves, Norfolk 1972-1976, Fascicule 1: Neolithic Antler picks from Grimes Graves, Norfolk and Durrington Walls, Wiltshire: A biometrical analysis*. London, British Museum Publications Limited.

Cosmetatou-Phoca, N. (2007). The terrestrial economy of a lake settlement: a preliminary report on the faunal assemblage from the first phase of occupation of Dispilio (Kastoria, Greece). *Anaskamma* 2, 47-68.

Curci, A. and Tagliacozzo, A. (2003). Economic and ecological evidence from the vertebrate remains of the Neolithic site of Makri (Thrace – Greece). In Kotjabopoulou, E., Hamilakis, Y., Halstead, P., Gamble, C. and Elephanti, P. (eds) *Zooarchaeology in Greece. Recent advances*, 123-131. Oxford, British School at Athens Studies 9. *175-176. ΕΜΘ 9μός Μακρy-125. gals in Archaeology: Teeth. Cambridge University Press. alamoti, S.M. Siridis, G. y 22: 99-140. g*

Darcque, P. and Treuil, R. (1997). Un bucrane Néolithique. *Dossier d'Archéologie* 222, 26-27.

Darcque, P., Koukouli-Chrysanthaki, Ch., Malamidou, D., Treuil, R. and Tsirtsoni, Z. (2007). Recent researches at the Neolithic settlement of Dikili-Tash, Eastern Macedonia, Greece: an overview. In Todorova, H., Stefanovic, M. and Ivanov, G. (eds) *The Struma/Strymon river valley in prehistory: proceedings of the International Symposium 'Strymon Praehistoricus', Kjustendil-Blagoevgrad (Bulgaria) and Serres-Amphipolis (Greece)*, 247-256. Sofia, Gerda Henkel Stiftung.

Davis, S.J.M. (1992). *A rapid method for recording information about mammal bones from archaeological sites*. Ancient Monuments Laboratory Report 19/92.

Davis, S.J.M. (1996). Measurements of a group of adult female Shetland sheep skeletons from a single flock: a baseline for zooarchaeologists. *Journal of Archaeological Science* 23, 593-612.

Demoule, J.P. (2004). Les récipients en céramique du Néolithique Récent (Chalcolithique): description, evolution et context regional. In Treuil R. (ed) *Dikili Tash, village préhistorique de Macédoine Orientale, vol. 2*, 63-270. Athènes, Bulletin de Correspondance Hellénique Supplément 37.

Demoule, J.P. and Perlés, C. (1993). The Greek Neolithic: a new review. *Journal of World Prehistory* 7 (4), 355-416.

Demoule, J.P., Gallis, K. and Manolakakis, L. (1998). Transition entre les cultures Néolithiques de Sesklo et de Dimini: les catégories céramiques. *Bulletin de Correspondance Hellénique* CXII, 1-58.

Driesch, A. von den. (1976). *A guide to the measurement of animal bones from archaeological sites*. Cambridge, Massachusetts, Harvard University Peabody Museum.

Driesch, A. von den and Enderle, K. (1976). Die Tiereste aus der Agia Sofi a-Magoula in Thessalien. In Milojcic, V. von den Driesch, A. Enderle, K. Milojcic von Zumbusch J. Kilian K. (eds) *Die deutschen Ausgrabungen auf Magulen um Larisa im Thessalien, 1966: Agia Sofi a-Magula, Karagyos-Magula, Bunar Baschi*, 15-54. Bonn, Rudolf Habelt.

Edwards, C.J., Bollongino, R., Scheu, A., Chamberlain, A. and Tresset, A. (2007), Mitochondrial history of the aurochs (*Bos primigenius primigenius*) in Europe. *Proceedings of the Royal Society B* 274, 1377-1385.

Efstratiou, N., Fumanal, M.P., Ferrer, C., Urem Kotsos, D., Curci, A., Tagliacozzo, A., Stratouli, G., Valamoti, S.M., Ntinou, M., Badal, E., Madella, M. and Skourtopoulou, K. (1998). Excavations at the Neolithic settlement of Makri, Thrace, Greece (1988-1996): a preliminary report. *Saguntum* 31, 11-62.

Evans, R.K. (1986). The pottery of Phase III. In Renfrew, C., Gimbutas, M. and Elster, S. (eds) *Excavations at Sitagroi: a prehistoric village in northeastern Greece, Volume 1* (Monumenta Archaeologica 13), 393-428. Los Angeles, California, Institute of Archaeology, University of California.

Evershed, R.P., Payne, S., Sherratt, A., Copley, M.S., Coolidge, J., Urem-Kotsu, D., Kotsakis, K., Özdoğan, M., Özdoğan, A.E., Nieuwenhuyse, O., Peter Akkermans, M.M.G., Bailey, D., Andeescu, R.R., Campbell, S., Farid, S., Hodder, I., Yalman, N., Özbasaran, M., BIçakcI, E., Garfinkel, Y., Levy T. and Burton, M.M. (2008). Earliest date for milk use in the Near East and southeastern Europe linked to cattle herding. *Nature* 455, 528-531.

Ewbank, J.M., Phillipson, D.W., Whitehouse, R.D. and Higgs, E.S. (1964). Sheep in the Iron Age: a method of study. *Proceedings of the Prehistoric Society* 30, 423-426.

Flannery, K.V. (1972). The origins of the village as a settlement type in Mesoamerica and the Near East. In Ucko, P., Tringham, R. and Dimbleby, D.W. (eds) *Man, settlement and urbanism*, 23-53. London, Duckworth.

Fotiadis, M. (1995). *Economy, ecology and settlement among subsistent farmers in the Serres basin, northeastern Greece 5000-1000 B.C.* Michigan, Ann Arbor University Microfilms International.

Fotiadis, M. (2001). Imagining Macedonia in prehistory, ca. 1900-1930. *Journal of Mediterranean Archaeology* 14, 115-135.

Fotiadis, M., Hondroyianni-Metoki, A., Kalogirou, A. and Ziota, C. (2000). Megalo Nisi Galanis (Kitrini Limni basin) and the Later Neolithic of northwestern Greece. In Hiller, S. and Nikolov, V. (eds) *Karanovo Band III Beiträge zum Neolithikum in Südosteuropa*, 217-228. Wien, Phoibos Verlag.

Gallis, K. (1990). Άτλας προϊστορικών οικισμών της ανατολικής θεσσαλικής πεδιάδας. *Θεσσαλικό Ημερολόγιο* 16, 16-144.

Gallis, K. (1996). Ο Νεολιθικός κόσμος. In Papathanasopoulos (ed) *Νεολιθικός πολιτισμός στην Ελλάδα*, 23-37. Αθήνα, Μουσείο Κυκλαδικής τέχνης.

Gejvall N.G. (1969). *Lerna, a Pre-classical site in the Argolid: Results of excavations conducted by the American School of Classical Studies at Athens. Vol. I: The Fauna.* Princeton N.J., American School of Classical Studies.

Gilchrist, M. and Mytum, H. (1986). Experimental archaeology and burnt animal bone from archaeological sites. *Circaea* 4, 29-38.

Gilman, A. (1981). The development of social stratification in Bronze Age Europe. *Current Anthropology* 22, 1-23.

Gimbutas, M. (1991). *The civilization of the goddess: the world of Old Europe.* San Francisco, J. Marler.

Gorczyk, J.M. (2013). *Communal consumption at Late Neolithic Sarnevo: faunal evidence from a pit site in central Bulgaria.* USA, Cornell University.

Götherström, A., Anderung, C., Hellborg, L., Elburg, R. and Smith, C. (2005). Cattle domestication in the Near East was followed by hybridization with aurochs bulls in Europe. *Proceedings of the Royal Society B* 272, 2345-2350.

Grammenos, D.V. (1991). Νεολιθικές έρευνες στη κεντρική και ανατολική Μακεδονία. Αθήνα, Αρχαιολογική Εταιρεία, Αρ. 117.

Grammenos, D.V. (1997). Κεφάλαιο Ε': Φυσική και ανθρώπινη οικολογία. In Grammenos, D.V. (ed) Νεολιθική Μακεδονία, 317-346. Δημοσιεύματα του Αρχαιολογικού Δελτίου, Αθήνα, ΤΑΠΑ.

Grammenos, D.V. and Kotsos, S. (2001). Ανασκαφή προϊστορικού οικισμού Νεώτερης Νεολιθικής και πρώιμης εποχής του Σιδήρου στο λόφο της Αγίας Λυδίας Ασπροβάλτας. Μακεδονικά 32, 393-441.

Grammenos, D.V. and Kotsos, S. (2002). Σωστικές ανασκαφές στο Νεολιθικό οικισμό Σταυρούπολης Θεσσαλονίκης. Θεσσαλονίκη, Αρχαιολογικό Ινστιτούτο Βορείου Ελλάδος.

Grammenos, D.V. and Kotsos, S. (2004). Σωστικές ανασκαφές στο Νεολιθικό οικισμό Σταυρούπολης Θεσσαλονίκης Μέρος ΙΙ (1998-2003). Θεσσαλονίκη, Αρχαιολογικό Ινστιτούτο Βορείου Ελλάδος.

Grammenos, D.V., Pappa, M., Ourem-Kotsou, D., Skourtopoulou, K., Giannouli, E., Maragou, Ch., Valamoti, S.M., Siridis, G., Marki, E. and Christidou, R. (1989). Ανασκαφή Νεολιθικού οικισμού Θέρμης Β και Βυζαντινής εγκατάστασης παρά τον προϊστορικό οικισμό Θέρμη Α: Ανασκαφική περίοδος 1989. Μακεδονικά 28, 381-501.

Grant, A. (1982). The use of tooth wear as a guide to the age of domestic ungulates. In Wilson, B., Grigson, C. and Payne, S. (eds) *Ageing and Sexing animal bones from archaeological sites*, 91-108. British Archaeological Reports British Series 109. Oxford, BAR Publishing.

Grayson, D.K. (1984). *Quantitative zooarchaeology.* New York, Academic Press.

Greenfield, H. (1986). *The Paleoeconomy of the Central Balkans (Serbia).* British Archaeological Reports International Series 304. Oxford, BAR Publishing.

Greenfield, H. (1988). Bone consumption by pigs in a contemporary Serbian village: implications for the interpretation of prehistoric faunal assemblages. *Journal of Field Archaeology* 15, 473-479.

Greenfield, H. (1991). Fauna from the Late Neolithic of the central Balkans: issues in subsistence and land use. *Journal of Field Archaeology* 18, 161-186.

Greenfield, H. (1999). The origins of metallurgy: distinguishing stone from metal cut marks on bones from archaeological sites. *Journal of Archaeological Science* 26, 797-808.

Greenfield, H. (2005). A reconsideration of the secondary products revolution in southeastern Europe: on the origins and use of domestic animals for milk, wool and traction in the central Balkans. In Mulville J. and Outram, A.K. (eds) *The zooarchaeology of fats, oils, milk and dairying*, 14-31. Oxford, Oxbow.

Greenfield, H. and Fowler, K. (2003). Megalo Nisi Galanis and the secondary products revolution in Macedonia. In Kotjabopoulou, E. Hamilakis, Y. Halstead, P. Gamble, C. Elephanti, P. (eds) *Zooarchaeology in Greece. Recent advances*, 133-143. Oxford, British School at Athens Studies 9.

Greenfield, H. and Fowler, K. (2005). *The secondary products revolution in Macedonia. The zooarchaeo-*

logical remains from Megalo Nisi Galanis, a Late Neolithic-Early Bronze Age site in Greek Macedonia. British Archaeological Reports International Series 1414. Oxford, BAR Publishing.

Gromova, V. (1950). Opredelitelj mlekopitajuščih SSSR po kostjam skeleta v.1: opredelitelj po krupnim trubčastim kostjam. *Trudi komisii poizučeniju četvertičnovo perioda, Moscow, Akademija nauk SSSR,* 1-105.

Gromova, V. (1960). Opredelitelj mlekopitajuščih SSSR po kostjam skeleta, v.2: opredelitelj po krupnim kostjam zapljusni. *Trudi Komisii po izučeniju četvertičnovo perioda, Moscow: Akademija nauk SSSR,* 1-116.

Halstead, P. (1989a). Like raising damp? An ecological approach to the spread of farming in southeast and central Europe. In Milles, A., Williams, D. and Gardner, N. (eds) *The beginnings of Agriculture, Symposia of the Association for Environmental Archaeology* No. 8, 23-53. British Archaeological Reports International Series 496. Oxford, BAR Publishing.

Halstead, P. (1989b). The economy has a normal surplus: economic stability and social change among early farming communities of Thessaly, Greece. In Halstead, P. and O'Shea, J. (eds) *Bad year economics,* 68-80. Cambridge, Cambridge University Press.

Halstead, P. (1990). Present to past in the Pindhos: diversification and specialization in mountain economies, *Rivista di Studi Liguri* 1-4, 61-80.

Halstead P. (1992). Dimini and the 'DMP': faunal remains and animal exploitation in late Neolithic Thessaly. *Annual of the British School of Athens* 87, 29-59.

Halstead, P. (1994). The north-south divide: regional paths to complexity in prehistoric Greece. In Hodder, I., Isaac, G. and Hammond, N. (eds) *Pattern of the past: studies in honor of David Clarke,* 195-219. Cambridge, Cambridge University Press.

Halstead, P. (1995). Plough and power: the economic and social significance of cultivation with the ox-drawn ard in the Mediterranean. *Bulletin of Sumerian Agriculture* 8, 11-22.

Halstead, P. (1996). Pastoralism or household herding? Problems of scale and specialization in early Greek animal husbandry. *World Archaeology* 28, 20-42.

Halstead, P. (1998). Mortality models and milking: problems of uniformitarianism, optimality and equifinality reconsidered. *Anthropozoologica* 27, 3-20.

Halstead, P. (1999). Neighbours from hell? The household in Neolithic Greece. In Halstead, P. (ed) *Neolithic society in Greece,* 77-95. Sheffield, Sheffield Academic Press.

Halstead, P. (2000). Land use in postglacial Greece: cultural causes and environmental effects. In Halstead, P. and Frederick, C. (eds) *Sheffield studies in Aegean Archaeology: Landscape and land use in postglacial Greece,* 110-128. Sheffield, Sheffield Academic Press.

Halstead, P. (2002). Agropastoral land use and landscape in later prehistoric Greece. In Badal, E., Bernabeu, J. and Martí, B. (eds) *Neolithic landscapes of the Mediterranean, Saguntum Papeles del laboratorio de Arqueología de Valencia,* 105-113. Universitat de Valencia, Department de Prehistoria I d'Arqueologia.

Halstead, P. (2005). Resettling the Neolithic: faunal evidence for seasons of consumption and residence at Neolithic sites in Greece. In Bailey, D., Whittle, A. and Cummings, V. (eds) *(Un)settling the Neolithic,* 38-50. Oxford, Oxbow.

Halstead, P. (2006). Sheep in the garden: the integration of crop and livestock husbandry in early farming regimes of Greece and southern Europe. In Serjeantson, D. and Field, D. (eds) *Animals in the Neolithic of Britain and Europe,* 42-55. Oxford, Oxbow.

Halstead, P. (2007). Carcasses and commensality: investigating the social context of meat consumption in Neolithic and Early Bronze Age Greece. In Mee, C. and Renard, J. (eds), *Cooking up the Past: food and culinary practices in the Neolithic and Bronze Age Aegean,* 25-48. Oxford, Oxbow.

Halstead, P. (2011). Farming, material culture and ideology: repackaging the Neolithic of Greece (and Europe). In Hadjikoumis, A., Robinson, E. and Viner, S. (eds) *Dynamics of Neolithisation in Europe: studies in honor of Andrew Sherratt,* 131-151. Oxford and Oakville, Oxbow.

Halstead, P. and Isaakidou, V. (2013). Early stock-keeping in Greece. In Colledge, S., Conolly, J., Dobney, K., Manning, K. and Shennan, S. (eds) *The origins and spread of domestic animals in southwest Asia and Europe,* 129-143. Walnut Creek, California, Left Coast Press.

Halstead, P. and O'Shea, J. (1989). *Bad Year economics: cultural responses to risk and uncertainty.* Cambridge, Cambridge University Press.

Halstead, P., Collins, P. and Isaakidou, V. (2002). Sorting the sheep from the goats: morphological distinctions between the mandibles and mandibular teeth of adult *Ovis* and *Capra. Journal of Archaeological Science* 29, 545-553.

Hamilakis, Y. (1999). The anthropology of food and drink consumption and Aegean archaeology. In Vaughan, S. and Coulson, W. (eds) *Palaeodiet in the Aegean,* 55-63. Oxford, Oxbow.

Hamilakis, Y. (2003). The sacred geography of hunting: wild animals, social power and gender in early farming societies. In Kotjabopoulou, E., Hamilakis, Y., Halstead, P., Gamble, C. and Elephanti, P. (eds) *Zooarchaeology in Greece. Recent advances,* 239-247. Oxford, British School at Athens Studies 9.

Hänsel, B., Schulz, H.D. and Willkomm, H. (1989). *Kastanas: ausgrabungen in einem siedlungshügel der Bronze und eisenzeit Makedoniens 1975-1979. Die grabung und der baubefund.* Berlin, Wissenschaftsverlag Volker Spiess.

Hart, R.H., Bissio, J., Samuel, M.J. and Waggoner, J.R. (1993). Grazing systems, pasture size and cattle grazing behavior, distribution and gains. *Journal of Range Management* 46, 81-87.

Hatting, T. (1974). The influence of castration on sheep bones. In Clason, A. (ed) *Archaeozoological studies*, 345-351. Elsevier, Amsterdam.

Hauptmann, H. and Milojcic, V. (1969). *Die funde der frühen Dimini-Zeit aus der Arapi-Magoula in Thessalien. Beiträgen zur ur und frühgeschichtlichen Arcäologie des Mittelmeer-Kulturraumes 9.* Bonn, Rudolf Habelt.

Helmer, D. (1997). Dikili Tash à l'époque Néolithique : faune sauvage et domestique. *Dossiers d'Archéologie* 222, 40-41.

Helmer, D. and Rocheteau, M. (1994). *Atlas du squelette appendiculaire des principaux genres Holocenes de petits Ruminant du Nord de la Mediterranee et du Proche Orient (Capra, Ovis, Rupicapra, Capreolus, Gazella).* Juan-les-Pins, Editions APDCA.

Helmer, D., Gourichon, L., Maamar, H.S. and Vigne, J.D. (2005). L'élevage des caprinés Néolithiques dans le sudest de la France: saisonnalité, des abattages, relations entre grottes-bergeries et sites de plein air. *Anthropozoologica* 40, 167-189.

Helmer, D., Gourichon, L. and Vila, E. (2007). The development of the exploitation of products from *Capra* and *Ovis* (meat, milk and fleece) from the PPNB to the Early Bronze in the northern Near East (8700-2000 BC Cal). *Anthropozoologica* 42, 41-69.

Heurtley, W.A. (1939). *Prehistoric Macedonia: An archaeological reconnaissance of Greek Macedonia (west of the Struma) in the Neolithic, Bronze, and Early Iron Ages.* Cambridge, Cambridge University Press.

Higgs, E.S. (1962). Fauna. In Rodden, R.J. (ed) *Excavations at the Early Neolithic site at Nea Nikomidia, Greek Macedonia (1961 season)*, 267-288. Proceedings of the Prehistoric Society 28.

Hiller, S. (1989). Neue ausgrabungen in Karanovo. In Srejovic, D. and Tasic N. (eds) *Vinča and its world. International symposium: The Danubian region from 6000 to 3000 B.C.*, 197-206. Belgrade, Smederevska Palanka.

Hillson, S. (1986). Teeth. Cambridge, Cambridge University Press.

Hillson, S. (1992). *Mammal bones and teeth: an introductory guide to methods of identification.* London, University College London Institute of Archaeology.

Hodder, I. (1990). *The Domestication of Europe: structure and contingency in Neolithic Europe.* Oxford, Blackwell.

Hondrogianni-Metoki, A. (2001). Εγνατία Οδός: ανασκαφή στη θέση Τούμπα Κρεμαστής Κοιλάδας Νομού Κοζάνης, ΑΕΜΘ 13, 399-413.

Hongo, H., Anezaki, T., Yamazaki, K., Takahashi, O. and Sugawara, H. (2007). Hunting or management? The status of *Sus* in the Jomon period in Japan. In Albarella, U. Dobney, K. Ervynck, A. Rowley-Conwy, P. (eds) *Pigs and humans: 10.000 years of interaction*, 109-130. Oxford, Oxford University Press.

Hourmouziadis, G. (1973). Burial costums. In Theocharis (ed) *Neolithic Greece*, 210-212. Athens, National Bank of Greece.

Hourmouziadis, G. (1996). *Το Δισπηλιό Καστοριάς.* Θεσσαλονίκη, Κώδικας.

Hourmouziadis, G. (2002). *The prehistoric research in Greece and its perspectives: theoretical and methodological considerations.* Thessaloniki, University Studio Press.

Iliev, N. and Spasov, N. (2007). Promachon-Topolniča: comparative study of the domestic and wild animals from sector Topolniča. In Todorova, H., Stefanovic, M. and Ivanov, G. (eds) *The Struma/Strymon river valley in prehistory: proceedings of the International Symposium 'Strymon Praehistoricus', Kjustendil-Blagoevgrad (Bulgaria) and Serres-Amphipolis (Greece)*, 509-521. Sofia, Gerda Henkel Stiftung.

Ingold, T. (1980). *Hunters, pastoralists and ranchers.* Cambridge, Cambridge University Press.

Isaakidou, V. (2006). Ploughing with cows: Knossos and the Secondary Products Revolution. In Serjeantson, D. and Field, D. (eds) *Animals in the Neolithic of Britain and Europe*, 95-112. Oxford, Oxbow.

Johanssen, N.N. (2005). Paleopathology and Neolithic cattle traction: methodological issues and archaeological perspectives. In Davis, J., Fabiš, M., Mainland, I., Richards, M. and Thomas, R. (eds) *Diet and health in past animal populations: current research and future directions (Proceedings of the 9th Conference of the International Council of Archaeozoology, Durham August 2002)*, 39-51. Oxford, Oxbow.

Johnson, M. (1996). Water, animals and animal technology: a study of settlement patterns and economic change in Neolithic southern Greece. *Oxford Journal of Archaeology* 15, 267-295.

Johnstone, C. and Albarella, U. (2002). *The Late Iron Age and Romano-British mammal and bird bone assemblage from Elms Farm, Heybridge, Essex (Site Code: HYEF93-95).* Centre for Archaeology Report 45/2002.

Johnstone, C. and Albarella, U. (2015). The Late Iron Age and Romano-British mammal and bird bone assemblage from Elms Farm, Heybridge, Essex. In Atkinson, M. Preston, S.J. (eds.) *Heybridge: A Late Iron Age and Roman Settlement, Excavations at Elms Farm 1993-5.* Internet Archaeology 40. http://dx.doi.org/10.11141/ia.40.1.albarella

Jordan B. (1975). *Die Tierknochenfunde aus der Magula Pevkakia in Thessalien.* Inaugural Dissertation, München, Ludwig Maximilians Universität.

Jovanović, B. (1980). The origins of copper mining in Europe. *Scientific American* 242 (5), 152–167.

Julien, R. (1992). Les moyens de subsistance: Les faunes domestique et sauvage. In Treuil R. (ed) *Dikili Tash, village préhistorique de Macédoine orientale, I. Fouilles de Jean Deshayes (1961-1975),* vol. 1, 147-153. Athènes, Bulletin de Correspondance Hellénique Supplément 25.

Karamitrou-Mentesidi, G. (2014). Περί προϊστορικών θέσεων στη Δυτική Μακεδονία: νομοί Κοζάνης και Γρεβενών. In Stefani, E., Merousis, N. and Dimoula, A. (eds) *A Century of research in Prehistoric Macedonia, proceedings of the International Conference,* 233-250. Thessaloniki, Archaeological Museum of Thessaloniki.

Karamitrou-Mentesidi, G., Efstratiou, N., Kaczanowska, M. and Koslowski, J.K. (2013). Early Neolithic settlement of Mavropigi in western Greek Macedonia. *Eurasian Prehistory* 12 (1-2), 47-116.

Karamitrou-Mentesidi, G., Lokana, H. and Anagnostopoulou, A. (2014). Δύο θέσεις της αρχαιότερης και μέσης Νεολιθικής στην Ποντοκώμη και Μαυροπηγή Εορδαίας. *AEMΘ* 2014, 39-52.

Kazantzis, G. (2009). *The faunal remains from the Greek sector of the Late Neolithic settlement of Promachon-Topolniča.* Unpublished Masters dissertation, University of Sheffield.

Kazantzis, G. (2014a). Preliminary results from a faunal assemblage in Greek central Macedonia: the case of the Late Neolithic Promachon sector, *Assemblage (Proceedings of the Postgraduate Zooarchaeology Conference, Sheffield, 2-4 November 2012),* 19-31.

Kazantzis, G. (2014b). The Vertebrate Fauna from a Late Neolithic settlement in eastern Macedonia: the case of Promachon Sector – preliminary results. In Stefani, E., Merousis, N. and Dimoula, A. (eds) *A Century of research in Prehistoric Macedonia, proceedings of the International Conference,* 437-451. Thessaloniki, Archaeological Museum of Thessaloniki.

Kazantzis, G. (2017). Animal husbandry and the use of space in the Greek sector of the Late Neolithic settlement of Promachonas- Topolniča. In Sarris, A., Kalogiropoulou, E., Kalayci, T. and Karimali, L. (eds) *Communities, Landscape and Interaction in Neolithic Greece, Proceedings of the International Conference Rethymno 29ᵗʰ 30ᵗʰ May 2015,* 291-315. International Monographs in Prehistory, Archaeological Series 20.

Kazantzis, G. and Albarella, U. (2016). Size and shape of Greek Late Neolithic livestock suggest the existence of multiple and distinctive animal husbandry cultures. *Journal of Archaeological Science: Reports* 9, 630-645.

Keighley, J.M. (1986). The pottery of Phases I and II. In Renfrew, C., Gimbutas, M. and Elster, S. (eds) *Excavations at Sitagroi: a prehistoric village in northeastern Greece, Volume 1* (Monumenta Archaeologica 13), 345-392. Los Angeles, California, Institute of Archaeology, University of California.

Kierdorf, H., Zeiler, J. and Kierdorf, U. (2006). Problems and pitfalls in the diagnosis of linear enamel hypoplasia in cheek teeth of cattle. *Journal of Archaeological Science* 33, 1-6.

Klein, R.G. and Cruz-Uribe, K. (1984). *The analysis of animal bones from archaeological sites.* Chicago, University of Chicago Press.

Kostov, D. (2006). Domestic and wild animals from the Neolithic period in the 'Azmaschka' settlement hill near Stara Zagora. *Trakia Journal of Sciences* 4, 55-60.

Kotjabopoulou, E., Hamilakis, Y., Halstead, P., Gamble, C. and Elephanti, P. (2003). *Zooarchaeology in Greece. Recent advances.* Oxford, British School at Athens Studies 9.

Kotsakis, K. (1999). What Tells can tell: social space and settlement in the Greek Neolithic. In Halstead, P. (ed) *Neolithic society in Greece,* 67-76. Sheffield, Sheffield Academic Press.

Kotsakis, K. (2002). Εισαγωγή. In Hodder, I. (ed) Διαβάζοντας το παρελθόν, 15-24. Αθήνα, Εκδόσεις του Εικοστού Πρώτου.

Kotsos, S. (1992). Ανασκαφή Νεολιθικού οικισμού Δροσιάς Έδεσσας. AEMΘ 6, 195-202.

Kotsos, S. and Urem-Kotsou, D. (2016). Langadas basin and the Neolithic settlement of Mikri Volvi. In Bacvarov, K. and Gleser, R. (eds) *Southeast Europe and Anatolia in prehistory, essays in honour of Vassil Nikolov on his 65ᵗʰ anniversary,* 117-129. Verlag Dr. Rudolf Hambelt, Gmbh, Bonn.

Koukouli-Chrysanthaki, Ch. (2000). Προϊστορικός οικισμός Προμαχώνας-Topolniča. *Αρχαιολογικόν Δελτίον* 50, 627-629.

Koukouli-Chrysanthaki, Ch. (2006). The Neolithic and Bronze Age of Eastern Macedonia: A review of the recent archaeological research. In Tasić N. Grozdanov C. (eds) *Homage to Milutin Garašanin,* 469-487. Belgrade, Serbian Academy for Science and Arts.

Koukouli-Chrysanthaki, Ch. and Basiakos, I. (2002). Non-slagging copper production of 5ᵗʰ millennium: the evidence from the Neolithic settlement of Promachon-Topolniča (eastern Macedonia, Greece). In: *8ᵗʰ EAA Annual Meeting 24-29 September 2002,* 193-194. Thessaloniki, Abstracts book.

Koukouli-Chrysanthaki, Ch., Aslanis, I. and Konstantopoulou, F. (1992). Προμαχώνας-Topolniča : Ένα πρόγραμμα ελληνοβουλγαρικής συνεργασίας. AEMΘ 6, 561-575.

Koukouli-Chrysanthaki, Ch., Aslanis, I. and Konstantopoulou, F. (1993). Προμαχώνας-Topolniča : Ελληνοβουλγαρικές έρευνες στον προϊστορικό οικισμό. ΑΕΜΘ 7, 505-512.

Koukouli-Chrysanthaki, Ch., Aslanis, I., Konstantopoulou, F. and Valla, M. (1995). Ανασκαφή στον προϊστορικό οικισμό Προμαχώνας-Topolniča κατά το 1995. ΑΕΜΘ 9, 435-439.

Koukouli-Chrysanthaki, Ch., Todorova, H., Aslanis, I., Bojadziev, J., Konstantopoulou, F., Vajsov, I. and Valla, M. (1996). Προμαχώνας- Topolniča: Νεολιθικός οικισμός ελληνοβουλγαρικών συνόρων. ΑΕΜΘ 10β, 745-767.

Koukouli-Chrysanthaki, Ch., Todorova, H., Aslanis, I., Bojadziev, J., Konstantopoulou, F., Vajsov, I., Valla, M. and Draganov, M. (1997). Promachonas-Topolniča settlement: program of Greek-Bulgarian cooperation. *10 Χρόνια Αρχαιολογικό Έργο στη Μακεδονία και στη Θράκη*, 123-127.

Koukouli-Chrysanthaki, Ch., Todorova, H., Aslanis, I. and Bojadziev, J. (1998a). Προμαχώνας-Topolniča: Πρόγραμμα ελληνοβουλγαρικής συνεργασίας. In Δήμος Σερρών (ed.), Οι Σέρρες και η Περιοχή τους απο την Αρχαία στη Μεταβυζαντινή Κοινωνία, Πρακτικά Συνεδρίου, Α' Τόμος, 7-24. Δήμος Σερρών.

Koukouli-Chrysanthaki, Ch., Aslanis, I., Konstantopoulou, F. and Valla, M. (1998b). Ανασκαφή νεολιθικού οικισμού Προμαχώνα-Topolniča. ΑΕΜΘ 12, 67-76.

Koukouli-Chrysanthaki, Ch., Aslanis, I., Konstantopoulou, F. and Valla, M. (1999). Ανασκαφή στον προϊστορικό οικισμό Προμαχώνας- Topolniča κατά το 1999. ΑΕΜΘ 13, 111-116.

Koukouli-Chrysanthaki, Ch., Aslanis, I. and Valla, M. (2000). Προμαχώνας-Topolniča 2000. ΑΕΜΘ 14, 88-98.

Koukouli-Chrysanthaki, Ch., Aslanis, I. and Valla, M. (2001). Προμαχώνας-Topolniča 2001. ΑΕΜΘ 15, 75-82.

Koukouli-Chrysanthaki, Ch., Aslanis, I., Vajsov, I. and Valla, M. (2003). Προμαχώνας-Topolniča 2002-2003. ΑΕΜΘ 17, 91-110.

Koukouli-Chrysanthaki, Ch., Todorova, H., Aslanis, I., Vajsov, I. and Valla, M. (2007). Promachon-Topolniča: a Greek-Bulgarian archaeological project. In Todorova, H., Stefanovic, M. and Ivanov, G. (eds) *The Struma/Strymon river valley in prehistory: proceedings of the International Symposium 'Strymon Praehistoricus', Kjustendil-Blagoevgrad (Bulgaria) and Serres-Amphipolis (Greece)*, 43-78. Sofia, Gerda Henkel Stiftung.

Koukouli-Chrysanthaki, Ch., Todorova, H., Aslanis, I., Vajsov, I. and Valla, M. (2014). Γεωφυσική Έρευνα και Αρχαιολογική Πραγματικότητα στο Νεολιθικό Οικισμό Προμαχών-Topolniča. In Stefani, E Merousis, N. Dimoula, A. (eds) *A Century of research in Prehistoric Macedonia, proceedings of the International Conference*, 251-260. Thessaloniki, Archaeological Museum of Thessaloniki.

Kratochvil, Z. (1969). Species criteria on the distal section of the tibia in *Ovis ammon f. aries L.* and *Capra aegagrus f. hircus L. Acta Veterinaria (Brno)* 38, 483-490.

Larje, R. (1987). Animal bones. In Hellstrom, P. (ed) *Para ddeisos: a Late Neolithic settlement in Aegean Thrace*, 89-118. Stockholm, Medelhavsmuseet (Memoir 7).

Larsson, G., Albarella, U., Dobney, K., Rowley-Conwy, P., Schibler, J., Tresset, A., Vigne, J.D., Edwards, C.J., Schlumbaum, A., Dinu, A., Bălăçsescu, A., Dolman, G., Tagliacozzo, A., Manaseryan, N., Miracle, P., Van Wijngaarden-Bakker, L., Masseti, M., Daniel, G., Bradley, D. and Cooper, A. (2007). Ancient DNA, pig domestication, and the spread of the Neolithic into Europe. *Proceedings of National Academy of Sciences USA* 104, 15276-15281.

Lazić, M. (1988). Fauna of mammals from the Neolithic settlements in Serbia. In Srejović, D. (ed) *The Neolithic of Serbia. Archaeological research 1948-1988*, 24-38. Belgrade, University of Belgrade, Faculty of Philosophy, Centre for Archaeological Research.

Legakis, A. and Marangou, P. (2009). *Red data book of threatened animals of Greece*. Athens, Zoological Museum, University of Athens.

Legge, A. and Moore, A. (2011). Clutching at straw: the Early Neolithic of Croatia and the dispersal of agriculture. In Hadjikoumis, A. Robinson, E. Viner, S. (eds) *Dynamics of Neolithisation in Europe: studies in honor of Andrew Sherratt*, 176-195. Oxford and Oakville, Oxbow.

Lespez, L., Tsirtsoni, Z., Darcque, P., Koukouli-Chrysanthaki, Ch., Malamidou, D., Treuil, R., Davidson, R., Kourtesi-Philippakis, G. and Oberlin, Ch. (2013). The lowest levels at Dikili Tash, northern Greece: a missing link in the Early Neolithic of Europe. *Antiquity* 87, 30-45.

Lister, A.M. (1996). The Morphological distinction between bones and teeth of fallow deer (*Dama dama*) and red deer (*Cervus elaphus*). *International Journal of Osteoarchaeology* 6, 119-143.

Lyman, R.L. (1994). *Vertebrate Taphonomy*. Cambridge, Cambridge University Press.

Mainland, I. and Halstead, P. (2002). The diet and management of domestic sheep and goats at Neolithic Makriyalos. In Davies, J. and Fabis, M. (eds) *Diet and health in past animal populations. Proceedings of the 9th ICAZ Conference, Durham 2002*, 104-111. Oxford, Oxbow.

Malamidou, D. (1996). *L'habitat et l'architecture du Néolithique Moyen en Macédoine Orientale. Le cas Limenaria (Thasos)*. Mémoire de DEA, Paris, Université de Paris I.

Malamidou, D. (1997). Ανασκαφή στον προϊστορικό οικισμό 'Κρυονέρι' Ν. Κερδυλλίων. *ΑΕΜΘ* 11, 509-538.

Malamidou, D. (2006). Στρωματογραφία, οργάνωση και χρήση του χώρου στον προϊστορικό οικισμό Λιμεναρίων. In Papadopoulos, S. Malamidou, D. (eds) Δέκα χρόνια ανασκαφικής έρευνας στον προϊστορικό οικισμό Λιμεναρίων Θάσου, 107-148. Hellenic Ministry of Culture (ΥΠΠΟ)-18th Ephorate of Prehistoric and Classical Antiquities (18η ΕΠΚΑ).

Malamidou, D. (2007). Kryoneri: a Neolithic and Early Bronze Age Settlement in the Lower Strymon Valley. In Todorova, H., Stefanovic, M. and Ivanov, G. (eds) *The Struma/Strymon river valley in prehistory: proceedings of the International Symposium 'Strymon Praehistoricus', Kjustendil-Blagoevgrad (Bulgaria) and Serres-Amphipolis (Greece)*, 297-308. Sofia, Gerda Henkel Stiftung.

Malamidou, D. (2016). Kryoneri, Nea Kerdyllia: a settlement of the Late Neolithic and Early Bronze Age on the lower Strymon valley, eastern Macedonia. In Tsirtsoni, Z. (ed) *The Human face of Radiocarbon: Reassessing chronology in prehistoric Greece and Bulgaria 5000-3000 Cal. BC*, 299-315. TMO 69, Lyon, Maison de l' orient et de la Méditerranée.

Malamidou, D. and Papadopoulos, S. (1993). Ανασκαφική έρευνα στον προϊστορικό οικισμό Λιμεναρίων Θάσου. ΑΕΜΘ 7, 559-572.

Maniatis, I. and Fakorellis, G. (2000). Αποτελέσματα ραδιοχρονολόγησης δειγμάτων απο τον Προμαχώνα-Topolnica. ΑΕΜΘ 14, 93.

Maniatis, I., Gogidou, K. and Kyriazi, M. (2004). Αποτελέσματα ραδιοχρονολόγησης δειγμάτων απο τον Προμαχώνα-Topolnica. ΑΕΜΘ 17, 101.

Maniatis, I., Kotsakis, K. and Halstead, P. (2015). Παλιάμπελα Κολινδρού: νέες χρονολογήσεις της αρχαιότερης Νεολιθικής στη Μακεδονία. *ΑΕΜΘ* 25, 149-156.

McCormick, F. (1992). Early faunal evidence for dairying. *Oxford Journal of Archaeology* 11, 210-209.

McGee, H. (1988). *On food and cooking: the science and lore of the kitchen.* New York, Collier.

Mlekuz, D. (2009). The materiality of dung: the manipulation of dung in Neolithic Mediterranean caves. *Documenta Praehistorica* 36, 219-225.

Munson, P.J. and Garniewicz, R.C. (2003). Age-mediated survivorship of ungulate mandibles and teeth in canid-ravaged faunal assemblages. *Journal of Archaeological Science* 30, 405-416.

Mylona, D. (1997). Παράρτημα: Οστά ζώων απο τα Νεολιθικά στρώματα του Κρυονερίου Σερρών, προκαταρκτική παρουσίαση. ΑΕΜΘ 11, 523-538.

Mylona, D. (2003). Archaeological fish remains in Greece: general trends of the research and a gazetteer of sites. In Kotjabopoulou, E., Hamilakis, Y., Halstead, P., Gamble, C. and Elephanti, P. (eds) *Zooarchaeology in Greece. Recent advances*, 193-200. Oxford, British School at Athens Studies 9.

Mylonas, G. (1941). The site of Akropotamos and the Neolithic period of Macedonia. *American Journal of Archaeology* 45, 557-576.

Mylonas, G. and Bakallakis, G. (1938). Ανάσκαφα νεολιθικού συνοικισμού Ακροποτάμου και Πολυστύλου. Πρακτικά, 103-106.

Nicholson, R.A. (1993). A morphological investigation of burnt animal bone and an evaluation of its utility in archaeology. *Journal of Archaelogical Science* 20, 411-428.

Nikolov, B. (1976). Gradesniča, *Acta Archaeologica Hungarica* 18, 22-54.

O'Connor, T. (1988). *Bones from the general accident site, Tanner Row.* London, Council for British Archaeology.

Orton, D.C. (2008). *Beyond hunting and herding: humans, animals and the political economy of the Vinča period.* Unpublished PhD Thesis, Cambridge, Faculty of Archaeology and Anthropology, University of Cambridge.

Orton, D., Gaastra, J. and Vander Linden, M. (2016). Between the Danube and the deep blue sea: Zooarchaeolgical meta-analysis reveals variability in the spread and development of the Neolithic farming across the western Balkans. *Open Quaternary* 2 (6), 1-26. http://dx.doi.org/10.5334/oq.28

Outram, A.K. (2002). Bone fracture and within-bone nutrients: an experimentally based method for investigating levels of marrow extraction. In Miracle, P. Milner, N. (eds) *Consuming Passions and Patterns of Consumption*, 51-63. Cambridge, McDonald Institute Monographs.

Özdoğan, M. (2001). Redefining the Neolithic of Anatolia: A Critical Overview. In Cappers, R.T.G. Bottema, S. (eds), *The dawn of farming in the Near East: studies in Early Near Eastern production, subsistence and environment*, 155-161. Berlin, Ex oriente.

Pales, L. and Lambert, C. (1971). *Atlas Ostéologique pour servir à l' identification des Mammiféres du Quaternaire.* Paris, Editions du Centre de la Recherche Scientifique Paris VII.

Pantelidou-Gofa, M. (1991). Η Νεολιθική Νέα Μάκρη: τα οικοδομικά. *Πρακτικά Αρχαιολογικής Εταιρείας* 119, 22-120.

Papadopoulos, S. and Malamidou, D. (2012). Δέκα χρόνια ανασκαφικής έρευνας στον προϊστορικό οικισμό Λιμεναρίων Θάσου. Hellenic Ministry of Culture (ΥΠΠΟ)-18th Ephorate of Prehistoric and Classical Antiquities (18η ΕΠΚΑ).

Papanthimou, A. and Papasteriou, A. (1993). Ο προϊστορικός οικισμός στο Μάνδαλο: νέα στοιχεία στη προϊστορία της Μακεδονίας. Αρχαία Μακεδονία 5, 1207-1216.

Papathanasopoulos, G.A. (1996). Νεολιθικός πολιτισμός στην Ελλάδα. Αθήνα, Μουσείο Κυκλαδικής τέχνης.

Pappa, M. (1993). *Στοιχεία για την οργάνωση του χώρου στη κοιλάδα των Βασιλικών, Αρχαία Μακεδονία, Πέμπτο Διεθνές Συμπόσιο Τόμος 2,* 1225-1238, Θεσσαλονίκη, Ίδρυμα Μελετών Χερσονήσου του Αίμου.

Pappa, M. (1999). Η οργάνωση του χώρου στους Νεολιθικούς *οικισμούς της βόρειας Πιερίας. Αρχαία Μακεδονία Έκτο Διεθνές Συμπόσιο Τόμος 2,* 873-876, Θεσσαλονίκη, Ίδρυμα Μελετών Χερσονήσου του Αίμου

Pappa, M. (2008). *Οργάνωση του χώρου και οικιστικά στοιχεία στους Νεολιθικούς οικισμούς της κεντρικής Μακεδονίας ΔΕΘ-Θέρμη-Μακρύγιαλος.* Unpublished PhD Thesis, Αριστοτέλειο Πανεπιστήμιο Θεσσαλονίκης.

Pappa, M. and Besios, M. (1995). Νεολιθικός οικισμός Μακρυγιάλου. ΑΕΜΘ 9, 175-176.

Pappa, M. and Besios, M. (1998). Ο Νεολιθικός οικισμός στο Μακρύγιαλο Πιερίας. Αρχαιολογικά Ανάλεκτα εξ' Αθηνών 23-28 (1990-1995), 13-30.

Pappa, M. and Besios, M. (1999). The Neolithic settlement at Makriyalos, northern Greece: preliminary report on the 1993-1995 excavations. *Journal of field archaeology* 26 (2), 177-195.

Pappa, M., Adaktylou, F. and Gerousi, S. (1998). Ο Νεολιθικός οικισμός στο Μακρύγιαλο Πιερίας. ΑΕΜΘ 12, 283-289.

Pappa, M., Adaktylou, F. and Nanoglou S. (2000). Νεολιθικός οικισμός Θέρμης 2000-2001. ΑΕΜΘ 15, 271-278.

Pappa, M., Halstead, P., Kotsakis, K. and Urem-Kotsou, D. (2003) Evidence for large-scale feasting at Late Neolithic Makriyalos, northern Greece. In Halstead, P. and Barrett J. (eds) *Food, cuisine and society in Prehistoric Greece*, 16-44. Oxford, The Alden Press.

Payne, S. (1972a). Partial recovery and sample bias: the results of some sieving experiments. In Higgs, E.S. (ed) *Papers in economic prehistory*, 49-64. Cambridge, Cambridge University Press.

Payne, S. (1972b). On the interpretation of bone samples from archaeological sites. In Higgs, E.S. (ed) *Papers in economic prehistory*, 65-81. Cambridge, Cambridge University Press.

Payne, S. (1973). Kill-off patterns in sheep and goats. *Anatolian Studies* 23, 281-303.

Payne, S. (1975). Partial recovery and sample bias. In Clason, A.T. (ed) *Archaeozoological studies*, 7-17. Amsterdam, North Holland Publishing Company.

Payne S. (1985a). Zooarchaeology in Greece: a reader's guide. In Wilkie, N.C. and Coulson, W.D.E (eds), *Contributions to Aegean Archaeology: Studies in honor of W.A. McDonald*, 211-244. London, Kendall/Hunt Dubuque.

Payne, S. (1985b). Morphological distinctions between the mandibular teeth of young Sheep, *Ovis* and goats, *Capra. Journal of Archaeological Science* 12, 139-147.

Payne, S. (1987). Reference codes for wear states in the mandibular cheek teeth of sheep and goats. *Journal of Archaeological Science* 14, 609-614.

Payne, S. and Bull, G. (1988). Components of variation in measurements of pig bones and teeth and the use of measurements to distinguish wild from domestic pig remains. *Archaeozoologia,* 2, 27-66.

Payne, S. and Munson, P.J. (1985). Ruby and how many squirrels? The destruction of bones by dogs. In Fieller, N.R.J., Gilbertson, D.D. and Ralph, N.G.A. (eds), *Palaeobiological investigations; research design, methods and data analysis*, 31-39. British Archaeological Reports International Series 266. Oxford, BAR Publishing.

Peristeri, A. (2002). Ανασκαφική έρευνα 2002 στον προϊστορικό οικισμό του Αρκαδικού Δράμας. ΑΕΜΘ 16, 131-136.

Peristeri, A. (2004). Ανασκαφική έρευνα 2004 στο Νεολιθικό οικισμό Αρκαδικού Δράμας στα αγροτεμάχια 542, 545, ιδιοκτησίας Φ. Χατζηγιαννίδη. ΑΕΜΘ 18, 25-32.

Perlès, C. (2001). *The Early Neolithic in Greece: The first farming communities in Europe.* Cambridge, Cambridge University Press.

Pernicheva, L. (1995). Prehistoric cultures in the Middle Struma valley: Neolithic and Eneolithic. *World Archaeology* 22, 99-140.

Pernicheva, L. (2002). Die prähistorische Siedlung Balgarcevo. In Lichardus, M., Lichardus, J. and Nikolov, V. (eds) *Beitrage zu jungsteinzeitlichen forschungen in Bulgarien*, 271-324. Saarbruken 2002.

Prummel, W. (1987). Atlas of identification of foetal skeletal elements of cattle, horse, sheep and pig. *Archaeozoologia* 1, 23-30.

Prummel, W. (1988). Distinguishing features of postcranial skeletal elements of cattle, *Bos primigenius* f. *taurus*, and red deer, *Cervus elaphus. Schriften aus der Archaologisch-Zoologischen Arbeitsgruppe Schleswig-Kiel* 12, 1-52.

Prummel, W. and Frisch, H.J. (1986). A guide for the distinction of species, sex and body side in bones of sheep and goats. *Journal of Archaeological Science* 13, 567-577.

Ray, K. and Thomas, J. (2003). In the kinship of cows: the social centrality of cattle in the earlier Neolithic of southern Britain. In Pearson M.P. (ed) *Food, Culture and Identity in the Neolithic and Early Bronze Age*, 37-51. British Archaeological Reports International Series 1117. Oxford, BAR Publishing.

Reese, D.S. (1994). Recent work in Greek Zooarchaeology. In Kardulias, P.N. (ed) *Beyond the site: Regional studies in the Aegean area*, 191-221. Lanham, University Press of America.

Reitz, E.J. and Wing, E.S. (2008). *Zooarchaeology*. Cambridge, Cambridge University Press.

Renfrew, C. (1969). The autonomy of the southeast European Copper Age. *Proceedings of the Prehistoric Society* 35, 12–47.

Renfrew, C. and Slater, E. (2002). Metal artefacts and metallurgy. In Elster, E. and Renfrew, C. (eds) *Prehistoric Sitagroi, excavations in northern Greece 1968-1970 Vol. 2 The final report*, 301-324. Los Angeles, Cotsen Institute of Archaeology, University of California.

Renfrew, C., Gimbutas, M. and Elster, E.S. (1986). *Excavations at Sitagroi: a prehistoric village in northeastern Greece, Volume 1* (Monumenta Archaeologica 13). Los Angeles, California, Institute of Archaeology, University of California.

Ridley, C., Wardle, K.A. and Mould, C. (2000). *Servia I*. Supplementary Volume No 32, The British School at Athens.

Ringrose, T.J. (1993). Bone counts and statistics: a critique. *Journal of Archaeological Science* 20, 121-157.

Rosenberg, M. (1999). Hallan Çemi. In Özdoğan, M. (ed) *Neolithic in Turkey*, 25-33. Istanbul, Arkeoloji ve Sanat Yayınları.

Rowley-Conwy, P. (2000). Milking caprines, hunting pigs: the Neolithic economy of Arene Candide in its West Mediterranean context. In Rowley-Conwy, P. (ed) *Animal bones, human societies*, 124-132. Oxford, Oxbow.

Rowley-Conwy, P. (2003). Early domestic animals in Europe: imported or locally domesticated? In Ammerman, A. and Biagi, P. (eds) *The Widening Harvest. The Neolithic Transition in Europe: Looking Forward, Looking Back*, 99-117. Boston, Archaeological Institute of America.

Rowley-Conwy, P., Albarella, U. and Dobney, K. (2012). Distinguishing wild boar from domestic pigs in prehistory: a review of approaches and recent results. *Journal of World Prehistory* 25, 1-44.

Runnels, C. and Murray, P. (2001). *Greece before history: an archaeological companion and guide*. Stanford, California, Stanford University Press.

Russell, N. (1993). Hunting, Herding and Feasting: human use of animals in Neolithic southeast Europe. Unpublished Ph.D. thesis, University of California at Berkeley.

Ryder, M. (1969). Changes in the fleece of sheep following domestication (with a note on the coat of cattle). In Ucko, P.J. and Dimbleby, G.W. (eds) *The domestication and exploitation of plants and animals*, 495-521. London, Duckworth.

Ryder, M. (1982). *Sheep and Man*. London, Duckworth.

Ryder, M. (1993). Sheep and goat husbandry with particular reference to textile fibre and milk production. *Bulletin on Sumerian agriculture* 7, 9-32.

Samartzidou, E. (2002). Παράρτημα 2: μελέτη παλαιοζωολογικών ευρημάτων από τη Νεολιθική θέση στην Ασπροβάλτα. *ΑΕΜΘ* 16, 185-186.

Samartzidou, E. (2015). Τα μυστικά της λίμνης: η κτηνοτροφία και οι κυνηγετικές δραστηριότητες στον νεολιθικό λιμναίο οικισμό του Δισπηλιού Καστοριάς. *ΑΕΜΘ* 25, 27-36.

Schmid, E. (1972). *Atlas for animal bones for prehistorians, archaeologists and Quaternary geologists*. Amsterdam, Elsevier Science Publishers.

Seferiadis, M. (1983). Dikili Tash: Introduction à la préhistoire de la Macédoine orientale. *Bulletin de Correspondance Hellénique* 107, 657-662.

Shaffer, J. and Lichtenstein, D. (1995). The concepts of 'cultural tradition' and 'palaeoethnicity' in South Asian archaeology. In Erdosy, G. (ed) *Indian Philology and South Asian Studies: The Indo-Aryans of Ancient South Asia: Language, Material Culture and Ethnicity*, 126-154. Berlin, New York, de Gruyter.

Shahack-Gross, R., Bar-Yosef, O. and Weiner, S. (1997). Black-colored bones in Hayonim cave, Israel: differentiating between burning and oxide staining. *Journal of Archaeological Science* 24, 439-446.

Sherratt, A. (2005). Settling the Neolithic: a digestif. In Bailey, D., Whittle, A. and Cummings, V. (eds) *(Un) settling the Neolithic*, 140-146. Oxford, Oxbow.

Shipman, P., Foster, G. and Schoeninger, M. (1984). Burnt bones and teeth: An experimental study of color, morphology, crystal structure and shrinkage. *Journal of Archaeological Science* 11, 307-325.

Siegel, J. (1976). Animal palaeopathology: possibilities and problems. *Journal of Archaeological Science* 3, 349-384.

Silver, I.A. 1969. The ageing of domestic animals. In Brothwell D. and Higgs, E. (eds) *Science in Archaeology: a survey of progress and research*, 283-302. London, Thames and Hudson.

Simpson, G., Roe, A. and Lewontin, R. (1960). *Quantitative Zoology*. New York, Harcourt, Brace and World.

Souvatzi, S. (2008). *A social archaeology of household in Neolithic Greece: an anthropological approach*. Cambridge, Cambridge University Press.

Speth, J.D. (1983). *Bison kills and bone counts: decision making by ancient hunters*. Chicago, University of Chicago Press.

Stratouli, G. (2004). Neolithic Avgi, Kastoria, 2003-2004. A new research programme. *ΑΕΜΘ* 18, 661–668.

Theocharis, D.R. (1993). *Νεολιθικός Πολιτισμός*. Αθήνα, Μορφωτικό Ίδρυμα Εθνικής Τραπέζης.

Theodorogianni, O. and Trantalidou, K. (2013). Η διαχείριση του ζωικού κεφαλαίου στη κοιλάδα του Στρυμόνα: δειγματοληπτική έρευνα στη κοιλάδα του Στρυμόνα. ΑΕΜΘ 23, 407-426.

Toufexis, G. (2003). Animals in the Neolithic art of Thessaly. In Kotjabopoulou, E., Hamilakis, Y., Halstead, P., Gamble, C. and Elephanti, P. (eds) *Zooarchaeology in Greece. Recent advances*, 263-271. Oxford, British School at Athens Studies 9.

Trantalidou, K. (1990). Animals and human diet in the prehistoric Aegean. In Hardy, D.A., Keller, J., Galanopoulos, V.P. and Flemming, N.C. (eds) *Thera and the Aegean world III. Proceedings of the Third International Conference, Santorini, Greece, 3-9 September 1989*, 392-405. London, Earth Sciences.

Trantalidou, K. (2001). Archaeozoology in Greece: a brief historiography of the science. *Archaeofauna* 10, 183-199.

Trantalidou, K. (2006). Companions of the oldest times: dogs in ancient Greek literature, iconography and osteological testimony. In Snyder, L.M. and Moore, E.A. (eds) *Dogs and people in social, working, economic or symbolic interaction (Proceedings of the 9th Conference of the International Council of Archaeozoology, Durham August 2002)*, 96-119. Oxford, Oxbow.

Trantalidou, K. (2010). Bovis skulls in southeastern European Neolithic dwellings: the case of the subterranean circular room at Promachon-Topolnica in the Strymon valley, Greece. In Campana, D., Crabtree, P., deFrance, S.D., Lev-Tov, J. and Choyke, A. (eds) *Anthropological approaches to zooarchaeology: complexity, colonialism, and animal transformations*, 213-219. Oxford, Oxbow.

Trantalidou, K. and Gkioni (2008). Προμαχών-Topolnica: Τα βούκρανα του μεγάλου υπόσκαφου χώρου: ζωολογικός προσδιορισμός και πολιτισμικά παράλληλα από την ανατολική Μεσόγειο. ΑΕΜΘ 20, 217-228.

Trantalidou, K., Skaraki, V., Kara, E. and Ntinou, M. (2006). Στρατηγικές επιβίωσης κατά την 4η χιλιετία: στοιχεία από την εγκατάσταση στην ανατολική όχθη του Αγγίτη. ΑΕΜΘ 19, 45-80.

Treuil, R. (1992). *Dikili Tash, village préhistorique de Macédoine orientale, I. Fouilles de Jean Deshayes (1961-1975)*, vol. 1. Bulletin de Correspondance Hellénique Supplément XXIV.

Treuil, R. and Darcque, P. (1998). Un 'bucrane' néolithique à Dikili Tash (Macédoine orientale): parallelés et perspectives d' interprétation. *Bulletin de Correspondance Hellénique* 122, 1-25.

Tringham, R. (2000). Southeastern Europe in the transition to agriculture in Europe: bridge, buffer or mosaic. In Price, T.D. (ed) *Europe's First Farmers*, 19-56. Cambridge, Cambridge University Press.

Troy, C.S., MacHugh, D.E., Bailey, J.F., Magee, D.A. and Loftus, R.T. (2001). Genetic evidence for Near-Eastern origins of European cattle. *Nature* 410, 1088-1091.

Tsirtsoni, Z. (1991). Morphologie et fonctions de la potterie, *Dossier d' Arcéologie* 222, 28-35.

Tsirtsoni, Z. (2000). Les poteries du début du Néolithique Récent en Macédoine I. *Bulletin de Correspondance Hellénique* 124, 1-55.

Tsirtsoni, Z. (2001). Les poteries du début du Néolithique Récent en Macédoine II: les fonctions des récipients. *Bulletin de Correspondance Hellénique* 125 (1), 1-39.

Tzevelekidi, V. (2012). *Dressing for dinner: butchery and bone deposition at Late Neolithic Toumba Kremastis Koiladas, northern Greece*. British Archaeological Reports International Series 2451. Oxford, BAR Publishing.

Tzevelekidi, V., Halstead, P. and Isaakidou, V. (2014). Invitatio to dinner: practices of animal consumption and bone deposition at Makriyalos I (Pieria) and Toumba Kremastis Koiladas (Kozani). In Stefani, E., Merousis, N. and Dimoula, A. (eds) *A Century of research in Prehistoric Macedonia, proceedings of the International Conference*, 425-436. Thessaloniki, Archaeological Museum of Thessaloniki.

Vajsov, I. (2007). Promachon-Topolnica: a typology of painted decorations and its use as a chronological marker. In Todorova, H., Stefanovic, M. and Ivanov, G. (eds) *The Struma/Strymon river valley in prehistory: proceedings of the International Symposium 'Strymon Praehistoricus', Kjustendil-Blagoevgrad (Bulgaria) and Serres-Amphipolis (Greece)*, 79-120. Sofia, Gerda Henkel Stiftung.

Valamoti, S.M. (2004). Η διατροφή στη Βόρεια Ελλάδα κατά την Προϊστορική περίοδο, με έμφαση στα φυτικά συστατικά της τροφής. ΑΕΜΘ 18, 417-427.

Valamoti, S.M. (2007). Agriculture and Use of Space at Promachon-Topolniča: preliminary observations on the archaeobotanical material. In Todorova, H., Stefanovic, M. and Ivanov, G. (eds) *The Struma/Strymon river valley in prehistory: proceedings of the International Symposium 'Strymon Praehistoricus', Kjustendil-Blagoevgrad (Bulgaria) and Serres-Amphipolis (Greece)*, 523-530. Sofia, Gerda Henkel Stiftung.

Valamoti, S.M., Mangafa, M., Koukouli-Chrysanthaki, Ch. and Malamidou, D. (2007). Grape-pressings from northern Greece: the earliest wine in the Aegean? *Antiquity* 81, 54-61.

Vigne, J.D. (2011). The origins of animal domestication and husbandry: a major change in the history of humanity and the biosphere. *Comptes Rendus Biologies* 334, 171-181.

Vigne, J.D. and Helmer, D. (2007). Was milk a secondary product in the Old World Neolithization process? Its role in the domestication of cattle, sheep and goats. *Anthropozoologica* 42, 9-40.

Viner, S. (2010). *A diachronic study of* Sus *and* Bos *exploitation in Britain from the Early Mesolithic to the Late Neolithic.* Unpublished PhD Thesis, University of Sheffield.

Wardle, K.A. Ed. (1996). *Nea Nikomedeia I: The excavation of an Early Neolithic village in Northern Greece 1961-1964,* Supplementary Volume No. 25. British School at Athens.

Watson, J.P.N. (1979a). Faunal remains. In Ridley, C. and Wardle, K.A. (eds) *Rescue excavations at Servia, 1971-1973: a preliminary report,* 228-229. Oxford, British School at Athens.

Watson, J.P.N. (1979b). The estimation of the relative frequencies of mammalian species: Khirokitia. *Journal of Archaeological Science* 6, 127-137.

Webb, Th. (2012). Faunal remains from Limenaria. In Papadopoulos, S. and Malamidou, D. (eds) Δέκα χρόνια ανασκαφικής έρευνας στον προϊστορικό οικισμό Λιμεναρίων Θάσου, 117-128. Hellenic Ministry of Culture (ΥΠΠΟ)-18th Ephorate of Prehistoric and Classical Antiquities (18η ΕΠΚΑ).

West, S. (1985). *West Stow: The Anglo-Saxon Village: Volume I: The Text.* East Anglian Archaeology 24, Bury St. Edmunds, Suffolk County Planning Department.

Whittle, A. (1996). Europe in the Neolithic: the creation of new worlds. Cambridge, Cambridge University Press.

Whittle, A. (2003). *The Archaeology of people: dimensions of Neolithic life.* London, Routledge.

Whittle, A. and Bartosiewicz, L. (2007). On the waterfront. In Whittle, A. (ed) *The Early Neolithic on the Great Hungarian Plain: investigations of the Körös culture site of Ecsgfalva 23, Co. Békés,* 727-752. Budapest, Institute of Archaeology, Hungarian Academy of Sciences.

Wright, E. (2013). *The history of the European aurochs (Bos primigenius) from the Middle Pleistocene to its extinction: an archaeological investigation of its evolution, morphological variability and response to human exploitation.* Unpublished PhD Thesis, University of Sheffield.

Yiannouli, E. (1989). Η νεολιθική Θέρμη Β: Τα δεδομένα απο τα οστά των ζώων (Ανασκαφική περίοδος 1989). In Grammenos, D., Pappa, M., Ourem-Kotsou, D., Skourtopoulou, K., Giannouli, E., Maragou, Ch., Valamoti, S.M., Siridis, G., Marki, E. and Christidou, R. *Ανασκαφή νεολιθικού οικισμού Θέρμης Β και βυζαντινής εγκατάστασης παρά τον προϊστορικό οικισμό Θέρμη Α (Ανασκαφική περίοδος 1989).* Μακεδονικά 28, 413-426.

Yiannouli, E. (1994). *Aspects of animal use in Prehistoric Macedonia, Northern Greece: examples from the Neolithic and Early Bronze Age,* Unpublished PhD Thesis, University of Cambridge.

Yiannouli, E. (1997). Dimitra interim report. In Grammenos, D.V. (ed) Νεολιθική Μακεδονία, 95-127. Δημοσιεύματα του Αρχαιολογικού Δελτίου, Αθήνα, ΤΑΠΑ.

Yiannouli, E. (2002a). Ήμερη και άγρια πανίδα από νεολιθικό οικισμό στη Σταυρούπολη Θεσσαλονίκης. In Grammenos, D.V. and Kotsos, S. (eds) Σωστικές ανασκαφές στο Νεολιθικό οικισμό Σταυρούπολης Θεσσαλονίκης, 693-744. Θεσσαλονίκη, Δημοσιεύματα του Αρχαιολογικού Ινστιτούτου Βόρειας Ελλάδας 2.

Yiannouli, E. (2002b). Παράρτημα Δ': Μεσημεριανή Τούμπα: τα ζωικά κατάλοιπα, in Grammenos, D.V. and Kotsos, S. (eds) Ανασκαφή στον προϊστορικό οικισμό «Μεσημεριανή Τούμπα» Τριλόφου Ν. Θεσσαλονίκης (ανασκαφικές περίοδοι 1992, 1994-1996, 2000, 2001), 321-334. Θεσσαλονίκη, Δημοσιεύματα του Αρχαιολογικού Ινστιτούτου Βόρειας Ελλάδας 1.

Yiannouli, E. (2003). Non-domestic carnivores in Greek prehistory: a review. In Kotjabopoulou, E., Hamilakis, Y., Halstead, P., Gamble, C. and Elephanti, P. (eds) *Zooarchaeology in Greece. Recent advances,* 175-192. Oxford, British School at Athens Studies 9.

Yiannouli, E. (2004). Σταυρούπολη Θεσσαλονίκης: νεότερα δεδομένα από την αρχαιοπανίδα του νεολιθικού οικισμού. In Grammenos, D.V. and Kotsos, S. (eds) Σωστικές ανασκαφές στο *Νεολιθικό οικισμό Σταυρούπολης Θεσσαλονίκης, Μέρος ΙΙ (1998-2003),* 489-526. Δημοσιεύματα του Αρχαιολογικού Ινστιτούτου Βόρειας Ελλάδας 6.

Yiannouli, E. (2013). The Brown bear in Greece: A brief review of bones and images in the Neolithic and Bronze Ages. In Brugal, J.P., Gardeisen, A. and Zucker A. (eds), *Prédateurs dans tous leurs états. Évolution, Biodiversité, Interactions, Mythes, Symboles, XXXIe rencontres internationales d'archéologie et d'histoire d'Antibes,* 269-284. Antibes, Éditions APDCA.

Yiannouli, E. and Trantalidou, K. (1999). The Fallow deer (*Dama dama L. 1758*) in Greece: archaeological presence and representation. In Benecke, N. (ed) *The Holocene history of the European vertebrate fauna. Modern aspects of research,* 247-281. Rahden/Vestf., Verlag Marie Leidorf Gmbg.

Zeder, M. (2005). A view from the Zagros: new perspectives on livestock domestication in the Fertile Crescent. In Vigne, J.D., Peters, J. and Helmer, D. (eds) *First Steps of Animal Domestication,* 125-146. Oxford, Oxbow.

Zeder, M. (2006). Reconciling rates of long bone fusion and tooth eruption and wear in sheep (*Ovis*) and goat (*Capra*). In Ruscillo, D. (ed) *Recent Advances in Ageing and Sexing Animal Bones,* 87-118. Oxford, Oxbow.

Zeder, M. (2008). Domestication and early agriculture in the Mediterranean Basin: origins, diffusion and impact. *PNAS* 11, 597-604.

Zeder, M., Emshwiller, E., Smith, B. and Bradley, D. (2006). Documenting domestication: the intersection of genetics and archaeology. *Trends in Genetics* 22, 139-155.

Zvelebil, M. (1992). Hunting in farming societies: the prehistoric perspective. In Grant, A. (ed) *Animals and their products in Trade and Exchange*, 7-18. Paris, HASRI.

Zvelebil, M. (1998). What's in a name: the Mesolithic, the Neolithic, and social change at the Mesolithic-Neolithic transition. In Edmonds M. and Richards C. (eds) *Understanding the Neolithic of North-Western Europe*, 1-36. Glasgow, Cruithne Press.

Appendix

Animal Bone Material

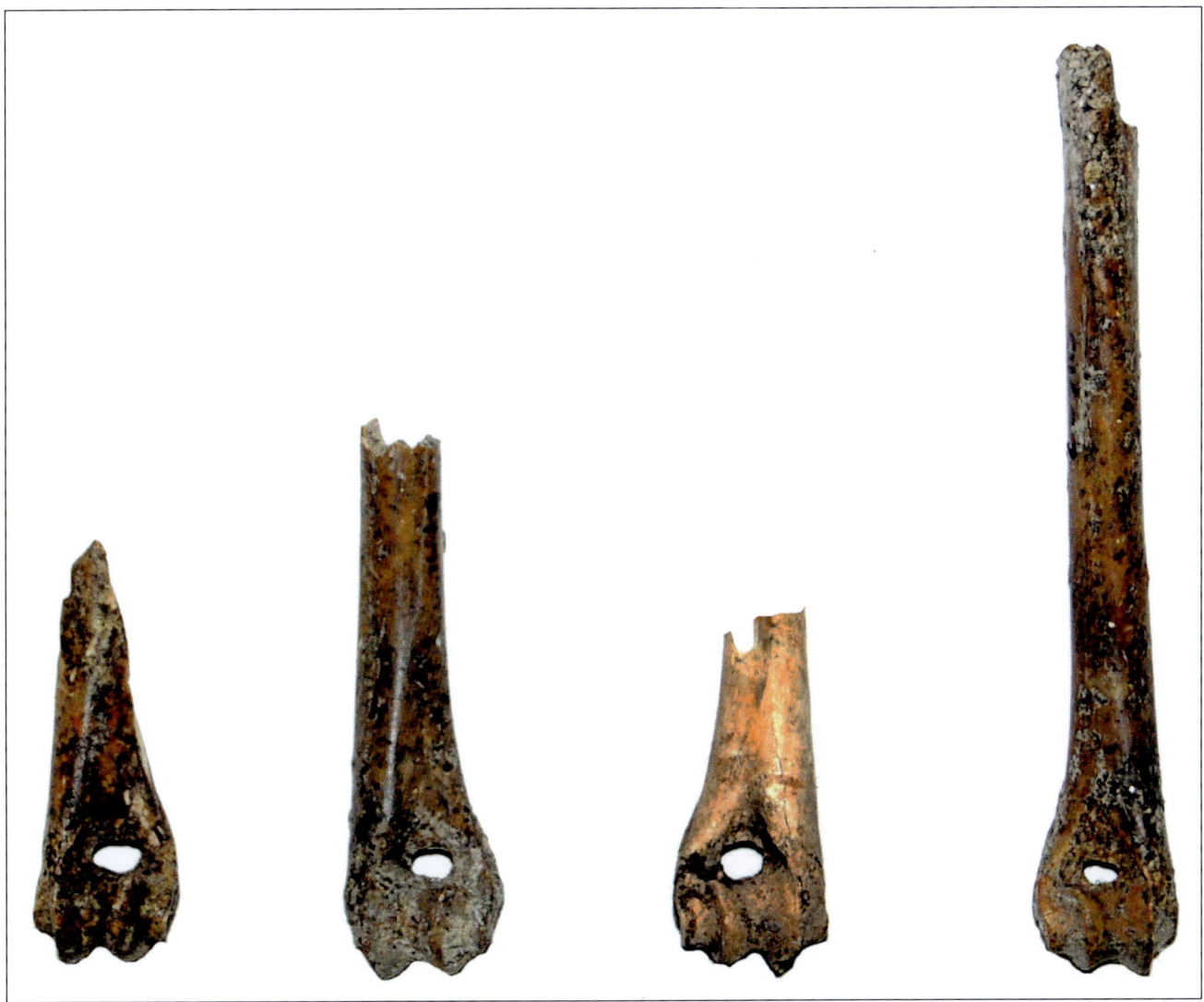

Figure A.1 *Lepus europaeus* (hare) humeri.

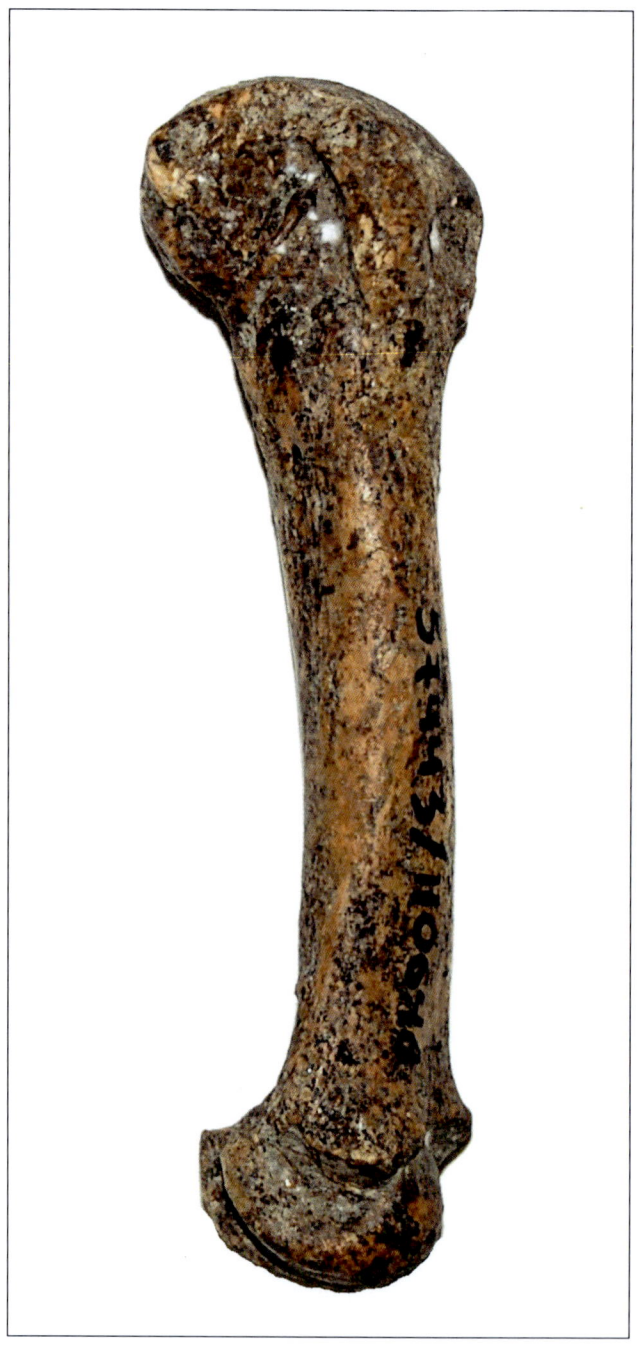

Figure A.2 *Ursus arctos* (bear) third metacarpal.

Figure A.3 *Canis familiaris* (dog) mandible with cutmarks on the ramus mandibulae.

Figure A.4 *Meles meles* (badger) ulna.

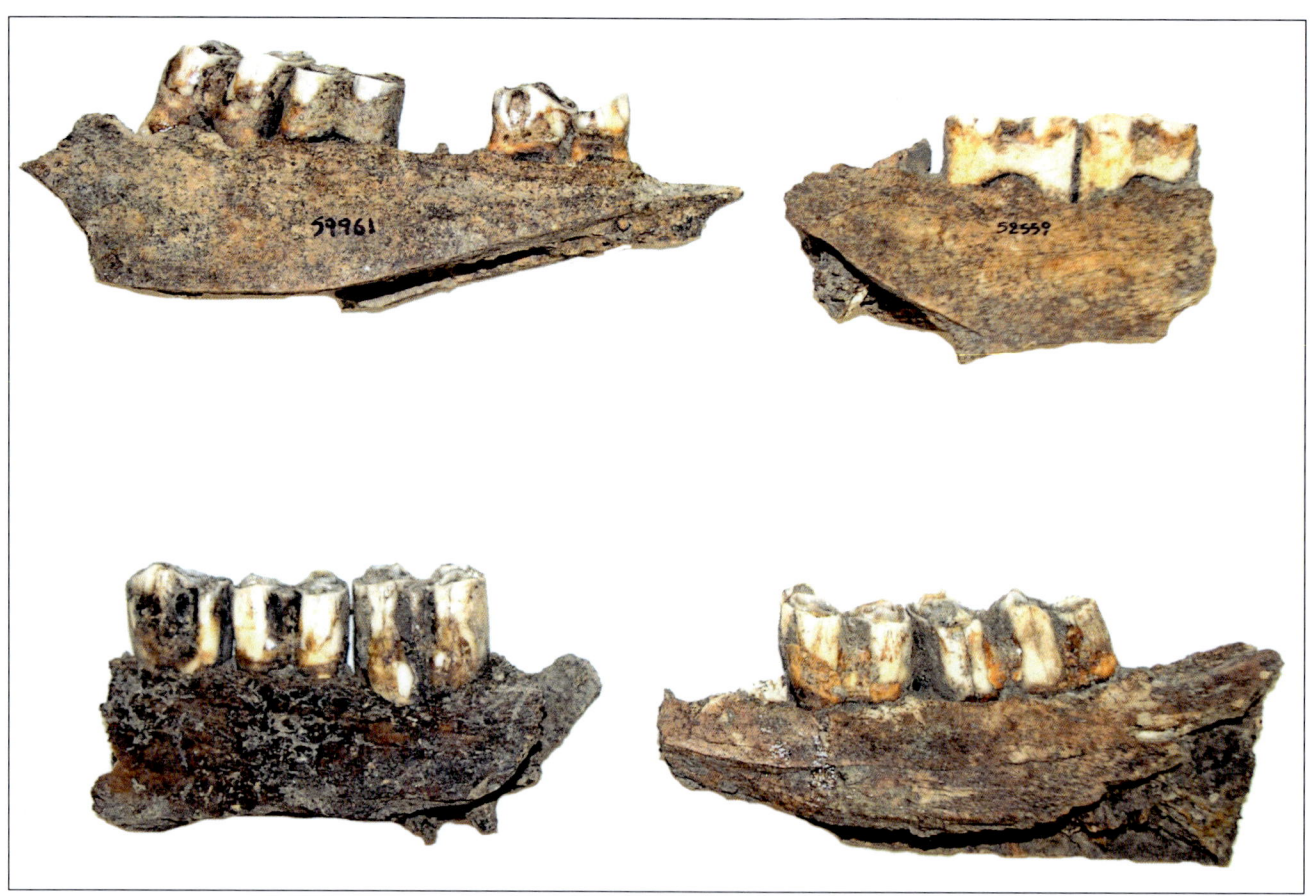

Figure A.5 *Bos taurus* (cattle) mandibles broken beneath the tooth root line for marrow extraction.

Figure A.6 Caprinae (caprine) humeri with traces of dismemberment; these are cutmarks, not fusion lines.

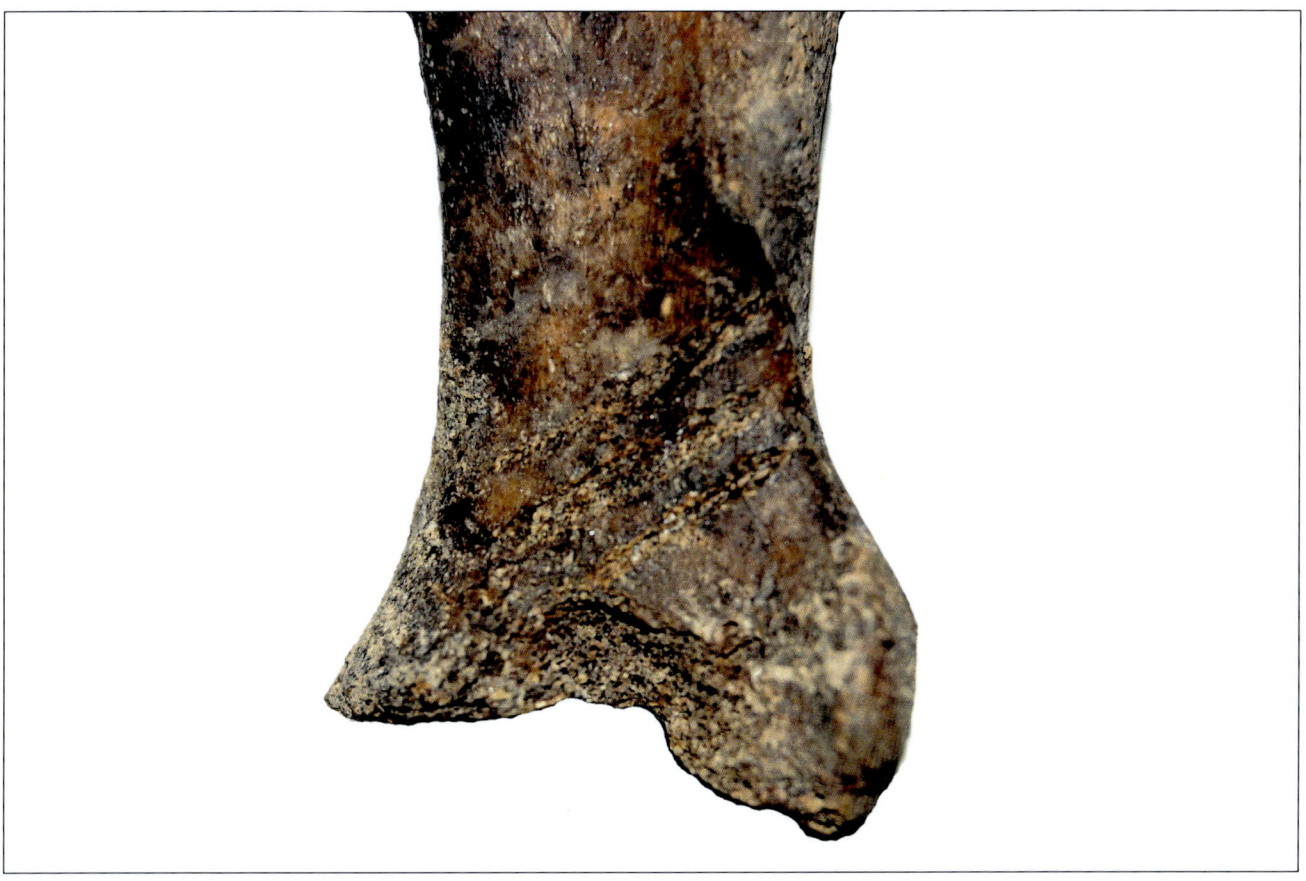

Figure A.7 *Sus* (pig) scapula with traces of chopping marks.

Figure A.8 *Sus* (pig) astragalus with traces of cutmarks.

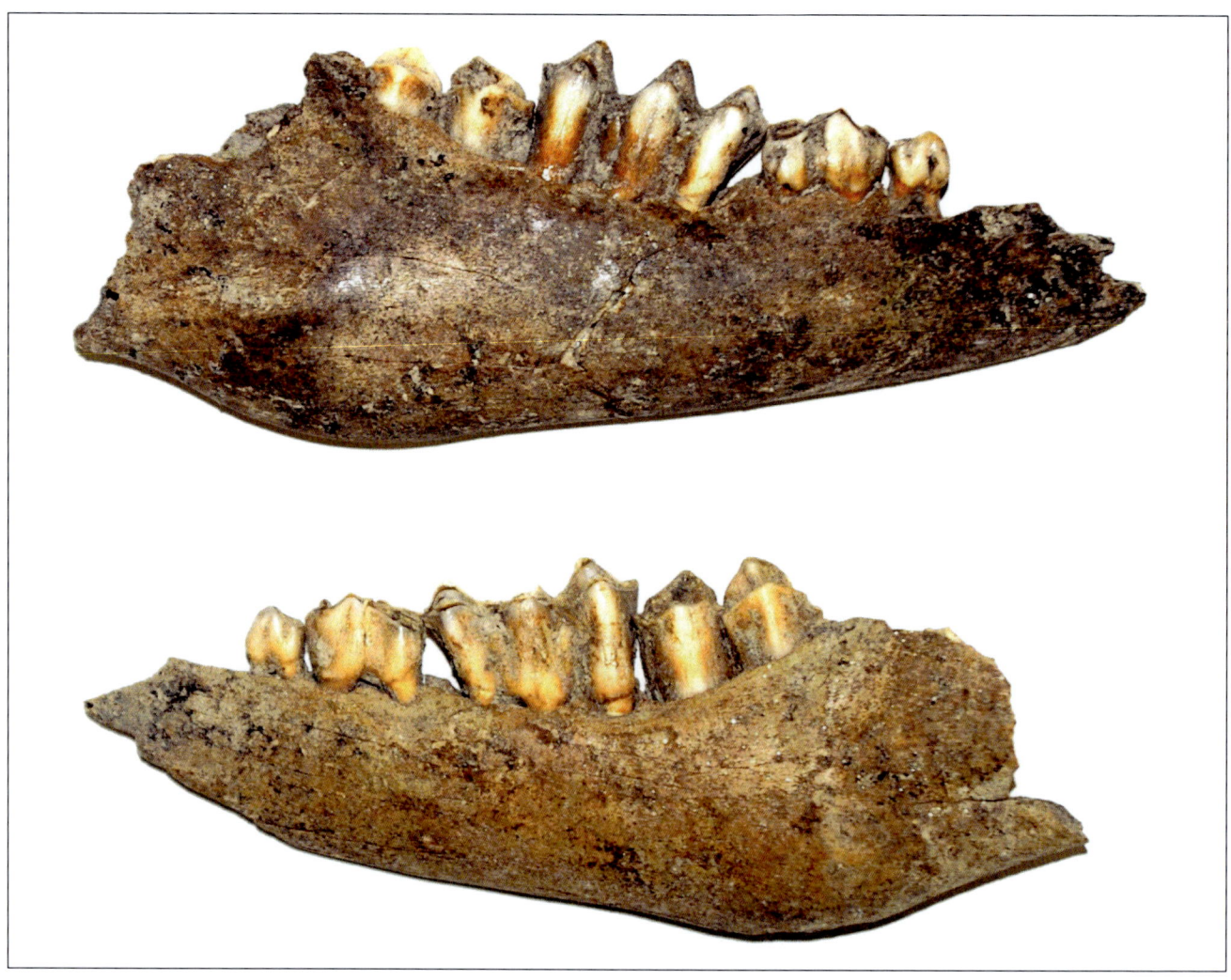

Figure A.9 *Bos taurus* (cattle) mandibles.

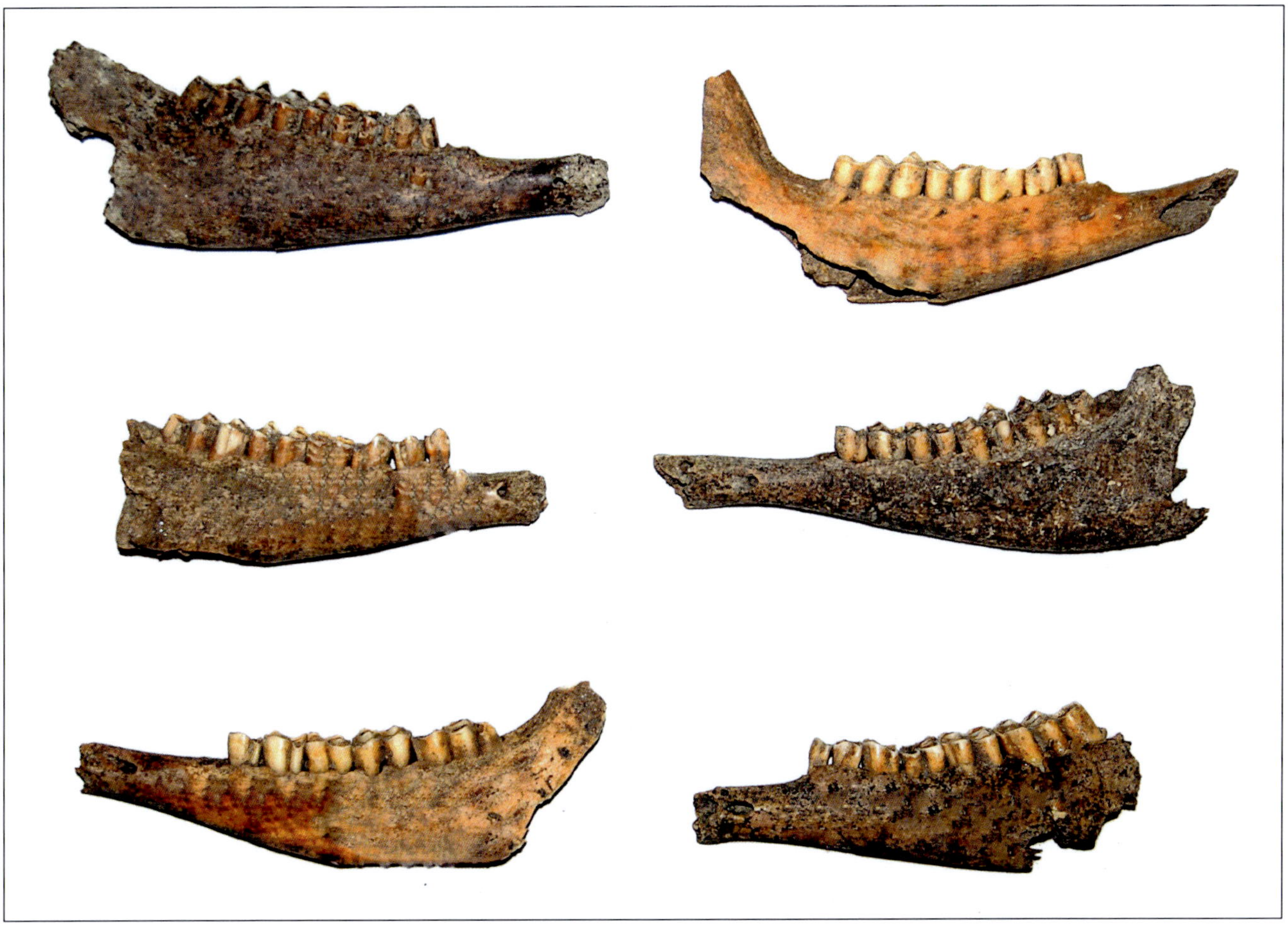

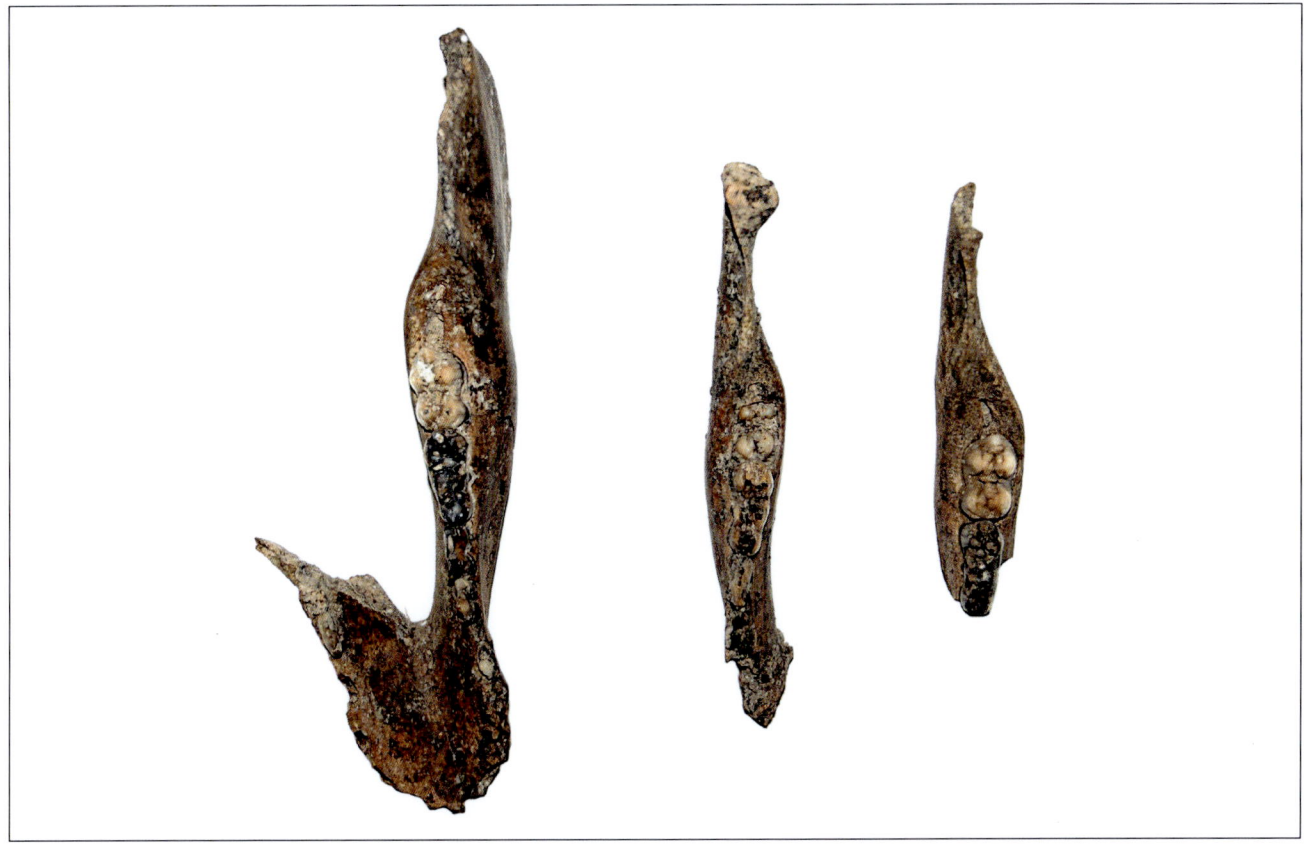

Figure A.10 Caprinae (caprine) mandibles.

Figure A.11 *Sus* (pig) mandibles.

Figure A.12 Caprinae (caprine) mandible with abscess development.

Figure A.13 Caprinae (caprine) teeth with root infection.